International Politics on the World Stage

International Politics on the World Stage

John T. Rourke
University of Connecticut, Hartford

Brooks/Cole Publishing Company
Monterey, California

For Meredith

Praising what is lost
Makes the remembrance dear.
Shakespeare, All's Well That Ends Well

Brooks/Cole Publishing Company
A Division of Wadsworth, Inc.

Printed in the United States of America

10 9 8 7 6 5 4 3 2 1

Library of Congress Cataloging-in-Publication Data

Rourke, John T., [date]
International politics on the world stage.

Includes index.
1. International relations. 2. World politics—1945- . I. Title.
JX1391.R588 1986 327 85-17429

ISBN 0-534-05808-6

Sponsoring Editor: *Marie Kent*

Marketing Representative: *Richard Giggey*

Editorial Assistant: *Amy Mayfield*

Production Editor: *Phyllis Larimore*

Manuscript Editor: *Rephah Berg*

Permissions Editor: *Carline Haga*

Interior and Cover Design: *Sharon L. Kinghan*

Cover Illustration: *Arnold D. Clapman*

Art Coordinator: *Michele Judge*

Interior Illustration: *Horvath & Cuthbertson*

Photo Editor: *Judy Blamer*

Photo Researcher: *Cris Pullo for Omni-Photo Communications, Inc.*

Typesetting: *Graphic Typesetting Service, Los Angeles, California*

Printing and Binding: *Malloy Lithographing, Inc., Ann Arbor, Michigan*

PHOTO CREDITS CHAPTER 1. 7, AP/Wide World Photos, Inc.; **11,** UPI/Bettmann Newsphotos; **15,** United Nations; **19,** Randy Taylor, SYGMA. **CHAPTER 2. 27,** United States Air Force; **33,** SYGMA; **37,** Culver Pictures, Inc.; **41,** Library of Congress; **43,** Owen Franken, SYGMA. **CHAPTER 3. 49,** United Nations; **53,** Fabian, SYGMA; **59,** UPI/Bettmann Newsphotos; **63,** John F. Kennedy Library; **69,** Leif Skoogfors, Woodfin Camp and Associates. **CHAPTER 4. 75,** United Nations; **81,** Alinari, Art Resources, New York; **85,** AP/Wide World Photos, Inc.; **87,** UPI/Bettmann Newsphotos. **CHAPTER 5. 99,** Michel Philippot, SYGMA; **101** and **109,** UPI/Bettmann Newsphotos. **CHAPTER 6. 123,** Jean Louis Atlan, SYGMA; **129,** UPI/Bettmann Newsphotos; **131,** AP/Wide World Photos, Inc. **CHAPTER 7. 143** and **147,** AP/Wide World Photos, Inc.; **153,** Robert Azzi, Woodfin Camp and Associates. **CHAPTER 8. 167,** AP/Wide World Photos, Inc.; **177,** Regis Bossu, SYGMA; **183,** Greard, SYGMA; **193,** Urraca, SYGMA. **CHAPTER 9. 205,** Yutaka Nagata, United Nations; **207,** Jimmy Carter Library; **209,** UPI/Bettmann Newsphotos. **CHAPTER 10. 229,** Atlan, SYGMA; **235,** UPI/Bettmann Newsphotos. **CHAPTER 11. 253,** Joe Crachlola; **259,** UPI/Bettmann Newsphotos. **CHAPTER 12. 277,** United Nations; **291,** Alain Nogues, SYGMA. **CHAPTER 13. 303,** Owen Franken, SYGMA; **313,** Yutaka Nagata, United Nations; **319,** J. K. Isaac, United Nations; **325,** Yutaka Nagata, United Nations. **CHAPTER 14. 337,** Culver Pictures, Inc.; **349,** United Nations. **CHAPTER 15. 363,** Reuters, Bettmann Newsphotos; **373,** SYGMA. **CHAPTER 16. 389,** R. Bossu, SYGMA; **397,** John Isaac, United Nations; **401,** Lofti Abou Zeid, CARE; **403,** United Nations; **409,** Bill Ross, Woodfin Camp and Associates.

Preface
Much Ado about Everything: A Beginning

The world familiar to us and unknown
***Shakespeare,* Henry V**

The text that follows is this author's attempt to introduce undergraduate students to the complex and compelling study of international politics. For someone who has taught the subject for years, the task turned out to be much more challenging than expected. One of the first choices that had to be faced was the question "Do I write this book for students or professors?" One of the perplexities of this endeavor is that a text has to appeal to two very different sets of consumers. In one sense, texts are bought by professors who assign them for their courses. For this group, a more sophisticated approach would often be the more appealing. But texts are actually read by students, and for that group, a more fundamental approach is most appropriate. The decision was to write for the student. That means using relatively straightforward prose, a format designed to facilitate notetaking, and a frame of reference that relates to students. To the professor/reviewer who couldn't understand why I would quote Robert Frost when I could have cited James Rosenau, my apologies.

A closely related question was where to pitch the text in terms of student sophistication. My basic assumption is that students taking this course know little about international politics. Study after study shows that, at the freshman/sophomore level, students have little sense of history or current events, much less of the basic forces that shape them. This text, therefore, operates from a reasonably *tabula rasa,* or blank slate, assumption. To the occasional student who has daily read the *New York Times* since age ten and is ready for a seventh-floor appointment at the State Department, again my apologies.

The next dilemma was what to cover and what to omit. My first-draft chapters were wonders of comprehensiveness—monsters, in fact. At the rate I was going, the text would have approached 1,000 printed pages. Obviously unacceptable. The choice was then either to touch on most of the significant aspects of international politics (but necessarily to do so only briefly, in the interest of space) or to omit many aspects and give those that remained an extensively detailed analysis. As will be plain, I opted for the former approach. There is no pretense here that the subjects I will address are covered exhaustively. They are not. This text, as the title says, is an introduction. If you really want to *know* about something, you will have to do a lot more than just read this book or even take this course. It is the author's hope that the text can thus serve as a base, a beginning. It is a base on which the instructor can build, enlightening his or her classes on the many subtleties that, necessarily, this text could not fully elucidate. The text is also meant to be a base from which student readers can begin further study of international relations. Footnotes hardly ever enter the average undergraduate's consciousness, but for those who wish to expand their understanding, footnotes are a valuable source of reference to more comprehensive studies.

Organizing the topics of this text was another interesting challenge. Someday someone will invent a modular, snap-together text that instructors can rearrange so that it will follow their own concepts and syllabus in exact order. Unfortunately, that day did not arrive before this text went to print. The general idea behind the organization of this text was borrowed from one of my excellent graduate school teachers, Susan Koch. She, in turn, was, I think, influenced by John Stoessinger and his earlier text *The Might of Nations,* all of which leaves me in pretty good company. The first three chapters focus on some of the bases of international politics and the study of that subject. Topics include why international politics is important globally and individually, who the actors are, and how the subject can be approached. Chapters 4, 5, and 6 discuss some of the basic motivational drives of international politics, including nationalism, ideas and ideology, and national interest. Chapters 7 through 11 focus on the "action," the way the world drama is played out. Power, force, diplomacy, and subversion are the divisions. It is, as we see, a world "full of sound and fury." The final four chapters, 12 through 16, look again at some of the world problems and areas of cooperation, such as organization, rules, arms, economics, and the human condition, and examine cooperation, the alternative to the all too common self-interested sound and fury.

For those many instructors whose organization differs from mine, care has been given to the table of contents and to the index in order to facilitate using the text for your syllabus. Economics, for one, is found in chapters 11 and 12 and in parts of chapters 1, 7, and 16. Arms and force are in chapters 8 and 15 and in parts of chapter 7.

It is also well that an author be clear about his or her basic orientations. As chapter 2 indicates, there are many approaches to the study of international politics. Which one an author adopts will heavily influence what is included in and excluded from a text and how the material is handled. I generally do not believe that any one of the approaches has all the answers. The text, therefore, is eclectic. It does, however, in its level of analysis, lean toward a state-centristic approach. That does not mean that systems analysis (a term we will explore) is irrelevant. Indeed, the world system is an important factor, and we will spend considerable time examining its nature and impact. The overall view taken here, though, is that the primary actor in international politics is and, for the foreseeable future, will remain the state (that is, the country) and that states are reasonably free to choose courses of action based on their international goals and domestic pressures.

This text also has something of a traditional approach toward emphasizing power politics as the most important characteristic of international politics. The world is, at best, a primitive political system in which self-interest—and the power-based pursuit of that interest—is the main concern of the primary actors, or states. There are, however, significant other trends in international politics, and we will spend a substantial amount of time exploring the possibilities of alternative processes and cooperation in areas such as international organization, international law, arms control, and a variety of transnational issues including human rights, environment, and resource preservation. In other words, although there is a slight emphasis on "what is" in terms of power politics and on the concerns and actions of the major powers, significant attention is also given to "what ought to be" for the survival of the world and also to the concerns and views of the less developed countries in the Third World.

Finally, some note should be made of this book's title, *International Politics on the World Stage,* and the Shakespearean quotations that begin each chapter and are from time to time used to highlight a point. The idea behind this motif is to convey some of the sweep and complexity of the world drama. No one who has ever read William Shakespeare can dismiss his masterpieces as easily understood or inconsequential. Similarly, the events on the world stage are full of drama—sometimes hopeful, often tragic, but always riveting. But the play analogy can be taken too far, and overdoing it would only obscure some of the issues that need to be dealt with in a straightforward manner. You, the reader, would also be mistaken to assume that the play analogy means that, as a member of the audience, you can be content to sit back and watch the plot unfold. Quite to the contrary, part of what makes the world drama so compelling is that the audience is seated on stage and is part of, as well as witness to, the action that is unfolding. Further, as in an improvisational play, the audience can become involved and, given the consequences of a tragic rather than a happy ending, ought to become involved, in its own self-interest. If there is anything this text preaches, it is that each and every one of us is intimately affected by international politics and that we have both a responsibility and an ability to become shapers of the script. As we shall see, our play has alternative scripts, and what the next scene brings depends in part on us. Last, with regard to the wholesale pilfering of the Bard of Avon's wisdom, there is no pretense here of creating an all-encompassing play construct. Rather, the quotations are meant as a literary vehicle to give some shape to my discussion and to show the timelessness of many concerns. They are meant to be pondered and enjoyed, but they are not a substitute for an analysis of the many subjects I will cover.

As a last note, this author is sincerely interested in getting feedback from the faculty members and students who use this text. My pretensions to perfection have long since been dashed, and your recommendations for additions, deletions, and changes in future editions will be appreciated and seriously considered. Students, in particular, are encouraged to write to me in care of Brooks/Cole Publishing Company, 555 Abrego, Monterey, CA 93940. This book, just like the world, can be made better, but its improvement depends heavily on whether you are concerned enough to think and act.

John T. Rourke

Acknowledgments

There are many involved in my immediate academic surroundings who contributed to this text. Russell Farnen, director of the University of Connecticut's undergraduate school on the Greater Hartford Campus, brought an atmosphere to that campus that has encouraged and allowed me, and others, to attempt what otherwise might never have been. And I am glad to have the opportunity to acknowledge an academic debt to my friend and colleague, J. Garry Clifford. Whatever I write, I know Garry will someday read, and my efforts are better for it.

This is the second book that Kathie Holmes has typed out for me, and she is a woman of tremendous skill and patience. Her role has been much closer to copyeditor than typist, and her suggestions and corrections were invariably on the mark. I also owe a debt to the librarians both of my home institution, the University of Connecticut, and Trinity College in Hartford. The Trinity staff's cooperation and their professional courtesy in giving me a work space provided important support.

During the gestation of this text, the ideas behind it and the manuscript changed extensively. A great deal of that evolution was due to the careful reading and thoughtful comments of the many reviewers who read parts or all of the manuscript. They will see, I am sure, that many of their suggestions were incorporated and the text, thus, improved. Colleagues who participated as reviewers are Robert Bledsoe, University of Central Florida; Abbott Brayton, East Tennessee State University; Garry Clifford, University of Connecticut; Paul Davis, University of Nevada; Raymond Duvall, University of Minnesota; Michael Fry, University of Southern California; Francis Hoole, Indiana University; Thomas Hovet, University of Oregon; Richard Katz, Johns Hopkins University; James Lebovic, George Washington University; Vincent Mahler, Loyola University; Ronald Meltzer, State University of New York at Buffalo; George Modeleski, University of Washington; Harold Molineu, Ohio University; James Murray, University of Iowa; Suzanne Ogden, Northeastern University; Ilan Peleg, Lafayette College; Neil Richardson, University of Wisconsin; Charles Taylor, Virginia Polytechnic Institute and State University; and Conrad Waligorski, University of Arkansas.

Saving some of my greatest debts for last, I would like to applaud the work of the staff at Brooks/Cole. Marquita Flemming was my first political science editor. She got me off the ground and through the first half of the manuscript. She is a woman of great talent, and I regard her with a mixture of affection and awe. When she left Brooks/Cole I was only consoled by the thought that it was for happy reasons. Distress at Marquita's departure was also eased by the arrival of Marie Kent. She has been a pleasure to work with personally and professionally. Given the tensions of publishing any book of this scope it may be rare to wind up liking one's editor, but I regard Marie with warm friendship as well as professional respect. I also found out that for all the grandiose titles like "author" and "editor" the real heroes of the publishing business are editorial assistants. Amy Mayfield, who is the "e.a." for political science, has worked very hard on this project and has helped turn the arduous into the bearable. She has responded to every need with dispatch and great good humor and can even understand why I'd rather be Marlin Perkins. In the production stage of the text, Phyllis Larimore has been my "boss." When I finished writing I thought I was finished. Wrong! Copyediting, galleys, page proofs, art, and a thousand other facets of publishing would have overwhelmed me without Phyllis' expert guidance. Rephah Berg, who did the copyediting, is an individual of tremendous skill. After getting over feeling as if I had been sent back to the first grade, I learned to appreciate the fineness with which she "tuned up" my work. I'll never again lightly use *which* instead of *that*. Judy Blamer coordinated the photo and cartoon effort. We both learned a lot about intranational as well as international relations, and I have discovered what an interesting and exacting process photo editing is.

Finally, anyone who has written will recognize that it is an intensely personal, as well as professional, experience. During the good times and the bad Eileen McNutt has been there to listen, to understand, to encourage. Thank you. I would also like to thank my son, John Michael. Teenagers have a great perspective, sometimes, and on occasion when he and I wound up at a football game or watching MTV together, I was refreshed and my balance restored.

To all of you,

I can no other answer make but thanks, and thanks, and ever thanks.

***Shakespeare,* Twelfth Night**

Contents

7

Power 136

8

Force 164

15

Disarmament and Arms Control 353

I

A Preview

An honest tale speeds best being plainly told.
***Shakespeare,* Richard III**

"All the world's a stage," William Shakespeare wrote in the second act of *As You Like It,* "and all the men and women merely players." The Bard of Avon was a wise political commentator as well as a literary great. Shakespeare's lines are used here because they help convey the mental picture the author has of this text. The characters are different, of course, the United States, China, and the Soviet Union replacing those of Shakespeare's time and imagination. Beyond that, though, there is a remarkable parallel between international relations and the master's plays. Both are cosmic and complex. The characters are sometimes heroic and at other times petty. The action is always dramatic and often tragic. As with any good play, the audience was drawn into the action at The Globe, the theater where Shakespeare staged his works. Similarly, in the global theater of international politics, we are all drawn in. Indeed, we are all seated on the stage, no matter how remote the action may seem or how much we may want to stop the world and get off. For better or worse, we and the world are stuck with each other. The progress of the play, even if it continues its long run or closes early, is something we will all enjoy—or perhaps endure.

Another quotation from Shakespeare—this time from *Macbeth*—is also worth thinking about here. A despairing Macbeth tells us that life "struts and frets his hour upon the stage" in a tale "full of sound and fury." Again the playwright hits the mark! The history and current state of world politics do not make for a peaceful scene. The view of this text is basically one of a world divided. The world drama has a cast of national actors at odds with one another. Although the actors, or countries, are often at peace, and although there are even elements of charity and humanity that can at times be found in them, they are also full of ambition, self-serving righteousness, and greed. It is a rare day when at least some of the actor states are not in open conflict. And even when they are not threatening one another, they are forever calculating what is good for themselves and then defining those ends in terms of universal justice and the common good of all humankind.

The last line from Macbeth's soliloquy is where this text and Shakespeare part company. The Bard pronounces the action of life as "signifying nothing." That thought has a gloomy and fatalistic appeal. It allows us to ignore our responsibility. "What the hell," we can say, "What can I do?" That approach may be easy, but it is also self-defeating.

In general, this text does not try to tell you what to think. That is neither appropriate nor likely to succeed. But one message is stressed here: the play is important and deserves our careful attention. We are not merely observers. We are inevitably actors because we are on the stage along with everybody else, great and small. What is more, the script is not set. It is an improvisational play with lots of room for ad-libbing, interpretation, and even changing the story line. Of course, most of us are bit players, many merely walk-ons with no lines, but we can speak up if we wish and join the action if we try. Capturing center stage is difficult, and even the great have not been able to hold it for long, but we can all play a part.

Why Study International Relations?

Well, you might say, if it is hard to become a "star," why bother? One "bit player," me, won't be missed. Besides, why should I even care? International politics is full of names and places I can't pronounce, which are far away, and which don't really affect me anyway. So why should I care?

The answer is that international politics does matter. It plays an important role in your life, and you should be concerned. To begin to see why, let's take a look at one leader who had the "it's far away, why bother" attitude.

The Danger and Futility of Ignoring International Politics

It was 1938 in Europe, and it was the last chance to stop Adolf Hitler. The Nazi Führer and his Third Reich threatened Czechoslovakia. But there was hope: the Czechs were well armed and were determined to remain free. Germany had not yet reached its full war potential. If only a major ally could be found to stand by Czechoslovakia and deter or defeat the Germans! Ah, the sad "might have beens" of history! Germany, of course, was not deterred and was defeated only seven years later at the cost of tens of millions of lives.

The decision whether to help the Czechs largely rested on the shoulders of British Prime Minister Neville Chamberlain. But Chamberlain would not help. Czechoslovakia, he told his countrymen, was "a faraway country about which we know little." Britons agreed. It did seem far away, and if Hitler subjugated the Czechs, well, that was a pity, but it did not really matter to Britain. Within two years, as Luftwaffe bombs fell on London, Chamberlain's thesis was disproved. Little or large, far or near, Czechoslovakia did matter.

In some ways we haven't learned much since 1938. Studies today show that Americans know very little about the places, people, or politics of the world. Like Czechoslovakia, countries such as El Salvador, Cambodia, Afghanistan, or Namibia are faraway countries about which we know little. Or are they?

International Politics and Your Pocketbook

Chamberlain was wrong then, and his views would be even less appropriate today. None of us is isolated from the impact of world politics. One way we are all affected is economically.

Intermestic Economics

The general impact of international economics on domestic societies expands as world industrial and financial structures become increasingly intertwined. Trade wins and loses jobs, we are dependent on foreign sources for vital resources, inflation is tied into foreign affairs, as is the domestic allocation of our own resources. The ties between national and international affairs are so close that one observer has coined a new word—**intermestic**—to symbolize the merger of *inter*national and do*mestic* concerns.[1]

Jobs and trade. In the United States one of every seven manufacturing jobs depends on foreign trade. One of every three farm acres is producing for export. Thus, international economics creates jobs. It can also cause the loss of jobs. In January 1982 over 290,000 American auto workers were out of work. At least part of their distress was due to the impact of foreign competition. By the end of 1981, over 27 percent of the American car market had been lost to imports.

Resource dependency. Economically, countries are also dependent on one another for a variety of resources. Some types of resource dependency, like oil, are obvious. The reliance of Japan, Europe, and the United States on foreign energy suppliers makes faraway and little-known countries like Saudi Arabia (which supplies about 25 percent of U.S. imports) or Nigeria (nearly 20 percent of U.S. imports) important to Americans.

Other import dependencies are less obvious. Take cobalt, for example. Cobalt, a mineral used to make high-strength alloys, is important to the defense and commerce of the United States. Cobalt is used in aircraft engines, and if the supply of this vital mineral were cut off, the United States would be unable to manufacture military and commercial jet engines. That would both adversely affect national defense and leave tens of thousands of aircraft workers jobless. The problem with cobalt is that the United States currently produces none. Zaire, however, produces 50 percent of the world's total and accounts for 75 percent of all cobalt shipped to the United States. What do you know about Zaire, another faraway, little-known country of great importance? Could you point to Zaire in Figure 1-1?

Inflation. The stability of the dollar, both at home and abroad, is another important international economic factor. The double-digit inflation that plagued the United States through the 1970s and into the 1980s resulted partly from the attempt of the Johnson and then the Nixon administrations to have both guns (in Vietnam) and butter (increased domestic programs at home). At the height of the war in 1968, the federal government had a deficit of $25.2 billion, against $153.7 billion in revenues. The United States spent 16.4 percent more than it took in. Interest rates soared as the government competed

with private sources to borrow money. As money became more expensive to borrow, industrial borrowing for plant expansion dropped off, the housing and auto industries faltered as consumers were unable or unwilling to bear the interest costs, and the trade deficit grew as American products became more expensive and the American dollar less desirable.

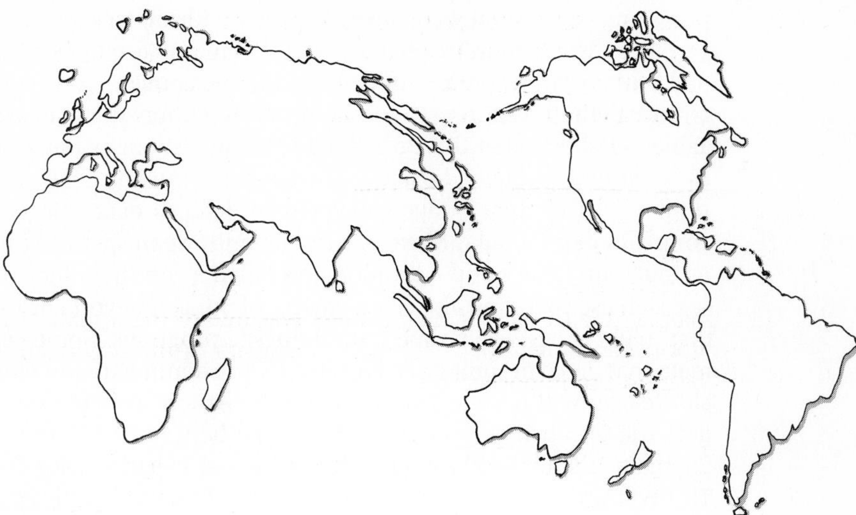

Figure 1-1. The world stage.

For many other countries inflation is an even greater problem. Compare the United States, which had an average inflation rate of 7.8 percent between 1970 and 1980, and Argentina, which had an average inflation rate of 119.2 percent—fifteen times the U.S. rate. Inflation there has become so bad that Argentina became the only country to print 1-million-unit currency. The million-peso bill is worth about $89 in U.S. dollars, and what forty years earlier would have been a fortune now buys an Argentine citizen a decent radio—if one can be found in the nearly empty shops.

Even that example pales when compared with what happened to Germany in the 1920s. Under demands by the Allies to pay reparations, the German economy fell apart. By August 1923 the German mark had soared to 4,600,000 to each U.S. dollar. By December of that year the figure stood at 4,200,000,000 marks to each dollar, for an annual inflation rate of almost 3,000 percent. After World War II the Hungarian unit of currency (the pengo), which had equaled 3.38 dollars in 1939, soared to a rate of 500,000,000,000,000,000,000 (500 million trillion) to one. Banknotes of 100 million pengos were printed, and a haircut in Budapest cost 800 trillion pengos. Could that happen to you? It is hard to believe it could, but the Germans and Hungarians did not think it could happen to them, either. It did, however, and was caused in part by international economics.

Domestic distribution of resources. A classic choice that governments have to make is between defense (guns) and domestic programs (butter). Defense and domestic spending do not vary inversely on a one-to-one ratio, but international relations do play an important role in determining how much governments can spend on domestic programs. In time of war, domestic programs are normally curtailed to provide for defense. If they are not, dangerous deficits and inflation can occur. Even in peacetime, however, the guns and butter options present difficult economic choices. Some countries devote almost all their resources to social programs. Others spend heavily on defense. Table 1-1 shows that the United States spends about as much on the military as on either health or education. The Soviet Union and China have even larger proportions of their budgets devoted to defense expenditures. By contrast, countries like Canada, Mexico, Austria, and Japan spend six to eleven times as much on health and education combined as on the military.

Defense spending also has a variety of impacts beyond its use of resources that might otherwise be spent on domestic programs. Some economists estimate that the arms buildup advocated by the administration of President Ronald Reagan will have a vast impact on the American economy. Beyond inflation, the $1.5 trillion spent on U.S. defense between 1982 and 1985 competes for materials, skilled workers, and industrial capacity with domestic needs. This will slow the development and supply of new domestic goods, hurt trade by leaving less available for export, and leave the United States with an inflexible economy that can continue to maintain itself only through high defense expenditures.

Individual Economics

On an individual level, each of us is probably more involved in international economics than we think. Many of us have jobs which are dependent on foreign sources or which are tied to defense spending. International economics affects the price of gasoline for your car, the availability of Datsuns or Toyotas, and even whether you can watch the Olympics. Defense-oriented budget deficits reduce the money available for educational loans and increase interest rates you pay for them. On an even more personal level, it would be worthwhile to survey your personal belongings. How many are foreign-made? Sony televisions, Panasonic radios, sweaters from China, European or Japanese

Table 1-1. Comparative Military and Social Per Capita Expenditures in Seven Countries, 1978.

	Military	*Education and Health*	*Ratio of Military to Education and Health*
United States	$499	$906	1:1.8
Soviet Union	394	271	1:0.7
China	26	21	1:0.8
Canada	174	1157	1:6.6
Mexico	8	78	1:9.8
Austria	93	814	1:8.8
Japan	80	878	1:10.9

Based on The World Bank, *World Development Report, 1981* (Washington, D.C.: 1981), table 24, p. 180.

Some would argue that the billions of dollars being allocated for the controversial B-1 bomber, shown here, would be better spent on domestic programs such as medicare, housing, or college scholarships.

cars, Italian shoes, and a host of other foreign manufactured items are likely to make up our individual inventories. International politics and economics, then, are really no farther away than our designer jeans—American-worn, French-named, and Hong Kong–manufactured.

International Politics and Your Life (Literally)

International politics can affect far more than your pocketbook. It can determine the quality and even the existence of your life.

The Environment

The growth of the world's population and its pressure on resources threaten to change the quality of life as we know it. It took 10,000 years for the world to reach its current 5 billion people. Projections are tricky, but it is reasonable to expect that by the year 2000 the world population will reach 6.3 billion. Within a century, at current rates, the population will have exploded to 28 billion people, a 700 percent increase (see Figure 1-2).

Americans will not be immune to this avalanche of humanity. The burning of fossil fuels to warm and propel this mass is raising the world carbon dioxide level, warming the atmosphere, and threatening to melt icecaps and flood low-lying areas of the world, including such places as Boston, New York, New Orleans, and Los Angeles. The chemicals spewed into the air cause disease and are also attacking the earth's atmosphere, which helps shield the earth

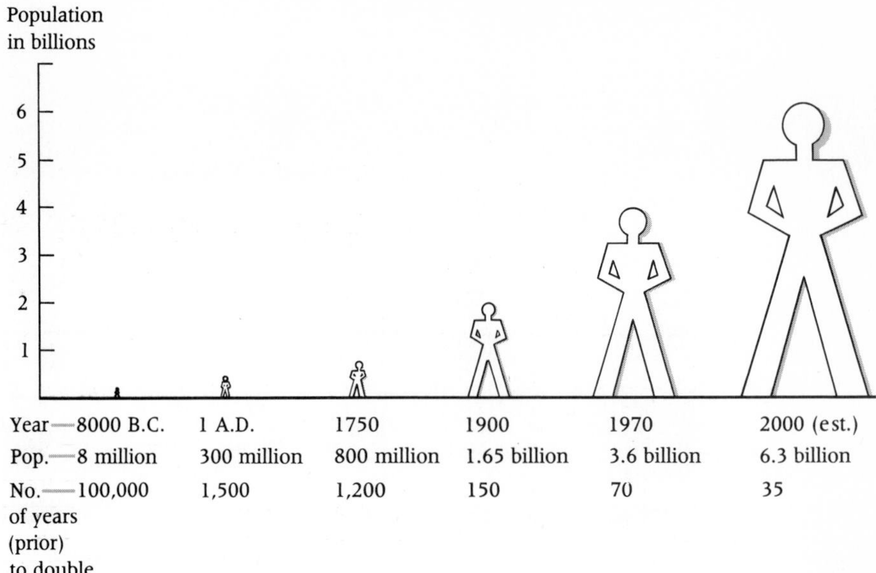

Figure 1-2. Estimated world population and doubling times, 8000 B.C. to 2000 A.D. *Adapted from Robert S. McNamara, "Population and International Security,"* International Security *3 (1977), pp. 116–136.*

from deadly ultraviolet rays. Fresh water supplies are also polluted and, in many areas, are insufficient to meet the exploding mass of humanity.

These ramifications are not the ravings of an ivory-tower academic: they are ongoing realities. A 1980 report submitted to the president by the Department of State and the Council on Environmental Quality warned that by the year 2000 the world would be "more crowded, more polluted, less stable ecologically, and more vulnerable to disruption than the world we live in now."[2] Among other possibilities, the report warned that the search for fuel alone could result in destruction of 40 percent of the world's remaining forests and extinction of 20 percent of the globe's plants and animals.

War

Plants and animals are not the only things facing extinction. Humans may also wind up on the endangered species list. International politics now has the potential of extinguishing most or all of the human race. Until recent times most people killed in wars were soldiers. Increasingly in the twentieth century, civilian casualties have risen and civilians have become a direct target of military operations. During World War II nearly as many civilians as soldiers were killed. In the next—nuclear—war, civilian casualties will far outnumber military deaths. The National Security Council has estimated that a nuclear exchange between the United States and the Soviet Union would kill a minimum of 140 million Americans and 113 million Russians.

Nuclear war has happened only once, when the United States dropped two atomic weapons on Japan in 1945. The fact that forty years have passed

Box 1-1. Ages of U.S. Marines Killed in Vietnam.

Age	*Deaths*
18–22	12,436
23–27	1,590
28–32	385
33–37	242
38–42	84
43–47	25
47+	11

It is the young who die in wars. College-age youth made up 84% of the Marine Corps dead in Vietnam.

Data based on Harry G. Lock, "Vietnam Casualty Statistics," *Marine Corps Gazette*, March 1985, p. 24.

without a recurrence may be partly luck as well as policy, and the odds of avoiding nuclear war are declining. Forty years ago there were no nuclearly armed countries. Now there are six, and the U.S. Energy Research and Development Agency estimated in 1977 that within ten years another thirty countries would possess the technical capability to produce a bomb. By the turn of the next century, countries with nuclear weapons could be the rule rather than the exception.

Individual involvement in war can also occur in circumstances less cataclysmic than atomic warfare. Many countries, including the Soviet Union and China, have a draft to staff their military services. The United States abandoned the draft in the early 1970s, but there is pressure to resume involuntary service, and draft registration is now required of all military-age males. The Supreme Court recently rejected a suit to require the registration of women on an equal basis with men, but the days of the all-male fighting force are probably numbered. Thus, most of the students reading this book could find themselves directly involved in world politics via the draft and an all-expenses-paid government trip to some exotic corner of the world. You can try to ignore it, but it may not ignore you.

World politics, then, does count. We are all involved environmentally and economically. Further, it can threaten our very lives. Wars have and will continue to happen. Young men—and probably young women—have been and will be drafted. Some will die. Perhaps you will be in the ranks or even among the casualties. In the worst possible circumstance, nuclear war, it will not make much difference whether you have been drafted or not.

Can We Make a Difference?

The next logical question is, so what? What can any individual do? Why not pay attention to something we can change? Fortunately, we can make a difference. It is true that we cannot all be president or secretary of state, but we can take action and we can make our views known. There are things we can do!

There are a variety of possible personal statements and actions on international politics. The sum of millions of individual actions, ranging from Jane

Fonda visiting Hanoi, through veterans burning draft cards in front of the White House, to students protesting and even dying on our campuses, helped end American involvement in Vietnam.

Fortunately, not all individual actions need to involve martyrdom or other forms of violence. Yellow ribbons tied around trees during the Iran hostage crisis, marches and other expressions in support of Poland's Solidarity Union, and donations to relief organizations in Ethiopia all are positive statements of concern and commitment.

Individuals can also work within democratic societies to influence foreign policy. The simplest way is by *voting* in elections. Presidential candidates Ronald Reagan and Walter Mondale differed on a variety of issues, including defense spending, arms negotiations, summit meetings, and specific weapons systems in world politics, as shown in Table 1-2.

Direct voting on international questions is also possible in some countries. British citizens, for example, voted in favor of joining the European Common Market. The citizens of Greenland recently voted against membership. Finally, *expressing your opinion,* orally or in writing, or even having your opinion sampled in a poll can have an impact. Public opinion polls are widely published in the United States, and political leaders keep a weather eye on public attitudes. Even the Soviets have recently taken up limited polling.

The point is that you can count. Protesting, donating, voting, even thinking can play a role. Few individual actions are dramatic, and by themselves few significantly change world politics, but the sum of many smaller actions can and does make a difference. Politics, then, is not best considered a spectator sport. Instead, it is a participant—even a contact—sport.

Evolution of the World System

For many of the students taking this course and reading this text, one frustration will be that at times it will seem like having come in after the movie started or the curtain went up. Things are happening and characters are strutting on the stage, and you are at a loss to know who they are or how they fit in. Unless you have had some strong courses in world history/current events,

Table 1-2. Positions of Mondale and Reagan on Selected Issues.

Issue	*Mondale*	*Reagan*
Summit with USSR	Immediate	When proper
Build MX missile	No	Yes
Nuclear freeze	Yes	No
Restrict auto imports (domestic content)	Yes	No
Build B-1 bomber	No	Yes
Aid to contra rebels in Nicaragua	No	Yes

This statue is part of the Vietnam memorial in Washington, D.C. To many Vietnam veterans, and others who lived through that controversial war, this statue represents the people—mostly of college age—who were killed there.

many of the events and individuals discussed in this text may be unfamiliar. To help remedy that, the following pages are devoted to a short explanation of the pivotal events and people that have played a part on the world stage.

We will pick up the action in the late 1700s with the American and French revolutions. That is somewhat arbitrary, but most political scientists and historians agree that this period marked a major watershed in the political path of the world.

A word of caution is in order before we proceed to our historical survey. The following pages make no pretense to being a definitive history of the last two centuries of world history. Among other things, there will be an emphasis on the particular themes, events, and personalities we will encounter in this text. That should suffice for a minimal understanding with particular reference to this text, but each reader is encouraged to find that old high school/college survey history text or take one out of the library and to spend some time refreshing his or her memory. The following discussion will make a lot more sense if you can put it into the proper historical context.

The Seventeenth and Eighteenth Centuries—the World Changes

The years of the late 1700s and 1800s were a time of major change for the world. The American (1776) and French (1789) revolutions began a process that changed the entire philosophy about the proper relations between those who governed and the people. *Democracies* were established on the principle that political power rests with the people rather than with the monarch. This view also changed and expanded the concept of *nationalism* to include mass identification with and participation in the affairs of the state (country). Among other symbols of this change was that Napoleonic France was the first country to have a true military draft and to raise an army a million strong.

From its beginnings in America and, particularly, France, democratic nationalism spread throughout Europe. Within just a little more than a century, monarchs (especially powerful ones) became the exception rather than the rule. The first two decades of the twentieth century marked the real end of monarchial government, with the collapse of the dynastic reigns in China, Germany, Austria-Hungary, Russia, the Ottoman Empire, and other, smaller states.

In the realm of international political relations among the major European powers, the century that extended from the final defeat of Napoleon (1815) to the outbreak of World War I was marked by a multistate *balance of power* system. In essence, that means that the major powers (Great Britain, France, Prussia/Germany, Austria-Hungary, Russia, and to a lesser extent Italy and the Ottoman Empire/Turkey) grouped themselves in shifting, equally balanced alliances that served to keep the peace. A related political assumption, but not specifically part of the balance of power, was that the major powers cooperated and compromised to exercise control over lesser powers. As a result, and although there were some limited clashes, Europe was free from a general conflict between the end of the Napoleonic wars and the beginning of World War I.

The 1800s were also a time of rapidly increasing *industrialization,* mainly in Europe and the United States. That had a number of impacts. One was a shift in the power of states, as those that most rapidly industrialized grew in power. Germany, in particular, benefited from this trend. So did the United States, but that would not be obvious for many years. A second impact of industrialization (and associated technological advances) was that the European powers gained strength compared with nonindustrialized Asia and Africa. Closely related to this disparity in development was the fact that the industrial countries needed to find resources and markets to fuel and fund their capitalist expansion. Economic expansion needed colonies. European countries and the United States also coveted colonies as a matter of prestige. France grabbed land to catch up with Great Britain, Germany colonized to gain "a place in the sun" with France, and Italy, the United States, Belgium, and others all followed suit. The result was an era of *imperialism* beyond anything that had been known in history. The losers, of course, were the peoples of Africa and Asia who fell under white domination. China, it should be noted, was never technically colonized, but after the 1840s that proud culture was divided into spheres of influence among the Western powers and had substantial territories taken away by the British (Hong Kong), Japan (Taiwan/Formosa), and Russia (about 1 million square miles in Central Asia and Pacific Siberia). This era was a period of "humiliation" for the Chinese, and some of their current foreign policy is a continuing reaction to this time of trial.

The Early Twentieth Century—the Old Order Totters

World changes usually evolve rather than occur suddenly, but by the beginning of the 1900s things were moving quickly. As mentioned, democracy was rapidly undermining dynastic monarchism. In 1900 there were still czars and kaisers, but they would be gone in less than two decades. *Nationalism* was similarly eroding the foundations of empires. World War I was, again, a pivotal point. Two major empires (the Austro-Hungarian and Ottoman) were among the losers. Among their ethnic subjects, there had been a great deal of nationalist/independence feeling, and that sentiment was further encouraged by President Woodrow Wilson's call in his Fourteen Points for "self-determination," or the right to self-rule by national groups. The result was the (re)establishment of countries such as Poland, Czechoslovakia, and Yugoslavia. Other countries like Syria, Jordan, Lebanon, and Palestine/Israel came under the mandate (control) of the League of Nations and finally became independent after World War II. As we will see in our recounting of that postwar period, the drive to national self-determination truly exploded in the second half of the twentieth century.

The *balance of power* that had governed European relations and had generally kept the peace during the 1800s broke down in the tragedy of World War I. The reasons were many and are still subject to dispute. We can say, however, that world systems change, but this particular alliance system became rigid rather than fluid and was not able to adjust adequately. After the defeat of the Central Powers (Germany, principally), there was an attempt to reestablish a balance-of-power system. After initially severe treatment in the 1920s by the Treaty of Versailles, Germany was allowed to rebuild its strength in the 1930s.

One reason that some were not dismayed by German revitalization was events that had occurred in Russia. In 1917 the czar had been deposed, and after some months the Bolsheviks under Lenin had taken power. There was a strong negative reaction in the West to communist power. There were some halfhearted attempts to overthrow the Bolsheviks, and the Soviets were generally treated as outcasts. Thus, a strong Germany was seen by some as a bulwark against the "Red menace."

Another cause of Germany's unimpeded restrengthening was the timorousness that World War I had instilled in Britain and France. Each almost literally had lost an entire generation of young men, and as Hitler came to power (1933) and rearmed his country, they often vacillated rather than risk a replay of the horror of vanquishing German arms. The *Munich Conference* (1938) became synonymous with this lack of will. Hitler demanded annexation of part of Czechoslovakia. The Czechs looked to France and Britain for support, but those countries refused to help. British Prime Minister Neville Chamberlain and other leaders met with Hitler in Munich and agreed to the dismemberment of Czechoslovakia in the hopes of *appeasing* Hitler and maintaining the peace. Needless to say, that failed. Hitler's aggression continued, and a year later World War II erupted when Germany invaded Poland.

A final trend of this period that should be noted was the expansion of the world community. Not only did self-determination result in new states, but many existing states that had previously been on the periphery of European-dominated diplomacy gradually began to play a more significant role. The rise of Japan and the United States is of particular note. Japan's coming of age was heralded by its defeat of a European power in the Russo-Japanese War (1905). As for the United States, it joined World War I in 1917, and its troops and industrial might added to the defeat of Germany. Many other non-European countries joined world diplomacy through membership in the League of Nations. The point is that international relations still focused on Europe during the first four decades of the 1900s, but a shift was underway.

After World War II—the Old Order Collapses Completely

World War II was a human tragedy of unequaled proportions. It also marked a major change in the world system.

The East/West confrontation. One shift involved the actors and, indeed, the nature of the system itself. Most of the major actors were devastated by the war, and they fell from the first rank of world politics. In their place, the United States emerged from the war as both a military and an economic *superpower.* The Soviet Union, though damaged beyond belief, emerged as the United States' chief rival. It could not match the United States economically, and for two decades or more the United States maintained a strong nuclear lead, but the Soviets possessed a huge conventional force that threatened Western Europe and an ideology that seemed to press American interests around the globe.

The exact causes of the Soviet/American confrontation, termed the *cold war,* are complex and controversial, but it is safe to say that varying economic and political interests and the power vacuum created by the collapse of the old balance-of-power system led to a new, *loose bipolar system,* in which a great deal of world politics was centered on the two superpowers and the *East/West confrontation* between them.

The most contentious point of conflict between the superpowers during the early postwar period was Eastern Europe, particularly Poland. At *Yalta,* a conference in February 1945 among Britain's Prime Minister Winston Churchill, America's President Franklin Roosevelt, and Soviet Premier Josef Stalin, the future of Poland was discussed. The Soviets, who already militarily occupied Eastern Europe, wanted to maintain their control. Defensiveness, expansionism, and ideology all played a part in the urge to dominate. Stalin thought that Roosevelt had given him tacit license to control the area. Americans, by contrast, thought Stalin had given assurances that the Soviets would allow free elections. That never happened, and what was said at Yalta and the status of Eastern Europe are still sore points between the superpowers.

The smiles on Churchill's, Roosevelt's, and Stalin's faces here at Yalta were a veneer that covered the coming East/West confrontation called *the cold war.*

The American reaction to the perceived world communist threat was the doctrine of *containment*. An offshoot of the lessons of Munich, containment held that the United States should try to counter Soviet/communist expansionism wherever it threatened. A somewhat later, related theory was the *domino theory*, which supposed that if communism conquered one country, then its neighbor would fall, then another, and another, just like a row of dominoes standing on end, until the chain reaction led to America's doorstep. The result of these strategic assumptions was that the United States moved from a prewar norm of isolationism to a postwar *global role*, diplomatically and militarily opposing the Soviet Union (and later Communist China) around the world.

The most serious direct confrontation, and the closest the world has ever come to nuclear war, occurred in Cuba in October 1962. *The Cuban missile crisis* erupted when the Soviets tried to station medium-range nuclear missiles in Cuba and the Kennedy administration resolved to force the missiles out. In the end, because the United States possessed a vast nuclear superiority and because it handled the crisis with some skill, the Soviet missiles were withdrawn. In the longer term, however, the crisis led to a major increase in Soviet military strength. The Kremlin was determined never again to be so humiliated. The Soviets began a massive nuclear armament program that soon brought them to parity with the United States. They also began a naval building program that eventually would lead them to a first-rank navy with the ability to project Soviet conventional military power around the world.

The containment doctrine also led to America's involvement in *Vietnam.* After World War II, the Vietnamese, led by nationalist/communist Ho Chi Minh, struggled for independence against the French. In 1954 Ho achieved victory, but the country was divided between his forces in the north and a pro-Western government in the south. Unification elections were supposed to occur soon, but the South resisted, and they did not. The struggle resumed in the early 1960s, and the United States, fearing a communist victory, intervened in behalf of the South. As the United States increasingly became involved, so did its prestige, and the American goal shifted to "peace with honor" more than preventing a communist victory.

The war, which was popular at first, soon became a domestic trauma for America as the violence and casualties mounted on all sides. The depth of the American domestic opposition to the war was tragically underlined by the death in 1970 of four students at Kent State University during antiwar clashes between demonstrators and Ohio National Guardsmen. War-weariness finally led to the complete disengagement of the United States, and within a short time the South fell (1975) to the North.

Vietnam led to a number of important changes in American attitudes about international relations. One was the reassessment of the need to fight communism everywhere. To some degree, the "lesson of Vietnam" that some drew was that the United States should fight nowhere, and in the 1970s America severely constrained its military power.

Second, and related to much wider developments, the United States saw more clearly that the world was no longer bipolar but had become a *multipolar system* or, perhaps, a new balance-of-power system. The communist "camp" was fragmented, with China more of an antagonist to than an ally of the Soviet Union. On the Western side, Japan and Europe had both recovered economically and (especially the Europeans) were increasingly inclined to follow foreign policies that sometimes diverged from those of the United States. President Nixon and his chief foreign policy adviser, Henry Kissinger, moved to better relations with both the Soviet Union (detente) and China in face of the new balance-of-power realities they perceived. U.S./Chinese relations have continued to improve gradually. U.S./Soviet relations, however, suffered a marked decline after the Soviet invasion of Afghanistan (1979) and the election of the more ideologically anticommunist, defense-minded Reagan administration (1980). The relations between the United States and Western Europe remain generally cooperative, but Europe continues to develop its own strength and foreign policy direction, especially through its main regional organization, the *European Communities*.

A nuclear world. One phase of detente was nuclear arms control. The world system was forever altered by the atomic flash over Hiroshima in August 1945. Atomic weapons not only brought total self-destruction within the range of human possibilities, they changed power relationships. They virtually divided the world into two classes of powers—the two superpowers, who had almost all the nuclear weapons, and everybody else. The possibility of nuclear war is

REPRINTED BY PERMISSION OF JOHN TREVER, ALBUQUERQUE JOURNAL.

THE LESSONS OF VIETNAM

so cataclysmic that a major focus of the current political system is avoiding Armageddon. Increasingly, nuclear arms talks have become an ongoing process—so much so, in fact, that when START arms talks broke off (in late 1983, only to be resumed in early 1985), the world was alarmed. The decades of arms talks have brought some, but limited, success. The 1963 Test Ban Treaty and the 1972 SALT I treaties brought some restraints but no reductions. The 1979 SALT II treaty was never fully ratified because of the decline in relations, but it has been tacitly followed by both superpowers.

Economic interdependence. World War II also signaled major shifts in world economics, in both *trade* and in *monetary relations*. The level of world trade had been gradually rising, but after the war it greatly accelerated. In addition to nonpolitical technological and economic factors, trade was encouraged by the belief that trade barriers had contributed to the economic collapse (world depression) that preceded and (some argued) helped to cause World War II. As a result, and in its own interest, the United States led moves to remove tariffs and other trade restrictions. The General Agreement on Tariffs and Trade (GATT) organization was a primary focus of that activity. One result of increased trade, as well as other factors, is increasing *economic interdependence:* almost all countries have economies that rely on foreign markets and sources of supply. The "free trade" philosophy still dominates Western thinking, although in recent years there has been restrengthened pressure to practice more "protectionism."

Monetary relations were also considerably revamped at the end of the war, primarily at a conference (1944) at Bretton Woods, New Hampshire. The resulting monetary arrangements, known as the Bretton Woods system, were based on the gold standard and the strength of the American dollar. That system lasted until the early 1970s, when a number of factors, including the weakening of the dollar and the unwillingness of the United States to sell gold at a fixed (and no longer realistic) rate, brought the world to a new system of currencies that generally "float"—that is, are exchanged on the basis of supply and demand conditions. The Bretton Woods structure also included the International Monetary Fund (IMF), which was designed to help stabilize currency exchange rates by loaning countries money to meet international currency demands, thereby keeping the supply and demand stable. The IMF continues to play a vital role in monetary relations.

Economic relations have become increasingly troublesome in the 1970s and 1980s. Trade and monetary tensions exist among the Trilateral countries (United States, Western Europe, Japan), with U.S./Japanese relations particularly troubled by the imbalance (in Japan's favor) of trade between the two. Monetary relations are also unsteady on a number of fronts. In recent years, the most serious problem has related to the massive loans made to the Third World/less developed countries (LDCs) and the difficulty those countries (especially in Latin America) are having meeting principal and interest payment schedules. On a broader scale, economic relations and international politics are increasingly concerned with the wide gap between the relatively wealthy industrialized states and the poorer LDCs.

North/South: Economic disparity. A basic world economic reality is that the substantial majority of people and countries are poor. These countries are designated the *South*. By contrast, world wealth is concentrated in a few industrialized countries (the *North*). Although some of the South's absolute economic (and related social) conditions are slightly improving, the gap between the North and South is widening. Increasingly, the poor countries are making demands that a *New International Economic Order* (NIEO) be established based on a greater sharing of wealth and the end to trade and monetary policies that favor the North. The response of the North has been limited to date, and the question of Third World development and North/South relations will remain a perplexing and contentious aspect of international relations for years to come.

Expansion of the world nation-state system. The Third World has also played a pivotal role in the expansion of the world's nation-state (country) system. The colonial systems established by the imperial Western powers collapsed after World War II, and in the ensuing years over one hundred new countries have gained independence (nearly tripling the previous number). Almost all these new countries are located in the Third World. Nationalism, once thought on the decline, has been reinvigorated, and the perspectives and demands of these countries have considerably changed the focus and tone of world political and economic debate.

Scenes such as this one are common throughout the Third World. The people of the less developed countries are becoming increasingly angry that they live in poverty while most of those in the developed countries, which are few in number, enjoy relative wealth.

International cooperation. While discord has continued to be a persistent theme of international relations, the period after World War II has also been notable for renewed attempts to further international cooperation. The United Nations, founded in 1945 as a successor to the League of Nations, has made contributions in peacekeeping and economic and social betterment. Its role, however, has been limited by the resistance of all countries to compromising their own interests for the common good. In addition to the UN, a wide array of *transnational* governmental and private organizations have been established that work to better the world's economic and social conditions. Many of these organizations also work to try to find solutions to the many environmental and resource problems that increasingly beset the world. The concept of international law has also made progress, although international law remains a primitive system.

Our Approach to Studying the World Drama

As a final step in this chapter, we will take a look at how we will go about studying the actors, plot, and action of world politics.

The goal of this text is to give its readers the beginning information and analytical tools to make sense of international politics and to form a foundation on which to found their opinions and actions. To organize that effort, the book has been divided into four parts.

The first three chapters are devoted to setting the stage. We have already addressed the question: Why care? Chapter 2 will set the stage and suggest ways to review the drama. We will see that international relations analysis is complex work. The subject has several important dimensions that demand our attention, and there are a number of approaches to studying our subject. Each of these approaches and dimensions will be discussed. Chapter 3, the last in this part, will introduce the actors. As we shall see, the world is truly a Cecil B. DeMille production: grand in scope, lavish in setting, and with a host of fascinating characters. States, private organizations, and individuals will all strut and fret across the stage. We will also find it necessary to analyze the stage—or "system"—because the stage, in itself, plays an important role in determining what the actors want to do, are likely to do, and find it possible to do.

In the second part of the text, Chapters 4 through 6, we look at the underlying plot of our play—the goals and motives that drive countries. Nationalism, ideology and ideas, and morality (yes, it exists) are all discussed. The summary concept of national interest in all its complexity is also considered.

Chapters 7 through 10 take up the play's action, the means by which countries pursue their ends. The underlying concept of power is taken up first. The two main components of power, military and economic strength, and their use are given individual treatment. The government-to-government interplay between countries, diplomacy, as well as the attempts by one government to undermine another, subversion, are also given special treatment. These aspects of the nature and use of power represent the basic action of our drama as it is played out today.

Like Shakespeare, some might add, however, that as it stands, international politics is "a tale told by idiots." Many have contended throughout history that power politics is wrong, and few could dispute that it is destructive. But up until now the potential for destruction has been limited. That is no longer true, and the voices urging world cooperation, while not new, are increasingly frightened and urgent. Power politics may be the norm, but it is not the only alternative.

Chapters 12 through 16 deal with the alternative script of international cooperation. Various types of international organizations, especially the United Nations, are considered. International law, disarmament and arms control efforts, and economic and social cooperation are also examined. They do not represent the predominant reality of today, but we struggle toward them. Which script we choose could very well determine whether, in the end, our play is a tragedy or not. In any case, it is great drama!

As in the novel and film *The French Lieutenant's Woman* there are two scripts and two possible endings. It is up to the actors—and we are they—to decide. As a final thought, and to thoroughly misapply an inescapable question posed by Ronald Reagan:

If not us, who?
If not now, when?

Summary

International politics is not a story of faraway people in faraway lands who matter little to us. To the contrary, international politics plays an important role in your life. Economically, it affects jobs, the supply of important natural resources, inflation, and how the government allocates its budget among domestic and foreign/national security programs. International politics also affects the environment, and it can even threaten your life by destroying you singularly or by annihilating your entire society.

The response to these realities should be action, not fatalistic passivity. There are many things, great and small, that we can do, singly and collectively, to change the course of international events. Like it or not, we are all involved in a momentous world drama. It is an improvisational play, however, and its script and climax are up to us.

Terms

Intermestic—The merger of *inter*national and do*mestic* concerns.

Resource dependency—Reliance by a country on foreign sources for an important natural resource.

Notes

1. Bayless Maning, "The Congress, the Executive and Intermestic Affairs," *Foreign Affairs* 57 (1979): 308.
2. Council on Environmental Quality, and Department of State, *The Global 2000 Report to the President,* vols. 1 and 2 (Washington, DC: U.S. Government Printing Office,1980).

2

The World Stage

I am amazed, methinks, and lose my way
Among the thorns and dangers of the world.
Shakespeare, **King John III**

International relations is a complex subject, and in the first half of this chapter we will examine some of the dimensions of our subject. In the second half we will look at the approaches that the reviewers of our drama, or political analysts, take in studying these complexities.

The Dimensions of World Politics

Our drama is complex, and its action is played out along several important dimensions. In the pages that follow, we will briefly preview each of these aspects of world politics. In these previews, however, you will be reading only "a little about a lot," but each of the dimensions will be discussed often as this book continues.

Conflict versus Cooperation

The world is essentially divided and conflictive. The political map is divided into more than 150 sovereign, self-interested states. Wars are fought, states maneuver for economic advantage, and diplomacy usually strives to gain political influence. Thus, conflict will be the main focus of the first three parts of this text.

Countering that main theme is cooperation. Global cooperation rather than national competition is still a secondary process in the world, but it is slowly growing. We will explore this hopeful trend in the last four chapters of our text. Concepts such as international law and organization are still in their infancy compared with domestic law and organization, but they do exist and have expanded their scope. Further, given the realities of declining resources and a mushrooming population and also the reality of our military ability to destroy ourselves, it is probable that international cooperation must continue to expand if the world is not to face economic, ecological, and/or nuclear catastrophe.

East versus West

The main focus of conflict since the end of World War II has been the struggle between the United States and the Soviet Union. This is termed the East/West conflict, or **East versus West**. Although the contest has its economic, ideological, and social aspects, it is primarily a military confrontation. The hopes for détente in the 1970s have faded into a new atmosphere of tension caused by Soviet actions in such places as Afghanistan and Poland and also by the election of the more "hard line" Reagan administration in the United States.

North versus South

During the last two decades a new geographic axis of tension has developed, **North versus South**. We will examine this dimension carefully in Chapter 12, but it is well to introduce the division here. The North symbolizes the wealthy, industrially developed countries, which lie mainly in the Northern Hemisphere. By contrast, the South symbolizes the less developed countries, the majority of which are near or in the Southern Hemisphere. The tension between the two groups is primarily economic and social. In 1980 the United States had a per capita gross national product of $11,596, West Germany's was $10,509, Britain's was $5,340, and the Soviet Union's was $4,820. In the South, Bolivia's per capita GNP was $692, Syria's was $988, Burma's was $186, and Uganda's was $256. Beyond the obvious poverty and hunger that those figures imply for the South, illiteracy and disease are rampant, and life itself is considerably shorter, as shown in Table 2-1.

The gap between the rich and poor countries is not new. What has changed is the awareness in the poor countries of their relative poverty. These countries have become less willing to accept a world system in which wealth is so unevenly distributed, and they are increasingly pressing the developed countries to share their resources. The tension between the countries on the two ends of the economic scale is just beginning to build, but it may become a crisis as populations expand, resources decline, and the South's military capability (especially nuclear) increases.

Reality versus Perception

There is a world as it is and a world as we see it. Sometimes reality is indisputable or inescapable. A Soviet T-72 tank, the level of U.S. steel production, and the 1 billion Chinese are all real. If the Soviets launched a nuclear

Table 2-1. Measures of Quality of Life in Selected Northern and Southern Countries, 1980.

	Life Expectancy (years)	*Illiteracy (percentage of population)*	*Population per Physician*
North			
United States	74	.5	621
West Germany	71	.5	503
United Kingdom	72	.5	761
Soviet Union	70	.5	299
South			
Bolivia	47	37	2,583
North Yemen	38	85	17,175
Laos	35	88	21,667
Uganda	49	65	24,700

Data from U.S. Department of Commerce, *Statistical Abstract of the U.S., 1981* (Washington, D.C.: U.S. Government Printing Office, 1981).

attack on the United States, that would also be real and could not be avoided, no matter what one thought. Often, however, world politics are not based on reality but, rather, on perception. The United States and the Soviet Union each perceive the other as the "bad guy," out to take over the world. Each also sees itself as the "good guy," wanting peace and beset by its enemies. Former Secretary of State Alexander Haig called the Soviets "dangerous because they are armed to the teeth" and prone to "foreign diversions." Secretary of Defense Caspar Weinberger believes the 1980s to be "a decade of danger" for the United States, and President Reagan told West Point cadets that they were part of a "chain holding back an evil force." Contrast that with the views the Soviets hold of the United States. The Soviet foreign minister charged that "American foreign policy now wears a heavy military steel helmet." A Soviet expert on America condemned the "wild scenarios by American strategists [which] breed suspicion and paranoia that serve to justify the arms race." And the editor of *Izvestia* has pointed out that "when civilian political figures talk about being able to fight and win a nuclear war, that's when we should all worry. Our politicians don't. Yours do!" Can both countries be correct?

The mutually perceived hostility reflected in these Soviet and American charges is called **mirror image**. This occurs when "two countries involved in a prolonged hostile confrontation develop fixed distorted attitudes of one another that are really quite similar. Each sees itself as virtuous, restrained, and peace-loving, and views its adversary as deceptive, imperialistic, and warlike."[1] Robert Jervis has suggested a number of general perceptions found in world politics.[2] Among these are the following:

1. *There is a tendency to see other countries as more hostile than one's own.* The reactions of Soviet and American officials to the other side certainly support that view.

2. *We tend to see the behavior of others as more centralized, disciplined, and coordinated than ours.* Both the Americans and the Soviets are convinced that the other side has a carefully planned, well-executed master strategy to expand its power and influence and to frustrate and defeat its opponents. By contrast, both sides view their own country as defensive and as responding on a piecemeal basis to the aggressive thrusts of the other side. Former Secretary of State Henry Kissinger described U.S./Soviet relations in terms of this perceptual phenomenon:

> The superpowers often behave like two heavily armed blind men feeling their way around a room, each believing himself in mortal peril from the other whom he assumes to have perfect vision. . . . Each tends to ascribe to the other side a consistency, foresight, and coherence that its own experience belies. Of course, over time even two armed blind men in a room can do enormous damage to each other, not to speak of the room.[3]

3. *It is hard to believe that the other side can see us as a menace.* Not only is each side convinced that it wears the white hats and that the other side wears the black hats, but it is hard to believe that the other side can doubt our

sincerity. When we propose a peace plan, how can they reject it? They can't be afraid of us. It must be that they really do not want peace, because if they did, they would accept our plan—the "good guy" plan.

The link between perception and world politics is the concept of **operational reality**. Not only is reality distorted by our (mis)perceptions, but we tend to act, or operate, on those perceptions. In the 1950s and 1960s, Americans viewed Vietnamese leader Ho Chi Minh as a communist whose victory in the war would further the worldwide communist movement and add to the threat faced by the "free world." Vice-President Lyndon Johnson told us that if we didn't stop the communists in Vietnam, someday we might have to fight them at the Golden Gate Bridge. Others saw Ho as primarily a nationalist leader who wanted to reunify the Vietnamese people and to free them from a century of foreign (French, then American) domination.

Whatever Ho's reality, communist or nationalist, the United States *operated* on the basis of the image of Ho as communist and waged war in Vietnam. The image, then, assumed a sort of *reality* because it motivated American action.

International politics is thus more than a matter of objective facts. It is a study of subjective judgments based on images of oneself and other international actors. It is something of an Alice in Wonderland tale in which what is important often is not what is but rather what seems to be.

Focus of Concern: What Is versus What Ought to Be

Another dilemma facing us is whether to focus on the study of "what is" in world politics or "what ought to be." In a rough classification, political scientists who study international affairs can be divided into those whose main concern is the current state of world politics and those who concentrate on their image of a future, better world community. The students of "what is" can be subdivided into two groups: (1) realists and (2) behavioralists. Similarly, the "what ought to be" futurists can also be subdivided into (1) idealists and (2) Marxists. It should be noted, parenthetically, that this four-category grouping paints many subtle ideas with a broad brush. Like most categories used herein, these are best understood as a teaching device, and a further reading of the scope of theorists will reveal rich and diverse perspectives.

Realists

During most of the post–World War II period to 1970, realist theory was the main theme of international relations theory. It also dominated and continues to dominate the thinking of most of the decision makers who practice international politics. **Realists** base their views on a number of assumptions:

1. Countries often have conflicting interests.
2. Differing interests can lead to war or other forms of conflict.

Whether Ho Chi Minh was really a communist or a nationalist, the American perception that he was a communist led to the operational reality of war in Vietnam.

3. A country's power is crucial in determining the outcome of conflict and also determines its influence over other countries.
4. Politics, then, is aimed at increasing power, keeping power, or demonstrating power.

Power, therefore, is the key concept for realists. In an early example of realist writings, Frederick Schuman characterized world politics as a process in which each country "necessarily seeks safety by relying on its own power and [views] with alarm the power of its neighbors."[4] Probably the most influential realist theorist of recent times has been Hans Morgenthau, who has defined politics as a "struggle for power." Morgenthau, like most realists, argues that human nature and societies are both imperfect and imperfectible. Therefore conflict is an inherent danger. Given that reality, decision makers should structure their policies and define national interest in terms of power. They should follow policies designed to maximize their power and should avoid policies that overstep the limits of their power.

Importantly, realists imply not only that international relations is based on power politics but that statesmen should follow the dictates of power or else they invite disaster. Thus the realists accept what is inevitable and argue that it is both impossible and dangerous to try to change reality.

It should be pointed out that realists are not warmongers. They desire peace but believe that peace can be achieved only through strength. Realists also believe that statesmen can avoid war by not pursuing goals they do not have the power to achieve. War can also be avoided by understanding the goals and power of your opponents, thereby not underestimating their abilities or threatening their vital interests.

Behavioralists

The behavioralist, or "scientific," school of political science is interested in recurring patterns and causal relations of international behavior. **Behavioralists** often use quantitative methods to arrive at and prove hypotheses that will explain both why certain events have occurred and under what circumstances they might occur again. They also often use cross-cultural analyses to test whether similar or divergent causal patterns occur between different political systems as well as over time.

A traditional belief in international relations is that domestic conflict (independent variable) might lead to external conflict (dependent variable) as a country's leaders tried to divert the focus of conflict to an external enemy. By doing so, the domestic leaders would encourage national unity and also help maintain their regime in power. The work of a number of behavioralist political scientists has generally shown that assumption to be wrong. Rudolph Rummel, for one, analyzed the levels of internal and external conflict in seventy-seven countries during the mid-1950s and found little relation between the two variables.[5] That does not mean that domestic unrest will not be followed by international aggressiveness. Indeed, other studies using behavioralist techniques have shown that in some cases domestic conflict is followed by international tension.[6] But the connection (causal relation) between the two circumstances is less certain than we once assumed.

Like realists, behavioralists have little interest in discussing what ought to be in world politics. Where they differ, beyond methodologies, is that realists accept what is and often advocate that statesmen should also accept and operate within the framework of power politics. Behavioralists, from their "value-free" or "scientific" perspective, are more disinterested in the good or ill of world politics. They tend to operate from a value-free posture, neither condoning nor condemning what is. They only describe what is and why and try to predict what will be. This value-free approach has been the source of some criticism of behavioralism by those who contend that the problems and stakes of the world are too great to be studied dispassionately. Behavioralists have also been criticized for studying only what is quantifiable and ignoring less quantifiable subjects. Finally, behavioralists have sometimes been disparaged for being more concerned with what is the best statistical formula to study a problem than with the resolution of that issue.

Idealists

Acceptance of the system of power politics is rejected by some students of international politics. The **idealists** are interested in *alternative world futures* and methods for changing the current state of international politics. Idealists start from a set of values and direct their efforts to moving the world in the direction they favor. Although they often focus on what is, they do so to show that it is unsatisfactory and may lead to disaster. Idealists assume that human nature and behavior can be changed for the better. Realists are skeptical of the human animal, and behavioralists make no assumptions at all. Idealists are interested in such things as strengthening world organization, spreading international law and morality, and achieving disarmament.

Idealists are particularly critical of political realism. They argue that power politics makes no sense in today's turbulent world of competing ideologies and potential nuclear and ecological catastrophe. Idealists also claim (but realists deny) that by concentrating on power, realists focus on means, with too little attention to ends. Finally, the idealists' main contention is that if the world continues to operate on the basis of national power, it may well be fated to repeat the wars and the economic and social dislocations of the past, with increasingly catastrophic results.

Marxists

Political scientists in many areas of the world and some in the United States have a Marxist orientation. Like idealists, **Marxists** are future-oriented, they operate from a set of prescriptive values, and they are optimistic about the nature of human beings. They also believe that the system of national states should and will wither away when world communism is achieved. Marxists believe that a historically inevitable series of pressures and counterpressures will lead to the destruction of capitalism and the triumph of communism. They analyze political conflict from the perspective of the control and distribution of economic resources. Marxists believe that international conflict results from the imperialist aggression of capitalist countries in their drive (1) to amass wealth and (2) to avoid their own inevitable collapse by destroying the communist wave of the future. Thus, like idealists, Marxists are *prescriptive* and *normative*. They advocate change according to their values. *Predictively,* however, idealists project what could happen if the world system does not change and, less clearly, predict what could be if the world did change. Marxists predict that the world will change and what it will be like when it does.

Levels of Analysis: System, State, Individual

Another major division among analytical approaches used by political scientists has to do with the level of focus. The essential question here is "What do we study?" One approach by political scientists has been to divide their foci of study into **levels of analysis**. These refer to levels of the factors that affect international politics. One early study[7] suggested two general levels of analysis. Other political scientists have refined and expanded that concept to include up to six levels of analysis, but for our analysis here we will adopt a middle ground by discussing three levels of analysis:[8]

(1) *Systems analysis*—a world view.

(2) *State-level analysis*—concern with the characteristics of an individual country and the impact of those traits on the country's behavior.

(3) *Individual analysis*—focus on people, which can be further subdivided into two categories:
   (a) the *biographical approach,* study of the attributes and views of individual decision makers, and
   (b) the *nature-of-humankind approach,* concern with biological and psychological explanations of the behavior of the human species.

Focus on one level of analysis does not mean exclusion of the others. Indeed, it would be best to think of the levels as occurring along a scale from the general (systems analysis) to the specific (individual analysis). It is possible to focus on one level and yet still use elements of the others. As will be clear as we go along, this text primarily uses state-level analysis but also includes elements of both systems and individual analysis.

Systems Analysis

Political scientists who take the **systems analysis** approach essentially adopt a "top down" approach to studying world politics. Their primary focus is the external events and world political environment that determine the pattern of interaction in any given system. Systems analysts believe that any system operates in predictable ways—that there are behavioral tendencies that the actor countries usually follow. An imperfect analogy might be a solar system.[9] In such a system, the planets and other celestial bodies move in regular and predictable patterns, which are determined by such factors as the size and gravitational pull of the sun and the size and distance of a planet from the center of the solar system. It can be noted, also, that a system can even have subsystems. A planet, for example, may have a number of moons that revolve around it, while the entire subsystem revolves around the sun.

If we follow this analogy, systems analysts can be thought of as political astronomers. What they focus on is determining the nature (size, shape, spatial relations between bodies, etc.) of the system and its subsystems. Even more important, systems analysts are interested in the interactive patterns within the system. How does it work? What are the relations between bodies? When and why do they collide or travel safely on? What can be predicted about future movements?

Systems Characteristics

A solar system has a variety of identifiable characteristics. It is a certain size and has existed for a finite period. The types and numbers of celestial bodies (suns, planets, moons, asteroids, comets) can also be described. The size of the bodies, their distances from one another, their relative movement, and a number of other relational characteristics are also important.

Similarly, political systems analysts are concerned with the characteristics of international systems and subsystems. These political scientists have not yet developed an agreed-on list of factors, but the most common possibilities include the following.

Number of actors or poles. A system with two major actors (bipolar) will differ in behavior from one with three (tripolar), which, in turn, will differ from a system of four or more (multipolar). One study found that a bipolar system has a medium chance of war, and a tripolar system has a relatively low chance of war. Multipolar systems have the highest probability of war, with five poles being the most unstable system.[10]

In a tripolar system, which is something like the current state of affairs, each of the major countries endeavors to make sure that it is not "odd man out." Systems analysts would point to the United States' normalization of relations with China as an example of the system at work. Richard Nixon, who had built a good deal of his political career on his adamant anticommunism, was the first president to visit China. Despite his personal views, Nixon recognized by the late 1960s that continuing to try to isolate China would leave the United States as "odd man out" if China and the Soviets became allies. As private citizen and presidential candidate, Ronald Reagan was a strong critic of "abandoning" Taiwan (Nationalist China) and an advocate of continuing military aid to Taiwan. As president, however, when he was faced with objections from the People's Republic of China to the sale of advanced fighter aircraft to Taiwan, Reagan backed down. China threatened to downgrade relations with the United States and, in a time of increased tension with the Soviet Union, leave the United States as odd man out in the tripolar system. Thus, according to systems analysis, U.S. domestic factors—such as a president's personal conservative views—mattered little. The system governed the American response to China in the tripolar world.

Distribution of power among the actors. The world pattern of military strength, industrial capacity, natural resources, and other power factors also determines the pattern of international interaction. The lack of sufficient oil in the United States and its abundance in Saudi Arabia has considerable impact on U.S. policy in the Middle East. When the Reagan administration proposed to sell AWACs (advanced-warning aircraft) to Saudi Arabia, there was heavy domestic opposition from those who were pro-Israeli and from those concerned about the security of the super-secret aircraft. In the end, however, the systemic distribution of resources prevailed. The United States could not afford to alienate its chief oil supplier. The AWACs were sold to Saudi Arabia.

Physical characteristics of actors. Systems analysts are also interested in such factors as location, size, and topography of the various actors. Technology may have reduced, but it has not eliminated, the importance of these factors. The fact that two of our three major actors, the Soviet Union and China, border on each other and that the United States borders on neither is important. Among other things, the Soviet Union or China could directly invade the other's territory. The two countries also have significant world border disputes. World politics would be considerably different if, let us say, the Soviet army were stationed on the Rio Grande.

Interaction of actors. How countries line up also interests systems analysts. Do alliances, for example, promote peace, or do they presage war? So far the answer is unclear. Alliances have acted differently at different times in history.[11] Another type of interaction is cultural interchange. Some systems analysts believe that increased intercultural contact between countries through modern travel and communications has decreased the chances of war.[12]

Factors That Cause Change

If we think about solar systems again, we will see that they are both stable and changing. The system we live in has existed for untold millennia and will probably remain pretty much the same for eons more. Thus it is relatively stable. But solar systems, ours included, are also dynamic. Usually these changes are evolutionary. Suns, for example, have a life cycle. They are born, expand, then gradually cool and die out. As that happens, over the ages, the system will slowly change.

Sometimes, though, the change can be revolutionary. A sun can explode, throwing the system into mayhem. It is also possible that "domestic" events on one of the planets could radically change the system. If, for example, the earth went on a craze of nuclear self-destruction, the cumulative effect of massive detonations might throw the globe off its axis. The result would be a missile weighing 588 quintillion (588×10^{30}) tons careering through the solar system with Lord only knows what impact.

International systems also change, usually slowly but sometimes rapidly. Accordingly, political scientists explore what causes systems to change. A list of possible factors, again meant to be illustrative rather than complete, follows.

Changes in the number/power of major actors. The collapse of the European powers (Great Britain, Germany, and France) and Japan as a result of World War II changed the existing multipolar system to a bipolar (U.S.–USSR) system. More recently, the perceived rise of China is changing the bipolar system to a tripolar system. Thus, a change in the number of major actors and/or their relative power may significantly change the rules of the game.

Change in technology. Changes in technology can alter systems. The development of nuclear weapons plus the ability to unleash them anywhere in the world via missile in a matter of minutes dramatically changed the system from what it had been in the 1930s. Systems analysts would say, for instance, that the United States did not abandon its isolationist stance and become an active internationalist actor after World War II by choice. Rather, the system, including the nuclear missile age, compelled the United States to extend its activities to maintain itself. It could no longer confidently hide behind oceans. In the future, the development of nuclear power and other alternatives to fossil fuels as energy sources will have a profound impact on the world system if countries become energy-self-sufficient and decrease their interdependency with the rest of the world.

During his tenure as a representative, a senator, and as vice president, Richard Nixon built his career on anticommunism. Here President Nixon smiles and waves on the Great Wall in (Red) China. Systems analysts would say he had little choice but to befriend the communists.

Domestic factors. Changes can also occur because of "crazy states."[13] Internal pressures can cause a country to act "abnormally," to break the norms of the system. This, in turn, can upset and even transform the system. The failure of the balance-of-power system that existed between World Wars I and II can be partly attributed to the German domestic factor of Adolf Hitler, who, to put it charitably, was not a rational statesman. The system was also changed by acute pacifism in Great Britain, which, in part, prevented that country from acting to keep the system in balance by restraining Germany. In more recent years, Iran, with its seizure of the American Embassy and its gruesome war with Iraq, is an example of a state whose acts do not follow system norms. Ideology can also be an important factor. Richard Rosecrance has commented that divergent ideologies, such as capitalism and communism, destabilize systems because they create different perceptions of the system, increase feelings of insecurity, and encourage actors to try to change the status quo.[14]

How Systems Work

One of the originators of systems theory, Morton Kaplan, identified six different systems.[15] Two, the "balance of power" and the "loose bipolar" systems, were based on historical observation. The other four, "tight bipolar," "universal," "hierarchal," and "unit veto" systems, were hypothetical, or possible, systems. Other political scientists have formulated different sets of systems, but Kaplan's work remains a classic. To explore both the different types of systems and how they operate, we will briefly examine Kaplan's ideas. All six systems will be defined, and we will focus on the "rules of the game" for the balance-of-power and loose bipolar systems.

Balance-of-power system. Kaplan defines this system as one in which there are five or more major actors. Historically it closely resembles the system of Great Britain, France, Germany, Russia, Austria-Hungary, and, to a lesser degree, Italy and Turkey, which existed in Europe in the 1800s. It is a relatively fluid and competitive system in which the countries involved form shifting alliances. All are interested in their own benefit and are primarily responsible for their own protection. Since too much strength for any one actor or even any one alliance would threaten all the other actors, there is a tendency to form counteralliances and to try to win allies away from the predominant coalition. The rules of the game for each actor are:

1. Increase power, but do so by negotiations rather than by fighting.
2. Fight rather than fail to increase power.
3. If fighting, stop short of destabilizing the system by destroying another major actor.
4. Oppose any actor or alliance that threatens to upset the balance by becoming preponderant.
5. Restrain (revolutionary) actors that do not subscribe to the system and do not play by the rules of the game.
6. Permit defeated major actors to maintain their status or, if a major actor is eliminated, find a new actor to take its place in order to maintain the potential for balance in the system.

Loose bipolar system. This system is characterized by two roughly equal coalitions of actors. There may be other important actors, either national or supranational (e.g., the United Nations), but they are neutral and do not threaten, either singly or in alliance, the two predominant blocs. This system closely resembles the system that existed for about two decades after World War II and featured the United States and its allies versus the Soviet Union and its allies. The rules of the game are:

1. Try to eliminate the other bloc.
2. Fight if necessary to eliminate the other bloc, but only if the risks are acceptable.
3. Increase power relative to the other bloc.
4. Fight to avoid elimination/subordination by the other bloc.
5. Attempt to bring new members into your bloc. Attempt to prevent other members from joining the rival bloc.
6. Nonbloc members act as mediators to reduce the danger of war between the blocs.

Tight bipolar system. This is a system in which all nonbloc national and supranational actors disappear. The world would be totally divided into two rival camps.

Universal system. In this system the principal actor would be a world organization, such as a much-strengthened UN. National actors or alliances with some local autonomy might also exist, but they would be subordinate to the universal organization on matters that affect other actors.

Hierarchal system. This system is even more integrated than a universal system. It comes close to a world government in which subunits would not be independent but might more closely resemble American states or the republics in the Soviet Union.

Unit veto system. In this system many or all actors possess the ability to destroy the others. This type of mutual checkmate system might occur when most of the world countries possess nuclear arms.

Individual Analysis

At the opposite end of the scale from broad systems analysis is **individual analysis**, which focuses on the role of humans in world politics. Individual analysis can be roughly subdivided into two approaches: the biographical approach and the nature-of-humankind approach.

The Biographical Approach

The biographical approach emphasizes the individuality of statesmen. It begins with the assumption that, in the last analysis, people make foreign policy decisions. Further, people differ and, therefore, different leaders make different decisions.

This view is represented in a recent book by John Stoessinger that argues that "a leader's *personality* is a decisive element in the making of foreign policy. . . . Differences in leaders' personalities thus may make or break a nation's foreign policy. It matters very much, in short, *who* is there at a given moment."[16] You might ask yourself what the communist revolution would have been like or whether it would have occurred at all if there had not been a V. I. Lenin in Russia or a Mao Zedong in China. Would World War II have occurred if Adolf Hitler had never lived? If John F. Kennedy had lived, would 50,000 Americans have died in Vietnam? The answers to these questions are, of course, unknowable. What is certain, however, is that history would have been different.

Advocates of the biographical approach are primarily interested in the *psychohistory* of individual leaders. The question is not *what* these persons decided. Rather, the question is *why* they chose certain paths. What are the internal, psychological factors that motivate decision makers?

The list of possible psychological factors is long and varies from analyst to analyst. For our discussion, though, we will consider four basic factors from the decision maker's point of view:

1. *How I feel*—What is the decision maker's physical and mental health?
2. *What I know*—What is the decision maker's view of history in general? What have been the experiences of his or her personal history?
3. *What I believe*—What are the individual's ideology, perceptions, and operational code?
4. *What I want*—What factors of ego and ambition affect the individual's decisions?

Mental and physical health. The mind and body can be important factors in decision making. According to Soviet Premier Nikita Khrushchev, his predecessor Josef Stalin suffered from severe paranoia. If it is true that "Stalin was a very distrustful man, sickly suspicious," that "everywhere and in everything he saw enemies," and that "Stalin had completely lost consciousness of reality," then it follows that Soviet policy after World War II might have been more cooperative with either a mentally healthier Stalin or a different Soviet leader directing foreign policy.[17]

The physical health of Stalin's American contemporary, Franklin Roosevelt, may also have affected Soviet/American relations. When Roosevelt met Stalin at Yalta in February 1945, the president's blood pressure was an astronomical 260/150 and he suffered from chest pains. It has been argued that FDR was too weak to stand up to Stalin. One scholar has written, "By the time of the Yalta Conference, Roosevelt was very seriously ill and unable to deal effectively with complex diplomatic issues to be discussed."[18] Two months later Roosevelt was dead. What might have been if a healthy Roosevelt had gone to Yalta?

History and personal experience. The past is another factor that helps shape a statesman's approach to world problems. It has been said that generals fight and statesmen try to prevent the last war. That is an oversimplification, but it has an element of truth. Decision makers often apply the "lessons" of *world history* to current situations. The "lesson of Munich" has done much to

What would the Soviet Union, indeed the world, be like if Lenin had never lived?

affect the actions of Western leaders since World War II. The British, in an attempt at **appeasement**, allowed Hitler to annex part of Czechoslovakia. This later became an obvious failure as Germany attacked the rest of Czechoslovakia, then Poland, and finally most of Europe. Munich serves as a symbol of what came to be regarded as a fatal series of concessions to the Germans, Italians, and Japanese that only encouraged aggression and finally led to World War II. The lesson (**Munich syndrome**) drawn by postwar statesmen was that you do not compromise with aggression—"Don't give 'em an inch, or they'll take a mile."

During the cold war years Western leaders repeatedly applied the lesson of the 1930s. When President Truman was faced with the North's invasion of South Korea, he drew a parallel in history:

> In my generation this was not the first occasion when the strong attacked the weak. I recalled some earlier instances: Manchuria, Ethiopia, Austria. I remembered how each time that the democracies failed to act it had encouraged the aggressors to keep going ahead. Communism was acting in Korea just as Hitler, Mussolini, and the Japanese had acted. . . . If this was allowed to go unchallenged it would mean a third world war, just as similar incidents had brought on a second world war.[19]

Truman decided for war.

In 1956 British Prime Minister Anthony Eden was faced with a crisis over Egypt's nationalization (seizure) of the Suez Canal. He drew on Munich as a lesson from history:

> Success in a number of adventures in the breaking of agreements in . . . the Rhineland, in Austria, in Czechoslovakia . . . persuaded Hitler . . . that the democracies had not the will to resist. . . . As my colleagues and I surveyed the scene . . . we were determined that the like should not come again.[20]

Eden decided for war.

In 1964 Lyndon Johnson faced a crisis in Vietnam. As he later remembered:

> Everything I knew about history told me that if I got out of Vietnam . . . then I'd be doing exactly what Chamberlain did in World War II. I'd be giving a big fat reward to aggression. . . . And so would begin World War III. [21]

Johnson decided for war.

A decision maker's *personal experiences,* as well as his or her understanding of world history, may also be an important influence on policy choices. The international and domestic policies followed by Mao Zedong can be partly understood from the story of his boyhood that Mao related to journalist Edgar Snow:

> One incident I especially remember [recalled Mao]. When I was about thirteen my father . . . denounced me . . . calling me lazy and useless . . . I cursed him and left the house . . . My father pursued me . . . I reached the edge of a pond and threatened to jump in if he came nearer . . . demands and counter demands were presented for the cessation of civil war . . . I learned when I defended my rights by open rebellion my father relented, but when I remained meek and submissive he only cursed and beat me the more . . . I learned to hate him, and we created a real united front against him.[22]

Belief system. What decision makers believe is a third personal element that influences foreign policy. *Ideology* is a key factor here. Ideology, which is discussed extensively in Chapter 5, forms a "lens" or "prism" through which we perceive reality. It helps precondition our images of both ourselves and others. It is common to think of ideology in terms of communism, but as used here *ideology* is a broader term referring to the preexisting images that decision makers hold. Try borrowing a pair of glasses from a friend. Look at the world around you. It becomes distorted, the degree of distortion depending on how thick the lenses are. Similarly, ideology acts as a perceptual lens, the degree of distortion related to the strength of the beholder's ideology.

A classic study of the role of belief systems has been done by Ole Holsti.[23] Holsti used content analysis techniques to examine 5,584 statements on the Soviet Union by Secretary of State John Foster Dulles. From these, Holsti was able to construct an *operational code* for Dulles. The study found that Dulles viewed the Soviets through a heavy ideological lens that told him that "the Soviet Union was built on the trinity of atheism, totalitarianism, and communism." From this perspective, Dulles saw the communist Soviets as unrelentingly hostile. Even when the Soviets showed a willingness to coexist, to compromise, or to shift their resources from military to domestic resources, Dulles interpreted their actions as signs of weakness or trickery rather than as good intentions. He was also unable to view Soviet policy from his opponent's perspective. He could see no legitimate Russian national interest, only the evil designs of godless communism. He once compared Soviet foreign policy to that of a hotel burglar who lurked in corridors, indiscriminately trying doors until he found one unlocked. Dulles' operational codification of Soviet foreign policy as always communist (and dangerous) and never as Russian (and perhaps legitimate) can be seen in an exchange he had with Senator Henry Jackson:

Jackson: Would you not agree on this: that international communism has been used as an instrument of Russian foreign policy since 1918?

Dulles: I would put it the other way around. Russian foreign policy is an instrument of international communism.[24]

What decision makers want. The fourth and final psychological factor that influences a statesman's point of view is personal motivation. Here the issue is not what a decision maker wants in terms of national interest. The point is what the decision maker wants in terms of personal interest. How do policy choices relate to the individual's ego and ambitions?

The Cuban missile crisis presents an instructive illustration of the ego involvements of Nikita Khrushchev and John Kennedy, the Soviet and American leaders. Khrushchev seems to have been partly motivated by the ego need to teach the much younger Kennedy who was the boss. At one point the Soviet premier dismissed the American president as "a man who is younger than my son." Faced with both foreign policy difficulties and domestic economic problems, Khrushchev, who was overthrown two years later, may also have wanted to shore up his domestic political position by taking advantage of a young, inexperienced president and a country that he considered "too liberal to fight."[25]

Kennedy also reacted personally to the crisis. His ego was wounded and his domestic political position was imperiled. One American official recalled that the installation of nuclear missiles in Cuba caught the administration "with our pants down." Further, the president's initial response to evidence of the missiles was an intensely personal "He [Khrushchev] can't do that to *me*!" Beyond the tender ego of a man who had been bullied at his Vienna summit with Khrushchev and who had been embarrassed over Cuba during the Bay of Pigs fiasco, Cuba was a domestic political liability for Kennedy. A close adviser characterized Cuba as Kennedy's "political Achilles' heel." The secretary of the treasury worried that, as a result of the crisis, "the next House of Representatives is likely to have a Republican majority." The president also worried that the crisis would help elect Republicans in the impending 1962 elections and might even catapult a Republican into the White House in 1964. Kennedy even half-imagined that he might not politically survive long enough to seek reelection. His brother Robert told him, "If you hadn't acted, you would have been impeached." "That's what I think," the President replied, "I would have been impeached." Getting the missiles out of Cuba, then, was motivated by more than the defense of the United States. It was also partly motivated by the ego and political defense of John F. Kennedy.[26]

The Nature-of-Humankind Approach

Like the biographical approach, the nature-of-humankind approach has a long history and focuses on the individual. The two approaches differ dramatically, though. Biographical studies emphasize the uniqueness of each individual. Nature-of-humankind studies look for commonalities in human behavior based on the nature of humankind. Many kinds of studies have been done from this perspective, but two types are of particular importance.

Psychological factors. Psychology is one possible source of human behavior. Here we mean the common psychological traits of humans, not the psychological makeup of an individual. Sigmund Freud theorized that individuals are torn between two instincts, *eros* (the life instinct) and *thanatos* (the death instinct). Death is attractive because it brings release from anxiety. Humans resolve the tension between eros and thanatos through *displaced aggression*. That is, people vent their destructive instincts on others rather than on themselves.

More recent psychological studies have focused on *frustration-aggression theory* as a source of international conflictual behavior. Theorists have contended that aggression can take many forms, including being aimed directly at the source of frustration, being displaced onto a scapegoat, or even being self-directed (suicide in the individual). Individual frustration-driven behavior can be amassed and projected through national aggressive behavior.

Biological factors. Biology is a second theoretical basis of human behavior. *Biopolitics* is concerned with the relation between humans' physical and political nature. One subdivision of this approach, ethology, argues that animal, including human, behavior is, at least to some degree, based on innate genetic characteristics. Ethology studies animal behavior and attempts to draw parallels with human behavior. Ethologists such as Konrad Lorenz *(On Aggression)*, Desmond Morris *(The Naked Ape, The Human Zoo)*, and Robert Ardrey *(The Territorial Imperative, African Genesis)* have raised provocative questions about the genetic basis of aggressiveness and other forms of human international behavior. Ardrey, as an example, contends that "territoriality—the drive to gain, maintain, and defend the exclusive right to a piece of property—is an animal instinct" and that "if man is a part of the natural world, then he possesses as do all other species a genetic . . . territorial drive as one ancient animal foundation for that human conduct known as war."[27]

Researchers have found that, in addition to conflict over food and sex, animals will fight to gain or maintain territory, will protect the young/family, will try to expel strange members of their species with whom they come into contact, will protect objects toward which they are possessive, will fight rather than be deprived of status, and will become more aggressive as they earn rewards through repeated success.

Soviet/American diplomacy, in general, and the Cuban missile crisis of 1962 were partly a result of the personal reactions of Premier Khrushchev and President Kennedy to one another. Here the two meet in Vienna in 1961.

Critics of ethology point out, correctly, that a great deal of human behavior is learned rather than instinctual. They also show that learning can modify behavior even if that behavior is partly genetic. The normal peaceful coexistence in domestic societies is an example. Still, ethology cannot be totally dismissed. When one considers, for example, the Grand Chaco War of the 1930s between Bolivia and Paraguay in which 100,000 people were killed in a dispute over an arid, desolate tract of essentially useless land, our animal roots seem a lot closer than we might wish to think.

State-Level Analysis

Focusing on the state as the primary international actor is the third and most common approach. **State-level analysis** is concerned with the study of foreign policy decision making. State-level theorists acknowledge that external (systems-level) factors influence decisions. They also agree that decision makers' responses are based partly on their personal (individual-level) traits. State-level theorists argue, however, that the key to understanding foreign policy is the *domestic environment* in which leaders operate.

Each of the world's more than 150 states is a complex structure, and the decisions that leaders make are heavily influenced by the domestic situations in their individual countries. Some analysts argue that each country and its policies are unique and can be understood or predicted only by a detailed study of that country. Other analysts contend that regularities between countries exist, and they use the comparative foreign policy approach in an attempt to find similarities in both the domestic structure and circumstances of various countries and the foreign policies pursued by those countries.

This dispute is not new, nor is it likely to be resolved soon. Indeed, neither side is completely correct, but both do have something to offer. On the one hand, the intensive study of an individual country can make a significant contribution, both through understanding that country and through gathering data that allow comparisons with other countries' domestic structures and foreign policies. On the other hand, comparative foreign policy analysts also make significant contributions to our understanding of world events. Various studies have found, for example, that there is little distinction between types of domestic government systems (e.g., democratic and dictatorial) and the peaceful or aggressive behavior of a country.[28] It can also be shown that dictatorial systems are no more likely than democracies to win wars or to achieve other foreign policy successes.

That does not mean, however, that dictatorships and democracies are the same in their foreign-policy-making processes. Analysts have argued that societal variables (such as public opinion) will be more important in decision making in democratic countries, while governmental variables (such as bureaucracy) will play a more powerful role in dictatorial systems.[29]

In a discussion of the state in Chapter 3, we will examine different domestic elements. Briefly, they are these:

Decision makers. Leaders are influenced not only by their individual characteristics (health, history, ideology, ego) but also by their role and by organizational behavior. Role behavior involves how people act because they occupy a certain position. Organizational behavior involves how people act in formal structures and how that differs from how they would act in a "free" (nonorganized) setting.

Bureaucracy. A country's bureaucracy is its governmental organization, especially the elements of the executive branch that are largely staffed by and led by nonelected officials. Bureaucracies (such as the military) are powerful actors in all types of domestic systems.

Legislatures. With rare exception, all countries have legislatures. The U.S. Congress, the USSR's Supreme Soviet, and China's National People's Congress are examples. The impact of legislatures varies greatly, however.

Political opposition. No decision maker or regime, even in the most dictatorial country, is free from real or potential opposition. Elections, coups, and rebellions are among the methods that elements of political opposition can use to gain power.

An aroused populace can affect foreign policy. Public pressure almost certainly helped persuade the Reagan administration to begin the Strategic Arms Reduction Talks. Here a million antinuclear demonstrators mass in New York City.

Interest groups. Most countries, particularly the more democratic systems, have a wide variety of organized interest groups that attempt to influence foreign policy. Interest groups are private (i.e., nongovernmental or nonbureaucratic) organizations that cluster around economic, ethnic, and other issues relevant to foreign policy.

The mass. Even in the most dictatorial system, the opinion of the mass (the general public) plays some role in foreign policy making. Public opinion, the media, and mass leaders (such as the clergy) all influence foreign policy.

International Politics—a Synthesis

What is the beginning student of international relations to make of these different approaches? Which is the most fruitful to follow? The answer is "All of them." All of these approaches combine to determine a country's actions and reactions. Each level of analysis has its place and can give us valuable insights. It is true that the exact weight of the factors on each level varies considerably over time, place, and circumstance. But explaining these variances is beyond the need or ability of a beginner and, indeed, has eluded the cleverest of professional political scientists.

What is important here is to view international politics as a synthesis of factors. If you look solely outside the state or concentrate exclusively on domestic factors, you will usually be seeing only part of the causal picture.

In line with the belief that international politics is a synthesis, this text utilizes each of the levels. Individual- and system-level influences have already been discussed and will be further illustrated in later chapters. The complexity of state-level analysis will be explored in Chapter 3. By considering each of these levels in complement, we can begin to understand not only *what* a state's foreign policy is and *how* it is carried out but also *why* that policy is adopted.

Summary

The world drama is complex. It is marked by both an East versus West and a North versus South struggle. Further, "what is" is often a function of our perceptions rather than of objective reality.

Wide disagreements exist on how to approach the study and conduct of international politics. There are realist, idealist, behavioralist, and Marxist approaches. Beyond these, there are three levels of analysis (system, state, individual). Thus, social scientists study international politics from many different perspectives. Each of these approaches makes contributions to our knowledge of international politics. The best way to view them, especially for the beginning student, is to concentrate on what they add, rather than worrying about which is "best." In that spirit, this study uses an eclectic approach, which draws on the scholarship of many analysts of various persuasions.

Terms

Appeasement—Trying to satisfy an aggressor by making concessions. See *Munich syndrome.*

Behavioralists—Analysts who look for scientific, usually quantitative evidence of recurring patterns over time and place in international politics.

East versus West—The cold war conflict between the Soviet Union and its allies and the United States and its allies.

Idealists—Analysts who reject power politics and argue that failure to follow policies based on humanitarianism and international cooperation will result in disaster.

Individual analysis—An analytical approach that emphasizes the role of individuals as either distinct personalities or biological/psychological beings.

Levels of analysis—Different perspectives (system, state, individual) from which international politics can be analyzed.

Marxists—Analysts who believe that international politics is governed by economic forces that will eventually lead to the fall of the aggressive and imperialistic system of capitalism.

Mirror image—The propensity of countries and people to have similar (good or bad) images of each other.

Munich syndrome—The "lesson" learned from the unsuccessful attempt to appease Hitler by giving the Germans part of Czechoslovakia at the Munich Conference (1938). Subsequent decision makers have used the lesson to justify a strong and immediate reaction to opponents.

North versus South—The growing tension between the few economically developed countries (North) and the many economically deprived countries (South). The South is demanding that the North cease economic and political domination and redistribute part of its wealth.

Operational reality—The process by which what is perceived, whether that perception is accurate or not, assumes a level of reality in the mind of the beholder and becomes the basis for making an operational decision (a decision about what to do).

Realists—Analysts who believe that countries operate in their own self-interest and that politics is a struggle for power.

State-level analysis—An analytical approach that emphasizes the actions of states and the internal (domestic) causes of their policies.

Systems analysis—An analytical approach that emphasizes the importance of world conditions (economics, technology, power relationships, and so forth) on the actions of states and other international actors.

Notes

1. James E. Dougherty and Robert L. Pflatzgraff, Jr., *Contending Theories of International Relations,* 2nd ed. (New York: Harper & Row, 1981), p. 282.
2. Robert Jervis, "Hypotheses on Misperception," *World Politics* 20 (1968): 454–479.
3. Henry Kissinger, *The White House Years* (Boston: Little, Brown, 1979), p. 1202.
4. Frederick L. Schuman, *International Politics,* 4th ed. (New York: McGraw-Hill, 1969), p. 271. Schuman's edition first appeared in 1933.
5. Rudolph J. Rummel, "Dimensions of Conflict Behavior within and between Nations," *General Systems Yearbook* 8 (1963). See Arthur Stein, "Conflict and Cohesion: A Review of the Literature," *Journal of Conflict Resolution* 29 (1976): 143–172, for a review of the literature.
6. Jonathan Wilkenfield has done work in this area in "Domestic and Foreign Conflict Behavior of Nations," in *Analyzing International Relations,* ed. William D. Coplin and Charles W. Kegley, Jr. (New York: Praeger, 1976), pp. 96–112, and (with Dina A. Zinnes) "An Analysis of Foreign Conflict Behavior of Nations," in *Comparative Foreign Policy,* ed. Wolfram F. Hanrieder (New York: McKay, 1971), pp. 167–213.
7. J. David Singer, "The Level-of-Analysis Problem in International Relations," in *International Politics and Foreign Policy,* ed. James N. Rosenau (New York: Free Press, 1969), pp. 20–29.
8. James N. Rosenau, *The Scientific Study of Foreign Policy* (New York: Free Press, 1971). Chap. 5 shows a six-level approach. The approach used herein resembles the classic work by Kenneth N. Waltz, *Man, the State, and War* (New York: Columbia Uni-

versity Press, 1959) in which Waltz uses three "images" to examine the causes of war.

9. The idea of a solar-system analogy is borrowed from Morton Kaplan, *Towards Professionalism in International Theory* (New York: Free Press, 1979), p. 94.
10. C. W. Ostrom and H. J. Aldrich, "The Relationship Between Size and Stability in the Major Power International System," *American Journal of Political Science* 22 (1978): 743–771.
11. J. David Singer and Melvin Small, "Alliance Aggregation and the Onset of War," in *Quantitative International Politics*, ed. J. David Singer (New York: Free Press, 1968), pp. 247–286.
12. Karl W. Deutsch, Sidney A. Burrell, Robert A. Kahn, Maurice Lee, Jr., Martin Lichterman, Raymond E. Lindgren, Francis L. Lowenheim, and Richard W. VanWagenen, *Political Community and the North Atlantic Area* (Princeton, N.J.: Princeton University Press, 1957).
13. Yeheckel Dror, *Crazy States* (Lexington, Mass.: Heath, 1973).
14. Richard Rosecrance, *Action and Reaction in World Politics* (Boston: Little, Brown, 1963), pp. 280–296.
15. Morton A. Kaplan, "Variants on Six Models of the International System," in *International Politics and Foreign Policy*, ed. James N. Rosenau, pp. 291–303.
16. John G. Stoessinger, *Crusaders and Pragmatists: Movers of American Foreign Policy* (New York: Norton, 1979), p. xv.
17. Quoted in Ivo D. Duchacek, *Nations and Men*, 3rd ed., (Hinsdale, Ill.: Dryden Press, 1975), p. 197.
18. Michael P. Riccards, "The Presidency in Sickness and in Health," *Presidential Studies Quarterly* 7 (1977): 226.
19. Quoted in Ernest R. May, *"Lessons" of the Past* (London: Oxford University Press, 1973), p. 32.
20. Ibid., p. x.
21. Doris Kearns, *Lyndon Johnson and the American Dream* (New York: Harper & Row, 1976), p. 264.
22. Quoted in Robert Isaak, *Individuals and World Politics* (Belmont, Calif.: Duxbury Press, 1981), p. 44.
23. Ole R. Holsti, "The Belief System and National Images: A Case Study," *Journal of Conflict Resolution* 6 (1962): 244–252.
24. Quoted in Duchacek, *Nations and Men*, p. 220.
25. Stoessinger, *Crusaders and Pragmatists*, p. 150.
26. These quotes taken from John T. Rourke, *Congress and the Presidency in U.S. Foreign Policy Making* (Boulder, Colo.: Westview Press, 1983), pp. 107–108.
27. Robert Ardrey, *African Genesis* (New York, Atheneum, 1963), pp. 12–14.
28. Melvin Small and J. David Singer, "The War-Proneness of Democratic Regimes, 1816–1965," *Jerusalem Journal of International Relations* 1 (1976): 50–69.
29. David W. Moore, "Governmental and Societal Influences on Foreign Policy in Open and Closed Nations," in *Comparing Foreign Policies*, ed. James N. Rosenau (Beverly Hills, Calif.: Sage, 1973), pp. 171–199.

3

The Actors

Mad world, mad kings, mad composition.
***Shakespeare,* King John II**

It is now time to introduce our cast of characters. As befits the complexity of our drama, its actors are many and diverse. We can, however, imprecisely divide the protagonists into two main categories. One of these, *system-level actors,* includes supranational organizations and transnational actors. The second category, *state-level actors,* consists of the states or countries themselves and their subcomponents.

System-Level Actors

Supranational Actors

The most broad-ranging international actors are **supranational organizations**. Their distinguishing characteristics are that (1) they have individual countries as members and (2) *theoretically,* the authority of the organization transcends that of its individual members. Many view supranational organizations as a "higher," more desirable form of international order than the current system of independent states. At the ultimate, some theorists envision a "United States of the World." In other words, a supranational organization is one in which the whole is greater than the sum of its parts, an organization to which countries surrender all or part of their sovereignty, and an organization to which member states are at least somewhat subordinate. There are several types of supranational organizations. These are discussed in depth in Chapter 13, but in brief, they are the following.

General-Purpose, Universal Organizations

The United Nations is the only existing general-purpose worldwide organization that, in theory, has some supranational characteristics. Not all countries are members, but the vast majority are. The UN also has a life and authority beyond the wishes of its individual members, and in theory, member states are bound to follow UN policy in many areas. As we will see in Chapter 13, however, there is a substantial gap between the ideal and reality.

Regional Organizations

A wide variety of regional organizations exist today. As their name implies, they are multipurpose (military, economic, social, and political) organizations centered in a given region of the world. The Organization of American States, the Organization of African Unity, the Arab League, the Association of South East Asian Nations, and the European Community are major regional organizations.

Alliances

Defensive associations that stress military cooperation are also a limited form of supranational organization. The key is that there are at least some aspects of transcendency. Member nations are expected to come to the aid of the collective and thus have, in theory, surrendered a part of their independence.

The United Nations is the leading example of a growing number of system-level actors.

The North Atlantic Treaty Organization and the Soviet bloc's Warsaw Pact are the two prime examples of multinational military alliances that have coordinating organizational structures. It should be noted that not all alliances constitute supranational organizations. The United States–Japan Security Treaty, for one, is a bilateral treaty and has neither the multinational or the organizational aspects necessary to warrant the name *supranational.*

Transnational Actors

Transnational organizations constitute a second group of system-level actors. There are both **intergovernmental organizations** (IGOs) and **nongovernmental organizations** (NGOs) that qualify as transnational actors insofar as they share three identifying characteristics: (1) They are organized, usually with identified leaders and a bureaucratic structure. (2) They are specialized, performing a limited number of defined tasks or functions. This functional perspective distinguishes transnational IGOs from multifunction, supranational IGOs. (3) They operate across international boundaries and have an orientation or allegiance that is, at least in part, not bound to the views or interests of any individual state.

The number of both IGOs and NGOs has grown tremendously during the twentieth century, particularly when compared with the growth of the number of states. Table 3-1 shows their approximate growth between 1900 and 1977. Furthermore, the influence and range of activities of transnational actors are growing as their numbers increase and as technological advances allow them to move and communicate more effectively across political boundaries.

Intergovernmental Organizations

IGOs perform a wide variety of functional, or nonpolitical, tasks in the world today. Many are *economic* in nature. One example, the International Monetary Fund (IMF), has 85 member countries and functions to keep world currencies stable. Other transnational organizations concentrate on *social* functions. The World Health Organization (WHO), with 156 member states, and the Food and Agriculture Organization (FAO), with 147 members, work in the fields their names imply. Indeed, IGOs are involved in an ever-increasing range of activities, as can be seen in Table 3-2.

Nongovernmental Organizations

The number of private organizations that operate internationally has grown phenomenally in the recent past. Like IGOs, they are involved in a wide spectrum of activities. Almost any classification scheme would omit some of the 2,500 NGOs, but a few of the more significant categories can be noted.

Table 3-1. Numbers of states, intergovernmental organizations (IGOs), and nongovernmental organizations (NGOs), 1900 and 1977.

	1900	*1977*	*Percentage Increase*
States	40	181	452
IGOs	11	242	2,200
NGOs	69	2,427	3,517

Figures based on Werner J. Feld and Robert S. Jordan with Leon Hurwitz, *International Organizations* (New York: Praeger, 1983), pp. 16–19. The number of states is debatable; this chart uses 181, the number given in *The Statesman's Year-Book, 1982–83*, ed. John Paxton (New York: St. Martin's Press, 1982), instead of 195, the figure given by Feld et al.

Table 3-2. Sample Intergovernmental Organizations.

Organization	*Members (1980)*	*Founded*	*Hqtrs.*	*Nationality of Chief Officer (1980)*
Intergovernmental Maritime Consultative Organization	121	1958	London	Indian
International Atomic Energy Agency	110	1956	Vienna	Swedish
International Labor Organization	147	1919	Geneva	French
International Criminal Police Organization (INTERPOL)	122	1923	Paris	French
Universal Postal Union	162	1875	Bern	Egyptian
World Meteorological Organization	154	1951	Geneva	Danish

Religious organizations. NGOs based on religion are widespread and active in world politics. The World Evangelical Alliance, founded in 1846, is an early example of a Protestant NGO. The Catholic church is by far the largest and most influential of current religion-based NGOs. The Vatican itself is, of course, a state, and the pope is a secular as well as a spiritual leader. The political influence of Catholicism, however, extends far beyond the Vatican itself.

The early 1980s have witnessed an interesting scene of the church asserting itself in some political areas and attempting to restrain the political activities of its clergy in other areas. The pope and other church officials have been active in the crisis in Poland. Polish patriotism and the church have been closely linked since the baptism in 966 of the country's first ruler, Prince Mieszko I. Some analysts have identified the visit of the first Polish pope, John Paul II, to his homeland in 1979 as one of the sparks that stirred Polish nationalism, which led, in part, to the Solidarity labor movement and resistance to the Soviet-supported communist government. During the ongoing crisis, the church has been deeply involved. Solidarity leader Lech Walesa met in the Vatican with the pope. The pope also sent an envoy to Poland to meet with representatives of Solidarity, the government, and the Communist party. At first the church seemed to be trying to play a mediating role, but after the imposition of martial law, the church became increasingly critical of the government and supportive of at least passive resistance. Many years ago when a subordinate cautioned Josef Stalin about risking the displeasure of the church, the communist leader was supposed to have dismissed the church's influence with the sarcastic question "How many [army] divisions does the pope have?"

The Soviet and Polish communists are finding out that the pope may have few divisions, but his legions are many.

In contrast to Catholic activism in Poland, the Vatican has been trying to restrain the "Pope's Marines." The Society of Jesus, the Jesuits, has become known for secular and religious liberalism and in recent years has become widely associated with leftist elements in Latin America and elsewhere. A number of Jesuits and other clergy, including nuns, have been killed in the recent unrest in Central America, and the pope has moved to rein them in. A papal emissary replaced the order's superior-general, and the order's leaders were summoned to Rome to hear of the pope's "wish" that they shun "secularizing tendencies." Whether the religious marines will retire to their barracks remains to be seen, but whether they do or not, the church will remain an influential transnational actor.

Business organizations. The expansion of international commerce has brought with it the rise of huge multinational corporations (MNCs), or companies with affiliates in more than one country. The role of MNCs is discussed in detail in Chapter 12, but suffice it to say that the economic power of these corporate giants gives them a substantial role in international affairs. There has been evidence of corporate manipulation of world oil supplies, involvement in antigovernment activities such as the overthrow of Chile's Marxist president Salvadore Allende in 1973, and bribery up to the level of the prince consort of the Netherlands and the prime minister of Japan. Some idea of the economic power of the MNCs can be gained from the fact that Exxon, the largest MNC, has a gross corporate product ($103 billion in sales, 1980) that is larger than the gross national product of the Netherlands ($99 billion), twice as large as the GNP of South Africa ($48 billion), three times as large as Finland's ($33 billion), four times as large as Egypt's ($24 billion), and five times as large as Portugal's ($20 billion).[1]

Banks are also a form of MNC. One measure of banks' economic strength worth pondering is their assets. The sum of the 1980 assets of the two largest U.S. banks, Citicorp ($114.9 billion) and Bank of America ($111.6 billion), exceeded the 1980 GNP of India ($137 billion) and approached that of Great Britain ($298 billion). There is a "golden rule" of politics that says, "He who has the gold makes the rules," and MNCs have plenty of gold.

Other transnationals. Other categories of transnational actors include humanitarian groups (Red Cross), political groups (Communist International), terrorist groups (Japanese Red Army), scholarly groups (International Political Science Association), and a host of others. They may not command the wide allegiance of the church or the economic muscle of the MNCs, but like those giants, they form part of the rapidly expanding network of international interactions, and many consider them part of the wave of the future.

The Catholic church, symbolized here by Pope John Paul II on a visit to Latin America, is an important actor on the world stage.

State-Level Actors

The State Defined

The most powerful actors on the world stage today are the states. Indeed, the state is so much the primary form of political organization and the focus of political loyalty that it is hard to imagine a political system based on any other unit. Yet, as we will see in Chapter 4, the state system is only a few hundred years old. And other forms of world order are possible based on organizations like those discussed in the section on system-level actors.

A **state**, or country, is a tangible entity. The United States, the Union of Soviet Socialist Republics, and the People's Republic of China are all states. So are Bahrain, Fiji, and Swaziland. What distinguishes a state, whether large or small, populous or not, is a set of six characteristics.

Sovereignty

The single most important political characteristic of a state is sovereignty. That term strongly implies political independence from any higher authority. Less certainly, sovereignty also suggests the idea of equality.

Independence. In the history of Western political thought and international law, sovereignty developed as the rulers of Europe broke away from the secular domination of the Holy Roman Empire and the theological authority of the pope after the Middle Ages. Independent states arose that exercised *supreme authority* over their territory and citizens. The basic idea, then, is that a sovereign state is free to order itself internally and to make and enforce domestic law without external interference.

Independence, however, is a relative term. We object and sometimes bring pressure when another state murders or tortures its citizens. Sometimes states must also compromise their independence if a stronger neighbor threatens. Finland, for example, can follow any foreign policy it wants—as long as it does not offend the Soviet Union. As Finland's president recently said, "Stable and confidential relations with the Soviet Union have been and will be a central element of Finland's foreign policy."[2] He could hardly have said anything else. Independence, then, is a key element of sovereignty, but not all sovereign states are equally independent.

Equality. Sovereignty also has an element of equality. If states recognize no higher authority, then it can be argued that they are all equal. That theoretical principle is given application in the UN's General Assembly, where each member state has one vote. Are all states really equal, though? Compare Tonga and China (Table 3-3). It is obvious that in many ways the two states are not equal. That reality is also recognized in the fact that the UN Security Council has five permanent members (the United States, the Soviet Union, China, Britain, and France), each of which possesses veto power. Finally, the question of equality has great practical import. As discussed in Chapter 13, the basis of representation is a sensitive question in current international organizations. Attempts to work toward even greater international cooperation and integration must someday deal with how to define *equal* and how to determine voting power.

Territory

A second characteristic of a state is territory. It would seem obvious that to exist, a state must have physical boundaries. Most states indeed have recognized boundaries, but on closer examination, the question of territory becomes

Table 3-3. Statistics on Tonga and China, Theoretically Sovereign Equals

	Tonga	*China*
Area (sq. mi.)	270	3,691,000
Population	94,000	983,578,000
GNP ($)	34,000,000	592,000,000,000
Military personnel	0	4,500,000
Vote in UN General Assembly	1	1

Data from *The Statesman's Year-Book, 1982–83,* ed. John Paxton (New York: St. Martin's Press, 1982).

more complex: numerous international disputes exist over border areas; territorial boundaries can expand, contract, or shift dramatically; and it is even possible to have a state without territory. Many current states recognize the Palestinians as a sovereign member of their fraternity, yet that nationality is scattered in other countries such as Lebanon and Jordan. Depending on one's view, the Palestinians either have no territory or have been expelled from the territory now occupied by Israel. It is also possible to maintain, as the United States currently does, that the Palestinians are not a state at all.

Population

People are an obvious requirement of any state. The populations of states range from a few thousand to a billion, but all states count this characteristic as a minimum requirement.

Diplomatic Recognition

One of the classic rhetorical questions is: If a tree fell in the forest and no one were around to hear it, would it make a sound? The same question governs the issue of statehood and the recognition of others. If a political entity declares its independence, and no other country grants it diplomatic recognition, is it really a state? The answer seems to be no. It would be difficult for any such aspirant to statehood to survive for long without recognition. Economic problems resulting from the inability to establish trade relations is just one example of the difficulties that would arise.

How many other countries must grant recognition before statehood is achieved is a more difficult question. When Israel declared its independence in 1948, the United States quickly recognized the country. Was Israel a state at that point? It certainly seems so. By contrast, consider the Republic of Transkei. This enclave within South Africa was established in 1976 by the white racist government of that country. The purpose was to settle the racial question in South Africa by segregating that country's black majority into several "independent" territories (the Republics of Bophuthatswana, Venda, Transkei, and Ciskei and others). These noncontiguous "countries" are in areas with no resource base and are economically dependent on South Africa. Even though they have been recognized by South Africa and recognize one another, for a total of five recognitions each, it is doubtful that they can be considered states. Thus, diplomatic recognition is needed but in itself does not necessarily confer statehood.

Internal Organization

It is generally conceded that states must have some level of political and economic structure. Most states have a government, but statehood continues even during periods of severe turmoil, even anarchy.

It is even possible for rival governments to claim that they legitimately represent the same state. China is an important example of one country (in theory) and two governments. The Nationalist Chinese on Taiwan and the

Communist Chinese on the mainland agree that the mainland and Taiwan are both part of the one China. Each claims to represent that China. Until 1979 the United States recognized the Nationalists. The United States then switched to the Communists but still treats Taiwan as an independent country. The result is a byzantine and troublesome political tangle.

Internal Loyalty

The final characteristic of a state is internal loyalty. This implies that a state's population has a feeling of positive identification with the state *(patriotism)* and that the population grants the state the authority to make rules and to govern *(legitimacy)*. It is possible that a political system can survive for a while by sheer force of arms. In Cambodia the Khmer Rouge ruled mostly by terror and killed 2 million Cambodians during its four-year rampage. Such control cannot last for long. Deserted by its own people, the Khmer Rouge was overthrown and again relegated to the status of guerillas by a Cambodian faction headed by Heng Samrin and backed by Vietnam's army. As we will see in Chapter 4, one of the major problems facing many world states and governments is winning and keeping the loyalty of their domestic populations.

State, Nation, Government

It is clear, then, that although an international state is defined by a number of distinct characteristics, those traits are often extremely complex in their application. The deeper you dig, the more complicated the questions become. Two other concepts need to be mentioned here and distinguished from the state. They are **nation** and **government**. These three terms, *state, nation,* and *government,* are often used synonymously, but they are really quite different.

Nation. In political science terminology, *nation* is a cultural term. It refers to a group of people who identify with one another politically because of common characteristics such as a common heritage, language, culture, religion, and race. A nation is intangible, a matter of mutual perceptions of cultural kinship, whereas a state is more tangible. Americans are a nation; the United States is a state. Many states and nations are not parallel. Canada, for one, contains both an English and a French nation. Chapter 4 discusses the international problems that result from the frequent lack of coincidence between states and nations, and in Chapter 7 we shall see that the interests of the nation are not always the same as the interests of the state.

Government. The term *government* can refer to either the system of government, such as the democratic system in the United States or the communist system in the Soviet Union, or it can refer to the specific regime, such as the Reagan administration or the government of Mikhail Gorbachev. In either case, governments are usually much more transient than either states or nations. It is not uncommon for leaders to confuse the interest of their government with that of the state and nation, as we will see in Chapter 7. As analysts of international politics, it is important that we keep the distinctions among the three concepts firmly in mind.

Inside the State

If we continue to dissect the state, we find that it is even more complex than the state/nation/government categorization just discussed. Indeed, the process by which a country arrives at its general foreign policy and its specific actions is a major focus of study among political scientists.

Franklin Delano Roosevelt in Lilliput

It is common to think of foreign policy in terms of decisions by presidents or prime ministers. They decide and it is done, or so we think. In reality, decision making is much less swift and sure. To see that, consider for a moment the authority of Franklin Delano Roosevelt.

FDR, we remember, was a president of immense power and stature. He was, after all, the leader who defeated both the Depression and Hitler, and he has been consistently rated by historians as among the three best American presidents. Obviously, he must have been very much in charge.

If you asked Roosevelt, however, you would get a different perspective. The bureaucracy, for one, restricted his ability to command. The N-A-A-A-V-Y, as FDR sometimes pronounced it with exasperation, was a particular thorn in his side. He despaired of getting it to do anything he wanted. "To change anything in the N-A-A-A-V-Y," the president once moaned, "is like punching a feather bed. You punch it with your right and you punch it with your left until you are finally exhausted, and then you find the damn bed just as you left it before you started punching."[3]

Sometimes the navy would not even tell the president what it was up to. "When I woke up this morning," FDR groaned on another occasion,

> the first thing I saw was a headline in the *New York Times* to the effect that our Navy was going to spend two billion dollars on a shipbuilding program. Here I am, the Commander-in-Chief of the Navy having to read about that for the first time in the press. Do you know what I said to that?
>
> No, Mr. President [the listener replied].
>
> I said: "Jesus Chr-rist!"[4]

Congress also hemmed Roosevelt in. Its isolationist members hampered FDR's attempts to aid the allies against the Axis powers before Pearl Harbor, and toward the end of the war, Congress threatened to block his dream of a United Nations. Career diplomat Charles "Chip" Bohlen has recalled how bitterly Roosevelt viewed the Senate, denouncing its members as "a bunch of

obstructionists" and declaring that "the only way to do anything in the American government [is] to bypass the Senate."[5]

Public opinion was a third of many restraints on Roosevelt. The British ambassador to Washington reported to London that FDR complained that "his perpetual problem is to steer between . . . (1) the wish of 70% of Americans to keep out of the war and (2) the wish of 70% of Americans to do everything to break Hitler even if it meant war."[6]

Roosevelt's evaluation of his own powers, then, was less grandiose than we remember. Indeed, he might have compared himself to Gulliver from Jonathan Swift's classic tale. The shipwrecked Gulliver was washed ashore in Lilliput. Although the Lilliputians were only a few inches high and he was a giant among them, Gulliver awoke to find himself bound by countless tiny ropes. He could have broken any one of them, but he could not free himself of all of them.

The purpose of these stories about Roosevelt and Gulliver is to point out that presidents, prime ministers, and even kings are not as free as we think they are. They are decision makers, but, like Gulliver, they operate within a complex web of governmental and societal restraints that make up the modern state. Our job in this section, then, is to see how the various components of a state affect the choices of individual decision makers.

Foreign Policy Making

Foreign policy is formulated by a decision-making process. In the last analysis, decisions are made by human beings, but, like Roosevelt, these decision makers do not exist in a vacuum. Instead, people make decisions within a complex political environment—the state.

The goal of this section is to explore the state-level influences on the choices of decision makers. To do that requires discussion of (1) the decision makers themselves, (2) bureaucracy, (3) legislatures, (4) parties and political opposition, (5) interest groups, and (6) the people. Each of these six groups is a substructure of the state, and each acts on the foreign policy process.

Decision Makers

The individuals who make decisions are influenced by (1) personal factors, (2) **role factors**, and (3) **organizational-person factors.**

Personal Factors

In Chapter 2 we reviewed the personal factors that influence a decision maker's perceptions and choices. Recall that individuals' ambitions, experiences, health, and beliefs help shape foreign policy. These personal factors, of course, properly belong to individual-level analysis rather than to the state-level analysis being discussed in this section. They are mentioned here again, however, because they tie into role and organizational-person factors.

Although President Roosevelt, pictured here with the chief of naval operations, was commander-in-chief, he often wondered just how much he really controlled the navy since he sometimes learned of its major decisions from the media.

Role Factors

We all play roles. As individuals, it may be that, for example, you and your professor are more alike than you think. Both you and your professor may like sports, enjoy Jack Nicholson movies, drink beer, make love, and have anxiety attacks. Yet, in class, the roles are well defined and different. You mostly sit, listen, and take notes. The professor talks and evaluates you. You probably wear jeans, sweatshirts, and sneakers to class. Most professors "dress up." If male, they wear uncomfortable suitcoats, strangely button their shirts around their necks, and wear vertical pieces of cloth called neckties. If you often cut class, your classmates probably won't mind. If the professor frequently cuts class, you will probably be angry. Why the differences in behavior and expectations? The answer is role.

Decision makers play roles just like students and professors. A role is a leader's conception of what is expected of him and what he expects of himself, not personally, but as a leader.

Take Harry Truman, for example. Almost everyone remembers Truman as a tough, feisty, confident president. And, indeed, Truman tried to convey that image and came to believe it himself. He put a sign on his desk that proclaimed, "The Buck Stops Here," and when a reporter asked how foreign policy was made, Truman decisively replied, "I make foreign policy."[7] That's how presidents are supposed to act! Truman knew it and played the role to the hilt.

But was that the "real" Harry Truman? Not exactly. Sometimes he was scared. A United States senator recalled that, on the day Truman was sworn in as president, "the tears ran right down [Truman's] cheeks. He kept saying, 'I'm not big enough for this job, I'm not big enough for this job.'"[8] But we never really saw that Truman—the self-doubting Truman. He publicly played the presidential role and acted as he was supposed to, not as he sometimes felt.

The impact of role playing on foreign policy is important. Sometimes Truman made decisions when he was uncertain of what was going on. Why? Because presidents do not get to say, "I don't know what to do!" We expect them to know what to do and how to act, and they expect the same of themselves. Truman also sometimes overcompensated for his anxieties by being too combative, and some historians have traced part of the cold war to Truman's truculence. President Reagan, by contrast, has toned down his rhetoric. He undoubtedly sees the Soviet Union as an "evil empire," but the role of presidents calls for a more temperate approach, and Reagan has learned to be (usually) more restrained, more presidential.

Organizational-Person Factors

People also act differently in organizations than they do as personal individuals or role individuals. Social scientists have found that the dynamics of group decision making often cause several characteristics. One analyst has labeled the process **groupthink**.[9] The theory of organizational decision making is extensive and complex, but one facet deserves particular mention here. That is the pressure on groups to *achieve consensus*, to agree on what should be done and to avoid dissent.

Leaders tend to seek consensus behind their policy because they believe that it is important to have a unified front against opponents. Consensus also enhances a politician's self-image as a national leader. Finally, leaders often seek consensus to maintain the loyalty and support of their staffs.

Subordinate group members also strive for consensus. Like leaders, they believe in a united front. They also don't want to be the dissenter, the "odd man out." Being the devil's advocate is psychologically uncomfortable because you do not "fit into" the group. Dissent also carries the risk of disapproval by group members or even future exclusion from the group: "Non–Team Players Need Not Enter." That fear of disapproval or banishment is especially strong for subordinate group members vis-à-vis the group leaders.

The drive for consensus has several ramifications. Three important results are lowest common denominator decision making, lack of coordination, and the urge to agree.

Lowest common denominator decision making. Groupthink tends to arrive at the lowest common denominator, or that policy which is least objectionable rather than optimal policy. In order to achieve consensus, presidents and premiers are apt to accept the recommendations of their subordinates and/or to make only marginal changes in previous policy.

Soon after entering office, President Kennedy had to decide whether to go ahead with the attempt to overthrow the Castro government in Cuba by the CIA-sponsored Bay of Pigs landing. Despite some personal doubts, Kennedy could not bring himself to reject a plan supported by his subordinates. He went ahead and disaster resulted. Kennedy's later reaction was "How could I have been so far off base? . . . How could I have been so stupid to let them go ahead?"[10]

Lack of coordination. A second result of consensus seeking can be *confusion* when the leader avoids dissent by working around some of his or her advisers, thus keeping them in the dark and/or alienated. Henry Kissinger has remembered that President Nixon used this method to avoid dissent but that it was "a poor system . . . even though I operated it. Nixon's strong distrust of his Cabinet members exaggerated their already strong will. Partly through ignorance and partly because they felt no commitment to policy they had not shaped, they consistently cut across our initiatives or challenged our strategies that had been clearly articulated."[11]

The urge to agree. A third possible result of consensus seeking is the reluctance of subordinates to oppose the preferences of their superiors or to suggest alternatives that do not fit the conventional wisdom.

The pressure to say yes to a superior is clearly illustrated by one of Lyndon Johnson's advisers who ruefully remembered:

> The President, in due course, would announce his decision and then poll everyone in the room. . . . "Mr. Secretary, do you agree with the decision?" "Yes, Mr. President." "Mr. X, do you agree?" "I agree, Mr. President." During the process I would frequently fall into a Walter Mitty-like fantasy: When my turn came I would rise to my feet slowly, look around the room, and then look directly at the President, and say very quietly and emphatically, "Mr. President, gentlemen, I most definitely do *not* agree." But I was removed from my trance when I heard the President's voice saying, "Mr. Cooper, do you agree?" And out would come a "Yes, Mr. President, I agree."[12]

The same "yes person" psychology intimidates people into accepting group decisions. Again referring to the Bay of Pigs operation, presidential adviser Arthur Schlesinger, Jr., has remembered that after the disaster he "bitterly reproached" himself "for keeping so silent" during group discussions before the landing. Schlesinger felt he could not "blow the whistle" on the "nonsense," because everyone else seemed agreed on the plan and he was afraid of gaining "a name as a nuisance."[13]

Bureaucracy

Every state, large or small, democratic or authoritarian, is heavily influenced by its **bureaucracy**. Although the dividing line between decision makers and bureaucrats is often hazy, generally we can say that bureaucrats are career governmental personnel, as distinguished from those who are political appointees.

In reviewing the foreign policy role of bureaucracies, we will be focusing on two basic points. The first is *bureaucratic perspective*. We will see that bureaucracies develop an institutional mentality, have their own set of values and priorities, and often favor and advocate policies based on their organizational view, rather than the national interest. Second, *bureaucratic methods*, or the means by which bureaucracies help to shape and carry out foreign policy, will be discussed.

Bureaucratic Perspective

Organizations often have policy preferences based on their missions and how a policy will affect them. The views of a country's military establishment on arms control are influenced by the fact that its size, equipment, and budget share will be reduced by any real arms reduction. According to Anatoli Dobrynin, Soviet ambassador to the United States, the Soviet Ministry of Defense had little use for the Strategic Arms Limitation Talks (SALT) and "put its most unimaginative and unenterprising general on the SALT delegation . . . to block any initiative put forward by the Foreign Ministry." Then Soviet Defense Minister Marshal Grechko reportedly told Dobrynin, "If you want my official opinion [on SALT], the standard answer is no."[14]

Bureaucratic Methods

An organization's perspective will cause it, consciously or not, to try to shape policy according to its views. Bureaucracies influence policy decisions in several ways.

Information filter. One method of influencing policy is by filtering information. Decision makers are dependent on their supporting organizations to tell them the "facts," but what facts they are told depends on what subordinates believe and what they want to pass on.

Decision makers depend on information provided by others and they can't consider what they do not know. Until concrete evidence such as this photo proved there were Soviet missiles in Cuba (1962), intelligence about the missiles was not given to President Kennedy.

The 1962 Cuban missile crisis exploded on October 14 when Soviet ballistic missiles were "discovered" in Cuba by U.S. spy planes. In fact, numerous intelligence reports for weeks had given clues about the introduction of missiles, but the information was considered erroneous by subordinate intelligence officials and never reached the attention of decision makers.

Information can also be suppressed or lost by bureaucratic rivalries. In the earlier Cuban misadventure, the April 1961 Bay of Pigs invasion, the CIA kept information from other foreign policy organizations and from the president, which, in the words of presidential adviser Arthur Schlesinger, "had the idiotic effect of excluding much of the expertise of government."[15]

Organizations even "spy" on one another. At one point in recent years a clerk in the office of the president's national security adviser was found to be passing information to the "enemy"—not the Russians but, rather, the U.S. Joint Chiefs of Staff. The same sort of rivalry for information occurs in the Soviet Union. A recent article on the Soviet military intelligence service, the GRU, described the attempts of that service and its Soviet rival, the KGB (equivalent to the CIA), to bug each other.[16]

Recommendations. Bureaucratic organizations also influence policy through their recommendations. Kissinger has related how bureaucracies often present options: "The standard bureaucratic device [is] leaving the decision-maker with only one real option, which for easy identification is placed in the middle. The classic case . . . would be to confront the policymaker with the choice of (1) nuclear war, (2) present policy, or (3) surrender."[17] If you are clever, then—and bureaucracies are—you present a decision maker with a series of choices, only one of which is reasonable. It resembles a multiple-choice exam question on which only one answer is correct. "All of the above" or "None of the above" is seldom included.

Implementation. It is obvious that decision makers must rely on their subordinates to carry out policy. Discrepancies between what decision makers think they said and what their subordinates actually do can result from genuine misunderstanding, unconscious misinterpretation based on subordinates' preferences, or conscious attempts to delay, change, or ignore a decision. In any case, practice is often different from policy. In 1968 President Johnson announced a peace initiative in Vietnam by halting the bombing in North Vietnam except in the area near the border. But the military defined the border area broadly and actually increased bombing in that area. To the North Vietnamese it must have seemed as if Johnson was lying or not in control. In either case, the war went on. Summing up the policy/implementation gap, Henry Kissinger has commented: "The outsider believes a presidential order is consistently followed out. Nonsense. I have spent considerable time seeing that it is carried out and in the spirit the president intended."[18]

Legislatures

Levels of influence. In all countries, the foreign policy role of legislatures is secondary to that of executive-branch decision makers and bureaucrats. That does not mean that all legislatures are powerless. They are not, but their exact influence varies greatly among countries.

In nondemocratic systems, legislatures generally rubber-stamp the decisions of the executive or, in the case of communist countries, party decision makers. Neither the Supreme Soviet of the USSR nor China's National People's Congress, for example, plays a significant role in foreign policy making.

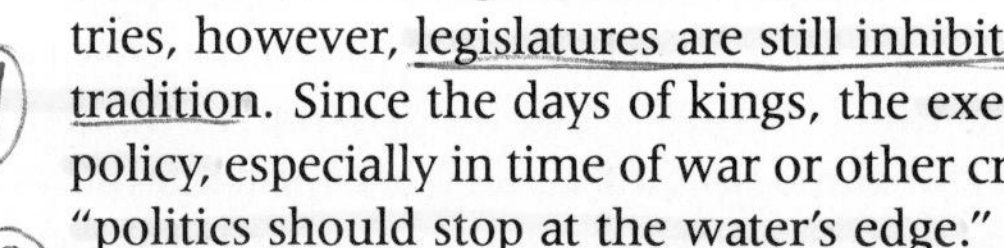

Restraints on legislative influence. Even in the more democratic countries, however, legislatures are still inhibited by many factors. One of these is tradition. Since the days of kings, the executive has traditionally run foreign policy, especially in time of war or other crisis. Second, there is the axiom that "politics should stop at the water's edge." The belief is that a unified national voice is important to a successful foreign policy. This is particularly true during a crisis, when there is a tendency to "rally around the chief" and to view dissent as bordering on treason. Third, the executive-dominant tradition has led to the executive's normally being given extensive constitutional power over foreign policy. In Britain, for example, a declaration of war does not require the consent of Parliament.[19]

Member of Congress Lee Hamilton recently listed some of the other reasons for legislative weakness:

- Diplomacy requires speed; Congress is slow.
- Diplomacy requires negotiation; Congress votes yes or no.
- Diplomacy requires secrecy; Congress leaks.
- Diplomacy requires expertise; Congress has little expertise for foreign affairs compared with the executive.
- Diplomacy requires strong leadership; Congress' leadership is scattered.[20]

Political Parties and Political Opposition

In every political system, those who are in power face rivals who would replace them, either to change policy or to gain power for themselves. In the more democratic systems, the opposition is legitimate and is organized into political parties. Rival politicians may also exist in the leader's own party. Opposition is less overt and/or less peaceful in nondemocratic systems, but it exists nonetheless.

In many European countries the number of parties and the range of issues they are based on are greater than in the United States. Many countries have both Communist and reactionary right parties that favor very different policies. Other parties grow up around specific issues. The "Green party" in Germany focuses in part on nuclear disarmament and played a role in the reorganization of the West German government in 1982. In any form, democratic parties serve as a source of criticism and alternative information to executive decision makers. Parties also help to contest elections, and as we saw in Chapter 1, it made a difference whether Democrat Walter Mondale or Republican Ronald Reagan was elected.

Parties also sometimes are part of the governing structure. In communist countries the party plays a very strong policy-making role—indeed, one that is stronger than or equal to that of the government itself. In other countries, such as Great Britain, parties play a lesser, but still substantial, role in influencing government policy, while in still other countries, like the United States, the parties play little role at all in directly setting policy.

Interest Groups

Interest groups are collections of people who have similar policy views and try to persuade the government to adopt those views as policy. Here the definition of interest groups will be private organizations. That eliminates bureaucracies from consideration here, although bureaucratic organizations certainly have interests they pursue.

Because foreign policy often has a unifying impact on a country's internal elements and because foreign policy sometimes has a limited effect on domestic groups, interest groups are generally less active on foreign policy questions than on domestic issues. Still, all political systems include interest groups that try to influence foreign policy.

Ethnic/racial groups. Many countries have ethnic or racial groups that have emotional or political ties to another country. American Jews, for one, have been extremely influential on the United States' sympathetic policy toward Israel. And in the early 1970s, when Pakistan brutally suppressed unrest among ethnic Bengalis in East Pakistan, India (which also has a large Bengali population) intervened and, as a result of the ensuing war, helped East Pakistan break away and establish itself as Bangladesh.

Business groups. One prominent type of economic group concerned with foreign affairs is business. With international trade increasing, foreign sales are vital to many companies, and they lobby their home governments both for favorable domestic legislation and for support vis-à-vis other governments. During the 1981 debate over whether to sell the Advanced Warning Aircraft System (AWACS) to Saudi Arabia, aircraft and oil companies were active (and successful) in trying to persuade Congress to allow the transfer. Businesses also press their governments to support them overseas. There are ongoing sensitive negotiations between Japan and the United States, as the former attempts to avoid restrictions on auto imports and other items and the latter presses for greater access to the Japanese market.

Financial institutions. Financial institutions, such as banks, are a related commercial interest group. International lending has become big business, and banks look to their home governments for protection of their interests. Crises such as the Polish Solidarity unrest, Mexico's 1982 devaluation, the Falkland Islands war, and the Iranian hostage seizure not only had important political ramifications but also involved billions of dollars in loans from U.S. and other Western banks to the nations involved. American banks, for example, argued that too much pressure on the Polish military government might lead Poland to default on its loans, resulting in a severe crisis for U.S. banking. That contention was a factor in the moderate U.S. stand on martial law in Poland.

Workers' groups. Unions and other workers' associations are a third type of economic interest group that affects foreign policy. In many countries unions are active on trade issues. They often favor policies that will protect workers and industries threatened by foreign competition. The activity of the United Auto Workers in the United States to restrict the importation of Japanese cars is but one example.

Worker groups can also pressure their governments to expand trade. In 1980 President Carter embargoed grain sales to the Soviets in retaliation against the Soviet invasion of Afghanistan. Ronald Reagan initially supported that policy, but soon after his election, pressure from farmers on the president and Congress persuaded Reagan to end the ban on grain sales.

Veterans' organizations. Groups of former military members and other military support organizations often lobby for a strong military posture and a conservative foreign policy. Retired military officers in Britain, for one, have been found to be influential on that country's defense policy. In the United States, veterans' groups like the American Legion and the Veterans of Foreign Wars have been active on a wide variety of foreign policy questions. Military support groups such as the Navy League and the Air Force Association have lobbied for their services.

Broad-based groups. A fourth type of foreign-policy-oriented interest group is not based on any narrow socioeconomic category, such as ethnicity or economics. Instead it draws its membership from those who have a common policy goal. The orientations of these groups run the gamut from the very general to the specific. In the United States, the Council on Foreign Relations draws together some 1,500 influential (elite) Americans who hold an internationalist, somewhat liberal point of view. The World Federalists desire a stronger United Nations. On the other end of the ideological scale, the Committee on the Present Danger urges a strong posture against the Soviet Union. For years the Committee of One Million was effective in blocking U.S. recognition of mainland China. In more recent years, the China-American Friendship Association has been promoting friendly relations between those two countries.

The People

The last source of domestic influence to consider is the mass, the vast majority of citizens in any country who have no direct say in policy making.

Influence on Public Opinion

The role of public opinion in foreign policy is complex, sometimes contradictory, and difficult to measure. Its role differs greatly among political systems: it is more important in open systems (such as the United States) and less important in closed systems (such as the Soviet Union and the People's Republic of China).

Politics in general, and international relations in particular, do not consistently command the attention of the average citizen. A series of Gallup Poll surveys in 1978 asked people in five countries to identify important political issues. Two of the countries, Canada and Uruguay, registered zero concern with international issues. Four percent of Brazilians were worried about the oil crisis, and 5 percent of the British were concerned with immigration issues. Only the Spanish showed a high degree of saliency, with 27 percent concerned about that country's entry into the European Common Market.[21]

What these figures indicate is that most of the people are not greatly concerned with foreign policy most of the time. They do not indicate that public opinion is unimportant: to sound Lincolnesque, some of the people (the attentive public) are interested in foreign policy all the time (and have influence), and almost all the people are interested in foreign policy some of the time.[22] Furthermore, as the policy process has become more democratic in at least some countries, and as the domestic impact of international affairs has become more obvious to people, there is evidence that public interest in and influence on policy has grown.

Still, the wider public is normally content to let leaders run foreign policy. In fact, the public regularly shifts its attitudes to favor announced government policy.[23] This pattern is particularly strong in time of crisis. A phenomenon of American foreign policy behavior is that in virtually every crisis the public has rallied behind the government and the president's popularity has soared. This has been true not only in times of success but also in times of failure, such as Kennedy's embarrassment at the Bay of Pigs and Carter's abortive attempt to rescue the hostages in Iran. It is instructive to consider the similar views of a Nazi leader and an American secretary of state, both of whom recognized the impact of an external crisis on public support. In the words of Hermann Goering: "Voice or no voice, the people can always be brought to do the bidding of the leaders. That is easy. All you have to do is tell them they are being attacked." John Foster Dulles concurred: "The easiest and quickest cure for internal dissension is to portray danger from abroad . . . from one or another of the nation-villains."[24]

Public opinion is not, however, always so passive and malleable. At times it can become an important factor in foreign policy formation. When it does, it can act in several ways.

Public Opinion and Pressure

Many of those who make foreign policy are essentially politicians. Although they are not slaves to public opinion, they keep a "weather eye" on it. The reaction of the American public to Vietnam is a good example. Henry Kissinger has explained that the Nixon administration felt the pressure: "The very fabric of the government was falling apart. The Executive Branch was shell-shocked. After all, their children and their friends' children took part in the demonstrations."[25]

Opinion polling is increasing the public's impact on decision making. It is difficult to prove scientifically, but it seems certain that the Reagan administration's disposition in 1981 to become involved in El Salvador was at least in part forestalled by polls that clearly showed that Americans strongly disapproved of any sort of direct intervention. Polling is more prevalent in open systems, but even the Soviets have begun to conduct some surveys of mass views.[26]

Public Opinion and Elections

National elections are not normally won and lost over foreign policy. One student of French politics, for instance, has suggested that elections in that country are never decided on international issues.[27] Sometimes, though, foreign policy can be very much an issue. Michael Brecher found that in Israel

Massive public protests were one factor that brought about the end of American involvement in the war in Vietnam.

foreign policy has dominated 40 percent of the national elections.[28] At times very specific issues are involved. Opposition in the U.S. Congress to the war in Vietnam was partly motivated by the belief, as Democractic Majority Leader Mike Mansfield reported to Lyndon Johnson, that "there is a strong conviction [among senators] that candidates of the Democratic Party will be hurt by the war" and that "if the war drags on, the party will suffer badly."[29]

Foreign policy concerns can also be part of the general electoral equation. President Carter did not lose the 1980 election because of foreign policy as such. Still, with only 23 percent of the public rating his handling of foreign policy as good or excellent (September 1980), with 60 percent disapproving of his handling of the Iranian situation, and with most Americans favoring more defense spending and a firmer stance vis-à-vis the Soviets, foreign policy leadership was certainly part of the public evaluation that led to Ronald Reagan's move to Washington, D.C., and Jimmy Carter's return to Plains, Georgia.[30]

A somewhat uncommon other type of "election" influencing policy is a referendum. In this procedure, the public is asked to indicate its views on an issue placed on the ballot by the legislature. France, for example, held a referendum in 1961 to endorse the peace settlement in the Algerian War and another in 1972 to approve a treaty opening the European Economic Community (EEC) to new members. In 1975, under heavy pressure from several domestic elements to withdraw from the EEC, Britain put the issue before its voters, who chose to remain associated with the Continent by a vote of 17.3 to 8.4 million.

Summary

There are a variety of types of actors in international politics. Supranational actors have member states and at least some theoretical authority over members. Transnational actors are specialized organizations composed of countries (intergovernmental organizations) or private groups/individuals (nongovernmental organizations) that operate across national boundaries.

States are traditionally the most important political actors. States are political organizations that enjoy at least some degree of sovereignty and have a number of observable characteristics (territory, population, and so on).

States are complex organizations, and their internal, or domestic, dynamics influence their international actions. Internal factors include decision makers, bureaucratic organizations, legislatures, political parties and opposition, interest groups, and the public. Each of these influences foreign policy, but the decision makers and bureaucratic organizations are consistently (though not always) the strongest factors.

Terms

Bureaucracy—The bulk of the state's administrative structure that continues even when leaders change.

Groupthink—See *organizational-person factors.*

Government—An organization that controls a state.

Intergovernmental organizations (IGOs)—Transnational actors composed of member countries.

Nation—A group of culturally and historically similar people who feel a communal bond and who feel they should govern themselves to at least some degree.

Nongovernmental organizations (NGOs)—Transnational organizations with private memberships.

Organizational-person factors—How an individual's membership in an organization/decision-making group influences his or her thinking and actions.

Role factors—How an individual's position influences his or her thinking and actions.

State—A political actor that has sovereignty and a number of characteristics, including territory, population, organization, and recognition.

Supranational organizations—Organizations that have countries as members and have at least some theoretical authority over the member countries.

Transnational organizations—Organizations that are not part of any single national government and that perform specialized functions across international boundaries.

Notes

1. *Fortune,* August 22, 1982, p. 70. GNP draws from *World Almanac, 1984* (New York: Newspaper Enterprise Association, 1983).
2. *Time,* February 2, 1982, p. 53.
3. Quoted in Robert E. DiClerico, *The American President* (Englewood Cliffs, N.J.: Prentice-Hall, 1979), p. 107.
4. Quoted in Robert Sherill, *Why They Call It Politics* (New York: Harcourt Brace Jovanovich, 1979), p. 217.
5. Charles E. Bohlen, *Witness to History: 1929–1969* (New York: Norton, 1973), p. 210.
6. Daniel Yergin, *The Shattered Peace* (Boston: Houghton Mifflin, 1977), pp. 45–46.
7. Louis E. Koenig, *The Chief Executive* (New York: Harcourt Brace Jovanovich, 1975), p. 213.
8. George Aiken Oral History, Harry S Truman Library, Independence, Mo.
9. Irving L. Janis, *Groupthink: Psychological Studies of Policy Decisions and Fiascoes,* 2nd ed., revised (Boston: Houghton Mifflin, 1983).
10. Irving Janis, "Groupthink in Action: A Perfect Failure at the Bay of Pigs," in *American Foreign Policy,* ed. William C. Vocke (New York: Free Press, 1976), pp. 81–94; Theodore Sorensen, *Kennedy* (New York: Harper & Row, 1963), p. 309.
11. Kissinger, *White House Years* (Boston: Little, Brown, 1979), p. 448.
12. Quoted in Russell Baker and Charles Peters, "The Prince and His Courtiers," in *Inside the System,* ed. Charles Peters and Nicholas Leman (New York: Holt, Rinehart and Winston, 1979), pp. 34–35.
13. Quoted in Janis, "Groupthink in Action," p. 87.
14. Excerpts from Kissinger's memoirs, *Time,* March 15, 1982, p. 41.
15. Quoted in Janis, "Groupthink in Action," p. 83.
16. Robert Moss, "Inside the GRU," *Parade Magazine,* September 16, 1981, pp. 6–9.
17. Kissinger, *White House Years,* p. 418.

18. Quoted in Morton H. Halperin, *Bureaucratic Politics and Foreign Policy* (Washington, D.C.: Brookings Institution, 1974), p. 245.
19. John E. Schwartz and L. Earl Shaw, *The United States Congress in Comparative Perspective* (Hinsdale, Ill.: Dryden Press, 1976), pp. 234–244.
20. Lee Hamilton, "Congress and Foreign Policy," *Presidential Studies Quarterly* 12 (1982): 133–137.
21. George H. Gallup, *The International Gallup Polls, Public Opinion, 1978* (Wilmington, Del.: Scholarly Resources, 1980), p. 127.
22. Gabriel Almond, *The American People and Foreign Policy* (New York: Praeger), 1965; Bernard C. Cohen, *The Public's Impact on Foreign Policy* (Boston: Little, Brown, 1973); William Wallace, *The Foreign Policy Process in Great Britain* (London: Royal Institute of International Affairs, 1975), p. 100.
23. Barry B. Hughes, *The Domestic Context of American Foreign Policy* (San Francisco: W. H. Freeman, 1978), pp. 38–39.
24. Quoted in Charles W. Kegley, Jr., and Eugene R. Wittkopf, *American Foreign Policy*, 2nd ed. (New York: St. Martin's Press, 1982), p. 285.
25. Kissinger, *White House Years*, p. 514.
26. Richard L. Merritt, *Foreign Policy Analysis* (Lexington, Mass.: Heath, 1975), p. 103.
27. Dorothy Pickles, "French Foreign Policy," *The Foreign Policy of the Power*, ed. F. S. Northedge (New York: Praeger, 1968), p. 189.
28. Michael Brecher, *The Foreign Policy System of Israel* (New Haven: Yale University Press, 1972), p. 125.
29. Senator Mike Mansfield to President Lyndon Johnson, September 29, 1966, National Security Files, Johnson Library, Austin, Tex.
30. Kegley and Wittkopf, *American Foreign Policy*, p. 295.

4

Nationalism

If this were played upon a stage now,
I could condemn it as an improbable fiction.
Shakespeare, King Henry VIII

When we mean to build,
We must survey the plot, then draw the model,
And when we see the figure of the house,
Then must we rate the cost of the erection.
Shakespeare, King Henry IV

Had I but served God with half the zeal
I served my king.
Shakespeare, Henry VIII

In Chapters 1 through 3, we explored our "playbill"—the setting and the actors of the world drama. The scenery is diverse. It ranges from the shining beauty of Planet Earth viewed from space to the charred stench of a battlefield. The states and other actors, like the world's population, are many and growing in number. Most play a limited or intermittent role in international politics while a few states dominate the stage. States, like the humans they encompass, can be benevolent. But they are also capable of self-interest and violence. Even when there is peace, the potential for danger is high in our improvisational play.

Chapters 4 through 6 will carry our dramaturgical expedition beyond the protagonists to the question of international goals and motives. Why do countries act the way they do? What is it that they want? What is the plot?

Some of that, of course, has been answered in the first three chapters. At a macroanalytical level, international politics occurs within the pressures and restraints of the international system. At a microanalytical level, policy is partly the result of the pressures caused by individual ambitions, perceptions, and other idiosyncrasies. Political rivalry, interest-group pressure, bureaucratic self-service, and a variety of other domestic factors also contribute.

Beyond these, Chapters 4 through 6 will deal with the more generalized causes of state-level international action. The first of these will be *nationalism.* More than any other force, nationalism is a symbol of our political identity. Politically, we are Americans, Chinese, Russians, Peruvians, Nigerians, Turks, or Swedes. We do not see ourselves as citizens of the world. Insofar as we are separate and insofar as we are self-interested, the potential for conflict exists.

The second generalized force we will examine is *ideas, ideology,* and *morality.* The fact that human beings think abstractly differentiates us from animals, and abstractions have been the source of both good and evil. The ethics of Judeo-Christian thought teach us to love our enemies and turn the other cheek. On occasion we have even tried that! By contrast, philosophies have been spread at times by the sword or symbolized by the gas chamber. It is debatable whether the pen is mightier than the sword, but it is certain that together they form a powerful combination.

Finally, in Chapter 6, we will address that slippery concept, *national interest.* In one sense national interest is an amalgamation of the nationalistic, ideological, and moral interests of the nation. But it can also be seen as an independent concept that deserves analysis as both an objective standard of evaluation and as a subjective standard applied in foreign policy decisions.

Thinking about Ourselves and Others

E.T.—the extraterrestrial being. Now, there was one strange-looking character. He—she?—had a squat body, no legs to speak of, a large shriveled head, saucer eyes, and a telescopic neck. And the color! Yes, E.T. was definitely weird. Not only that, there was a whole spaceship, and presumably a whole planet,

There are many ways to organize differences and similarities. E.T., for example, might see all these people as very similar, while you may discern ethnic and religious differences among them. Division according to national identity—nationalism—is currently at the center of world politics.

full of those characters—all looking alike, waddling along, with their necks going up and down.

Or did they all look alike? Maybe they did to us, but maybe they didn't to one another. Perhaps on their distant planet there were different countries, ethnic groups, and races of E.T.s. Maybe they had different-length necks, were varied shades of greenish-brown, and squeaked and hummed with different tonal qualities. It's even possible that darker green E.T.s with longer necks from the country of Urghor felt superior to lighter-shade, short-necked E.T.s from faraway Sytica across the red Barovian Sea.

Further, we might wonder whether E.T. could differentiate among us earthlings. Was he aware that some of those he met were boys and some were girls, that some were black and others white, and that an assortment of ethnic Americans chased him with equal-opportunity abandon? Maybe we all looked pretty much the same to E.T. If he had been on a biological specimen-gathering expedition and had collected a Swede, a Nigerian, a Peruvian, and a Laotian, he might have thrown three of the four away as unnecessary duplication.

The point of this academic whimsy is to get us thinking about the world, the human beings who populate it, how different and how similar we are, and how we divide ourselves up perceptually and politically. What we will see is that people tend to see themselves as different. We do not have an image of ourselves as humans; rather, we divide up ethnically into Poles, Irish, Egyptians, Thais, and a host of other "we-groups." Further, there is a strong tendency to organize, or try to organize, politically around that ethnic connection. People overwhelmingly adopt their country as the focus of their political identity. If you think about it, you see yourself politically as a citizen of the United States or perhaps Canada. You might even be willing to fight and die for it. Would you do the same for Peoria, Illinois? Or the earth?

This country-level focus is nationalism. As we shall see, national identification is not a given. It has not always been, nor, probably, will it always be. Yet, for the time being, it is. Nationalism is a powerful force which has had an important impact on world politics for several centuries and which will probably continue to help shape people's minds and affairs in the foreseeable future. That prospect brings mixed emotions because, like the Roman god Janus, nationalism has two faces. It has been a positive force for political integration and building. It has also brought despair and destruction to the world. It is, in essence, both a uniting and a dividing force in international politics.

Nationalism: A Slippery Concept

One of the things this book tries to do is avoid jargon—the unnecessary use of fifty-cent words with specialized meanings. Sometimes, however, it is important to be quite precise about what a word means so that we will have a common basis of discussion. This is one such place, and we need a definition of *state, nation, nation-state,* and *nationalism* before their roles and impact can be examined.

States and Nations

As discussed in Chapter 3, a **state** is a tangible, objective political entity. It has territory, people, organization, and other observable characteristics. The United States, Angola, and Bolivia are states.

A **nation** is often a far less certain phenomenon. Three factors must exist before a group of people qualifies as a nation. First, the group must share certain *similarities.*[1] Often these are demographic characteristics, such as language, race, or religion, that can be easily identified and quantified. But the similarities can also include less measurable aspects, such as a common historical experience, regular social/economic/political interaction and cooperation, and common values. These latter factors allow a demographically diverse people, such as Americans, to come together as a nation. In the last analysis, the American nation is the outcome of McDonald's, CBS, Valley Forge, interstate commerce, the Super Bowl, Michael Jackson, voting for and then getting rid of Richard Nixon, and a host of other factors.

This leads us to *perception,* which is the second factor that creates a nation. For all the similarities a group might have, it is not a nation unless it feels like one. Over a century ago, a French scholar defined a nation as "a soul, a spiritual quality."[2] What he meant is that those within a group must perceive that they share similarities. Further, these perceived similarities must lead to a *feeling of community*. This sense of being a "we-group" is, of course, highly subjective, but it can be objectively measured by social scientists through attitudinal surveys.

The third factor necessary for a nation to exist is some level of a *desire to be separate*, especially an urge to be politically independent or at least autonomous. In the United States there are many groups of "hyphenate Americans" (Italian-Americans, black-Americans, Mexican-Americans) that share the first two factors of a nation. They have similarities and a sense of mutual identification. They do not have a separatist impulse, however. Thus, they are ethnic or subcultural groups. This is an important distinction, and it separates states that are demographically diverse (the United States) from states that are nationally divided (Cyprus, Lebanon).

Nation-States

A third phenomenon, the **nation-state,** combines the previous two concepts in our search for the meaning of nationalism. A nation-state is, in theory, the natural outgrowth of a nation's desire to have and maintain its own state and to govern itself independently. The nation-state is represented by many symbols such as flags, national anthems, or animals (eagles, bears, dragons). It is the object of patriotic loyalty, and we view it as the "highest form of political authority."[3]

In practice, as we shall soon see, the nation-state concept diverges from the ideal in three ways. First, many states contain several nations within their boundaries. Second, many nations overlap one or more international borders. This lack of "fit" between nations and states is often a source of international conflict. Third, as two scholars noted, "Nations and states . . . do not necessarily evolve simultaneously; . . . it is impossible to say, as an inflexible rule, which one comes first."[4] In Europe, nations generally came together first and only later coalesced into states. In Africa and Asia, by contrast, many states are the result of earlier boundaries drawn by colonial powers and do not contain a single, cohesive nation. Often the people within a former colonial state are of different tribal and ethnic backgrounds and find little to bind them to one another once independence has been achieved and the common enemy (the colonial power) has been defeated.[5] This lack of cohesion often results in civil discord and regime instability and carries the potential for spreading to international conflict.

Nationalism

The fourth and final phenomenon, **nationalism** itself, is a coming together of the concepts of state, nation, and nation-state. One scholar has observed that the "core nationalist doctrine" includes the "far-reaching propositions" that

1. Humanity is naturally divided into nations.
2. Each nation has its peculiar character.
3. The source of all political power is the nation, the collective whole.
4. For freedom and self-realization, people must identify with a nation.
5. Nations can only be fulfilled by their own states.
6. Loyalty to the nation-state overrides other [political] loyalties.[6]

Nationalism, then, is both a cohesive and a divisive force. It has allowed and continues to allow larger political entities to form where feudal, tribal, and other local loyalties had once existed. But nationalism has also been destructive. It makes us see ourselves as essentially different from (and often superior to) other nationalities, it promotes the idea of self-interested sovereignty, and it blocks the path to a global consciousness and loyalty that some claim to be the wisest course for the future.

Nationalism: Past, Present, Future

There is not enough space in this text to give a complete review of the development of nationalism.[7] Instead, the goal of this brief historical survey is to show that nationalism has not always existed as a primary political focus, nor is it necessarily the best course for the future. It is also worthwhile to consider some of the "faces" of nationalism, to see that it is a varied and changing phenomenon.

The Rise of Nationalism—to 1945

Given the strength of our nationalistic political focus, it is difficult to envision almost any other system of loyalties. But consider this: Only seventy years ago (until the end of World War I) most of the nation-states of central Europe, such as Poland and Czechoslovakia, were all or in part within the realm of the Austro-Hungarian Empire. Only a little earlier than that, there was no Germany or Italy. We often suppose countries like that always existed, but they did not. Before the 1860s Germany was a collection of dozens of kingdoms, principalities, and other small entities. Italy was in part controlled by France and Austria and also was subdivided into Sardinia, Lombardy, Parma, Moderna, Tuscany, the Papal States, and the Kingdom of the Two Sicilies.[8]

Before the age of nationalism, political organization was generally characterized by *universalism,* on the one hand, and *localism,* on the other. At the macropolitical end of the extreme, there existed a series of great empires. The Roman Empire was the most universal, but after its decline it was followed in the West by the empire of Charlemagne, then the Holy Roman Empire, and finally the Austro-Hungarian Empire. In the early Middle Ages, the overarching authority of the Catholic church was also present. Farther to the east, the Byzantine Empire and then the Ottoman (Turk) Empire rose and fell. To the north of those, the Russian Empire was expanding, and this multiethnic conglomerate still exists in many ways. In Asia, the Chinese Empire dominated the continent. There were also empires at this time in the yet "undiscovered" Western Hemisphere, such as the Aztecs and Incas, and also in Africa, including those of Ashanti, Mali, and Benin.[9]

On the micropolitical end of the scale, organization was localized in its focus. People saw themselves as attached to tribal, village, or provincial groups. The patchwork feudal systems that existed were dominated by the lesser nobility. In many areas, beneath the imperial canopy, a mosaic of autonomous political structures held sway. It was true, as Voltaire quipped, that the Holy Roman Empire was "neither holy, nor Roman, nor an empire."

Origins. Some scholars trace the origins of nationalism to the Hebrew tribes and ancient Greeks, but full-blown nationalism did not truly begin to emerge for almost another two millennia. Gradually during the Middle Ages and the Renaissance, nationalism began to take hold, in part as a result of economics and technology. As manufacturing, trade, transportation, and communications grew, larger economic units were needed for efficiency, and people became more aware of and cooperative with their ethnic kin in other areas.[10] The Protestant Reformation (1517) began to break down the authority of the papacy, and the break of Henry VIII (1509–1547) from the church was a pivotal point in the growth of English nationalism. Military technology, especially gunpowder, made the feudal estate indefensible.[11] There was also a growing sense of national identity as people associated and identified with their larger ethnic groups. That sense of nation can be seen in the plays of Shakespeare, who in 1595 had his exiled Richard II proclaim:

> ***Where'er I wander, boast of this***
> ***I can,***
> ***Though banished, yet a true-born***
> ***Englishman.***

During the next several centuries, as economic and social interaction expanded and as monarchs such as Louis XIV of France, Frederick II of Prussia, and Peter the Great of Russia expanded and consolidated their domains, the genesis of nationalism continued. It still lacked one key element, however. Missing was the concept that the state was an embodiment of the nation, not a possession of the king, who ruled by divine right. Symbolic of that God-given dominion, Louis XIV of France could proclaim: "L'etat, c'est moi [I am the state]." Also symbolically, it was the French Revolution that ended that monarchial assumption.

Modern nationalism. Because of its violence and the dramatic shift from aristocratic privilege to relative "liberty, equality, fraternity," the French Revolution (1789) is considered by many scholars to be a landmark in the growth of nationalism. French thinkers such as Rousseau, Voltaire, and Montesquieu were the philosophers of popular power, and the idea's influence spread far beyond France's borders. Adding the sword as an ally to the pen, in 1792 the National Convention proclaimed that "The French nation . . . will treat as enemies every people who, refusing liberty and equality . . . treat with a prince and privileged class."[12] Within a decade, Napoleon's legions were forcibly spreading the philosophy of the democratic-national revolution throughout Europe.

The growth of popular nationalism sometimes occurred through both evolution and revolution. Its growth in England was mostly evolutionary, and by the time of the French Revolution, the power of the English parliament (and people) over the king was established. Also predating the French Revolution, Americans had proclaimed their independence in favor of a government of, by, and for the people.

From its beginnings in England, France, and the United States, the idea of popular sovereignty spread around the globe until, by the middle of the twentieth century, virtually all of Europe and the Western Hemisphere had been divided into nation-states, and the colonies of Africa and Asia were beginning to demand their own identity. Nationalism reigned supreme; despite Winston Churchill's bravado statement, the sun was setting on the age of empires.

Nationalism after World War II

Obituary notices. While visiting London in 1897, Mark Twain was astonished to read in the paper one morning that he had died. Reasonably sure that in fact he was alive, Twain hastened to assure the world: "The reports of my death are greatly exaggerated."

That anecdote and World War II relate to nationalism because in the aftermath of the second world conflict, there were reports that nationalism was dead or dying. In Twain's terms, those predictions were greatly exaggerated.

The assumptions of a postnationalist period were based on the belief that we had learned from the horrors of war that the anarchistic system of sovereign states could no longer continue. E. H. Carr suggested in 1945 that "certain trends . . . suggest that . . . nations and international relations are in the process of undergoing . . . clearly definable change. . . . [Current nationalism] can survive only as an anomaly and an anachronism in a world which has moved on to other forms of organization."[13] The development of nuclear weapons, in particular, led scholars such as John Herz to theorize that the sovereign state could no longer carry out the primary task of protecting the nation and therefore was doomed.[14] The emphasis on free trade and growing economic interdependence also seemed to augur an end to the nationalist age. Finally, the newly established (1945) United Nations served as a symbol of progress away from conflictive nationalism and toward cooperative universalism.

Delacroix's famous painting of Liberty storming the barricades symbolizes the French revolution and the growth of democratic nationalism.

Resurgent nationalism. The trouble with these rosy projections is that they turned out to be wrong. Nationalism not only refused to die, but it has been rejuvenated as a world force. The primary force behind the resurgence of nationalism has been the anti-imperialist independence movement in the Third World. As Figure 4-1 indicates, the numbers of new nation-states gaining independence have accelerated greatly.

If anything, nationalism in the newly emergent states has been more strident than in their older counterparts. The newer countries have been undergoing rapid modernization, which breaks down old ties (nuclear family, tribe, etc.) and promotes nationalism; they have a history of colonial rule, which makes them assertive of their independence; they are struggling to regain their traditional cultures; the lack of ethnic unity in many makes the conversion to nationalist feeling vital for stability; and economic, social, and political difficulties tempt regimes to encourage national pride and unity by emphasizing outside enemies.[15] Each of these factors spurs strong nationalist feelings, so that nationalism continues as a strong force driving modern countries.

It should also be noted that there is resurgent nationalism in the West. Countering the trend toward European unification, a number of nationalist movements are reasserting their emotional pull. Great Britain has Irish, Welsh, and Scottish separatist sentiments. Spain has Basque and Catalan movements,

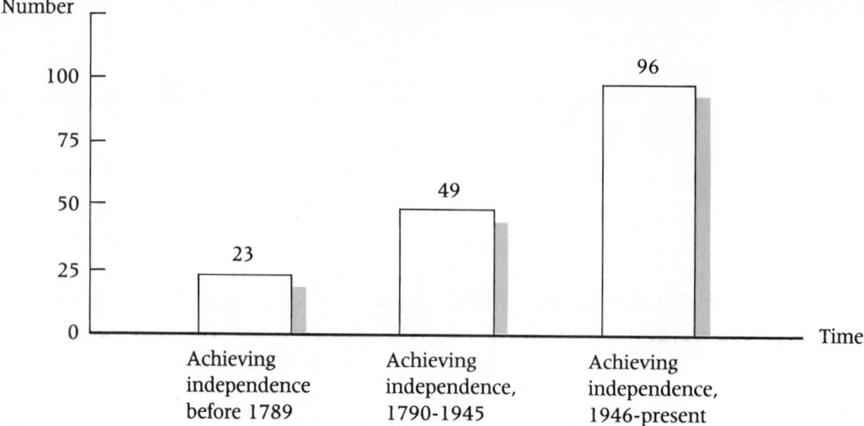

Figure 4-1. Number of independent states at three periods in history. *Based on John Paxton, ed.,* The Statesman's Year-Book, 1982–83 (New York: St. Martin's Press, 1982).

and Belgium (Flemish and Walloon) and Yugoslavia (Serbs and Croatians) are strained by group conflict.[16] In the Western Hemisphere, the French Canadians of Quebec are demanding greater cultural and political self-direction.[17]

As John Herz, in a commendable reevaluation of his earlier prophecy, admitted, "Developments have rendered me doubtful of the correctness of my previous anticipations. . . . There are indicators pointing . . . to retrenchment . . . to a new self-sufficiency . . . toward a 'new territory'"[18]—in short, to a new nationalism.

The issue of microstates. The rapidly growing number of independent countries, many of which have a marginal ability to survive on their own, has increasingly raised the issue of the reasonable limits to the principle of self-determination. At what point does a lofty principle become pragmatically unrealistic? The basic issues revolve around the wisdom of allowing the formation of what have been called **microstates**, or countries with tiny populations, territories, and/or economies. In one sense, such countries have long existed, with Monaco, Andorra, and San Marino serving as examples. But in recent years, as colonialism has become discredited, more of these microstates have become established. Table 4-1 lists three such states and some of their characteristics.

Table 4-1. Characteristics of Three Microstates.

	Tonga	*Maldives*	*Seychelles*
Population (1979)	94,000	143,000	63,000
Territory (sq. mi.)	270	115	156
Cash exports	copra, coconuts, bananas, swamp taros	bonito	copra, cinnamon bark, guano (bird droppings), coconuts, frozen fish

Table 4-2. Characteristics of a Microstate, a U.S. State, and a U.S. City.

	Seychelles	*Rhode Island*	*Phoenix*
Population (1979)	63,000	974,000	764,000
Territory (sq. mi.)	156	1,214	325

Many of the current microstates do not have the economic or political ability to stand as truly sovereign states. Let's compare the Republic of Seychelles, the smallest American state, Rhode Island, and Phoenix, Arizona (Table 4-2).

Tanzania's President Nyerere once made the sexist but vivid comment that "small countries are like scantily clad women—they tempt the wicked." In that vein, countries like the Seychelles, which are unable to defend themselves and which have a marginal economic existence, invite outside interference by and clashes between stronger powers. The Seychelles, in fact, have been invaded twice by pirates and barely fended off those attacks. In the latest foray, a group of mercenaries led by the infamous Colonel "Mad" Mike Hoare flew into the islands in 1981 on a commercial jetliner in an attempt to seize the government. They were defeated, but an earlier commando raid was overturned only by France's intervention.

If countries are unable to defend their own existence, they invite meddling by outside powers. That has the potential for conflict. Certainly, in a truly peaceful and beneficent world, impoverished nationalities would be helped and their weakness would not tempt aggression. Unfortunately, that sort of world does not exist, and microstates create a power vacuum that threatens to draw more powerful states into confrontation.

It is easier, of course, to raise the issue of microstates than to supply the answers. In an ideal world, where the lambs and lions lay down together and where universal mutual responsibility reigned, independence for any self-identifying group would be admirable. In the real world, that idea is not only unattainable, it is destabilizing. It may well be that levels of domestic autonomy and guarantees of human and political rights for subcultural groups are a wiser course than the support of self-determination to the point of *reductio ad absurdum*.

Nationalism: Builder and Destroyer

Earlier in this study Janus, the two-faced Roman god of gates through which roads passed, was mentioned. To unconscionably mix historical images, Janus had two faces because, in Robert Frost's terms, "two roads diverged" and wayfarers had to choose which to travel by. Janus might well have been the god of nationalism because that concept, that movement, has taken the world in two divergent directions, one of harmony and one of conflict.

The Beneficent Face of Nationalism

Most scholars agree that in its philosophical and historical genesis nationalism was a positive force. It has a number of possible beneficial effects.

Nationalism promotes democracy. One analyst points out that through nationalism "the concept of popular sovereignty replaced the concept of the divinely or historically appointed ruler; the concept of citizen replaces the concept of subject."[19] In short, nationalism promotes the idea that political power legitimately resides with the people and that governors exercise that power only as the agents of the people.

Nationalism encourages self-determination. In modern times, the notion that nationalities ought to be able to preserve their cultures and govern themselves according to their own customs has become widely accepted. The English utilitarian philosopher John Stuart Mill (1806–1873) argued that "where the sentiment of nationality exists . . . there is a *prima facie* case for unity of all the members of the nationality under . . . a government to themselves apart."[20] Self-determination was also a key element of Woodrow Wilson's Fourteen Points, and in recent years it has been especially strong in the Afro-Asian countries.

Nationalism allows for economic development. Many scholars see nationalism as both a facilitator and a product of modernization. Nationalism created larger political units in which commerce could expand. The prohibition of interstate tariffs and the control of interstate commerce by the national government in the 1787 American Constitution is an example of that development. Further, as modernization, with its industrialization and urbanization, broke down the old parochial loyalties of the masses, they needed a new focus—and that was the nation-state.[21]

Nationalism allows diversity and experimentation. A related argument is that regional or world political organization might lead to an amalgamation of cultures or, worse, the suppression of the cultural uniqueness of the weak by the strong. Diversity of culture and government also promotes experimentation. Democracy, it could be said, was an experiment in America in 1776, and it might not have occurred in a one-world system.

The Troubled Face of Nationalism

Despite its possible good, many contend that nationalism has become primarily a destructive force. Pope John XXIII, in his 1963 encyclical *Pacem in Terris,* reviewed nationalism and sovereignty and found that "the present system of organization and the way its principle of authority operates on a world basis no longer correspond to the objective requirements of the universal common good." The ills that nationalism brings are many and serious and can be subdivided into three categories: (1) how we relate to others, (2) the lack of fit between states and nations, and (3) the issue of microstates, which has already been discussed.

Colonel "Mad" Mike Hoare, pictured here after his capture, led a group of mercenaries that attempted to seize the Seychelles, one of the many microstates with only a minimal ability to defend themselves.

How We Relate to Others

Nationalism can lead to insularity. Because we identify with ourselves as the "we-group," we tend to consider the "they-group" as aliens. Our sense of responsibility—of even human caring—for the "theys" is limited. This is an especially pronounced effect of the American national experience. Isolationism was a standard sanctioned by George Washington and Thomas Jefferson that lasted for a century and a half. It has retreated somewhat, but the isolationist impulse still can be felt. Some 40 percent of Americans still favor a "fortress America" foreign policy.

Domestically, we Americans accept the principle that we have a responsibility to our least fortunate citizens. The social welfare budget in the United States is in the hundreds of billions of dollars, and we engage in countless acts of charity, from donating blood to distributing toys for tots. Internationally, to be blunt, most of us don't give a damn. A tidal wave kills hundreds of thousands in Bangladesh, an earthquake kills a million in China, disease and hunger debilitate millions in Africa and Asia, and, well, yawn—"I wonder what's at the movies." We may give a few pennies for UNICEF to Halloween kids or donate a few dollars at religious services for international relief work, but all in all, these Asians, Africans, and others seem far away, not like us at all, and certainly not our responsibility.[22]

Nationalism often leads to a feeling of superiority. It is a small step from feeling different and liking your group to feeling superior. At its extreme, this manifestation festered in Nazi Germany. The German nation—or race—was at the top of the ladder, which descended downward to where, at the bottom, Slavic peoples were to be kept as virtual and expendable slaves in segregated and degrading conditions, and Jews and Gypsies were "nonpeople" and "racial vermin" to be exterminated.[23]

Nationalism may lead to xenophobia. **Xenophobia** is a suspicion or fear of other nationalities. The belief that other nationalities are hostile is widespread and leads to world tension. Xenophobia is also related to regular disruptions as alien residents are expelled from one country or another. Whether the issue is Mexican workers in the United States, Turks in Europe, Chinese in South Asia, Ghanaians in Nigeria, or (before that) Nigerians in Ghana, banning or expelling aliens has caused human misery and conflict between the host country and the they-group's country of origin. As the international migration of labor increases, this cause of conflict is likely to become more pronounced.

Nationalism is jingoistic. Too often nationalism leads to **jingoism**, the belief that your country can do no wrong. It combines with patriotism—or love of country—to the point that a Stephen Decatur can say, to our applause, "Our country! . . . may she always be in the right; but our country right or wrong."

Nationalism can be messianic. If you like yourself or your we-group too much, it is easy to imagine that your fate—indeed, your duty—is to "save" others and bring them to the "way of truth"—that is, your way. This is, essentially, **messianism**. Consider, for example, the messiah complex found in Feodor Dostoevsky's *The Possessed*: "If a great people did not believe that truth is only to be found in itself alone, if it did not believe that it alone is destined to save all the rest by its truth, it would . . . not remain a great people. But there is only one truth, and therefore only a single one out of the nations can have the true God. That is the Russian people."[24]

Nationalism can be aggressive. Feelings of xenophobia, superiority, jingoism, and messianism can easily lead to aggressive behavior. Again, Hitler's Germany and the supposed destiny of its Aryan super-race to be master of the world is an especially strong example. But there are many others. Nation-

Nationalism run amok led to a belief in Aryan superiority and the inferiority of Jews and others who were sent to extermination camps such as Buchenwald, shown here.

alism has been a major factor in the aggressiveness of the United States, the Soviet Union, and, to a lesser degree, China and has led each of these powers to expand, colonize, and/or try to dominate its neighbors.

The Lack of Fit between States and Nations

Nations and states often do not coincide. As we have seen, the concept of a nation-state in which ethnic and political boundaries are the same is more ideal than real. In fact, most states are not ethnically unified, and many nations are not politically unified or independent. This lack of "fit" between nations and states is a significant source of international (and domestic) tension and conflict. There are two basic disruptive patterns: (1) one state, multiple nations, (2) one nation, multiple states.

States with more than one nation. The number of **multinational states** far exceeds that of nationally unified states. One study found that only about 9 percent of all countries truly fit the nation-state concept, as Figure 4-2 shows. The rest of the countries fall short of the ideal by at least some degree, 29.5 percent having no national majority.

We are, for example, used to thinking of Soviet citizens as Russians. Yet, in fact, only about 50 percent of the people in the USSR are ethnic Russians. Additionally, there are fifteen major nationalities and many smaller national/ethnic groups. Some of these groups are closely akin to Russians, but others

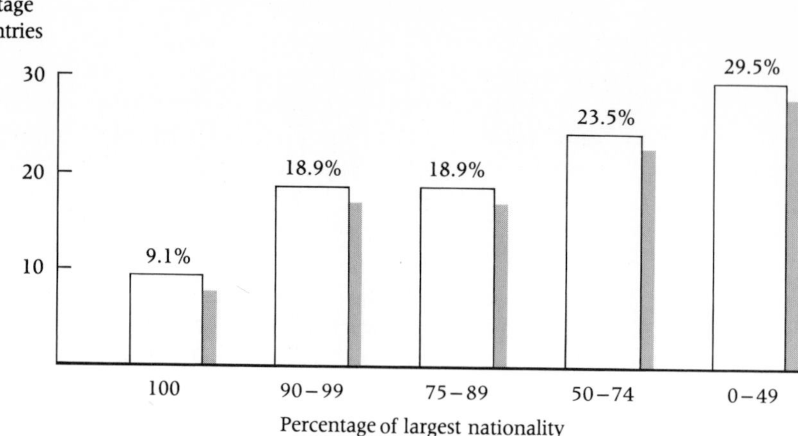

Figure 4-2. Percentage of countries in which the largest nationality makes up each of various percentages of the population. *Based on Walter Connor, "Nation-Building or Nation-Destroying," in* The Theory and Practice of International Relations, *5th ed., ed. Fred A. Sondermann, David S. McLellan, and William C. Olson (Englewood Cliffs, N.J.: Prentice-Hall, 1979), pp. 20–21.*

are quite dissimilar and have different religious heritages, languages, and racial/ethnic physical characteristics.

Many multinational states are unstable because the various ethnic groups perceive that they have little in common, and one or more may wish to establish an independent political entity. Indeed, in many African and Asian countries "nationality" is largely a fiction based on colonial boundaries. Nigeria, Africa's most populous country, is a prime example. When Nigeria became independent in 1960, there were few within its borders who truly considered themselves Nigerians. As one political leader put it, "Nigeria is not a nation. It is a mere geographical expression. . . . The word 'Nigerian' is merely a distinctive appellation to distinguish those who live in Nigeria from those who do not."[25] Instead of being a nation, Nigeria's 50 million people were divided into a number of ethnic groups with different languages, religions, histories, cultures, and subracial backgrounds. Once independence was gained from Great Britain, the semblance of unity built around anticolonialism began to break down. Within a few years divisions among the Hausa, Yoruba, Ibo, and other ethnic groups had become more pronounced, and in May 1967 the Ibo nation declared its independence and established the Republic of Biafra. The result was a tragic civil war that led to 1.5 million deaths before the Ibo independence movement was crushed in 1970.

A civil war, like Nigeria's, is of course a domestic event and not formally a part of international affairs. But very often the discord within a country threatens to draw outside powers in as supporters of the various factions. A combination of cold-war politics, Nigeria's oil production, and humanitarian concern created considerable international jockeying for position although, happily, intervention was largely avoided.[26]

In other cases, outside powers have been drawn in. In 1971 Pakistan dissolved into civil war when the Bengalis of East Pakistan declared their independence and established Bangladesh. In the ensuing struggle India (which lay between East and West Pakistan) joined the struggle against the dominant Punjabis of West Pakistan, thus internationalizing the civil war.[27]

Another possible link between multiethnicity and international behavior is based on the theory that leaders may use international conflict to unify a country by diverting attention from internal problems such as ethnic divisions. Studies on this point are, so far, inconclusive. One analysis found that between 1815 and 1939 approximately half of the international wars were preceded by domestic unrest in one of the belligerent countries.[28] Other studies have found little connection between domestic factors and international conflict, while still others have concluded that some types of countries (dictatorial and developing) were more subject to the link between internal and external conflict than others.[29] Thus we cannot say that domestic instability necessarily leads to international adventurism, but we can say that it creates a temptation to which troubled leaders sometimes succumb.

Nations in more than one state. A second type of departure from the nation-state ideal involves **multistate nationalities**. This phenomenon occurs when a nation overlaps the borders of two or more states. One pattern that can be found is a nation-state with elements of its national group in one or more surrounding states.

Figure 4-3 depicts such a situation in which state B and nationality X form a nation-state. Nationality X, however, also forms a minority group in multinational states A and C, which are dominated by nationalities Z and Y respectively. Such a situation creates the potential for conflict. The nation-state (B-X) serves as a magnet for the minorities (A-X, C-X), who want to separate and join the "fatherland."

This situation also fosters claims by the nation-state that the minority areas (A-X, C-X) should be part of a greater B-X nation-state. This type of national feeling is called *irredentism,* after the phrase *Italia irrendenta* ("Italy unre-

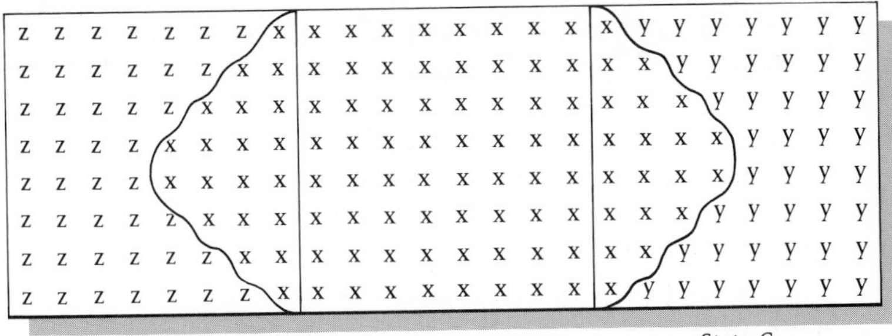

Figure 4-3. One type of situation involving multistate nationalities. Nationality X has its own nation-state, state B, and is also found as a minority group in states A and C.

deemed"). Further, if the X nationality in state A or C is oppressed as a minority group by the Zs or Ys, the Xs in state B may try to intervene on behalf of their national kin. This pattern was a major cause of conflict before World War II as Germany sought to incorporate the German nationals in the Sudetenland (Czechoslovakia), Austria, Poland, and other areas into a greater Germany. Illustrating the protection of ethnic brethren, Turkey invaded Cyprus in 1974 and nearly became involved in a war with Greece over the issue of the oppression (according to Turkey) of the Turkish-Cypriot minority by the Greek-Cypriot majority.

In another variation of the multistate nationality phenomenon, a nationality is a minority in two or more states and has no nation-state of its own, as in Figure 4-4. Palestinians, who are spread throughout Israel, Lebanon, Jordan, and Egypt, are a current conflictual example, as are Kurds, who live in Iran, Iraq, Turkey, Syria, and the Soviet Union.[30] In such cases, there may be conflict between the separatist nationality and the states in which it is a minority or even the states themselves as they try to deal with the nationalist agitation.

Finally, there is the pattern of a nationality split between two states and being a majority in both, as in Figure 4-5. North and South Vietnam, North and South Korea, East and West Germany, and the two Yemens are or were examples. Such a division causes almost a natural urge to reunite, but there is usually conflict over which of the two political systems will dominate. This has led to armed conflict in three of the examples (Korea, Vietnam, Yemen) and considerable cold-war tension over Germany.

Overall, then, the lack of fit between nations and states has been a major source of conflict. Given the rampant nationalism that still exists, it is likely to continue as a problem. One study, for instance, found some sixty-one national groups with separatist potential.[31] Areas like Africa are such a patchwork quilt of nations and states that the Organization of African Unity has refused to give aid to secessionist movements. As President Julius Nyerere of Tanzania put it, "African boundaries are so absurd that they need to be recognized as sacrosanct."[32] That may be a good thought for states that are, but it will surely meet with violent objection from nations that wish to be.

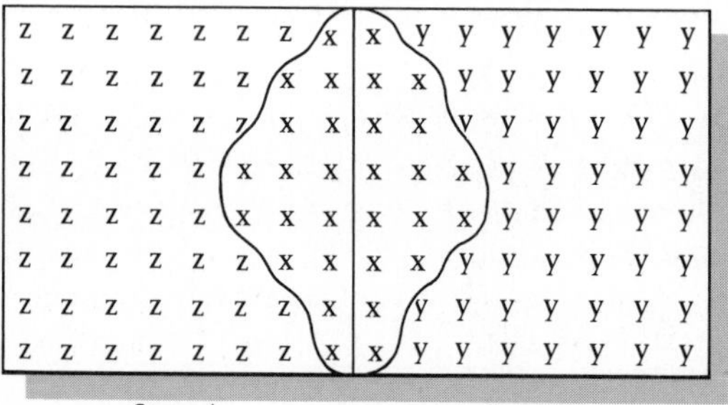

Figure 4-4. Another type of multistate nationality situation. Nationality X forms a minority in states A and B and has no nation-state of its own.

x	x	x	x	x	x	x	x	x	x	x	x	x	x	x	x
x	x	x	x	x	x	x	x	x	x	x	x	x	x	x	x
x	x	x	x	x	x	x	x	x	x	x	x	x	x	x	x
x	x	x	x	x	x	x	x	x	x	x	x	x	x	x	x
x	x	x	x	x	x	x	x	x	x	x	x	x	x	x	x
x	x	x	x	x	x	x	x	x	x	x	x	x	x	x	x
x	x	x	x	x	x	x	x	x	x	x	x	x	x	x	x
x	x	x	x	x	x	x	x	x	x	x	x	x	x	x	x

State A State B

Figure 4-5. A third type of multistate nationality situation. Nationality X has two nation-states, A and B.

Nationalism: Tomorrow and Tomorrow

This discussion of nationalism began with the observation that nationalism has not always been, nor will it necessarily always be, the world's principal form of political orientation. What will follow it and when, however, is difficult to predict. At least for the immediate future, barring a major upheaval, nationalism seems to have a firm grip on our consciousness. We still revere Nathan Hale for regretting that he had but one life to lose for his country, and we still sympathize with Philip Nolan, the tragic figure in Edward Everett Hale's *Man without a Country*.

There are voices, however, that see nationalism as a weakening philosophy and those who advocate its end. Louis Snyder, one of the leading scholars on nationalism, has listed the arguments of those who see a coming end to nationalism: (1) Increased cross-cultural interaction is lessening the nationalistic we/they image of other peoples in the world. (2) The **intermestic** (merging of *inter*national and do*mestic* issues) nature of politics is creating a heightened sense of internationalism. (3) The nation-state can no longer cope with problems such as ecology, food production, and disease prevention. (4) In a supersonic, nuclear age, the nation-state can no longer protect its people. (5) Given its history of causing conflict, nationalism is condemned by the moral judgment of history. (6) Multinational corporations and interdependence are ending economic nationalism. (7) There is an indefinable, but real, psychological trend toward a new world order. International organization is expanding, and transnational philosophies (such as communism) have a strong appeal.[33]

Still, Snyder concludes that, for a variety of reasons, nationalism remains the world's most powerful and resilient "ism." We can bemusedly tolerate a politically powerless Albert Einstein saying, "It is beyond me to keep secret my international orientation. The state to which I belong as a citizen does not play the least role in my spiritual life; I regard allegiance to a government as a business matter, somewhat like the relationship with a life insurance company."[34] But it is a different story when a presidential candidate like Jerry

Brown in 1976 tells us that we all live together on "spaceship earth" and should have to sacrifice for humanity's common good. In that case, we sighed and wrote Brown off as one of those overly mellow Californians. A peanut farmer seemed a much safer presidential choice.

Summary

Nationalism is one of the most important factors in international politics. It defines where we put our primary political loyalty, and that is in the nation-state. Today, the world is divided and defined by nationalism and nation-states. That focus has grown for about five centuries. After World War II, some predicted an end to nationalism, but they were wrong. Today nationalism is stronger, and the independence of the Afro-Asian nations has made it even more inclusive.

Nationalism has both positive and negative aspects. On the plus side, it has promoted democracy, self-government, economic growth, and social/political/economic diversity and experimentation. On the negative side, nationalism can lead to isolationism, feelings of superiority, suspicion of others, jingoism, messianism, and aggressiveness. Further, nationalism can cause instability when there is a lack of fit between states and nations. Domestic instability and foreign intervention are often the result.

In a world of transnational, global forces and problems, many condemn nationalism as outmoded and perilous. Some even predict its decline and demise. Such predictions are, however, highly speculative, and nationalism will remain a key element and powerful force into the future.

Terms

Intermestic—The merger or intermingling of foreign and domestic concerns. See Chapter 1.

Jingoism—An aggressive attitude combined with excessive patriotism.

Messianism—The belief that you are just/holy/good and have a duty/right to save others, even from themselves.

Microstate—A country which cannot economically survive unaided or which is inherently so militarily weak that it is an inviting target for foreign intervention.

Multinational states—Countries in which there are two or more significant nationalities.

Multistate nationalities—Nations whose members overlap the borders of two or more states.

Nation—A group of people who share certain similarities, have a sense of community, and desire a degree of self-governance. Ethnic or other subcultural groups have the first two of these characteristics but not the third.

Nationalism—The belief that the nation is the ultimate basis of political loyalty and that nations should have self-governing states.

Nation-state—A country (state) in which national self-identification and patriotism toward the state intermix or even become synonymous.

State—An independent political entity that has territory, people, organization, and other observable characteristics. See Chapter 3.

Xenophobia—Fear of others, "they-groups."

Notes

1. Karl Deutsch, *Nationalism and Social Communication* (Cambridge, Mass.: M.I.T. Press, 1966) represents this approach. Also see Deutsch's *Tides among Nations* (New York: Free Press, 1979).
2. Ernest Renan, "Qu'est-ce qu'une Nation?," in *The Dynamics of Nationalism,* ed. Louis L. Snyder (New York: D. Van Nostrand, 1964), p. 9.
3. Boyd C. Shafer, *Faces of Nationalism* (New York: Harcourt Brace Jovanovich, 1972), p. 15.
4. Mostafa Rejai and Cynthia H. Enloe, "Nation-States and State-Nations," in *The Theory and Practice of International Relations,* ed. Fred A. Sondermann, David S. McLellan, and William C. Olsen (Englewood Cliffs, N.J.: Prentice-Hall, 1979), p. 15. For a study of nations before political development, see John A. Armstrong, *Nations before Nationalism* (Chapel Hill: University of North Carolina Press, 1982).
5. Gerald Heeger, *The Politics of Underdevelopment* (New York: St. Martin's Press, 1974), pp. 21, 55.
6. Anthony D. S. Smith, *Theories of Nationalism* (London: Duckworth, 1971), pp. 20–21.
7. Shafer, *Faces of Nationalism,* is an excellent study.
8. For a review of European nationalistic movements see Louis L. Snyder, ed., *The Dynamics of Nationalism* (New York: D. Van Nostrand, 1964), chaps. 6–11. Also excellent is the older study by the Royal Institute of International Affairs, *Nationalism* (London: Oxford University Press, 1939).
9. To remedy the all too common "blank" in African history prior to colonization, see Roland Oliver and Anthony Atmore, *The African Middle Ages, 1400–1800* (Cambridge: Cambridge University Press, 1981).
10. Deutsch, *Tides among Nations,* p. 17.
11. John H. Herz, "The Rise and Demise of the Territorial State," *World Politics* 9 (1959): 473–493.
12. Quoted in Louis L. Snyder, *Varieties of Nationalism* (Hinsdale, Ill.: Dryden Press, 1976), p. 77.
13. Edward H. Carr, *Nationalism and After* (London: Macmillan, 1945), p. 34.
14. Herz, "Rise and Demise."
15. Snyder, *Varieties of Nationalism,* chap. 10; Heeger, *Politics of Underdevelopment,* chap. 1, pp. 21–22; and Rupert Emerson, *From Empire to Nation: The Rise and Self-Assertion of African and Asian Peoples* (Cambridge, Mass.: Harvard University Press, 1960).
16. Anthony D. S. Smith, *Nationalism in the Twentieth Century* (New York: New York University Press, 1979), Chap. 6.

17. David Cameron, *Nationalism, Self-Determination, and the Quebec Question* (n.p.: Macmillan of Canada, 1974).
18. John H. Herz, "The Territorial State Revisited," in *International Relations and Foreign Policy,* ed. James N. Rosenau (New York: Free Press, 1969), p. 77.
19. Eugene Kamenka, "Political Nationalism—the Evolution of the Idea," in *Nationalism: The Nature and Evolution of an Idea,* ed. Eugene Kamenka (New York: St. Martin's Press, 1976), p. 14.
20. John Stuart Mill, "Of Nationality, as Connected with Representative Government" (1861), in Snyder, *Dynamics of Nationalism,* p. 4.
21. Snyder, *Varieties of Nationalism,* p. 11.
22. This is not meant to belittle the private humanitarian aid that is given. Those who give are to be admired, and their efforts do help. The problem is that too few help and too few are helped.
23. Smith, *Nationalism in the Twentieth Century,* p. 77.
24. Quoted in Snyder, *Varieties of Nationalism,* pp. 213–214.
25. Quoted in Frederick A. O. Schwartz, Jr., *Nigeria: The Tribes, the Nation, or the Race—the Politics of Independence* (Cambridge, Mass.: M.I.T. Press, 1965), p. 3.
26. John M. Stremlau, *The International Politics of the Nigerian Civil War, 1967–1970* (Princeton, N.J.: Princeton University Press, 1977).
27. Subrata Roy Chowdhury, *Genesis of Bangladesh* (New York: Asian Publishing House, 1972).
28. Geoffrey Belainy, *The Causes of War* (New York: Free Press, 1973), p. 71.
29. R. J. Rummel, *War, Power, and Peace,* vol. 4, *Understanding Conflict and War* (Beverly Hills, Calif.: Sage, 1979), p. 345; Patrick J. McGowan and Howard B. Shapiro, *The Comparative Study of Foreign Policy* (Beverly Hills, Calif.: Sage, 1973), pp. 81–82; Jonathan Wilkenfield, Gerald W. Hopple, Paul J. Rossa, and Stephen J. Andriole, *Foreign Policy Behavior* (Beverly Hills, Calif.: Sage, 1980), p. 172.
30. On the Kurds, see A. R. Ghassemlou, M. Nazdar, A. Roosevelt, and I. S. Venly, *People without a Country: The Kurds and Kurdistan* (London: Zed Press, 1980).
31. Raymond Gastil, "The Comparative Survey of Freedom," cited in Lloyd Jensen, *Explaining Foreign Policy* (Englewood Cliffs, N.J.: Prentice-Hall, 1982).
32. Quoted in Jensen, *Explaining Foreign Policy,* p. 58.
33. Snyder, *Varieties of Nationalism,* pp. 266–269.
34. Quoted in Snyder, *Varieties of Nationalism,* p. ix.

5

Ideas, Ideology, and Morality

Thrice is he armed that hath his quarrel just.
Shakespeare, King Henry VI

The devil can cite Scripture for his purpose.
Shakespeare, The Merchant of Venice

The great French philosopher René Descartes defined the essence of being a human when he wrote, "I think, therefore I am." People can think abstractly. They can conceive of what they have not experienced, and they can group ideas together to try to explain existence and to chart courses of action.

This chapter is about the force of ideas in international relations. The essential task is to look at the great "causes" that help shape world politics. We have already covered the force of ideas in a number of contexts. The role of individual perceptions is one example. Nationalism has also been classified as an ideological force by some scholars, and, in fact, some aspects of nationalism, such as messianism, could just as well be included in this chapter as in the previous one.

The ideas and ideologies we will explore here, however, are distinguished by several characteristics. First, they are transnational. That means that large numbers of people hold a similar concept and that adherents are not confined to a single country. Second, they are internationally action-oriented. They urge a course of action on their believers. Third, they have a coherent set of symbols. Often such "gospels" have a "bible" such as the Koran or the *Communist Manifesto*. Prophets, be they Mohammed or Marx, are another symbolic anchor. Other ideas, such as democracy, are less focused, but they still have their important writings and philosophers.[1]

We will explore these motivational forces by first discussing several broad categories: (1) religious, (2) social, (3) economic, (4) political, and (5) humanitarian and moral ideas. A second important point will be discussion of the role ideas play in world events.

Before going further, it is wise to define and distinguish between ideas and ideology. Ideas are less complex than ideologies. Hitler's belief that Aryans were the master race and should rule the world was an idea. An **ideology**, by contrast, is "a more or less interrelated collection of beliefs that provide the believer with a fairly thorough picture of the entire world."[2] Communism is an ideology. It is primarily an economic doctrine, but it also has profound political implications as well as social, religious, and humanitarian consequences. Of course, the line between a simple idea and a complex ideology is fuzzy in practice. A religion, such as Islam, is not an ideology in the strictest sense, but it certainly involves conceptual complexity with impact on the secular as well as spiritual life of the world. This is particularly true when the spiritual force is activated and takes on political goals, whether they be missionary-inspired colonialism or current pan-Islamic assertiveness.

Types of Ideas and Ideologies

When "ideology" is mentioned, it is probable that "communism" is the word association you draw. In fact, communism is only one, and a recent one at that, of the many ideas that have shaped the world.

Religion

Religion is one of the most ancient forces influencing world events. It has played a dual role in world politics. In one sense it has been the source of humanitarian concern and pacifism. The role of the Catholic church, or elements therein, as part of the antinuclear movement and as a sponsor of social reform in Latin America was discussed in Chapter 3. The 1982 Oscar-winning film *Gandhi* focused on the pacifism that has a strong current in India's Hinduism.[3] The virtually universal condemnation by Islamic countries of the Soviet invasion of Afghanistan is another example of religiously inspired attempts to counter violence.

At the other extreme, religion has played a role in some of the bloodiest wars in history. The expansion of Islam following the death of Mohammed (570?–632 A.D.) and the doctrine of the *jihad,* or holy war, set off a series of clashes including the Crusades (eleventh through thirteenth centuries) between the equally expansionist Islamic and Christian worlds that lasted—quite literally—for a thousand years. The Protestant Reformation (1517) divided Christianity, and the conflict between Catholic and Protestant included the Thirty Years' War (1618–1648) and others. Religion also played a role in the imperial era. Catholic and Protestant missionaries were early European explorers and colonizers of North America, Africa, Asia, and the Pacific. Whatever its good intent and works, the missionary movement also served in many cases to promote and legitimize the political, economic, and cultural subjugation of local people by outsiders.[4]

Religious conflict, despite its archaic sound, is not a thing of the past. Religious differences continue to be the source of conflict or to serve as an aggravating factor. When Britain gave up its colonial control of the Indian subcontinent after World War II, that area was divided between the Moslems of Pakistan and the Hindus of India. Countless members of each faith were killed in the ensuing conflict and in the subsequent wars between India and Pakistan. In more recent times, Sikh/Hindu discord within India has led to attacks and reprisals, including the assassination of Prime Minister Indira Gandhi and threats to destabilize India and the region. Divisions within religions also continue to cause conflict. The split between the Sunni and Shi'ite sects of Islam, discussed further below, played a role in the war between Iran and Iraq. Finally, religion serves to help define and sharpen ethnic and national differences. The Jews versus the Moslem Arabs, the split between the Christians, Moslems, and Druze in Lebanon, and the struggle between the Catholics and Protestants of Northern Ireland are three examples of current importance.

Of all the dimensions of the interaction between religion and politics that exist in today's world, none is so important as *the role of Islam.* Given the importance of the Middle East, where Islam was founded and where it is still centered, given the strength of recently resurgent Islamic fundamentalism and assertiveness, and given the fact that the Western secularization of politics makes the idea of any religion acting as an autonomous political force a novel thesis, it is worth pausing for a moment to examine this ancient yet modern force.[5]

There are in this world 832 million Moslems, or about one fifth of all humanity. They are a majority not only in the Middle East but also in countries like Pakistan, Turkey, Indonesia, Iran, and Algeria. There are other countries, such as Nigeria and the Philippines, in which Moslems constitute an important political force. Indeed, only about one of every four Moslems lives in the Middle East. Wherever their location, during most of this century they were dominated by non-Islamic powers. Direct political domination ended with the collapse of colonialism, and later, economic domination was at least partly eclipsed by the growth of oil power. Along with these changes, there has been a growth of Islamic fundamentalism, pride, and militancy that has interacted with and supplemented the nationalism of Islamic countries.

The impact of Islam on world politics has been sharp and can be divided into two phenomena. One is *interreligion impact* and is based on the interaction of Islamic and non-Islamic countries. The previously mentioned antagonism between Israel and the Arabs and between India and Pakistan has persisted. In addition to these at least partly religious conflicts, we can add the strains and clashes between other countries (for example, Turkey versus Greece, Somalia versus Ethiopia) and also tensions within countries (Chad, the Sudan, the Philippines, Cyprus, Lebanon) between Moslems and other religious groups.

The second aspect of the effect of religion on politics is *intrareligion impact.* On the one hand, religion promotes *unity.* There are some signs of pan-Arab sentiment among Middle East Moslems. That feeling of pan-Arab nationalism has led to the establishment of some regional cooperation (for example, the Arab League) and other cooperation such as the support of Afghan rebels against the Soviet occupation. On the other hand, there are also *divisions* within Islam that are significant factors in today's politics. All the various sects and subsects condemn outside intervention in Islamic affairs, but they also struggle among themselves. In particular, there is tension between the long-dominant Sunni and the Shi'ites who have been inspired by the leadership of the Ayatollah Khomeini. The Iranian revolution not only encompassed anti-Western (and anti-Soviet/communist) elements, it also invigorated a populist movement that threatens the established elites in the Persian Gulf area. It is one of the causes of the Iran/Iraq war,[6] as well as Islamic rivalries in Lebanon, the assassination of moderate Egyptian President Anwar Sadat, and the temporary seizure of the Grand Mosque of Mecca in 1979 by fundamentalist extremists. The ongoing tension is aptly captured by the comment of one Persian Gulf state ruler who expressed a preference for dealing "with ten communists rather than with one Muslim fundamentalist."[7]

The message here is not that religion and politics are an explosive mix. That is not true. In some cases, such as the position of the American Catholic bishops on nuclear arms, religion is a force for peace. It is also not true that resurgent Islam is an aggressive, violent movement. To a substantial degree, it is merely reacting against the imperialistic wrongs of the recent past and attempting to uplift the status and circumstances of Moslems everywhere.

The Easter Sunday funeral of two Irish Republican Army members who starved themselves to death in prison is part of the ethnic and religious violence that has tormented Northern Ireland.

The point is that religion, with its political and social ramifications, is an important factor in international relations. Like any set of coherent ideas, it helps define who is on which side, and it often plays a powerful role in shaping the perceptions of political leaders and the actions of the countries they command.

Social Theories

Social theories—theories about the nature of world society and about the roles and the importance of various types of people—have also had an impact on world politics. Racism, for example, combined with nationalism to help encourage and justify imperialism. The ideas of biologist Charles Darwin in *The Origin of Species* were thoroughly corrupted to allow the exploitation of the "unfit" (nonwhites) by the "fit" (whites).[8] Racism also joined with religion to build a case in the Western mind that subjugation was in the interest of the uncivilized and pagan—that is, nonwhite, non-Christian—societies. Symbolic of this racist self-justification is Rudyard Kipling's "White Man's Burden," penned in 1899 to urge Americans to seize the Philippines.[9]

Take up the White Man's burden—
Send forth the best ye breed—
Go bind your sons to exile
To serve your captives' need;
To wait in heavy harness
On fluttered folk and wild—
Your new-caught sullen peoples,
Half devil and half child.

Take up the White Man's burden—
In patience to abide,
To veil the threat of lesson
And check the show of pride
By open speech and simple
An hundred times made plain
To seek another's profit
And work another's gain.

Take up the White Man's burden—
The savage wars of peace—
Fill full the mouth of Famine
And bid the sickness cease;
And when your goal is nearest
The end for others sought
Watch Sloth and heathen Folly
Bring all your hopes to naught.

Take up the White Man's burden—
And reap his old reward:
The blame of those ye better
The hate of those ye guard—
The cry of hosts ye humor
(Ah, slowly!) toward the light:—
"Why brought ye us from bondage,
Our beloved Egyptian night."

Take up the White Man's burden—
Have done with childish days—
The lightly proffered laurel,
The easy, ungrudged praise.

Iran's Ayatollah Khomeini is a charismatic leader who has inspired both interreligious and intrareligious conflict.

Comes now, to search your manhood
Through all the thankless years,
Cold-edged with deal-bought wisdom
The judgment of your peers!

That sort of bastardized **social Darwinism** also reared its head as a component of Italian fascism[10] and the related German credo of National Socialism. The Führer proclaimed that war and conquest were "all in the natural order of things—for [they make] for the survival of the fittest."[11] Race was a particular focus of conflict because, Hitler asserted in *Mein Kampf,* "all occurrences in world history are only expressions of the races' instinct of self-preservation."[12] This racist social theory was an important part of the Nazi *Weltanschauung* (world view) and gave Hitler what one scholar called "a universal missionary objective" that helped determine his foreign policy.[13]

Horribly laughable as that sort of doctrine may seem, we should not delude ourselves into thinking it died in the ashes of the Third Reich. It is, among other places, alive and well in South Africa. The white South African policy of *apartheid,* or race separation/segregation, is, in the strictest sense, a domestic issue. It has become internationalized, however, (1) because human rights have become more of a world concern, (2) because of growing tension with black African countries, and (3) because under the guise of "separate development" the South African government has tried to set up "independent" black homelands (Transkei, Bophuthatswana, Ciskei, and Venda).[14]

Economic Theories

The role of economic thought as an expression of nationalism has already been noted in Chapter 4. Beyond that limited application, though, **economic theories** have become one of this century's most important ideological forces. **Communism** is, in its origins, essentially economic in nature. It is an important factor in the foreign policies of the Soviet Union, China, and other communist-dominated countries. **Capitalism**, though a more amorphous doctrine, also has its committed adherents and affects world politics. These ideologies will be discussed fully below, but for the moment, it is sufficient to note that the clash between communism and capitalism has been a main element of the East/West struggle referred to in Chapter 1.

Communism

As one of the most powerful forces of the twentieth century, communism deserves our attention here. Before we look at this far-reaching ideology, though, three caveats must be noted. First, communism is a complex set of ideas. We will be concentrating only on those with international political ramifications. Second, communism is not monolithic. Whatever its "pure" roots, it has been interpreted over time, place, and circumstance to meet the perspectives and needs of its adherents. Third, communism is flexible and is only one part of the foreign policy equation in communist countries. You cannot understand Soviet or Chinese policy by only studying communism. But, equally, you cannot understand it unless you take communist perceptions into account. That does not mean communism has been rendered meaningless as a doctrine. It does mean that analysts must treat communism as a relative rather than an absolute force.[15]

Communist ideology, associated with Karl Marx, tells its believers that history proceeds by means of a historical dialectic, or clash of opposing ideas (thesis versus antithesis), with a resulting new order, or synthesis. Communists also believe that the economic (material) order determines political and social relationships. Thus, history, the current situation, and the future are determined by the economic struggle, termed dialectical materialism.

The first Soviet Communist Party chief, V. I. Lenin, applied dialectical materialism to international politics. Lenin argued that capitalist, bourgeois leaders had duped their proletariat workers into supporting the exploitation of other proletariat peoples through imperialism. Thus, the material dialectic was transformed, in part, from a domestic class struggle to an international struggle between bourgeois and proletariat countries and peoples.

Stemming from these ideas, communism suggests several principles and perceptions that influence the foreign policy of its believers.

First, it disposes communist leaders to view events in terms of *world struggle*. Until the mid-1950s, Soviet communist doctrine tended to assume that inevitably the communist and capitalist systems would clash militarily. In the face of nuclear arms, Soviet leader Nikita Khrushchev backed away from that idea and called for "peaceful coexistence." That did not mean acceptance of capitalism, however. It and the later term *detente* mean only that the Soviets are willing to carry on the struggle politically and economically while waiting for the capitalist system to collapse.

Second, and given the sense of struggle, communism lends a sense of *insecurity.* The Soviet and Chinese view themselves as surrounded by hostile capitalist and heretical, revisionist communist countries. Thus, the assumption of struggle causes a curious mixture of aggressiveness and defensiveness in communist foreign policies.

Third, communism is *universalistic* in that it looks to a world proletariat system. This aspect of communist ideology underwrites Soviet or Chinese activity in support of the "proletariat revolution" in all parts of the world.

Fourth, communist ideology has a *messianic* element. Its believers not only believe, they feel that the conversion of nonbelievers, by gospel or by sword, is legitimate. Accordingly, ends (the victory of the movement) are the greater morality, and means can be justified in terms of those ends.

The messianic component also has implications for relations among communist countries. Just as in some religions, many communists believe there can be only one "true faith." That conviction has led to bitter rivalries, especially between the Soviet Union and China, over which country's interpretation of Marxism-Leninism is correct. In fact, again as in religion, there is something of a tendency to look at heretics (revisionist communists) as even more evil and dangerous than heathens (capitalists).

Capitalism

Perhaps more than any other "ism" that we cover, capitalism is an amorphous set of ideas. Many of the current texts on ideologies do not treat capitalism as a separate subject. But the idea of private enterprise as the main characteristic of a country's economic structure has played a role in world politics. The United States, in particular, has often equated economic capitalism with political freedom and has often confused economic socialism with the political suppression usually found in communist states.

This political opposition to noncapitalist states was most pronounced in the 1950s, and has since declined. It has made something of a comeback, however, under President Reagan. He has blamed the problems of many Third World countries on their socialist systems. In particular, the Reagan administration has argued that greater reliance on private enterprise, competition, and the profit motive, rather than foreign aid, is the route to economic development for the less developed countries. It is the administration's position, as the president told the World Affairs Council in 1981, that "Free people build free markets that ignite dynamic development." As such, Reagan argues, the "emphasis" of American aid should be on "market-oriented policies" and on "improving the climate for private capital flow, particularly private investment."

Political Theories

Although it has its own chapter in this book, nationalism, in its theoretical sense, has been treated by many scholars as a political ideology.[16] Insofar as it is one, nationalism has had a tremendous impact during this century as the world rapidly changed from a system of a few states to a system of many. Another political ideology with an important historical role was *monarchism.* As a belief system, dynastic monarchism, which held that political loyalty should extend to the monarch, who ruled by right, struggled against liberal nationalism, which tended to favor democracy with power resting with the nation. For most of the 1800s the outcome hung in the balance. At times monarchism won out, as in the case of the restoration of the Bourbon monarchy in France in 1815 and the crushing of Hungarian nationalism by the czar's troops in 1848. By the end of World War I, however, with the overthrow of the German kaiser, the Austro-Hungarian emperor, and the Russian czar, the idea of dynastic monarchism was permanently eclipsed.

Next to nationalism, *democracy* is the political ideology with the greatest impact in the twentieth century. Although belief in and advocacy of democracy has not been confined to the United States, that country has been a particular champion. From the time that Woodrow Wilson called on Americans to follow him to war in order to "make the world safe for democracy," the United States has strongly, if not consistently, judged others by the standards of its democratic-liberal ideals. Even when the American government has supported authoritarian regimes, it has often faced a drumfire of domestic criticism. In recent years such events as the slackening of U.S. support and the fall of the regimes of the Shah in Iran and President Anastazio Somoza in Nicaragua have been linked to the democratic impulse. Political freedom has not yet quite joined basic human rights as a universally acclaimed (if not practiced) standard, but democracy is a benchmark of legitimacy to many people.

Moral/Ethical/Humanitarian Ideas

Morality as a force in international politics is both part of and also very much different from the ideas we have been examining. In one sense specific concepts of moral behavior may stem from religious beliefs or any one of the secular "isms." But here we will also be looking at morality in a different, broader sense. There are several issues we will need to examine: (1) whether ethical concepts affect world politics, (2) some of the difficulties in determining what is moral and what is not, and (3) the age-old debate over whether moral principles can—or even should—be applied to international politics.

Ethics—Who Cares?

Ethical concepts do play a role in world politics. It is madness, given the wars, starvation, and violations of human rights that occur, to imagine that morality is a predominant force. Yet it is there.

Stanley Hoffmann has defined three great ethical issues facing the world: the use of violence, violations of human rights, and the maldistribution of economic resources.[17] It is important not to exaggerate the progress, but strides have been made. Violence is gradually moving from being considered legitimate—even glorious—to unfortunate (even when "necessary") or even reprehensible. Some weapons, such as poison gas, have been outlawed; although there have been occasional reports of use of poison gas in Laos, Cambodia, Afghanistan, Yemen, and Iraq in recent years, the potential world shock keeps its employment limited. The Nuremberg and Tokyo war trials established the principle that individuals could be tried and executed for war crimes. Ethical considerations can also affect immediate decisions. At the time of the Cuban missile crisis, Robert Kennedy argued that bombing Cuba would be a Pearl Harbor in reverse and make the president as bad as Japanese Prime Minister Tojo. Kennedy's contention helped carry the day for restraint, and a blockade was applied instead.[18]

Advances have also been made in the area of human rights. By the latter part of the 1800s, the international slave trade had been halted by international action.[19] There have been actions and agreements condemning genocide, setting down principles of human rights, and condemning violations in South Africa and elsewhere. Again, this has not halted offenses, but governments are warier of violations. Forty years ago Soviet dissidents were shot. Twenty years ago they were sent to Siberia. Now they are sometimes deported to the West. Moral pressure also helped end the racist rule in Zimbabwe (Rhodesia) and is pressuring the South Africans to find an alternative to apartheid. The progress is slow, but it exists.[20]

The problem of resource redistribution has been the area of the least progress, but here again there have been advances. Organizations such as the

United Nations Conference on Trade and Development have been working to press the developed "North" countries to take on more responsibility for the less developed countries (LDCs) of the "South." In a step with promise for the future, eight industrialized and fourteen developing countries met at Cancun, Mexico, in October 1981 on "global negotiations" to assist the poorer nations. Although the meeting met with wide criticism, especially because of the U.S.'s desire to stress private economic investment, it did help establish the principle that the "North" has a responsibility for as well as an interest in aiding the LDCs.

Moral Uncertainties

Despite the slow growth of moral behavior, many questions remain concerning the basic nature of morality.

Is there any universal morality? Some scholars argue that it is difficult or impossible to develop universal moral standards, for the world is too diverse and there are too many different cultures to allow agreement. Former presidential adviser Arthur Schlesinger, Jr., contends that "[we] may eventually promote a world moral consensus. But for the present, national, ideological, ethical, and religious divisions remain as bitterly intractable as ever."[21]

Although most advocates of the development of moral standards would not be foolish enough to claim that such norms are in place, many are hopeful that they can be developed.[22] Indeed, for over 2,000 years philosophers, scholars, and theologians have been attracted by the notion that rational humans could come to a common conception of moral behavior.[23] One basis is the concept of **natural rights**, which contends that people carry into a society the same rights—such as the right to life—that they had in a "state of nature" before communities were organized.[24]

Is there one standard of morality that applies to both individuals and states? It is common practice for states to act legitimately in ways that would be reprehensible for individuals. Capital punishment is administered to murderers because of their terrible crimes. If you shoot five people you are a mass killer. Join the Air Force and shoot down five enemy pilots, and you are an ace. Of course, we recognize differences between justifiable and inexcusable actions, but where is the line? Some have argued that the state cannot be held to individual moral standards. Niccolò Machiavelli wrote in the sixteenth century that "a prudent ruler ought not to keep faith when by doing so it would be against his interest. . . . A prince . . . cannot observe all those things which are considered good in men, being often obliged, in order to maintain the state, to act against faith and charity, against humanity, and against religion."[25]

The controversy between the convergence and divergence of individual and state morality is more than a theoretical dispute. In 1793, when France was at war, it and the United States debated whether to honor the alliance that had earlier brought France to the aid of the revolutionary American colonies. The problem for the United States was that to side with France would mean war with England and place America in peril. Secretary of the Treasury Alexander Hamilton argued against honoring the treaty:

> The rule of morality . . . is not precisely the same between nations as between individuals. The duty of making its own welfare as the guide of its actions is much stronger [for countries]; in proportion to the greater magnitude and importance of national compared to individual happiness. . . . Millions . . . are concerned with the present matters of government; while the consequences of the private actions of an individual ordinarily terminate with himself.[26]

Secretary of State Thomas Jefferson held that the United States was morally obligated to honor the treaty:

> The moral duties which exist between individual and individual in a state of nature accompany them into a state of society and the aggregate of the duties . . . constitutes the duties of that society toward any other; so that between society and society the same moral duties exist as between the individuals composing them.[27]

Jefferson, by the way, lost the argument, and President Washington proclaimed neutrality.

Do ends justify means? Another philosophical problem with real-world impact is the means/ends controversy. What if you, a psychic with knowledge of the future, had had a chance to assassinate Adolf Hitler in 1932? Avoiding World War II plus the genocide of 6 million Jews would certainly be a lofty end. But assassination/murder?

When is war justified? Judeo-Christian tradition has predominantly believed in "just wars," but under what conditions?[28] Most crucially, under what conditions would nuclear war, particularly the first use of nuclear weapons, be morally justified? In the 1950s a controversy in the United States was whether it would be better to be "dead or Red." That dilemma still stands and would have to be faced if nuclear weapons were needed to save Washington from communism—or Moscow from capitalism.

The Argument against Moral Standards

These uncertainties and other issues have led some to argue that it is futile, even dangerous, to attempt to govern policy by moral standards. One such argument is that states should act in their citizens' interests. Leaders should act in the national interest, not according to an egocentric concept of morality. A second contention is that because not all states act morally, those who do are at a disadvantage: "Nice guys finish last." It can also be said that requiring that others act morally is **cultural imperialism**, since we always apply our own moral standards. If, for example, we demand free elections before giving foreign aid, we are imposing our standards. Democracy is not highly valued in some cultures. A fourth argument against applying morality holds that since there is no universal morality, its invocation is a self-serving sham invoked retrospectively to justify the unjustifiable. Yet another objection to applying morality is that insisting on one form of moral behavior violates other states' sovereignty. Americans are quick to condemn the Soviet Union's treatment of Jews, South Africa's treatment of its blacks, or El Salvador's treatment of political prisoners. But how would Americans react to a Russian investigation of Ku Klux Klan marches, a South African inquiry into the death of Martin Luther King, or an El Salvadoran condemnation over the jailing of draft registration resisters?

Some also contend that other evils are greater than violations of some civil rights. Ernest Lefever, once nominated as Reagan's assistant secretary of state for humanitarian affairs, argues that civil rights violations by friendly regimes should be sometimes downplayed because "the greatest threat to human rights comes from messianic totalitarian regimes."[29] That sort of attitude is nothing new. An aide once supposedly complained to Franklin Roosevelt about dealing with a certain Latin American dictator. "The man's a son-of-a-bitch!," the aide objected. "Ah, yes," FDR replied, "but he's our son-of-a-bitch."

A seventh and last objection to applying morality is that it may be counterproductive. The United States pressured the regime of the Shah to give more freedom to dissidents in Iran. That in part led to the revolution that brought the Ayatollah Khomeini to power and resulted in the seizure of the American embassy and the political and religious persecution of an untold number of Iranians.[30]

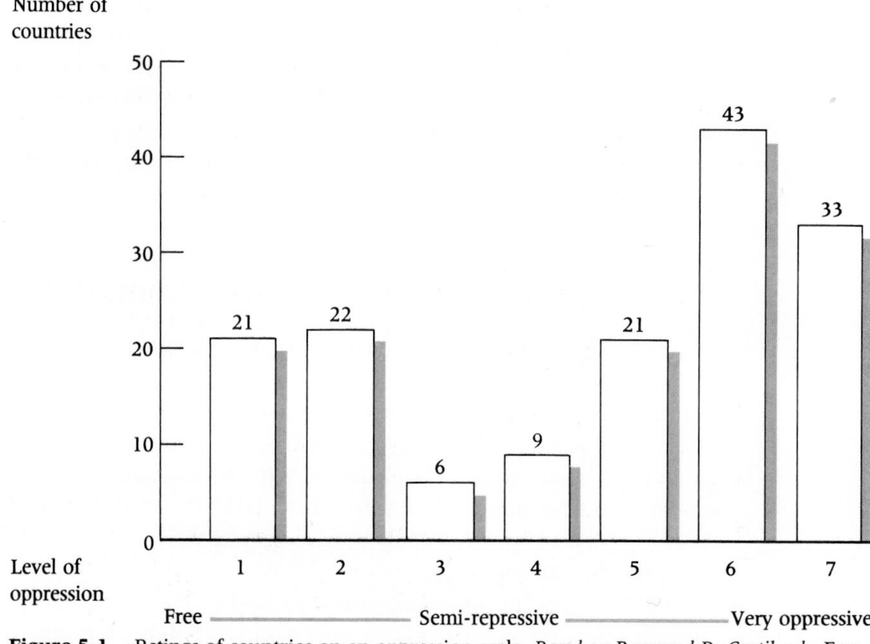

Figure 5-1. Ratings of countries on an oppression scale. *Based on Raymond D. Gastil, ed.,* Freedom in the World: Political Rights and Civil Liberties, 1978 *(Boston: G. K. Hall, 1978), p. 16.*

If it were the 1930s and you could forsee the horrors of World War II, would you be justified in assassinating Adolf Hitler? Would the end justify the means?

The Argument for Moral Standards (pro)

Despite the obvious problems with applying morality, there are also excellent reasons for doing so. One is that the dignity of the human race demands it. Perhaps the strongest argument for demanding moral responsibility by states, both internationally and domestically, involves the basic tenets of civilized behavior. Internationally we have witnessed aggressive war, the use of chemical warfare, genocide, and a host of other atrocities. Domestically, racism, religious and political persecution, and the brutal denial of civil rights and the economic rudiments of human existence are regularly reported. Indeed, one study, rating countries' civil liberties from 1 (good) to 7 (terrible), 4 being regularly semi-repressive, found a distressing state of affairs (see Figure 5-1). Sixty-nine percent of the countries were ranked 4 or above on the oppression scale.

These numbers are dry and do not convey the gruesome reality of life in some police states. To bring the figures to life, consider part of Amnesty International's 1981 report on Chile:

> [Thirty-three prisoners] were kept hanging upside down by their feet for hours at a time; they were stripped naked and then taken outdoors where icy jets of water from a high-pressure hose were turned on them (it was winter in Chile); they were punched and kicked, and given electric shocks in the most sensitive parts of their bodies. . . . [Some were] treated with particular cruelty . . . forced to swallow human excrement and urine.[31]

Proponents of morality would argue, first, that people have an obligation to oppose the continuance of these conditions. Neither national interest nor sovereignty legitimizes crimes against humanity. Second, they would argue that it is possible to work toward and arrive at a universal morality. The slow growth of internationally acclaimed (if not always practiced) norms of behavior has been mentioned. Proponents argue that standards like the Universal Declaration of Human Rights and the International Covenant on Civil and Political Rights, which declares, "No one shall be subjected to torture or to cruel, inhuman, or degrading treatment or punishment," are beginning to form at least basic agreement on moral conduct.[32]

A third argument is that greater justice is necessary for world survival. This argument, mentioned in Chapter 1, basically deals with resource distribution. It contends that it is immoral to maintain a large part of the world both impoverished and without self-development possibilities. The inevitable result will be a world crisis that will destroy order. "The reasons for making such a right [not to be impoverished] universal are now pragmatic and moral," Richard Barnet tells us. "Unless such clear norms are created and supported by an overwhelming international consensus, the politics of scarcity . . . will keep the world in a permanent state of grotesque and dangerous conflict."[33]

Finally, one can argue that pursuing moral policy is good power politics. The heart of this line of thought is that being moral can win you friends and dismay your enemies. Critics of U.S. policy, for example, say that the gap between America's moral preaching and cynical practice have damaged its reputation. They argue that a more righteous stand in deed as well as word would win widespread world support and draw a sharp distinction between the United States and its international opponents. One scholar told Congress, for example, that President Carter's stress on human rights "placed the Soviet government on a defensive both at home and abroad."[34]

Is Morality Absolute?

The preceding argument on using moral standards in international conduct does not mean that proponents are moral and "good" and opponents are immoral and "evil." It is, rather, a discussion of standards and priorities. "What ought to be" is highly subjective, a matter of philosophy more than of concrete fact.

It should also be noted that you do not have to choose one standard or the other—morality or amorality. There is a middle ground. Kenneth Thompson, who writes a great deal on these issues, suggests adopting the standard of *"practical morality,"* which he defines as "the reconciliation of what is morally desirable" with what is "politically possible."[35] That may sound like mumbling rather than deciding, and Thompson admits that practical morality "offers few absolutes." It does, however, offer "many practical possibilities." Prudence would be the cardinal precept of Thompson's approach, which would allow statesmen to consider ethics as a component of their decisions without making it the only factor. Two questions, then, "What is ethical?" and "Is it prudently possible to be moral?," would influence decisions.

The Impact of Ideas and Ideology

Identifying categories of ideas is easier by far than analyzing their precise, or even general, impact. No nations and few decision makers are *pure ideologues* who make choices based solely on theoretical correctness. Even if a decision maker is an ideologue, it is likely that reality will rudely intrude to disrupt his or her theoretical world. A classic example involves Russia's surrender to Germany in 1918. The newly-in-power Bolsheviks, even in the face of the total dissolution of the Russian army, refused at first to act defeated. The Bolsheviks expected social unrest to spread to Germany, and when they arrived at the negotiations, they handed out leaflets to the German guards calling on them to join the workers' revolution. The Soviets proclaimed the war a capitalist conflict, declared that they would no longer participate, and called on Germany to withdraw. When the Germans pressed for capitulation, the Russian foreign commissar, Leon Trotsky, said they would neither surrender nor fight. "We interrupt the war and do not sign the peace; we demobilize the army" was Trotsky's formula—no war, no peace. "Unerhört!" ("Unheard of") was the German reaction. The German armies began to move forward again, and the Bolsheviks learned their first diplomatic lesson. Within days they agreed to Germany's terms.[36]

At the other extreme from being an ideologue, it is also rare to find people who operate without any belief system. Some leaders like to imagine themselves pure power pragmatists, but it is self-delusion. They are not only influenced by their idiosyncratic beliefs (see Chapter 2), they are also part of and affected by their nation's belief system. As Richard Sterling has noted, ideology, whether it be "translated as doctrine, creed, belief system, [or] social myth," is "an essential component of social organization and, as such, cannot be eliminated from human existence."[37]

Between the two unlikely poles—pure ideologue and pure pragmatist—ideology plays several important roles.[38]

First, belief systems act as *prisms*. A prism is a lens that distorts reality, and deeply held beliefs have a similar effect. They help us, for example, define enemies. Leftist regimes in Cuba in the 1960s, Vietnam in the 1970s, and Nicaragua in the 1980s all met with American hostility. "Good" and "communist" seem to be a contradiction in terms. Similarly, when communist countries view the policies of capitalist countries, they are prone to see them in negative and threatening terms. A bit surprisingly, ideological similarity does not necessarily mean friendship. One study found that between 1815 and 1939 ideological similarity did not predict the stability of alliances.[39]

Indeed, the Sino-Soviet split shows that intraideological competition can be just as conflict-causing as interideological competition.

Belief systems also *restrict options*. A country's belief system makes it difficult or even impossible for it to select certain policy options, even if they make more pragmatic sense. Syria has, for instance, threatened Jordan on several occasions in recent years. Syria and Israel are also enemies. A case could be made for Jordan and Israel to ally themselves against Syria. It probably won't happen, though. Religion would make it extremely difficult for Islamic Jordan to join Jewish Israel against Islamic Syria.

Additionally, belief systems provide a level of *continuity*. For good or ill, ideas and ideology provide some predictability to foreign policy. Because of ideological differences, it is predictable that the United States and the Soviet Union will not become allies. For the same reason, it is predictable that the United States will not help leftist guerrillas overthrow the government of El Salvador. Similarly, for at least partly ideological reasons, any real threat to the Polish communist government by Solidarity or other "reactionary" factions will cause a violent Soviet reaction.

Belief systems also often *rationalize and legitimize policy*. Especially in an era when gunboat diplomacy and the naked, self-interested use of power have become déclassé, ideology has become a legitimizing standard by which policy makers can justify their actions to themselves, to their domestic populations, and to the world. Because ideologies are a secular religion, they are useful as a simplified explanation (we must avoid a communist takeover of South Vietnam). They also seem to elevate what otherwise would seem reprehensible. Invading, killing, and conquering in the name of power or economic gain is damnable. Invading, killing, and conquering in the name of communism, freedom, Islam, or the white man's burden cloaks the aggressor in an aura of self-righteousness.[40]

Finally, belief systems serve to *differentiate*. The world's diverse religious, social, political, economic, and moral belief systems help perpetuate our feeling of distinctiveness. Here the divergent ideas act much like nationalistic concepts. They make us see ourselves not only as different but also often as superior to, hostile to, and threatened by those of differing and, especially, opposing philosophies.

In sum, then, ideas and ideologies are part of the complex of international and domestic forces that affect world politics. Decision makers and nations are neither devoid of belief systems nor completely captivated by ideological tenets. Between those extremes, the role of ideas varies greatly. Ideas are most potent, for example, in revolutionary times when new ideas challenge established ideas.[41] Scholars have also found that belief systems are more important in establishing general policy but less relevant to decisions on particular issues. Finally, ideology may be more important than such domestic factors as economics,[42] but it is usually less important than power and national security factors.[43]

Summary

The single most important factor that separates humans from animals is that we can think abstractly. That ability to carry ideas in our heads profoundly affects world politics. In this chapter, we have seen that many types of ideas based on religion, social, political, and economic theories and on concepts of morality help structure our perceptions and actions.

Important as they are, though, ideas do not exist in a vacuum. Time, events, and individual predispositions all interact with ideas. Ideas, then, are not often absolute guides to action. Rather, they are flexible parts of a number of factors that create mind sets and determine action. Most important, ideas influence perception. They dispose policy makers to view other actors, events, and possible policies from a predetermined perspective. Thus ideas limit options and point in the "proper" policy direction.

Terms

Capitalism—An economic system based on the private ownership of real property and commercial enterprise, competition for profits, and limited government interference in the marketplace.

Communism—A wide-ranging and diverse economic doctrine, with origins in Marxism-Leninism, that has significant political ramifications.

Cultural imperialism—The belief and practice that others should be judged according to how closely their beliefs and actions parallel our own.

Economic theories—Beliefs about economic forces and their impact on politics and society.

Ideology—A set of related ideas, usually founded on identifiable thinkers and their works, that offers a more or less comprehensive picture of reality.

Natural rights—The belief that humans have inalienable rights which existed before societies and which cannot be legitimately denied by society.

Social Darwinism—A social theory that argues it is proper that stronger races will prosper and will dominate lesser peoples.

Social theories—Beliefs about the nature of world society and the importance of various types of people.

Notes

1. Lloyd Jensen, *Explaining Foreign Policy* (Englewood Cliffs, N.J.: Prentice-Hall, 1982), pp. 71–72. See subsequent notes, especially, 2, 5, and 7, for individual works on political philosophy.
2. Lyman T. Sargent, *Contemporary Political Ideologies: A Comparative Analysis*, 3rd ed. (Homewood, Ill.: Dorsey Press, 1975), p. 3.

3. Jensen, *Explaining Foreign Policy*, p. 95.
4. Benjamin J. Cohen, *The Question of Imperialism* (New York: Basic Books, 1973), p. 69.
5. A good short study is Daniel Pepes' "Understanding Islam in Politics," *Middle East Review* 16 (Winter 1983/84): 3–15. Also see Pepes' more complete *In the Path of God: Islam and Political Power* (New York: Basic Books, 1983).
6. See Sheikh R. Ali, "Holier than Thou: The Iran-Iraq War," *Middle East Review* 17 (Fall, 1984): 50–57.
7. Quoted in James A. Bell, "Resurgent Islam in the Persian Gulf," *Foreign Affairs* 63 (1984): 111. It should be noted that Islamic fundamentalism includes both Sunni and Shi'ite elements, and neither the fundamentalist movement nor the sects are monolithic. It is, however, the Shi'ites who are in the vanguard of the more radical political aspects of the movement.
8. William Montgomery McGovern, *From Luther to Hitler: The History of Fascist-Nazi Political Philosophy* (New York: Houghton Mifflin, 1941), chap. 10.
9. Richard W. Sterling, *Macropolitics: Foreign Relations in a Global Society* (New York: Knopf, 1974), p. 209.
10. A. James Gregor, *Contemporary Radical Ideologies* (New York: Random House, 1968), p. 310.
11. Ibid., p. 186.
12. Ibid., p. 188.
13. William T. Blum, *Ideologies and Attitudes* (Englewood Cliffs, N.J.: Prentice-Hall, 1971), p. 212.
14. For a comparison of fascism and apartheid see Heribent Adam, *Modernizing Racial Domination: South Africa's Political Dynamics* (Berkeley: University of California Press, 1971), chap. 3; also Gregor, *Contemporary Radical Ideologies*, chap. 6.
15. This section relies on Judson Mitchell, *Ideology of a Superpower: Contemporary Soviet Doctrine on International Relations* (Stanford, Calif.: Hoover Institution Press, 1982), and Adam Ulam, *The Unfinished Revolution: Marxism and Communism in the Modern World* (Boulder, Colo.: Westview Press, 1979). The impact of ideology on Chinese foreign policy is discussed in such works as Grey O'Leary, *The Shaping of Chinese Foreign Policy* (New York: St. Martin's Press, 1980), and J. D. Armstrong, *Revolutionary Diplomacy* (Berkeley: University of California Press, 1977).
16. Sargent, *Contemporary Political Ideologies*, chap. 1
17. Stanley Hoffmann, *Duties beyond Borders: On the Limits and Possibilities of Ethical International Politics* (Syracuse, N.Y.: Syracuse University Press, 1981), pp. 5–6.
18. John C. Bennett and Harvey Seifert, *U.S. Foreign Policy and Christian Ethics* (Philadelphia: Westminster Press, 1977), p. 62.
19. J. E. S. Fawcett, "The International Protection of Human Rights," in *Political Theory and the Rights of Man*, ed. D. D. Raphael (Bloomington: Indiana University Press, 1967), p. 67.
20. Jan Pettman, "Race, Conflict and Liberation in Africa," in *Moral Claims in World Affairs*, ed. Ralph Pettman (New York: St. Martin's Press, 1979), pp. 131–146.
21. Arthur Schlesinger, Jr., "Morality and International Politics," in *World in Crisis*, 4th ed., ed. Frederick Hartmann (New York: Macmillan, 1973), p. 72.
22. For the work of two leading scholars of this view, see Kenneth W. Thompson, *The Moral Issue and Statecraft* (Baton Rouge: Louisiana State University Press, 1966); and Hoffmann, *Duties beyond Borders*.

23. Walter Lippmann, "The Eclipse of the Public Philosophy," in *The Puritan Ethic in United States Foreign Policy,* ed. David L. Larsen (Princeton, N.J.: D. Van Nostrand, 1966), pp. 51–57.
24. On the nature of human beings and political organization and rights, see Joseph Cropey, *Political Philosophy and the Issues of Politics* (Chicago: University of Chicago Press, 1977), especially part 4 and pp. 221–230. A particularly good review of non-Western ideas can be found in Dorothy Rae Dodge and Duncan H. Baird, eds., *Continuities and Discontinuities in Political Thought* (New York: Wiley, 1975), pp. 7–36.
25. Niccolò Machiavelli, *The Prince and the Discourses* (New York: Random House, 1950), pp. 64–65.
26. Norman A. Graebner, ed., *Ideas and Diplomacy* (New York: Oxford University Press, 1964), p. 61.
27. Ibid., p. 55.
28. Bennett and Seifert, *Christian Ethics,* pp. 88–92.
29. Ernest W. Lefever, "The Trivialization of Human Rights," in *The Theory and Practice of International Relations,* 5th ed., ed. Fred A. Sonderman, David S. McLellan, and William C. Olsen (Englewood Cliffs, N.J.: Prentice-Hall, 1979), p. 357. As United Nations ambassador, Jeane Kirkpatrick has also made this case, and it is one basis of Reagan administration attitudes.
30. Henry Kissinger, "The Politics of Human Rights," *Trialogue,* no. 19 (1978), p. 3.
31. *Amnesty International Report, 1981* (London: Amnesty International).
32. Ibid., pp. 1–9. Also see Hedly Bull, "Human Rights and World Politics," in Pettman, *Moral Claims,* p. 84.
33. Richard Barnet, "Human Rights Implications of Corporate Food Policies," in Pettman, *Moral Claims,* p. 48.
34. Bohdan R. Bociurkiw's contribution in U.S. Congress, Senate Committee on Foreign Relations, *Perceptions: Relations between the United States and the Soviet Union* (Washington, D.C.: U.S. Government Printing Office, 1979), p. 389.
35. This and subsequent quotations are from Kenneth W. Thompson, "The Ethical Dimensions of Diplomacy," *Review of Politics* 46 (1984): 387.
36. Ronald Segal, *Leon Trotsky* (New York: Pantheon Books, 1979), pp. 196–212. It should be noted that there is disagreement on Trotsky's motives. Some scholars claim he was cleverly stalling for time. Additionally, others, especially Lenin, were more realistic. As a balance, still others, such as Karl Radek and Nikolai Bukharin, were even more radical.
37. Sterling, *Macropolitics,* pp. 157–158.
38. There is dispute over the impact of ideology, some arguing it has become unimportant. See, for example, Daniel Bell, *The End of Ideology* (New York: Free Press, 1962). This author disagrees. For a discussion, see Ronald H. Chilcote, *Theories of Comparative Politics* (Boulder, Colo.: Westview Press, 1981), pp. 30–35. The following discussion of the functions of belief systems relies heavily on Jensen, *Explaining Foreign Policy,* pp. 72–75.
39. John D. Sullivan, "International Alliances," in *International Systems,* ed. Michael Haas (New York: Chandler, 1964), pp. 100–122, cited in Jensen, *Explaining Foreign Policy,* p. 74.
40. This use of ideology to deceive oneself and others is argued by a number of thinkers, such as Marx and Karl Mannheim. See H. M. Drucker, *The Political Uses of*

Ideology (New York: Harper & Row, 1974), chap. 2; Chilcote, *Theories of Comparative Politics*, p. 31.

41. Warner Levi, "Ideology, Interests and Foreign Policy," *International Studies Quarterly* 14 (1970): 1–18.
42. See Patrick J. McGowan and Howard B. Shapiro, *The Comparative Study of Foreign Policy* (Beverly Hills, Calif.: Sage, 1973), p. 126.
43. Bruce M. Russett and Elizabeth C. Hansen, *Interest and Ideology: The Foreign Policy Beliefs of American Businessmen* (San Francisco: W. H. Freeman, 1975), p. 227; Jensen, *Explaining Foreign Policy*, p. 163.

6

National Interest

Out of this nettle, danger,
We pluck this flower, safety.
Shakespeare, King Henry IV

I do perceive here a divided duty.
Shakespeare, Othello

National interest is one of those terms that drive political scientists to distraction. It is widely used by political leaders to explain their actions. What politician has ever announced a policy or action and declared it "not in the national interest"? Atomic attacks, conventional invasions, and subversive activities have all been declared in the national interest. Peace treaties, foreign aid, and the insistence on humanitarian conduct have also been described as fulfilling the national interest.

This use of the term to describe every conceivable sort of policy for good or evil has led some political scientists to discount the term as meaningless. Others say that it is so elastic and ambiguous that it is of little use in describing what has happened, predicting what will happen, or prescribing what policy ought to be adopted.[1]

Political scientists have also been generally confounded in their attempts to devise "scientific" criteria and measurements for the national interest. Several scholars have tried to look beyond the self-serving, rationalizing use of the term by politicians, but progress has been slow in constructing objective outlines of what national interest is or ought to be.

The combination of diverse use of the term by decision makers plus academic conceptual difficulties has led many scholars simply to ignore national interest. Indeed, one recent look at the subject has accused the academic community of "copping out."[2]

Whether or not that charge is fully true, it is plain, at least to this writer, that we cannot afford to ignore national interest. First, if it is true, as this study holds, that nation-states are the prime movers in international politics, and if, as is surely true, these actors have interests, then national interest is a vital topic. However it is used or abused, it is an important source of international behavior. Second, and more important, we need to develop our own systematic concept so that we will not have to accept the definition of regime leaders. As responsible citizens, we can begin to develop an overall view of "what ought to be," and we can begin to evaluate individual policy options according to those standards and priorities. Even a limited ability to do that will elevate your analytical ability above that of some reactive, narrow-perspective decision makers.

In this chapter we will examine several aspects of national interest. First, we will look in detail at problems with the concept. Why is it so slippery? Second, we will look at some attempts by scholars to arrive at useful definitions and dimensions of national interest. Third, we will explore an approach to the subject that will help the reader begin evaluating policies by a more sophisticated set of standards.

Issues and Problems

In one of the best essays in recent years on national interest, Fred Sondermann has outlined the major difficulties that political scientists face when they try to discuss the subject.[3]

Vagueness

Sondermann's first argument is that the term *national interest* lacks precision. French political philosopher Raymond Aron contends that national interest is a concept beyond meaningful comprehension, that "the plurality of concrete objectives and ultimate objectives forbids a rational definition of national interest."[4]

Even those who do not find a definition of *national interest* impossible concede that it is difficult to "operationally define in the sense that empirical referents can be identified easily."[5] In simpler words, that means that *national interest* has not been defined in terms which are clear and widely acceptable and which also can be applied to describe, predict, and prescribe the real-world actions of countries.

Ends/Means Confusion

In international politics, we often confuse ends (goals) and means (methods). The concept of "power" is particularly important here. Hans Morgenthau has argued that "statesmen think and act in terms of interest defined as power."[6] Without delving into all the controversy caused by Morgenthau's formulation, we can point out that, in part, power becomes an end in itself. But power is also a means insofar as its possession allows a country to achieve other ends, such as security. Thus, power presents an ends/means ambiguity. Is it in the

national interest to acquire power, or is power a tool to achieve the national interest?

Whose Interests? Determined by Whom?

The problem here is that *national interest* is a highly subjective term. As used by decision makers, it is a projection of the perceptions of a particular regime or even a single political leader in a given international or domestic environment.[7] It has been argued, for example, that the Soviet communist regime follows an aggressive policy in order to maintain itself in power. On the individual level, it has also been argued that President Kennedy engaged in the Cuban missile confrontation partly to save his own political skin. Thus, the national interest can be interpreted, all or in part, in terms of a régime's interest

or an individual's interest.

Retroactive Justification

Ideally, a decision maker should fashion policies to meet the national interest. In practice, leaders often react to events with less than perfect rationality. Top American leaders defined South Korea as outside the perimeter of American interests in 1950. Yet when North Korea invaded its neighbor, President Truman's feisty personality led him to resist militarily. It was only later, with hindsight, that justifications on the basis of national interest were made to Americans and the world.

Existence and Transcendency

Numerous scholars have argued that national interest does not really exist. Their point is that a society is a collection of subgroups, each with its own set of interests.[8] It can also be said that the "intermestic" mingling of international and domestic issues has increased both the number of subgroups concerned with foreign affairs and the level of the stakes involved, thus making the search for a single national interest even more difficult.[9] Beyond this problem, and even if a nationwide interest does exist, the question of transcendency remains. The issue is whether the national interest takes priority over the interests or rights of subgroups or individuals. Jews are oppressed in the Soviet "national interest." The World War II confinement of Japanese Americans in concentration camps was also justified by that lofty term. The question is, then, what is the balance between majoritarianism and minority rights?

National Egocentrism

A last issue is one of operation rather than definition. Some students of world politics charge that, as it is used in the world, national interest is a destructive phenomenon. This indictment is closely related to the attack on nationalism discussed in Chapter 4. According to this view, the concept as used has become a "synonym for national egoism" and must be abandoned to avoid world-shattering conflict.[10] In the estimation of one critic, "The bird's-eye view of the political will of mankind in relation to global problems and their solutions does not present an encouraging picture. People are intent on their immediate material benefits, [and] leaders play the game of power and wealth while the clouds of doom gather overhead."[11]

National Interest: What It Is, What It Ought to Be

One way to begin to find our way out of all this confusion is to admit that national interest cannot be approached from a single perspective. Instead, it must be viewed in two ways, each of which is important to our understanding of international politics.

The first way to study national interest is to analyze various countries to ask whether there are any consistent ways that they define what their **subjective national interest** is. In other words, **"what is"** a country's perceived national interest? It is true that political leaders almost always justify what they do in terms of national interest, but no matter how subjective these claims are, they do represent a form of reality. Unless we characterize a given country's foreign policy as random, then we must concede that there are certain principles, norms, or concepts that give some structure and consistency to the actions of that country. It follows, then, that by examining the claims and actions taken in the name of national interest, we can begin to understand a country's past actions, current policy, and, perhaps, future policy. What we find will be far from foolproof, but it will give some valuable clues.

The second way to approach national interest is to ask **"what ought to be."** This question addresses the issue of whether there is any such thing as **objective national interest** and, if so, what it is. The value of this approach is that it allows us to *independently* analyze the policy of our own country for ourselves and ask whether it fits in with our own systematic concept of the "real" national interest.

In the following pages, national interest is analyzed from these two directions. First, we will examine the way national interest is applied as an instrument of political actions. Then, we will explore concepts that will help you form independent judgments of what the national interest of your country is.

National Interest: What It Is

The term *national interest* has been used for good or ill in many ways. It is impossible to account for every policy followed by every decision maker, but we can begin to try to understand that the policies of countries do have some level of consistency. In part, that consistency is caused by continuing themes of national interest. The way that your, or any, country defines its national interest is heavily influenced by an intermingling of historical experiences, ideas and ideology, and current needs. The sort of national history and continuing ideas that have been covered in the last two chapters are the roots of currently defined national interest.

We cannot possibly survey the perceived national interests of all the world's countries, but we can briefly look at some of the consistent themes in the psyches of the United States and the Soviet Union as two examples.

National Interest, American Style

A great deal of American policy is influenced by the ideas and experiences of the past. These, of course, are not static. Instead, they are evolutionary and are modified by intervening experiences and current needs. Americans have never really had to protect their territory from serious conquest, for instance, but that, of course, is a base interest of any country and can be seen in deterrence and other defense policies. The convergence of these influences leads to some consistencies in the United States' particular definition of its national interest.

Protection of trade is one important component of American national interest. From its beginning, the United States has been a trading nation, and this factor worked against early isolationism and thrust the country outward. Unlike isolationism, however, trade continues to be a significant and growing American national interest. The United States' economy and its national security are heavily dependent on trade. Protection of American trading partners in Western Europe and Japan is a mainstay of current American policy. Energy dependence also makes the Middle East/Persian Gulf area a vital concern, and even as noninterventionist a president as Jimmy Carter warned that he would move militarily to keep that region's oil flowing to the United States and its major trading partners.

Maintaining a ***sphere of influence*** consisting of the Caribbean, Central America, and (to a lesser degree) South America is another basic tenet of U.S. national interest.[12] Rejection of Old World influence and belief in the special status of the New World led, in part, to the formulation of the *Monroe Doctrine,* which proclaims that the New World should not be dominated by the Old and that the United States has a special role in ensuring that no such domination be allowed to develop or persist. Since Franklin Roosevelt announced the Good Neighbor Policy, the United States has in theory stopped trying to be the hemisphere's police officer, but in practice American troops or U.S.-supported rebels have moved against the governments of Cuba, the Dominican Republic, Grenada, Nicaragua, and others in recent history.

Containment of communism is a third basic part of America's perceived national interest. Almost everything about communism as practiced runs counter to American tradition and ideals. Soviet-style communism is atheistic and totalitarian and thus is antithetical to American democratic-liberal ideals about free government, freedom of religion, and other civil and political liberties. Communism is also dedicated to the overthrow of capitalism, or the free-enterprise system and private property, which is the basis of the American economic system. Added to all this, communism is wedded to the Soviet Union, which means that it is a physical as well as a spiritual and economic threat. As such, the United States has long opposed communism. Woodrow Wilson refused to recognize Lenin's government and sent troops to Russia soon after its 1917 revolution, in at least an indirect attempt to topple the Bolsheviks. More important, containment has been a major part of America's post–World War II policy.

The reverses in Vietnam and the obvious rivalries within the communist world modified some of the automatic anticommunist reactiveness. They did not end it, though, and with Ronald Reagan in the White House, the now unspoken commitment to containment persists.[13]

Making the world like America is another aspect of the American impulse. Americans believe in themselves and their system, and their heritage convinces them that they can and should bring the blessings of the American political and civil libertarian system to the world. Despite the warnings of John Kennedy (1962) and others that "we must reject . . . the theory that the American mission is to remake the world in the American image," the result is a tendency to try to pressure others to live up to American ideals. This can

The United States has intervened repeatedly in Latin America to maintain its sphere of influence. Here American troops patrol Grenada after they overthrew the leftist government there in 1983.

be condemned as "ugly Americanism" or applauded as "humanitarianism," depending on one's views, but the basic urge is the same.

National Interest, Soviet Style

Just like the United States, the Soviet Union has a history of ideas and experiences that combine with current needs to influence its concepts of national interest.

Defense of the motherland is a key element of Soviet thinking. All countries, of course, emphasize defense of the home territory, but the Soviets share a sense of impending danger unknown to Americans and many others. Conflict is a mainstream of Russian history. War has been the exception in American history. Peace has been the exception in Russian history, and the Russians have suffered staggering losses. In this century alone, they have gone through a major revolution and borne the brunt of two world wars. During World War II, for example, seventy-five Russians died for every American who was killed. Thus, in part because of their expansionism but in larger part because they have been repeatedly bludgeoned from nearly every direction, the Russians have some reason to regard danger and struggle as the norm of international relations.

The Soviet Union's adoption of communism has enhanced this feeling of struggle and of being surrounded by hostile capitalist forces. The rise of China as a power, particularly against a history of earlier conflict with Asiatic peoples, and as an ideological rival further adds to Soviet fears and defensiveness.

The Soviet stress on massive military might is one result of this defensive psychology. The Soviets' long refusal to allow on-site nuclear inspections and their 1984 downing of a South Korean jet airliner are probably further examples of their suspicious fear of outsiders.

Domination of Eastern Europe and other buffer states is a related key element of Soviet policy. To a large degree, the Soviets perceive Eastern Europe as a defensive buffer against NATO. If there is to be another war in Europe, they mean to have it fought far from the Soviet border. Afghanistan, Outer Mongolia, and Soviet Siberian areas in dispute with China are, in the same sense, buffers against danger from that quarter. The 1979 Soviet invasion of Afghanistan, for example, can be interpreted as an extension of Russian interest in that area since the clashes with colonial India's British raj in the rugged Hindu Kush.

Somewhat paradoxically, the Soviets also still pursue *expansionism*. Russian history is a record of expansionism. From its beginning 500 years ago as

Figure 6-1. 500 years of Russian expansion.

the 15,000-square-mile Duchy of Moscovy, half the size of Maine, the Soviet Union has grown to be the world's largest country (Figure 6-1). Thus, the Russians have a long history of expanding their borders and areas of control. Recent history has witnessed a traditional increase in the size of the Russian state.

The messianic element of communism also helps drive Soviet expansionism.[14] What has changed is that communism and the growth of Soviet power have urged and allowed that country to project its influence far from its borders.

The desire to be a true superpower in influence as well as in might also stems from the Soviet Union's reaction to its own sense of inferiority. Because they were so often besieged, and because they lagged behind Europe culturally and economically, Russians not only are suspicious of outsiders but also have strong pride and insecurity that make them react very negatively to any sense of being second and to any real or perceived insult. They intend to put their country in a position where no one can ever look down on them again.

The triumph of communism is another basic Soviet goal. The Russians have a long messianic tradition. This urge to "spread the belief" manifested itself in the early Russian idea that their system inherited the mantle of Rome (the word *czar* is a derivative of *Caesar*) and was obligated to protect Western civilization and, in particular, Christian orthodoxy. In somewhat later times, the messianic tradition spurred the belief among Russians that they had a special mission to protect their ethnic Slavic cousins in Eastern Europe, a belief that, in part, led to World War I.

The belief that the Russians should spread communism fits in with their disposition toward messianism. The Soviets believe in and work toward the eventual spread and success of their economic and political system. This means that they continue to support "liberation" movements, hope to neutralize and eventually convert Western Europe, and desire increasingly to isolate and weaken the United States.

Like all messianic movements, communism also leans toward the idea of one truth and one focus of leadership, and the Soviet struggle with China over leadership of the world communist movement is another ideologically inspired aspect of Soviet national interest.

National Interest: Limits to Understanding

The themes outlined above in Americans' and Russians' conceptions of their national interest are far from absolutes. They are, in the first place, only tendencies. Like all rules, they have exceptions, and individual leaders or unusual circumstances may cause a country to depart from the norm. In addition, they sometimes conflict with one another. In the United States, for example, one of the continuing policy struggles is whether support should be given to anticommunist regimes (such as the Philippines or Chile) that violate American standards of political and civil liberties. Examining any country's conceptions of national interest, then, can provide some guidelines for understanding and even predicting policy, but it can never be a substitute for good analysis.

National Interest: What It Ought to Be

Understanding how national interest is perceived in the "real" world is important, but it gives us no standards to use in evaluating the national interest claims of our own country or other countries. It leaves us in the position of having to accept at face value the policies of decision makers or, if we reject them, of doing so without applying any systematic criteria of our own. Falling into that trap leaves us rightfully subject to the charge that our concept of how the national interest "ought to be" defined is no more valid than anybody else's.

Thus, if we want to be informed, rather than just opinionated, it is important to be able to evaluate any given policy within the broad context of our country's national interest. In this section we will explore some ideas that can help us accomplish that task.

National Interest—as in Nation

Before going further it is necessary to clearly understand what is meant by *national*. The existence of the nation-state has caused the two parts of that hyphenate to be confused or considered synonymous. As discussed earlier,

states and nations are very distinct, the state being a physical, political entity and the **nation** being a people who have common characteristics and experiences and a perceived sense of kinship.

When we speak of national interest, we mean the goals of the state and its regime based on its representation of the nation. What we are not discussing is the interests of the state or its regime, as such. In other words, the function of the state is to act as an agent of the nation, or, as another author put it, the state's "principal, if not its only care, is the welfare of its citizens. . . . The test of its utility is the faithfulness with which it reflects" the nation's interest.[15]

The focus on the nation (the people), not on the physical state or the political regime, is a critical point in understanding what national interest ought to be. *Public interest* is a term that has been suggested to clarify whose interest is properly considered.[16] Whatever the term, the point is that the interests of the state and the nation are not synonymous. They are normally closely related, but they are not identical.

It is, for instance, possible for the demise of the state as such to be in the national interest. Imagine a situation in which the Soviets got the nuclear drop on your country. The president faces two stark choices: surrender or be annihilated. Can a war that kills almost everyone be in the national interest? Would you rather be Red or dead?

If we focus on the concept of nation, it is possible to identify various dimensions of national interest. Inasmuch as a nation is (1) a people (2) with feelings of kinship (3) based on common cultural characteristics, then the national interest is whatever enhances those three factors. Policies that foster physical safety, economic well-being, and the freedom of a people to order their own sociopolitical processes can be properly identified as in the national interest. In subsequent sections we will see how these can be included in a working definition.

National Interest—Majoritarian

To form our concept of national interest, we also have to deal with the contention that there is no *single* set of interests in any society. Several points can be made in response. First, the diffusion of interests within a nation does not mean that an interest cannot be national. It is axiomatic that in most cases different subgroups will have varying interests. Not all these can be met all the time. That is true for any policy, domestic or foreign.

Instead, national interest can properly be defined as goals that will benefit all if possible but, when that is impossible, will (1) either maximize positive results or minimize negative results for the majority and also (2) either minimize negative results for the minority or minimize the size of the minority that suffers negative results.

Basically this comes down to **majoritarianism** as the primary guideline for goal selection, with minority protection an important, but secondary, standard. Given the function of a state, any other guideline would be inconsistent with the proper state/nation relationship. Obviously, this does not establish a precise standard between majority and minority interests or clearly delineate which policy benefits the majority. That is properly left to the political process. It does, however, objectively eliminate policies that serve the interest of politically powerful individuals or small groups at the expense of the majority. Majoritarianism also does not imply following every mass whim. As the next section shows, there are long- and short-term interests, and the former should prevail.

Principles of Evaluation

Once we have some concept of "whose" interest we are considering, our next step is to formulate some principles that we can use to judge the policies that we and others proclaim to be in the national interest. The following three principles can be applied to evaluating any such claim.

1. Place the *burden of proof* on the claimant. "Show me—I'm from Missouri" is a prudent stand to take in the face of claims to the national interest.
2. Apply the principle of *consequence*. Consider *all* the various dimensions of national interest. It is not enough to say a policy will enhance trade. The impact on security and other factors must also be considered.[17]
3. Finally, consider the principle of *generalization*. This standard posits that what is right or wrong for one actor must also be right or wrong for any actor in similar circumstances. It is, for example, incompatible, by this prin-

ciple, for the U.S. to intervene in El Salvador (U.S. sphere of influence) while condemning Soviet interference in Poland (USSR sphere of influence).

This somewhat existential standard of conduct also helps unravel some of the issues of consequences for domestic majorities and minorities. We cannot ask farmers not to sell wheat to Russia unless other segments of the economic community are also ready to suffer financially. Domestically and internationally, then, ganders need to be ready to accept the same sauce they advocate for the geese.

Dimensions of National Interest

With these preliminary principles in mind, the next step is to consider the possible dimensions of national interest. Some contend that there are so many complex and often conflicting national interests that ordering them is beyond human capability. National interest is, indeed, a complex phenomenon, but it is not beyond comprehension. Frederick Hartmann, for one, has argued that there is an "irreducible core" of interests based on the function of the state.[18] And Hans Morgenthau has similarly identified a "hard core" of interests that are relatively permanent. What is needed, then, is to devise a hierarchy of interests that will at least begin to allow us to order our priorities. That is the task of this section, which explores the work of scholars toward that goal.

Hans Morgenthau, a pioneer in this area, described interest in a variety of terms. These can be broken up into four basic groups according to priority, time frame, specificity, and compatibility (with the interests of other countries). The categories are shown in Table 6-1.

More recently, Donald Neuchterlein has contributed a study outlining five dimensions of national interest: basic interests, defense of homeland, economic well-being, favorable world order, and promotion of values (such as ideology or humanitarianism). These are combined with the four levels of intensity (survival, vital, major, peripheral) to form an analytical matrix.[19]

These efforts and the current author's own work[20] can also be combined into a matrix that can be used to help evaluate national interest. It contains four **issue areas** of national interest: physical safety, material well-being, political environment, and national cohesion. The matrix also distinguishes between two time frames: long-term and short-term. Finally, the matrix includes

Table 6-1. Dimensions of National Interest According to Morgenthau.

Priority:	Primary Secondary	*Specificity:*	General Specific
Time Frame:	Permanent Variable	*Compatibility:*	Identical Complementary Conflicting

Based on Thomas W. Robinson's analysis of Morgenthau's work in "National Interests," in *International Politics and Foreign Policy,* rev. ed., ed. James N. Rosenau (New York: Free Press, 1969), pp. 184–185.

The Friends of the Earth, who towed this whale by London's Tower Bridge, oppose whaling. Many of those employed in the fishing industry favor whaling. Determining what is in the national interest can be difficult when subgroups have different interests and favor different policies.

two levels of importance: primary and secondary. The combination of these three dimensions is shown in Table 6-2, and its use and terms are explained more fully in the pages that follow.

Issue areas. Our four issue areas of national interest are objective in that each is a direct requirement of the welfare of the nation and, therefore, a legitimate goal of the state.

1. *Physical safety.* This issue is largely self-explanatory. The essence of a nation is its people, and the physical survival of the people is an irreducible

Table 6-2. Matrix for Categorizing National Interest Issues.

	Long-Term		Short-Term	
	Primary	Secondary	Primary	Secondary
Physical safety				
Material well-being				
Political environment				
National cohesion				

element of national interest.[21] It should be noted that this does *not* necessarily include territory preservation or regime maintenance. The safety of the nation is more important than the state or its government, as such. Ask yourself this question: If a U.S. president had to either surrender the United States to Moscow or face the certainty of the total annihilation of the nation, which choice should she or he make?

2. *Material well-being.* The state also has an obligation to ensure that its citizens enjoy adequate food, housing, clothing, medical care, and other human needs. It is unlikely, for example, that the West could long tolerate a complete cutoff of Mideast oil. Subsistence is primary; opulence is secondary.

3. *Political environment.* This dimension is akin to a nation's liberty to choose its own sociopolitical structure[22] or favorable world order.[23] When, in 1984, Mikhail Gorbachev was criticized by a British member of Parliament for the oppressive Soviet system, the communist leader shot back, "You govern your society, and you leave us to govern ours." There is an element of free choice here, but it is not necessarily synonymous with sovereignty. It is possible to argue, for example, that a form of world federal order that allowed only limited autonomy would better ensure a favorable political environment than the current Darwinian process of survival of the fittest.

4. *National cohesion.* This is probably the most controversial of the issue dimensions. It is related to Neuchterlein's "promotion of values," which he equates with ideology or the protection and furtherance of a set of values that citizens share and believe to be good.[24]

Considering again the nature of a nation, we can see that perceived mutual identity is a crucial element. Without that sense of mutuality, potential nations do not form and existing nations dissolve. It follows, then, that any goal or action that contravenes a nation's values and thereby fosters disintegrative forces has a deleterious effect on the nation. The Vietnam War, for one, was one of the most traumatic attacks on the American self-image in the nation's history. Whatever other interests were involved, it is reasonable to argue that U.S. disengagement was necessary to avoid a further tearing of the national fabric.

In the sense in which it is used here, the national cohesion dimension includes ideas, ideology, and morality as discussed in the preceding chapter. It allows for the introduction of moral, humanitarian goals even if they are self-sacrificing.[25] These types of goals have been described as "transcending"

The war in Vietnam began to tear apart American society as witnessed here at Kent State University where thirteen antiwar protesters were wounded or killed by National Guardsmen.

the national interest, but insofar as they promote national cohesion or, as will be discussed presently, are in the long-term national interest, then values are not necessarily self-sacrificing at all.

Finally, by looking to national values, we avoid the swamp of controversy surrounding universal values. By combining the principle of generalization with nationally generated ideals, we thus have a valid set of values.

Time frames. It is also important to distinguish between time frames. Long-term interests clearly outrank short-term interests (all other factors being equal). At the time of the hostage crisis, many advocated military action against Iran. Retrieving the hostages and/or smiting the Ayatollah may have been in the United States' short-term interest, but a stable, independent Iran, given its economic and geostrategic position, is in the United States' long-term interest.

Considering time frames also helps to meet some of the objections that idealists raise about the concept of national interest. As the well-known scholar Inis Claude recently pointed out, idealists and realists are not necessarily divided over *whether* there is a national interest; they differ over *what* the national interest is.[26] If, however, we approach the search for world order (based on humanitarianism, limited sovereignty, and peaceful coexistence) as necessary for the long-term survival of civilization, then that goal clearly falls within both idealist and realist values. Disarmament is a long-term interest, while arms spending to stimulate the domestic economy is short-term. Concern with world socioeconomic development through such vehicles as foreign aid is a long-term interest. Cutting aid to balance the budget or economically exploiting developing countries is a short-term goal. Clearly, the former, long-term ends should prevail.

Levels of importance. It is, finally, necessary to establish *priorities*. The choice of Morgenthau's "primary" and "secondary" over other, more complex schemes of intensity is based mainly on simplicity. The line between primary (essential to national continuance; can be compromised only *in extremis*) and secondary goals is sufficient for our purposes here in an introductory text.

The issue of Poland provides an apt illustration of how this priority dimension might be used. What if Poland revolted and called for help by U.S. paratroopers? That might help Poland gain true independence. It also would run the risk of starting World War III. Both alternatives affect America's interest, but avoiding war is primary, whereas an independent Poland is secondary. American decision makers were faced with exactly that choice during the 1956 Hungarian uprising, and President Eisenhower refused to intervene. It is likely that a similar choice in Poland in the 1980s would bring a similar (non)reaction.

Possibilities and limits. It is important not to overestimate the utility of the matrix presented in Table 6-2. It is a beginning tool for understanding and evaluating the use and abuse of national interest. By plugging in what decision makers say, we can gather evidence on why they acted or how they might act.

We can also use the matrix as a tool for planning and evaluation. Is overthrowing Castro in Cuba in the national interest? What are the long- and short-term consequences? Are the impacts primary or secondary?

Finally, use of the matrix helps ensure that we follow the principle of consequences. We need to consider *all* the consequences *all* the time. Stringing up the Ayatollah in 1979 would have felt "good" to a lot of Americans, but would it have been worth it? *All* things considered, probably not.

There are also distinct limits to the matrix. Assigning policy questions to one or another category (short, long; primary, secondary) will often be debatable. Making trade-offs between interests will also be controversial. What if two primary, long-term interests are mutually exclusive? No matrix can account for all possibilities or substitute for informed, rational judgment. In real life, though, such dilemmas exist and choices must be made, and a matrix helps us see the myriad factors. Finally, calculating consequences cannot be accomplished by this or any matrix. By seeing how a policy will affect another country's interest—whether the interests will be "identical, complementary, or conflicting"—we can begin to estimate reactions and consequences, but we can only begin.[27] In short, there is no mechanical substitute for insight. That is what the study of world politics is all about.

Summary

National interest is one of the most difficult concepts for international relations analysts to define and evaluate. In the first place, it is used in two different ways: subjectively, as a rationale for political action, and objectively, to evaluate goals and policies.

Second, even from an objective viewpoint, there are many troubling questions that complicate attempts to come to a meaningful conceptualization of national interest. Many dismiss any such attempt on the grounds that, as a concept, national interest is hopelessly vague, confuses ends and means, is necessarily subjective, and ignores the diversity of elements in society.

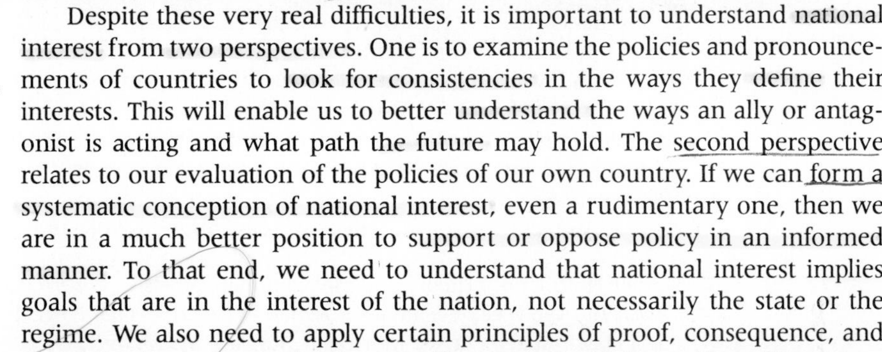

Despite these very real difficulties, it is important to understand national interest from two perspectives. One is to examine the policies and pronouncements of countries to look for consistencies in the ways they define their interests. This will enable us to better understand the ways an ally or antagonist is acting and what path the future may hold. The second perspective relates to our evaluation of the policies of our own country. If we can form a systematic conception of national interest, even a rudimentary one, then we are in a much better position to support or oppose policy in an informed manner. To that end, we need to understand that national interest implies goals that are in the interest of the nation, not necessarily the state or the regime. We also need to apply certain principles of proof, consequence, and generalization to our evaluation. Finally, we need to define various dimensions of national interest according to issue area, time frame, and level of importance.

These steps will not allow us to predict flawlessly what policy will be, nor will they yield a foolproof formula for evaluating policy. What the steps will do is organize our thinking so that we can reach conclusions on a systematic and informed basis.

Terms

Issue areas—Substantive categories of policy that must all be considered when evaluating national interest.

Majoritarianism—A belief that the will and the interest of the majority should prevail.

Nation—A people with a mutual and political identification based on common characteristics and experiences.

Objective national interest—Policies and goals that can be identified by neutral analysts as being in the interest of the nation.

Sphere of influence—A region dominated by a great power.

Subjective national interest—Preferred policies and goals of an individual or regime that spring from a particular set of views and predispositions.

"What is"—Subjective national interest; that which "is" practiced.

"What ought to be"—Objective national interest; that which "ought to be" practiced.

Notes

1. Alexander L. George and Robert Keohane, *Report* of the Commission on the Organization of Government for the Conduct of Foreign Policy (Murphy Commission), vol. 2, appendix 2 (Washington, D.C.: U.S. Government Printing Office, 1976).
2. Donald E. Neuchterlein, "The Concept of 'National Interest': A Time for New Approaches," *Orbis* 23 (1979): 74.
3. Fred A. Sondermann, "The Concept of National Interest," *Orbis* 21 (1977): 121–138.
4. Raymond Aron, *Peace and War: A Theory of International Relations,* trans. Richard Howard and Annette Baker Fox (Garden City, N.Y.: Doubleday, 1966), pp. 91–92.
5. Richard C. Snyder, H. W. Bruck, and Burton Saipin, "Decision-Making as an Approach to the Study of International Politics," in *Foreign Policy Decision-Making,* ed. Richard C. Snyder, H. W. Bruck, and Burton Saipin (Glencoe, Ill.: Free Press, 1962), p. 129.
6. Hans J. Morgenthau, *Politics among Nations,* 5th ed. (New York: Knopf, 1973), p. 5.
7. Stanley Hoffmann, "Theory and International Politics," in *International Politics and Foreign Policy,* rev. ed., ed. James Rosenau (New York: Free Press, 1969), p. 33.
8. For a classic statement see Morton A. Kaplan, *System and Process in International Politics* (New York: Wiley, 1957), pp. 152–165.
9. J. Martin Rochester, "The 'National Interest' and Contemporary World Politics," *Review of Politics* 40 (1978): 77–96.
10. Sondermann, "Concept of National Interest," p. 123.
11. John Herz, "Political Realism Revisited," in *International Studies Quarterly*'s Symposium in honor of Hans J. Morgenthau, 25 (1981): 182–197.
12. Cecil V. Crabb, Jr., *The Doctrines of American Foreign Policy* (Baton Rouge: Louisiana State University Press, 1982), especially chaps. 1 and 6.
13. Robert E. Osgood, "The Revitalization of Containment," *Foreign Affairs* 60 (1982): 465–502.
14. Adam Ulam, *Dangerous Relations: The Soviet Union in World Politics, 1970–82* (New York: Oxford University Press, 1983), pp. 130, 139.
15. Clive Perry, "The Function of Law in the International Community" in *Manual of Public International Law,* ed. Max Sorensen (New York: St. Martin's Press, 1968), p. 6.
16. Frederick Kratochwill, "On the Notion of 'Interest' in National Relations," *International Organization* 36 (1982): 4.
17. Kratochwill, "Notion of 'Interest,'" p. 5, discusses both the principle of consequences and the principle of generalizations.
18. Frederick Hartmann, *The Relations of Nations,* 2nd ed. (New York: Macmillan, 1962), p. 5.
19. Neuchterlein, "National Interest," p. 75, especially table 1.
20. John T. Rourke, "National Interest: Toward an Operational Definition," unpublished paper, 1971.

21. George and Keohane, *Report,* p. 67.
22. Ibid., p. 68.
23. Neuchterlein, "National Interest," p. 74.
24. Ibid.
25. On "self-abnegating" goals see Arnold Wolfers, "The Pole of Power and the Pole of Indifference," in *International Politics,* ed. Rosenau, p. 178.
26. Inis Claude's "Comment" on Herz's "Political Realism Revisited," *International Studies Quarterly* 25 (1981): 200.
27. The terms are Morgenthau's. See Thomas W. Robinson, "National Interests," in *International Politics,* ed. Rosenau, p. 185.

7

Power

Two stars keep not their motion in one sphere.
Shakespeare, Henry IV

Then, everything includes itself in power,
Power into will, will into appetite;
And appetite, a universal wolf
So doubly seconded with will and power,
Must make perforce a universal prey,
And last eat up himself.
Shakespeare, Troilus and Cressida

A Prologue to Chapters 7–12

This chapter brings us to the action of our world drama. The actors have been cast in Chapters 1 through 3 and their motivations established in Chapters 4 through 6. Now it is time to bring down the house lights, raise the curtain, and begin the play.

In Chapters 7 through 12 we will look at the way the principal actors—states—play out their parts. Our primary focus will be the *means* states use to accomplish their ends. Our subjects will include force and coercion, diplomacy, penetration and subversion, and economic methods. We will examine how each of these means is employed to accomplish national ends.

Before approaching those subjects, however, it is necessary to discuss the concept of power. That concept forms a backdrop to all the means. Power is not everything in world politics. Some states even act and survive without much of it, but their actions are limited and their survival rests on the sufferance of others.

Power: Another Slippery Concept

Power is a crucial factor in world politics. Indeed, some analysts argue that it is *the* single most important element in determining the course of international interactions.[1] Most political scientists agree that that view is an overstatement, but it does serve to emphasize the importance of power. National goals and interests often conflict, and when they do, whose interests will prevail becomes a central question. The resolution of that issue is heavily influenced by power.

Like a number of other terms we have covered, *power* is used in a variety of ways. The academic debate over its various uses is complex, and we cannot resolve it here.[2] It is, however, important to come to a clear understanding of how this text uses the word so that we can proceed from a common point.

Ends and Means

In the preceding chapter we looked at the confusion of ends and means—or goals and methods—and considered power as an example. In the discussion here, the term *power* should be understood as a means. Not that countries do not seek to enhance power as an end in itself—they certainly do. Here, though, we are concerned with power as a resource, or, perhaps, a tool, that enables countries to successfully pursue their national interests.[3] Some authors have distinguished between power and influence, with the former a key factor in conflictive situations and the latter operating in cooperative relations.[4] The relation between the two terms is complex, but here power is conceived of as the larger, more inclusive term. Power, whether it be obvious military armament or more subtle diplomatic skill, gives one country the ability to bend a second country to its will. Whether that is done by coercion or by persuasion, the success or failure of the first country is based on its power.

Actual versus Potential Power

To be effective, power normally must have the capacity to be used. It does not have to be actually employed to count, but there must be either the real or the perceived possibility of its use. **Potential power** is less of a factor in world politics than **actual power**. China has oil reserves off its coast, and Brazil has extensive mineral deposits deep within its Amazon region. Their ability to extract these resources, however, is limited, and consequently the resources are only potential power factors. Prior to both world wars, the United States had vast military potential, but its readiness was at a low ebb. When asked for his evaluation of the American military in 1917, a German admiral replied, "Zero, zero, zero." Potential power was not enough to deter the U-boat campaign; only after American power was activated did it contribute to Germany's defeat.[5]

Real versus Perceived Power

We have seen on several occasions that international politics is influenced both by what is true and by what others believe to be true. **Real power**, or the power that you objectively possess and can use, is, of course, a major factor. Yet, insofar as power has to do with making others conform to your wishes, it may be sufficient for them only to believe that you have both the *capacity* and the *will* to act. When a robber confronts a bank teller with his hand in his jacket pocket, the teller's decision to hand over the money or not will depend on whether the threat is believed.

This **perceived power** also occurs on a global level. Richard Nixon and Henry Kissinger long argued that unilateral U.S. withdrawal from Vietnam would damage American power. In his memoirs Kissinger writes: "Rightly or wrongly—I am still convinced rightly—we thought that capitulation . . . would usher in a period of disintegrating American credibility that would only accelerate the world's instability."[6] Measuring the loss of power is difficult, but it is hard to escape the conclusion that the defeat in Vietnam and the subsequent uncertainty of U.S. foreign policy did diminish world perceptions of American power in terms of resolve and purpose. That decline almost certainly emboldened the country's adversaries and alarmed its friends.

The gap between objective and subjective power and its impact on influence were documented by one researcher who compared capability and influence during the period 1925–1930. Kenneth Holsti[7] found that the seven great powers at the time ranked by capability were:

1. United States
2. Germany
3. Great Britain
4. France
5. Russia
6. Italy
7. Japan

With respect to influence, however, the rankings were quite different:

1. France
2. Great Britain
3. Italy
4. Germany
5. Russia
6. Japan
7. United States

As can be seen, the United States, which ranked first in objective measurement of capability, scored last in its ability to extend influence.

Power as Money

In trying to characterize power, Karl Deutsch has written that "just as money is the currency of economic life, so power can be thought of as the currency of politics."[8] It is useful to equate power and money because both are assets that can be used to acquire things you want. Economically, money buys things. Politically, power causes things to happen.

Even Deutsch, however, is careful to caution that "the similarities between power and money should not be overstressed."[9] As another analyst points out, "Political power resources tend to be much less liquid than economic resources."[10] That liquidity factor means that it is harder to convert power than money. Among other differences, power, unlike money, has no standard measurement that allows all parties to agree on the amount involved.

Measuring Power

The difficulty of agreeing on the "value" of power brings us to the last issue of this section—how do we measure power? Candidly, the answer is that political scientists have not been very successful at doing that.[11]

One problem, as will be discussed in the next section, is that power is multifaceted and also varies from situation to situation. That means that "estimates of capabilities covering all [countries] . . . in all imaginable contingencies would run to millions of combinations and permutations."[12] Second, measuring things like number of guns, oil production, or population is easy.

Measuring other aspects of power, such as leadership or morale, is much more difficult.[13] When you add in the perceptual factor of how others evaluate your capacity, you have an unimaginably complex equation.

These difficulties have not deterred some political scientists from trying to measure power. By far the most ambitious and comprehensive approach was formulated by Ray Cline. According to Cline's formula, perceived power (P_p) equals critical mass (C), comprising population and territory, plus economic capability (E), plus military capability (M), times strategic purpose (S), or coherent planning, plus will to pursue national strategy (W).[14] In symbolic representation, then,

$$P_p = (C + E + M) \times (S + W)$$

Using that formula as a basis, Cline compiled numerous indicators of power components and arrived at a final estimation of national power for 1978. Table 7-1 shows Cline's ratings for selected countries and their rankings among the seventy-seven countries evaluated.

It must be stressed that Cline's formula is at best a guideline and is subject to all the qualifiers discussed in the next section. How to count even the tangible factors (C + E + M) is highly controversial. Quantifying the intangible factors (S + W) is *beyond our current capability and may well be impossible.* Thus, in the final analysis, trying to use Cline's formula as a measuring device includes many, many subjective assessments. Still, there is value in Cline's formula both as a pioneering effort and because it emphasizes the fact that sheer numbers of things (C + E + M) must be modified by such intangible factors as strategy and will (S + W) in order to truly evaluate power.[15] The United States, according to Cline, has the highest C + E + M rating, yet Cline's substantially higher evaluation of the USSR's S + W total leaves that country with a stronger final P_p rating. Cline highly rates Soviet strategy because he believes that, "whatever current tactics might be at any moment, Soviet strategy toward the outside world is coherent and clear."[16] By contrast, Cline contends that U.S. strategy is characterized by "drifting and passivity" and is "reactive," designed in response to situations created by other nations.[17] China, which has the third-highest C + E + M, ranks only seventh (P_p) because Cline gives it a very low will rating (W = 0.2) based on post-Mao leadership instability.[18]

Power: A Definition

For all the various problems in defining and measuring power, it is still important to arrive at a common understanding of the term. As we use it here, power is equated with national capabilities. Power is a multifaceted, ever-changing political resource and is the sum of the various elements that allow one country to have its interests prevail over the interests of another country.

In short, national power is *the sum of the attributes that enable a state to achieve its goals even when they clash with the goals and wills of other international actors.*

Table 7-1. World Power Rating, 1978.

Rank	Country	Perceived Power (P_p)	=	Power Weights (C + E + M)	×	Strategy (S)	+	Will (W)	Total (S + W)
1	Soviet Union	458		382		0.7		0.5	1.2
2	United States	304		439		0.3		0.4	0.7
3	Brazil	137		98		0.6		0.8	1.4
4	West Germany	116		77		0.7		0.8	1.5
5	Japan	108		77		0.6		0.8	1.4
6	Australia	88		73		0.5		0.7	1.2
7	China	83		129		0.4		0.2	0.6
8	France	74		82		0.4		0.5	0.9
9	Great Britain	68		68		0.5		0.5	1.0
10	Canada	61		87		0.3		0.4	0.7
12	Taiwan	49		29		0.8		0.9	1.7
14	Egypt	46		38		0.6		0.6	1.2
16	Vietnam	39		39		0.8		0.2	1.0
18	Israel	39		23		0.9		0.8	1.7
20	India	36		71		0.3		0.2	0.5
21	Italy	34		48		0.4		0.3	0.7
22	Argentina	32		40		0.5		0.3	0.8
26	Pakistan	22		28		0.5		0.3	0.8
27	Nigeria	22		28		0.4		0.4	0.8
28	Mexico	22		32		0.3		0.4	0.7
33	Poland	20		28		0.5		0.2	0.7
35	Turkey	18		36		0.2		0.3	0.5
41	Syria	15		15		0.5		0.5	1.0
59	Greece	6		8		0.4		0.4	0.8
70	Cuba	2		2		0.7		0.5	1.2

Source: Ray S. Cline, *World Power Trends and U.S. Foreign Policy for the 1980s* (Boulder, Colo.: Westview Press, 1978), pp. 173–174. P_p rounded. Reprinted with permission.

Characteristics of Power

Power is anything but a simple phenomenon. Indeed, it is very much a political chameleon, constantly changing even while it remains the same. The complexity of power can be seen by examining four of its characteristics.

Power Is Relative

In his discussion of power, Hans Morgenthau has observed that "it is one of the most elemental and frequent errors in international politics to neglect . . . [the] relative character of power and to deal instead with the power of a nation as though it were an absolute."[19] When assessing capabilities, then, **relative power**, or the comparative power of the national actors, must be considered.

We cannot say the United States is powerful unless we specify *in comparison to whom*. If, as stated above, power is the ability to prevail, then the United States generally is not as powerful compared with the Soviet Union as it is in a contest with Cuba.

A related issue is whether power is a *zero-sum game*. The question is whether a gain in the power of one country inevitably means a loss of power of other actors (zero-sum) or whether an increase in power for one does not necessarily mean a loss of power for the others (non-zero-sum).[20] Without delving too far into that controversy, we can say that the relative nature of power implies that, at least potentially and in times of conflict, power changes approach zero-sum. However, it should also be noted that the situational nature of power, which will be discussed next, means that power changes can at times be non-zero-sum. If we agree that, even if provoked, the United States is unlikely to use nuclear weapons against Cuba, then increases in the American atomic arsenal do not affect the U.S./Cuban power relationship.

Power Is Situational

A country's power varies according to the situation, or context, in which it is being applied. A country's **situational power** is often less than the total inventory of its capabilities. During the Iranian hostage crisis, the preponderance of American military power was virtually useless given the goal of freeing the hostages alive. Similarly, the U.S. defeat in Vietnam did not occur because the communists were more powerful as such. Rather, it happened, in part, because the U.S. was restrained. Air Force General Curtis Lemay once suggested bombing North Vietnam "back into the Stone Age," and the United States had the resources to do it. It did not, however, have the "will" to annihilate the Vietnamese, and, therefore, its power was dissipated. Will, as such, might be equated with "price." Power is modified by our willingness to "pay the price," economically, physically, or spiritually, to achieve an end. There is no implication here that lack of will implies weakness in a macho sense. Indeed, prudence is often laudable. But inevitably, right or wrong, lack of will decreases power.

The horror of nuclear war and, indeed, the rising world opinion against force in any context are having the general effect of decreasing the weight of military might as a power factor. The ability of the two superpowers to destroy each other has, to a degree, rendered the huge nuclear stockpiles impotent. As Henry Kissinger once exclaimed, "What, in the name of God, is strategic superiority? What is the significance of it politically, militarily, operationally at these levels of numbers? What do you do with it?"[21]

On the conventional level, some analysts have also observed that although armed force is far from ended, there is a growing reluctance to use it.[22] It can be argued that had the Polish or Nicaraguan/El Salvadoran situations occurred decades earlier, the Soviets and the United States would have intervened militarily, as they did in Czechoslovakia (1968) or the Dominican Republic (1965).

Power is situational. For all the power these Soviet rockets represent, they cannot be used to defeat the rebel forces in Afghanistan.

The 1980s are different, however, and so far the two Goliaths have blustered, but they have not invaded Poland or Nicaragua.

Power Is Dynamic

The complexity and relativity of power make it a very dynamic phenomenon. Even simple measurements show that power is constantly in flux. Economies prosper or lag, arms are added or become outmoded, resources are discovered or are depleted.

Normally, power changes are evolutionary. For example, Soviet military and economic capabilities have developed slowly during this century. At times, though, change can be dramatic. Wars and revolutions often rapidly create and destroy power. The explosion of the first atomic bomb in June 1945 instantaneously and radically altered U.S. power. The rise or fall of a strong leader—de Gaulle of France, China's Mao, Egypt's Sadat, or Nixon in the United States—can also quickly alter power. Whether the change is slow or fast, however, power is always in flux.

Power Is Multidimensional

A last characteristic of power is that it is multifaceted. People often think of international power only in terms of military capability. As we have seen, though, military might cannot always be used, is costly for all involved, and is only one of a number of power factors. We must be careful, when analyzing power, to avoid what Morgenthau calls "the fallacy of the single factor," or "attributing to a single factor an overriding importance, to the detriment of all the others."[23]

Just as we did with national interest, it is important to consider *all* the aspects of power *and* to place them in their proper relative and situational contexts. Only then can we begin to answer the question of who is powerful and who is not. To help with that process, our next step is to identify the various elements of national power.

Elements of Power

Attempts to categorize political phenomena are almost always frustrating. The real world is a subtle place, and applying categories to concepts is often more of a teaching tool than a meaningful task in any real sense. This difficulty is especially acute for power. Scholars have grouped power factors according to a variety of categories and subcategories, but the most common distinction is between tangible and intangible facets of power.

For our purposes here, we will follow the tangible/intangible dichotomy. The elements of **tangible power** are those that can be readily measured. Population, industrial output, and number of soldiers are examples. Elements of **intangible power** are those that cannot be measured easily. Leadership is an example, as is morale. A word of caution is that even such a simple division leaves questions. Consider, for example, education. An educated populace is an asset, but is it tangible or intangible? We can measure how many people are educated and at what level, but what is the quality of education? Are there Soviet or Chinese equivalents of M.I.T. or Cal Tech? Morale is generally listed as an intangible factor, but modern opinion-survey techniques now give us the ability to at least begin to measure that factor. The point is, be concerned with the elements and their impacts. The categories are important only to help you organize your thinking.

Tangible Elements of Power

Our discussion will include seven tangible elements: (1) a state's physical characteristics, (2) demographics (population characteristics), (3) natural resources, (4) industrial output, (5) agricultural output, (6) information/communications capabilities, and (7) military capabilities. Several of these factors are also discussed, with a focus on application, in the chapters on force (Chapter 8) and economics (Chapters 11 and 12).

Before discussing these elements, it would be well to mention *technology.* Some classifications list technology as a separate element. The view here is that technology affects all the tangible elements. Air conditioning modifies the impact of weather, computers are revolutionizing education, robotics is speeding industry, synthetic fertilizers expand agriculture, new drilling techniques allow for undersea oil exploration, microwaves speed information, and lasers bring the military to the edge of the Buck Rogers era. Thus, technology is an overarching factor and will be discussed as part of all the tangible elements.

Physical Characteristics

Shakespeare's King Henry VI proclaimed:

> ***Let us be backed with God and with the seas***
> ***Which he hath given for a fence impregnable, . . .***
> ***In them and in ourselves our safety lies.***

Henry's homage to God and the English Channel, the latter of which, at least, has helped save England from European conquest for nine centuries, is an apt reminder of the importance of a country's physical characteristics.

The advent of air power, missiles, and nuclear weapons has changed and, in some ways, lessened the relationship of geography to power. Other modern factors, however, have increased the importance of geography. Expanding trade, for example, has made the control of sea-lane "choke points," such as the Cape of Good Hope, off South Africa, an increasingly important concern. Dependence on oil also has geographic ramifications, with, for instance, the location of Iran on the Soviet Union's southern border a potentially significant factor.

Geopolitics. Within the more general discipline of political geography, the study of geopolitics is concerned with the interrelationship of geography, power, and international politics. First associated with German geographer Friedrich Ratzel (1844–1904) and Swedish geographer Rudolph Kjellen (1864–1922), geopolitics fell into disrepute because of its use by Karl Haushofer (1869–1946) and the Nazis to justify German expansion in order to gain *Lebensraum* (living space). Haushofer believed, as Ratzel and Kjellen had, that the state had an "organic" dimension and that it had to expand or die.[24] That theory has been discredited, as has the idea that geography necessarily determines power and policy.

Other geopolitical theories have also influenced history and continue to have currency among some scholars and practitioners. On the grandest scale, there have been a number of writers who have formulated general geopolitical theories. Alfred Thayer Mahan (1840–1919), an American naval officer, argued that world power was determined by control of the seas and the acquisition of colonies for that purpose. Mahan's theory supported both British and American imperial expansion. Kaiser Wilhelm II was also influenced by Mahan, leading to Germany's naval expansion and search for colonies in the years before World War I.

Taking the opposite view, British geographer Sir Halford Mackinder (1861–1947) classified Europe, Asia, and Africa as the "world island" with the Eurasian "heartland" at its center. Control of the heartland was vital because

Who rules East Europe commands the Heartland
Who rules the Heartland commands the World Island
Who rules the World Island commands the world.

Nicholas J. Spykman (1893–1943) took a geopolitical position between Mahan's and Mackinder's. Spykman, an American, emphasized the "rimlands" of Europe, the Middle East, Africa, South America, and Asia as the keys to U.S. security. These lands form a sort of fence that can be used to wall the Eurasian powers out of the New World or, conversely, if controlled by a hostile power, to encircle the United States. More contemporarily, Saul Cohen has divided the world into "geostrategic regions," with the two dominant areas, the maritime and the Eurasian continental, confronting each other in the Middle Eastern and Southeast Asian "shelterbelts."[25]

National geography. Whether or not one subscribes to broad geopolitical theories, it is hard to escape the impact of geography on individual countries. These factors comprise (1) location, (2) topography, (3) size, and (4) climate.

The *location* of a country, particularly in relation to other countries, is significant. The fact that China and the Soviet Union share a border has power implications for both. The huge Chinese army can do little at present to threaten the United States. By contrast, the People's Liberation Army can walk into Siberia. Some have argued that an American military intervention in El Salvador would be another Vietnam, but the proximity of Central America, in contrast with Vietnam's distant location and its border connection with China, implies that the outcome might be very different in El Salvador.

Location can be an advantage or a disadvantage. Spain was able to avoid involvement in either world war in part because of its relative isolation from the rest of Europe. Poland, sandwiched between Germany and Russia, has a distinctly unfortunate location. The Israelis would almost certainly be better off if their promised land were somewhere—almost anywhere—else.

A country's *topography*—its mountains, rivers, and plains—is also important. The Alps, for example, have helped protect Switzerland from its larger European neighbors and spared the Swiss the ravages of both world wars. Topography can also work against a country. The broad European plain that extends from Germany's Rhine River to the Ural Mountains, which separate Europe from Asia in the Soviet Union, has been an easy invasion avenue along which the armies of Napoleon, Kaiser Wilhelm, and Hitler have marched. In the current era, topography has been of major importance in the Middle East, where such points as the Suez Canal, Golan Heights, Jordan River, and Straits of Tiran have played crucial roles, and in Afghanistan, where the rugged terrain works to the guerrillas' advantage.

A country's *size and shape* can be an advantage, a disadvantage, or both. The immense expanse of the Soviet Union, for example, has saved it in each of the major invasions of the modern era. Overwhelmed at first, the Russian armies were able to retreat into the interior, buying time with geography while

The rugged mountainous terrain has made it possible for these lightly armed Afghan guerrillas to withstand assaults from the more mechanized Soviet occupation forces.

they regrouped their forces. That saving distance, however, has also proved a liability. During the Russo-Japanese War (1904–1905) the Russian armies had to traverse thousands of Siberian miles to engage the Japanese along the Pacific coast. Similarly, the Russian navy had to sail more than halfway around the world from its European base to threaten Japan (and, as it happened, to get sunk). By contrast, Israel's size gives it no room to retreat, and, in particular, its east-west narrowness leaves it in constant danger of being cut in two.

A country's *climate* also plays a power role. The tropical climate of Vietnam, with its heavy monsoon rains and its dense vegetation, made it difficult to use effectively much of the superior weaponry possessed by the Americans. At the other extreme, the bone-chilling Russian winter has allied itself with size to form a formidable defensive barrier. Napoleon's army literally froze to death during its retreat from Moscow, and 133 years later the German Wehrmacht was decimated by cold and ice during the sieges of Leningrad and Stalingrad.

Demographics

A second national power factor is a country's human characteristics. Demographic subcategories include population in sheer numbers, age distribution, and such measurable quantitative factors as health and education.

Population. Because a large population supplies military personnel and industrial workers, sheer numbers of people are a positive power factor. It is unlikely, for instance, that Kiribati (pop. 60,000) or Liechtenstein (pop. 30,000) will ever achieve great-power status.

Table 7-2. World Age Distribution.

Country	***−15 (percent)***	***15–64 (percent)***	***65+ (percent)***
China	36	58	6
United States	33	61	6
Soviet Union	26	65	11
Jordan	52	45	3 (most −15)
Mali	48	51	1 (least 65+)
East Germany	21	63	16 (most 65+)
West Germany	20	65	15 (least −15)

Source: The World in Figures (New York: Facts on File, 1981), p. 17.

Pure numbers, however, are not directly translatable into power. It is important that the population be in balance with resources. If it is not, then people can become a negative factor. India (pop. 730 million) has the world's second-largest population, yet because of the country's poverty (1979 GNP per capita: $190), it must spend much of its energy and resources merely feeding its people.

Age distribution. It is an advantage for a country to have a large number and percentage of its population in the productive years (roughly fifteen to sixty-five). Some countries with booming populations have a heavy percentage of children who must be supported. In other countries with limited life expectancy, many people die before they complete their productive years. Finally, some countries are "aging," with a geriatric population segment that consumes more resources than it produces. Table 7-2 shows age distribution figures for selected countries, including the world leader in each category. Figure 7-1 takes the extreme cases of Jordan and West Germany and analyzes their age distribution. It is obvious that West Germany is aging, while Jordan is a very "young" society. Neither extreme is a balanced population.

Other factors. There are a variety of ways to measure the strengths of a population. It goes without saying that an educated, healthy population is important to national power. Table 7-3 illustrates selected countries' educational and health factors, plus an "economic-social standing" based on GNP and a variety of health and education statistics.

As a final comment, it should be noted that such statistics are helpful but not conclusive. Educationally, for example, they do not tell us how good the schools and teachers are. Medically, physician-training standards and equipment availability vary widely throughout the world.

Natural Resources

The possession or lack of natural resources has become an increasingly important power factor as industrialization and technology have advanced.

Among the myriad raw materials needed to become a modern industrial power, petroleum, iron, and coal are the most important (Table 7-4). But

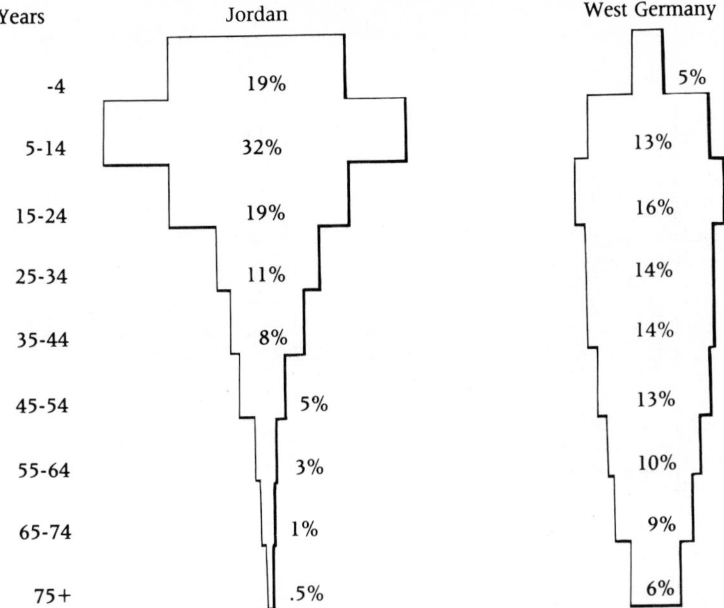

Figure 7-1. Population distribution: percentage of total population by age group. Figures from *Demographic Year Book, 1982* (New York: United Nations, 1984).

there is also a host of other natural resources that are important. Some of these, such as bauxite (for aluminum), copper, and lead, are all well known. Others, including manganese, tungsten, and cobalt, are more exotic. They are all necessary, however, for a strong economy.

In the power equation, natural resources have an impact in four related ways: (1) The greater a country's *self-sufficiency* in vital natural resources, the greater its power. In other words, the relation between output and consumption is important. (2) Conversely, the greater a country's *dependency* on foreign sources for vital natural resources, the less its power. (3) The greater a country's *surplus* (over domestic needs) of vital resources needed by other countries, the greater its power. (4) The greater a country's *reserves* in terms of ability to meet future (especially emergency) needs, the greater its power.

Each of these four related points plays a key role in determining international relationships. The Soviet Union, for example, is self-sufficient in each of the "big three" resources mentioned above. Japan, by contrast, has been able to construct a strong economic base because of its efficient industrial capacity, but it is built on quicksand. The Japanese import virtually all their oil and have become increasingly dependent on foreign sources for coal and iron ore because of depletion of their own resources.[26] Hence, if its resource supplies were cut off—say, by Soviet naval action—Japan would be in perilous straits, especially since it has scant reserves.

A vital resource surplus is a third power factor that the world imbalance of oil production and consumption has dramatically underlined. Not only have the oil resources of the Middle East allowed that region's countries to amass

Table 7-3. Health and Education Factors of Selected Countries.

	Education:			*Health*		
Country	***Literacy (%)***	***Percentage of 5–19 pop. in school***	***Teachers/ 1,000 pupils***	***Life expectancy***	***Physicians/ 100,000 pop.***	***Econ.-Soc. Standing Rank***[a]
Argentina	94	58	37	68	192	37
Burma	25	10	3	44	3	116
China	70	62	18	68	33	88
Egypt	44	45	13	54	92	83
Ethiopia	8	12	3	38	1	141
France	99	68	41	74	164	8
India	36	42	13	46	26	115
Iran	50	52	20	57	39	68
Israel	88	62	50	74	277	25
Italy	95	61	42	70	208	20
Japan	99	72	25	76	119	11
Mexico	74	64	19	64	57	59
Nigeria	25	37	7	47	7	101
Poland	98	54	27	70	166	30
Soviet Union	99	90	37	69	346	23
Sweden	99	74	46	75	178	1
United States	99	85	43	74	176	7

[a]Economic-social rankings in *World Almanac,* p. 589, based on Ruth Leger Sivard, *World Military and Social Expenditures* (Leesburg, Va.: World Priorities, 1982).
Based on *The World Almanac & Book of Facts 1983* (New York: Newspaper Enterprise Association, 1983).

Table 7-4. Coal, Iron, and Oil Production in the United States, the Soviet Union, and China, 1967.

	Coal		Iron		Oil	
Country	1,000 tons	World rank	1,000 tons	World rank	1,000 tons	World rank
United States	585,680	1	48,398	3	401,594	3
Soviet Union	494,000	2	130,700	1	520,000	1
China	450,000	3	34,000	6	85,000	11

Based on data in *The World in Figures* (New York: Facts on File, 1980), pp. 29–33.

huge financial reserves, but oil has also increased diplomatic power. By turning off the oil tap, or threatening to, the Arabs have been able to gain a stronger voice in world affairs. More subtly, control of this vital resource has also given a psychological uplift to the Arab world both in their own eyes and in the perceptions of others. They used to get very little respect—now they demand and receive much more.

It should finally be noted that simple production figures should be handled gingerly. There are, for example, many grades of crude oil, and some, like China's (with a high paraffin content), are harder to refine. In addition, production must be compared with consumption. The United States is the world's  third-largest oil producer. Its consumption (1982), however, was almost 35 percent higher than its production, and that detracts from American power.

Industrial Output

Even if a country is bountifully supplied with natural resources, its power is limited unless it can convert those assets into industrial goods. Both China and India are considered to have extensive reserves of iron and coal, and China is finding new oil possibilities, but because of their limited industrial capacity, those countries have not been able to effectively transform potential into power.

Japan, by contrast, efficiently converts imported resources and has become an industrial power despite its lack of natural assets. Despite, for example, the disparity in iron-ore mining between Japan and the United States (the United States producing approximately 150 times as much), the Japanese in 1980 exceeded U.S. steel production by about 10 percent or 10 million metric tons.[27]

Table 7-5 illustrates a variety of economic production statistics, including per capita gross national product, that serve as measures of industrial capacity.

Agriculture

It is common to equate steel production or numbers of soldiers with power; it is less common to think of food in those terms. Yet a country's agricultural capacity is an important factor. As with natural resources, the contribution of agriculture to power depends on whether a country can adequately supply its domestic needs and on whether it has a surplus of a commodity others need.

A third factor is the percentage of its total economic energy that a country must devote to feeding itself.

Self-sufficiency varies widely in the world. The United States is basically able to supply its own needs. With less than 6 percent of the world's population, it produces (1981) 17 percent of the world's wheat, 18 percent of its corn, and 63 percent of its protein-rich soybeans. Other countries are less fortunate.[28] Some are able to import to meet their needs; others face widespread hunger. In 1972–1974, for example, Africa as a whole had a food consumption figure that was 28 percent below the minimum caloric intake needed for good health. The figure for the Far East was −29 percent. Lack of  an adequate diet requires countries to devote their economies to more agriculture rather than industry and to expend financial reserves on imports. During 1983-1984, for example, the non-self-sufficient countries of Africa, Asia, and Latin America needed to import an estimated 48 million tons of food to meet minimum dietary requirements.[29] In the most deficient countries, agricultural deprivation also affects the health of the populace.

By contrast, a surplus of food can be a plus, primarily by helping in the balance of trade. As a diplomatic "weapon," food has not proved highly successful. An attempt by the United States, for example, to withhold wheat and other grains from the Soviet Union in retaliation for the invasion of Afghanistan was ineffective. The Soviets were able to "tighten their belts," to buy grains from other countries, and even to get U.S. grain transshipped through third countries (that is, U.S. grain goes to, say, French importers, who, in turn, sell it to the Soviets).[30]

Another significant agricultural factor is the percentage of a country's total economic effort that it must devote to feeding itself. India and Italy provide a ready comparison in Table 7-6, which presents percentage of the total work

Table 7-5. Industrial Indicators.

Country	***Per Capita GNP ($U.S.)***	***Aluminum (000s metric tons)***	***Cement (000s metric tons)***
Brazil	1,748	186	23,244
China	516	300	62,540
Egypt	470	100	3,028
Germany (West)	10,690	784	33,959
India	202	202	19,626
Italy	4,117	493	38,232
Japan	8,253	1,722	84,822
Mexico	1,434	43	14,150
Nigeria	615	0	15,141
Poland	4,071	100	21,651
Soviet Union	3,700	1,670	126,956
United States	10,752	5,876	77,548

Data except GNP from United Nations *1979/80 Statistical Yearbook* (New York: United Nations, 1981). All figures except GNP are for the year 1978. GNP from *Handbook of the World* (1981).

Oil has brought power and wealth to the oil rich states symbolized here by the King of Saudi Arabia.

force engaged in agriculture, tractors used, and fertilizers consumed per hectare. As can be seen, Italy's agricultural effort is much more efficient, using more tractors and fertilizers per hectare and a much smaller percentage of its

Table 7-5. *(continued)*

Pig Iron (000s metric tons)	***Crude Steel (000s metric tons)***	***Motor Vehicles (1,000s)***	***Electricity Production (million kwh)***
10,530	12,120	1,063	112,575
34,790	31,780	140	256,550
300	601	0	15,150
30,417	41,253	4,219	353,429
9,718	10,018	98	110,130
11,593	24,283	1,657	175,041
88,102	102,105	9,269	563,990
5,058	6,712	379	55,864
0	0	0	4,848
11,409	18,566	419	115,558
110,702	151,453	2,074	1,201,896
79,542	124,314	12,458	2,285,880

Table 7-6. Measures of Agricultural Self-Sufficiency, India and Italy, 1980–1981.

Country	*Agric. Workers as a Percentage of Labor Force*	*Tractors Used*	*Lbs. Fertilizer Used/ Cultivated Hectare*
India	63	418,000	60
Italy	11	1,072,168	370

Data from United Nations Food and Agricultural Organization, *Production Yearbook, 1981.* Figures rounded.

work force. This leaves Italy free to concentrate on industry, while India struggles to feed itself.

Information/Communications Capabilities

A country's information and communications capabilities are becoming increasingly important. The advent of satellites and computers has accelerated the revolution begun with radio and television. Enhanced technology in this area increases the ability of a society to communicate within itself and remain cohesive. It also increases efficiency and effectiveness in industry, finance, and the military. The trilateral countries (Western Europe, United States, Japan) have a wide advantage in this area. Eastern Europe and the Soviet Union are a distinct second. Some Third World countries such as India, which launched a communications satellite in 1983, have some capability, but most have not entered the microchip age. Table 7-7 shows some representative figures for selected countries and is one indication of the ability of these countries to communicate and disseminate information internally.

Military

The final category of tangible power that we will consider is the military. Throughout the world, countries are scrambling to increase their military might. In contrast to the few countries like Costa Rica, which has almost no

Table 7-7. Information/Communications Capability (per 1,000 population) in Eight Countries.

Country	*Newspaper Circulation*	*Radios*	*Televisions*	*Telephones*
United States	274	2,000+	739	748
Soviet Union	396	450	223	80
China	36	152	1.2	unknown
India	15	26	1.6	3.7
Italy	123	230	218	32
Mexico	58	250	77	67
Nigeria	1.0	1.7	neg.	2.0
Poland	351	236	214	90

Based on *The World Almanac & Book of Facts, 1983* (New York: Newspaper Enterprise Association, 1983). China does not report its telephone statistics.

army as such and which relies on the strategy that it would be too embarrassing for an aggressor to invade it, there are dozens of countries with a ravenous appetite for weaponry. We will look at the use and effectiveness of force in the next chapter, but we first need to consider the level of national armament and the fact that the military is the world's largest single economic consumer.

Levels of spending. In the century between 1865 and 1965, the proportion of the gross world product devoted to military expenditures rose from 2.6 percent to 6.8 percent.[31] During the 1970s alone, military expenditures rose 27 percent (in constant dollars). By 1984, total annual world military spending stood at nearly $970 billion, with less developed countries spending nearly $200 billion that otherwise could have been devoted to economic development.[32]

Of 1982's total expenditure, the Soviet Union accounted for 31 percent ($257 billion), and the United States accounted for 24 percent ($196.5 billion). China's expenditures were $49.5 billion, or 6 percent of the global total. The expenditures of NATO countries ($308 billion, 37 percent) and the Warsaw Pact countries ($311 billion, 38 percent) were roughly equal.[33]

Another telling set of statistics is the percentage of GNP devoted by many countries to military expenditures. Table 7-8 shows these percentages for countries grouped according to per capita GNP. Overall, 13 percent of all countries spend 10 percent or more of their GNP on arms, and 37 percent spend 5 percent or more. It can also be seen that the poorest ($0–999) countries, with crying domestic needs, spend proportionally as much on arms as the wealthiest ($3,000+) countries.

Quality versus quantity. One of the classic debates in military thinking is the issue of quality versus quantity. There is, for example, some point in numerical odds where even the most modern armed soldier will be overwhelmed by numerous opponents with sticks and stones. Where that point is, however, is extremely difficult to estimate. The point is that the reader

Table 7-8. Relative Burden of Military Expenditures against Per Capita GNP.

Military Expenditures as a Percentage of GNP (1980)	*GNP $0–999 No. of Countries*	*GNP $1,000–2,999 No. of Countries*	*GNP $3,000+ No. of Countries*
10%+	6	5	7
5–9.99%	19	5	11
2–4.99%	24	9	20
1–1.99%	10	7	5
<1%	6	6	3

Source: U.S. Arms Control and Disarmament Agency, *World Military Expenditures, 1971–1980* (ACDA Publication 117, April 1984), p. 4.

should bear in mind that military statistics should be treated with caution. Technology, training, morale, and leadership all greatly alter the impact of numbers.

It should also be remembered that the effectiveness of soldiers and military hardware is very situational: it depends on circumstances. In Vietnam, the United States possessed vastly superior weaponry and its troops were excellent. Yet it lost the war, in part because technology was limited by the war-zone environment and in part because some weapons (such as nuclear devices) were inappropriate.

Still, numbers are important. They have an impact on the battlefield when force is used. Even when force is only threatened or merely forms a brooding backdrop to negotiations, numbers count because they affect the perceptions and calculations of friend and foe alike. Table 7-9 compares the armed forces of the world's ten leaders in annual (1982) military expenditures.

Military sales and transfers. Another facet of military power is the advantages a country gains through the grant or sale of its weapons. The supplying country often has the opportunity to gain contacts in the receiving country by stationing technical advisers overseas or bringing representatives of the recipient's military home for training. The supplying country can also manipulate the supply of ammunition, repair parts, and replacements. The degree, for instance, to which the Soviet Union supplies Syria with weaponry has a major influence on Syria's bellicosity in the Middle East. Similarly, U.S. arms sales to Arab customers have been generally limited to defensive weapons that cannot be used to strike Israel.

The movement of arms and ammunition, then, has important policy potential. In 1982 total world arms transfers stood at $36.5 billion and were rising at a rate of $1.42 billion a year. The leading arms exporters were the Soviet Union (30.1 percent of the world market), the United States (26.2 percent), France (8.8 percent), and Great Britain (5.5 percent). Brazil is the largest Third World arms exporter (sixth overall), with 1982 sales estimated at $600 million. The Middle East took in 41.9 percent of the total 1982 world imports, eight of the world's ten largest importers coming from that region.[34]

Intangible Elements of Power

Though difficult or impossible to measure, the intangible elements of power are important to a country's international position. Next, we will examine various qualitative power elements of the government, the civilian population, and the military.

The Government

Power is partly determined by the degree to which a country's government is administratively competent, demonstrates individual leadership, and has an international reputation for being resolute and skillful.

Table 7-9. Military Expenditures and Inventories of Ten Countries, 1982.

Country	*Military Expenditures ($ billions)*	*Personnel (millions)*	*Long- and Medium-Range Nuclear Missiles and Planes*	*Fixed-Wing Combat Aircraft*	*Artillery*	*Major Naval Combatants*	*Tanks*
Soviet Union	257.0	4.3	3,908	11,350	22,700	553	45,000
United States	196.3	2.1	2,728	6,119	6,500	285	11,400
China	49.5	4.5	79	5,300	18,000	32	11,000
Great Britain	27.4	0.3	110	720	290	90	1,717
France	25.6	0.5	164	606	837	65	1,454
Saudi Arabia	24.8	0.06	0	139	54	3	630
West Germany	24.4	0.5	0	552	2,295	45	2,350
Poland	13.5	0.4	0	650	900	5	3,560
Japan	12.2	0.2	0	350	1,400	64	700
Iraq	11.7	0.5	0	300	800	1	2,100

Data for military expenditures and personnel based on U.S. Arms Control and Disarmament Agency, *World Military Expenditures and Arms Transfers, 1971–1982* (ACDA publication). Other figures based on the International Institute for Strategic Studies, *The Military Balance, 1983–1984* (London: International Institute for Strategic Studies, 1983).

Administrative competence. To fully utilize its power potential, a state must have a well-organized and effective administrative structure. A government that is disorganized, sluggish because of overbureaucratization, or corrupt seriously weakens a state's power. Writing about Italy, as a negative example, one analyst describes its bureaucracy as characterized by low morale, absenteeism, moonlighting, and inefficiency, leading to a "mediocre quality of services rendered . . . [and a] spreading laxity that was the rule of life in all sectors of the civil service."[35] Among other results, this ineptness contributed to the stagnation of the Italian economy and the general instability of the government.

By contrast, the Japanese bureaucracy has been portrayed as purposeful and efficient, working with business to build the modern Japanese industrial empire.[36] It should be pointed out that, contrary to public myth, authoritarian states have no advantage in efficiency over democratic states. Rather, there are pros and cons for each system in terms of power creation and utilization.[37]

Individual leadership. The charisma and ability of an individual leader can provide a nation with inspiration and direction. France in 1958 was in serious trouble. The country, which only a half century before had been considered the world's leading land power, had been devastated by two world wars, had lost its colonial empire, and was faced with revolt in the streets. There was, quite literally, only one man who could save the day, and that was Charles de Gaulle. "Le Grande Charles," as the World War II hero has been called, assumed the French presidency, called on the French people to join him in reasserting France's "grandeur," and started the country back on the road to stability and self-assurance. It was, one observer writes, a demonstration of "the triumph of will over personal and national conflict, over inner doubts and external dramas."[38]

The Populace

A second group of the qualitative power elements involves a country's populace.

General characteristics. Some scholars use the term *national character* to describe the basic social characteristics of a people.[39] There is considerable debate about the nature or even the existence of national character, and it should be stressed that, insofar as national character exists, it is a set of learned rather than innate traits.[40] It is also true, though, that some national groups seem more industrious, cooperative, and goal-oriented than others. Such factors as excellence of education, rather than quantitative literacy, are also intangible assets. As the bumper sticker on many an American's car says, "If you think education is expensive, try ignorance."

Morale. A more specific, almost measurable, intangible factor is a population's morale. The end of World War I came as much because of the loss of the national will to fight as because of military events. In 1917, war-spurred revolution took Russia out of the war. A year later, the weary populaces of Germany and Austria-Hungary drove their respective emperors from their thrones. For France, the internal collapse of their enemies came not a moment too soon, for there was also popular unrest in Paris.

At the opposite extreme, World War II demonstrated the power of strong civilian morale. Early in the war, Great Britain and the Soviet Union reeled under a tremendous pounding by the Nazi forces. Yet the allies hung on. As Winston Churchill told the British nation during the darkest days of 1940, "Death and sorrow will be the companions of our journey; hardship our garment; constancy and valor our only shield. We must be united, we must be undaunted, we must be inflexible."[41]

And they were, and they held, and they prevailed.

The Military

A country's armed might is a third element of national power that is significantly shaped by qualitative factors.

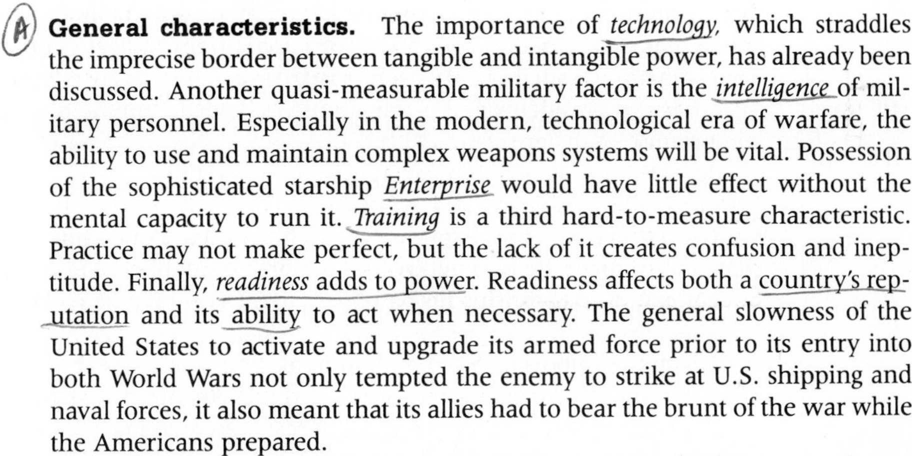

General characteristics. The importance of *technology,* which straddles the imprecise border between tangible and intangible power, has already been discussed. Another quasi-measurable military factor is the *intelligence* of military personnel. Especially in the modern, technological era of warfare, the ability to use and maintain complex weapons systems will be vital. Possession of the sophisticated starship *Enterprise* would have little effect without the mental capacity to run it. *Training* is a third hard-to-measure characteristic. Practice may not make perfect, but the lack of it creates confusion and ineptitude. Finally, *readiness* adds to power. Readiness affects both a country's reputation and its ability to act when necessary. The general slowness of the United States to activate and upgrade its armed force prior to its entry into both World Wars not only tempted the enemy to strike at U.S. shipping and naval forces, it also meant that its allies had to bear the brunt of the war while the Americans prepared.

Leadership. Military leadership, in the form of both inspiration and tactical skills, plays a significant role. It is difficult, for instance, to understand the long resistance of the southern Confederacy to the overwhelming numerical superiority of the Union unless the brilliant generalship of Robert E. Lee is considered. By contrast, French generals in the middle part of this century made a series of classic errors. In the 1930s they relied on the fortified, but static, Maginot Line and were routed in 1940 by the Germans' more creative coordination of a highly mobile and mechanized army with air support. In 1954, again relying on a static defense, the French garrison at Dien Bien Phu in Indochina was surrounded and decimated by Vietnamese forces under the command of the able General Giap.

Morale. A third intangible military factor is morale. An army that will not fight cannot win. The Soviet-trained and well-equipped Afghan army has been almost totally ineffective against the poorly armed, but highly motivated, rebel forces. Large numbers of regular army troops have deserted, and Soviet soldiers have had to do most of the fighting. The Afghan soldiers on both sides are no different except that the army is fighting for an unpopular government backed by an alien army, while the rebels are highly dedicated to a popular cause.

Reputation

A fourth element of intangible power is a country's reputation. Whatever real power a country may possess, its ability to exert that power and influence others will depend partly on how those others perceive its capacity and will. Even if inaccurate, those perceptions will at least initially become the operational reality.

Statesmen commonly believe that weakness will tempt their opponents, while a reputation for strength will deter them. Although there is evidence that a strong reputation does not always dissuade an enemy or encourage a friend, it is clear that decisions are made based on the images of others.[42] That idea, sometimes called the **Munich syndrome**, has strongly affected Western diplomacy, as presidents and prime ministers have drawn the line rather than compromise with "aggressors."

Nonwestern leaders also recognize the operational importance of reputation. Soviet Premier Nikita Khrushchev once observed, "It is quite well known that if one tries to appease a bandit by giving one's purse, then one's coat, and so forth, he is not going to be more charitable because of this. He is not going to stop exercising his banditry. On the contrary, he will become ever more insolent."[43]

Given the importance of reputation, an important aspect of diplomacy is projecting an advantageous image of power. If you are truly strong, you will usually want to convey that to opponents accurately so that they will give way without a struggle. If you are weak, then you may want to mislead others into believing that you are stronger than you actually are. We will examine these strategies in Chapter 9, on diplomacy.

Summary

Power is a key concept in a conflictual world. It is, in essence, the ability to get one's way even when opposed by others who have different interests and goals. Beyond that sort of simple characterization, the study of power becomes quite complex.

To fully understand power, one must consider all its aspects. Actual power, which can be used now, is important, but potential power also plays a role.

Real power, that which you possess, is another key element, but so is perceived power, or how others evaluate your capacity and will.

Measuring power is especially difficult. In this chapter we looked at one analyst's attempt to do so, but his effort is more notable for the attempt than for any real success in accurately measuring power. The power-measurement formula is also valuable because it highlights the fact that power is both tangible and intangible. Tangible elements of power, such as tanks or petroleum production, are relatively easy to visualize and measure. Intangible elements of power, such as morale and reputation, are much more difficult to operationalize.

It is also necessary to remember that power is dynamic and ever changing. It is also relative, which means that its effectiveness depends partly on the power possessed by other (particularly opposing) international actors. Finally, power is situational. Not all types of power can be used in all situations, and, therefore, only applicable power can be validly considered.

For all its complexity, a thorough understanding of power is crucial to a sophisticated analysis of international relations. It is prudent policy to have goals that are in realistic balance with one's power. Overly ambitious goals invite disaster. If goals and power are not in sync, then either the goals should be modified or an effort should be made to enhance one's power. In either case, a realistic assessment of both national interest and power is a necessity to the successful pursuit of international relations.

Terms

Actual power—Power which currently exists and which can be utilized.

Intangible power—Elements of power that are relatively difficult to observe or measure, such as leadership and morale.

Munich syndrome—A belief among post–World War II leaders, particularly Americans, that aggression must always be met firmly and that appeasement will only encourage an aggressor. Named for the concessions made to Hitler by Britain and France at Munich during the 1938 Czechoslovakian crisis.

Perceived power—The power that others think you have, whether it actually exists or not.

Potential power—Power that can be developed in the future, such as untapped natural resources or untrained workers.

Real power—Power which objectively exists, which can be established as a fact.

Relative power—Power measured in comparison with the power of other international actors.

Situational power—The power that can be applied, and is reasonable, in a given situation. Not all elements of power can be applied to every situation.

Tangible power—Elements of power that are relatively easy to observe and measure, such as factories and soldiers.

Notes

1. For several such views associated with *Realpolitik*, see James E. Dougherty and Robert L. Pfaltzgraff, *Contending Theories of International Relations*, 2nd ed. (New York: Harper & Row, 1981), p. 87.
2. This is discussed in Dougherty and Pfaltzgraff, *Contending Theories*, pp. 89–90. Also see R. J. Rummel, *Understanding Conflict and War*, vol. 2, *The Conflict Helix* (Beverly Hills, Calif.: Sage, 1976), pp. 163–165.
3. Karl W. Deutsch, *The Analysis of International Relations*, 2nd ed. (Englewood Cliffs, N.J.: Prentice-Hall, 1978), pp. 49–51.
4. Klaus Knorr, *The Power of Nations* (New York: Basic Books, 1975), p. 4.
5. David A. Baldwin, "Interdependence and Power: A Conceptual Analysis," *International Organization* 36 (1980): 498.
6. Henry Kissinger, *The White House Years* (Boston: Little, Brown, 1979), p. 292.
7. Kenneth J. Holsti, *International Politics: A Framework for Analysis* (Englewood Cliffs, N.J.: Prentice-Hall, 1977), pp. 170–171, cited in Lloyd Jensen, *Explaining Foreign Policy* (Englewood Cliffs, N.J.: Prentice-Hall, 1982), p. 200.
8. Deutsch, *Analysis*, p. 46.
9. Ibid., p. 47.
10. David A. Baldwin, "Power Analysis and World Politics," *World Politics* 31 (1979): 164.
11. For a discussion, see Jensen, *Explaining Foreign Policy*, p. 201.
12. Harold and Margaret Sprout, quoted in Baldwin, "Power Analysis," p. 167.
13. Stephen B. Jones, "The Power Inventory and National Strategy," in *The Theory and Practice of International Relations*, 5th ed., ed. Fred A. Sondermann, David S. McLelland, and William C. Olson (Englewood Cliffs, N.J.: Prentice-Hall, 1979), p. 57.
14. Ray S. Cline, *World Power Assessment, 1977* (Boulder, Colo.: Westview Press, 1977), p. 34. Also see Cline's *World Power Trends and U.S. Foreign Policy* (Boulder, Colo.: Westview Press, 1980).
15. For a critique of Cline, see Baldwin, "Power Analysis," p. 173.
16. Cline, *World Power Trends*, p. 153.
17. Ibid., pp. 157, 162. In subsequent works, Cline has upgraded the U.S. S + W equation.
18. Ibid., pp. 153–157. On the difficulty of future power projections, see Klaus P. Heiss, Klaus Knorr, and Oskar Morgenstern, *Long-Term Projections of Power: Political, Economic, and Military Forecasting* (Cambridge, Mass.: Ballinger, 1973).
19. Hans Morgenthau, *Politics among Nations*, 5th ed. (New York: Knopf, 1973), p. 154.
20. See Baldwin, "Power Analysis," p. 186.
21. Quoted in Theodore Draper, "Appeasement and Détente," in *At Issue: Politics in the World Arena*, 2nd ed., ed. Steven L. Spiegel (New York: St. Martin's Press, 1977), p. 192.
22. For example, "1981: The Powers That Tie Down the Superpowers," in *World Politics 82/83* (Guilford, Conn.: Dushkin, 1982), p. 28.
23. Morgenthau, *Politics among Nations*, p. 158.
24. Jack C. Plano and Roy Olton, *The International Relations Dictionary*, 3rd ed. (Santa Barbara, Calif.: ABC-Clio, 1982). On Haushofer see Andreas Dorpalen, *The World of General Haushofer* (New York: Farrar & Rinehart, 1942).

25. Saul B. Cohen, *Geography and Politics in a World Divided* (London: Oxford University Press, 1973).
26. Japan's 1976 production of ore iron was only 26 percent of its 1960 total, and its coal mining from the same period was 36 percent (*The World in Figures,* 1980, p. 177).
27. U.S. Department of Commerce, Bureau of the Census, *Statistical Abstract of the United States, 1982–83,* p. 876.
28. For an overview, see U.S. Congress, Senate Committee on Agriculture, *Global Food Assessment—1980,* Report of the Subcommittee on Foreign Agricultural Policy, 96th Cong., 2nd sess. (1980).
29. U.S. Department of Agriculture, *Agricultural Outlook,* July 1983, p. 13.
30. John C. Roney, "Grain Embargo as Diplomatic Lever: A Case Study of the U.S.-Soviet Embargo of 1980–81," in U.S. Congress, Joint Economic Committee, *Soviet Economy in the 1980s,* Part II, 97th Cong., 2nd sess. (1982).
31. Stanley Hoffman, *Primacy of World Order* (New York: McGraw-Hill, 1978), p. 209.
32. U.S. Arms Control and Disarmament Agency, *World Military Expenditures and Arms Transfers, 1971–1980,* Publication 117, April 1984, p. 3.
33. Ibid. Estimates of Soviet defense expenditures are highly controversial. For a view that Soviet spending is not so alarming, see Franklyn D. Holzman, "Myths That Drive the Arms Race," *Challenge* 27, no. 4 (October 1984): 32–36.
34. Ibid., p. 7.
35. Norman Kogan, *A Political History of Postwar Italy* (New York: Praeger, 1981), p. 135.
36. Marshall E. Dimock, *The Japanese Technocracy* (New York: Walker/Weatherhill, 1968).
37. See Jensen, *Explaining Foreign Policy,* pp. 117–129, for a discussion.
38. Stanley Hoffman, *Decline or Renewal? France since the 1930's* (New York: Viking Press, 1974), p. 203.
39. Morgenthau, *Politics among Nations,* p. 128.
40. See Jensen, *Explaining Foreign Policy,* pp. 46–53, and see Chapter 4 of the present text.
41. Report to the House of Commons, October 8, 1940.
42. See Robert Jervis, *Perception and Misperception in International Politics* (Princeton, N.J.: Princeton University Press, 1976), chap. 3.
43. Quoted in Jervis, *Perception and Misperception,* p. 61.

8

Force

Cry "havoc," and let slip the dogs of war.
Shakespeare, Julius Caesar

The naked, poor, and mangled peace.
Shakespeare, Henry V

It is February 1945. Marine Sergeant John Stryker, played by John Wayne, dashes across the beach after ninety minutes of celluloid heroics in *The Sands of Iwo Jima.* A machine gun barks, the sand spurts up at his feet. The leatherneck falls, a few telltale dark spots on his fatigues. There is just enough time for one last speech, a tribute through stoically clenched teeth to God, glory, and the girl back home. Fade to an image of the Stars and Stripes waving bravely over Mount Suribachi and the stirring strains of the Marine Hymn. Goosebumps, applause, lights up, go home safe and sound!

This 1949 classic is a typical image of war. There is an air of nobility, plumed knights, dashing air aces, and, of course, Sergeant Stryker.

There is another image of war. It is Marines with crushed skulls, mangled testicles, and charred bodies. It is naked and frightened Vietnamese children, Lebanese parents wailing over their fallen sons, and widowed mothers around the world whose babies will never know their fathers. War is ear-shattering, mind-warping, terrifying, and dirty, and it has a stench all its own. "I am tired and sick of war," General William Tecumseh Sherman told a class of graduating military cadets in 1879. "Its glory is all moonshine. It is only those who have never fired a shot nor heard the shrieks and groans of the wounded who cry aloud for blood, more vengeance, more desolation. *War is hell* [emphasis added]."

War: The Human Record

Politically, war is a paradox. It has been condemned by almost all leaders during every period of history. Further, the monetary and human costs of war are becoming ever higher, and we may have come to the eve of Armageddon. There is truth in the recent observation that "either man is obsolete or war is."[1]

Yet it is also true that wars are fought almost as regularly as they are condemned. One survey counted 208 instances of major (more than 1,000 deaths) international and civil war between 1816 and 1977.[2] Another study estimated that during the entire 5,500-year history of "civilization" there have been only 292 years of total peace in the world. During the 95 percent of the time that there was conflict somewhere in the world, the study estimated, humans had waged 14,500 wars and directly or indirectly slaughtered 3.5 billion of their own kind.[3]

In addition to the overall impact of war, it is important to consider its frequency and severity. *Frequency* is the least gloomy news. The odds that a country will become involved in an international war in any given year have steadily declined from 1 in 43 in the mid-1800s to 1 in 62 around the turn of the century to 1 in 166 since World War II.[4] Likelihood of civil war declined from 1 in 55 (1850–1870) to 1 in 73 (1946–1965) to 1 in 147 (1966–1977).[5]

It should be carefully noted that this frequency decline is not an unmitigated sign for optimism. The increasing number of states in the international system has decreased the annual average number of wars per country. In absolute terms, though, the 1850–1870 period averaged 1.61 new international and civil wars per year, 1891–1914 averaged 1.42, and the 1946–1977 average was 1.79.[6] Thus, while any given country is less likely to be at war, the worldwide incidence of war is relatively constant.

Severity is truly bad news. Not only have we become much more efficient at killing soldiers, we also now kill larger numbers of civilians as part of the war effort. During World War I, 8.4 million soldiers and 1.4 million civilians died. World War II killed 16.9 million troops and 34.3 million civilians, for a staggering 8 million deaths per year.[7] The worst news of all is for the future. A general nuclear exchange between the superpowers would certainly escalate the casualty count from millions per year to millions per minute. General Sherman's cataclysmic characterization will have literally come true.

The Causes of War: Three Levels of Analysis

Why war? That question has challenged investigators over the centuries. Philosophers, world leaders, and social scientists have come to many conclusions. A survey of their divergent findings brings the inescapable conclusion that there is no single reason that people fight. Instead, there are many causes of war, which, for our purposes here, can be classified according to the three levels of analysis discussed in Chapter 2.[8] As we look at the different types of war later in this chapter, we will also consider causal factors specifically related to each class of conflict.[9]

Human Behavior and War

The idea that the roots of war lie in the nature of human beings, either individually or as a species, has a long history.

Humans as animals. It is clear that human behavior is predominantly learned, but there are also behavioral links to the primal origins of humans. Territoriality, which we examined in Chapter 2, is one such instinct.

Stress, frustration, anxiety, and aggression. Some social psychologists argue that human aggression, individually or collectively, can stem from stress, anxiety, or frustration. The reaction of the German society to its defeat in World War I and subsequent humiliation is one possible example.

Sociopsychological need for power. At least some leaders have a power drive that may lead them to aggressive behavior. The Hitlers of history are more easily understood from this perspective.

There is no nobility in war. War is hell.

Misperception. The inability of leaders and nations to perceive events objectively is caused, in part, by factors that are inherently human. The proclivity for seeing your opponent as more hostile than you are is one example.

The State and War

War may also result from causes related to the political dynamics of individual countries.

Internal conflict. There is great academic debate over the linkage between domestic unrest and external aggressiveness. Among other factors, political regimes will sometimes engage in war to rally the populace and divert attention from domestic problems. We can say that at least under some circumstances internal conflict may lead to external conflict, as happened when the unstable military junta in Argentina moved against the Falkland Islands in 1982. Domestic conflict may also lead to outside intervention.

Economic factors. Marxists argue that capitalism causes imperialism. Others contend that the military-industrial complex or other domestic economic factors foster aggressive behavior.[10]

National growth. Growth is related to both internal conflict and economics. Various growth factors, such as population expansion and economic modernization, may lead to pressures and dislocations that cause aggressive behavior.

Nationalism. Ethnocentrism, xenophobia, and the strains caused by the lack of fit between states and nations are common causes of conflict.

The System and War

Finally, wars may be caused by a number of factors that are related to the general nature of the world's political structure.

Persistent crisis. There is a contagion theory that argues that persistent crisis or recurrent warfare breeds further hostility because of, for example, heightened tension or the tendency to become inured to violence.

Distribution of resources. The uneven distribution of world resources and the needs of strong/weak or rich/poor nations can cause conflict. Colonial conquest is an example.

Distribution of power. Numerous studies have found that power vacuums can cause conflict, as opposing powers move to fill the void. Some scholars have also argued that relative equality may cause conflict because each side calculates it can win. This factor can involve either individual countries or alliance systems.

Changes in power. Many studies have found that periods of power transition are conflictive. Dominant states may be tempted to strike a rising rival. Declining states may act to try to preserve or regain their glory. Changes in power will often lead to miscalculation of the actual power of the states involved. In an era of rapid technological innovation this factor is especially important and led the Soviets to the brink of a preemptive strike against China in 1969.

Arms races. At least to some degree, the world arms spiral is a systemic reactive model. Countries acquire arms in part because other countries do, creating a cycle of escalating arms → tensions → arms → tensions, until a flash point is reached.

Anarchy. Finally, some systems analysts argue that war occurs because there is little to prevent it. Unlike domestic societies, the international society has no effective system of law creation, enforcement, and adjudication.

The Conduct of War

Because of its causes, its continuance, and its consequences, war is the focus of ever-increasing research. Indeed, the research is so extensive that there are even bibliographies of bibliographies on the subject.[11] For all that effort, though, political scientists have only begun to be able to identify the causes, conditions, and consequences of conflict. It may be that social scientists in the future will be able to write of war in the past tense, but for the present we must recognize conflict as a fact of international politics. Having discussed the human record, we should also consider levels of violence, the effectiveness of war, and the changing nature of warfare.

Levels of Violence

A country's military may be used in several escalating ways: (1) gaining prestige and perceived power by enhancing military potential, (2) threatened use of the military against an opponent, (3) limited demonstrations of military power, and (4) direct use of military force to defeat an opponent.

Prestige. Military power does not have to be used or even threatened to be effective. Its very existence may persuade potential opponents not to risk confrontation. This is especially true when there is gross inequality—when losing for one side is certain—or when both antagonists have a great deal of relatively equal power and, thus, face not only a 50/50 chance of losing but almost certain significant damage, win or lose. The calculation of these "odds," it should be noted, is highly subject to decision-maker misperception, especially during periods of power fluctuation.[12]

Active threat. The next level of military application is overtly threatening an opponent. This may be done verbally, or it may involve shifts in the readiness or deployment of a country's armed forces. During the 1973 Arab-Israeli War, for example, the Soviets readied airborne brigades and threatened to intervene if Israel attempted to annihilate the encircled Egyptian army. The prospect caused sufficient alarm in Tel Aviv and Washington to restrain the Israeli forces.

Limited demonstration. A third military option is a limited demonstration of capability and commitment. This involves actual combat use of the military but is aimed at intimidating rather than defeating an opponent. The U.S. naval blockade during the 1962 Cuban missile crisis is an example in which action was taken but shots were not fired. The United States' downing of two Libyan fighters over the Mediterranean in 1981 served as a message that American naval forces would neither observe Tripoli's claim to extended territorial waters nor tolerate harassment.

Direct action. The most violent option is using force to defeat an opponent. Within that context, the level of violence can range from highly constrained conventional conflict to unrestricted nuclear war.

A multiple menu. The four choices are often exercised concurrently. While fighting in South Vietnam (action), for example, the Nixon administration mined the North's Haiphong Harbor (demonstration) and issued warnings (threat) that the Communists had to either negotiate more seriously or face the full force of American arms (prestige).

Effectiveness of War

Measurement. There are two ways of measuring the effectiveness of war. One is by trying to apply *cost/benefit analysis.*[13] Was the result "worth it" in terms of the loss of life, human anguish, and economic destruction? Although such trade-offs are made in reality (see Chapter 6), it is impossible to arrive at any objective standards that can equate the worth of a human life or political freedom with dollars spent or territory lost. A pacifist would argue that no political objective is worth taking a human life. A militarist would argue that war actually improves the human condition, or, as Benito Mussolini declared, "War alone brings up to its highest tension all human energy and puts the stamp of nobility upon the people who have the courage to face it."

The second way to judge the effectiveness of force is in terms of *goal attainment.* The issue is whether the accumulation and use of military power achieve the desired results. Political science is on firmer ground from this perspective, although the amount of empirical research available is still scanty.

There is little doubt that military force does work. Clear victors in the past few decades have included the North Vietnamese in their now unified country, the Soviets in Czechoslovakia, the British in the Falklands, the Americans in Grenada, and the Israelis against any number of Arab opponents.

It is equally clear that initiating military force sometimes backfires. Egypt's attack across the Suez Canal (1973) and Argentina's seizure of the Falkland Islands (1982) are two examples in which the countries that chose action were routed militarily.

Conditions for success. The next question, then, is: When does force succeed and when does it fail to accomplish its goals? Several studies have begun to outline some of the conditions for successful application of conventional force. Two studies, one by Alexander George[14] and the other by Barry Blechman and Stephen Kaplan,[15] have analyzed instances of threatened or actual use of the U.S. military. George's analysis of the Laos (1961), Cuban (1962), and Vietnam crises found that U.S. success was dependent on (1) strong U.S. determination, (2) a less determined opponent, (3) clear U.S. goals, (4) a sense of urgency to accomplish those goals, (5) adequate domestic political support, (6) usable military options, (7) fear of U.S. escalation by the opponent, and (8) clarity concerning the terms of peaceful settlement. In the Laotian and Cuban crises, all eight elements were present, and the United States was successful. In Vietnam only two elements (nos. 1 and 6) were in evidence, and failure followed.

Blechman and Kaplan's study, asking somewhat different questions, arrived at some additional conclusions as well as reinforcing George on some points. The military option was most successful when viewed as a short-term measure designed to supplement diplomacy and give diplomacy time to seek more permanent solutions. Among their other conclusions, Blechman and Kaplan found the military instrument most successful when:

1. The opponent finds the threat credible (related to George's finding no. 7).
2. The other state is not yet fully committed to a course of action (George, no. 3).
3. The goal is maintaining the authority of a particular regime abroad.
4. Force is used to offset force by another power (George, no. 6).
5. The goal is reinforcing rather than modifying current behavior (that is, as a deterrent).
6. The action is consistent with prior policy (George, no. 1).
7. There has been previous U.S. action in the area (George, no. 1).
8. U.S. involvement begins early in the crisis (George, no. 1).
9. Military action is taken rather than threatened (George, nos. 6, 7).
10. Strategic forces become involved, thus signaling seriousness of purpose (George, nos. 1, 7).

As the authors of both studies acknowledge, these correlations between military action and success are preliminary. They do, however, give some indication of the factors that contribute to successful use of the military instrument.

The Changing Nature of War

The nature of war has changed greatly over the centuries. Two factors, technology and nationalism, have radically altered the scope and strategy of war.

Technology. It goes without saying that the technological ability to kill has escalated rapidly. Successive "advances" in the ability to deliver weapons at a distance (hand-held, then thrown, then bow and arrow, then rifle, then cannon, then plane, then missile) and in killing power (individual, then gunpowder, then TNT, then nuclear) have resulted in climbing casualties, both absolutely and as a percentage of soldiers and civilians of the countries at war.[16]

Nationalism. Before the nineteenth century, wars were generally fought between noble houses with limited armies. The French Revolution changed that. War began to be fought between nations, with increases in intensity and the numbers involved. Napoleon's Grand Army was the first to rely on a mass draft and the first to number more than a million men.

Scope. As a result of technology and nationalism, entire nations have become increasingly involved in wars. Before 1800, no more than 3 of 1,000 (.3 percent) people of a country participated in a war. By World War I, the European powers called up 1 of 7 (14 percent) of their populations to arms.[17]

Technology increased the need to mobilize the population for industrial production and also increased the capacity for and rationality of striking at civilians. Nationalism made war a movement of the masses, increasing their stake and also giving justification for attacking the enemy nation. Thus, the lines between military and civilian targets have blurred.

Strategy. Finally, the strategy of war has changed. Two concepts, the power to defeat and the power to hurt, are key here.[18] The **power to defeat** is the ability to seize territory or overcome enemy military forces and is the classic goal of war. The **power to hurt**, or coercive violence, is the ability to inflict pain outside the immediate military sphere. It is hurting some so that the resistance of others will crumble. The power to hurt has become increasingly important to all aspects of warfare.

Traditionally wars were fought with little reference to hurting. Even when hurting was used, it depended on the ability to get at civilians by defeating the enemy's military forces. During the American Revolution, for example, the British could have utilized their power to hurt—to kill civilians in the major cities they controlled—and they might have won the war. Instead they concentrated on defeating the American army (which at first they could not catch, then which grew stronger) and lost.

In the modern era, the power to defeat has declined in importance relative to the power to hurt. Guerrilla and nuclear warfare both rely extensively on terror tactics to accomplish their ends. Even conventional warfare relies partly on terror tactics to break down the opponent's morale.

Conventional War

Having completed a general survey of the incidence, causes, levels of violence, effectiveness, and changing nature of war, we can now consider the types of war and the specific issues regarding each. The first type of conflict is conventional war, which is defined for our purposes as an overt international conflict that does not include nuclear weapons. This level of warfare is also sometimes called "limited" because even at its extreme, World War II, a few restraints were followed.

Goals and Conduct

The classic statement on the proper goal of war was made by the nineteenth-century German strategist Karl von Clausewitz. He argued that "war is not merely a political act, but also a political instrument, a continuation of political relations, a carrying out of the same by other means" (*On War,* 1833).

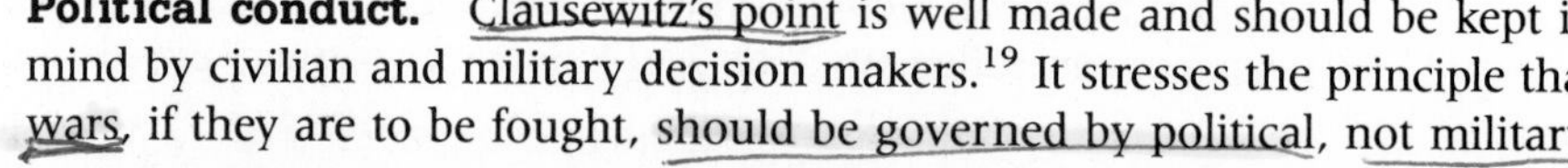

Political conduct. Clausewitz's point is well made and should be kept in mind by civilian and military decision makers.[19] It stresses the principle that wars, if they are to be fought, should be governed by political, not military,

considerations. Often commanders chafe under restrictions, as General Douglas MacArthur did in Korea over his lack of authority to attack China. When generals become insubordinate, as MacArthur did, they should be removed from command, as he was.[20]

Political goals. Clausewitz's statement also emphasizes that war should be fought with clear political goals in mind. When those goals are subordinated to military factors or when the flush of victory escalates those goals, disaster looms. Harry Truman's accomplishment of firing MacArthur is offset by the president's earlier error in crossing into North Korea. After the North's invasion of the South, Truman's stated aim was to drive the communists out and restore the border. The spectacular victory at Inchon and subsequent disintegration of North Korean forces, however, emboldened the president to move north of the border. That brought in China, with a resulting cost of two years and tens of thousands of casualties in a war that had already been "won" according to initial U.S. goals.

Ongoing negotiations. Finally, Clausewitz's statement includes the idea that war is not a substitute for diplomacy. During combat, channels of communication to the opponent should be kept open in an attempt to limit the conflict and to reestablish peace.

Rules of the Game

The idea of limits is inherent in conventional war. At times, as in World War II, near-total war occurs, but even then weapons such as gas were not used in combat. Most writers have observed that conventional wars have a number of explicit or implicit rules of the game by which they are fought. These include limits on objectives, weaponry, targets, geography, mobilization, and direct superpower confrontation.[21]

Goals are limited, usually falling short of eliminating the opponent as a sovereign state. Even where unconditional victory is the aim, obliteration of the enemy population is not a goal. *Weapons* are also restricted. The use of nuclear, chemical, and biological weapons has generally been avoided despite their ready availability. This is the principle that the level of force used should be no greater than the minimum necessary to accomplish war aims. Conventional wars also usually have *target* restrictions. Despite their close proximity, the Arabs and Israelis have never tried to bomb each other's capitals.

Additionally, there is often an attempt to limit *geographical scope*. American forces were restrained from invading China during the Korean War. On a more global scale, the Soviets passed up the temptation to blockade Berlin in 1962 in response to the U.S. blockade of Cuba. Geographical limits thus help define and confine conventional war. Further, by limiting the extent to which they *mobilize* their troops and economic power, countries assure their opponents that rapid escalation is not in the offing. Since 1945 another mark of limited war has been *avoiding big-power armed clashes*. Often the superpowers have used lesser powers, such as Israel and Syria, to test their arms against one another. Even where one is involved directly, care has been taken to avoid a clash. One reason the United States did not invade North Vietnam, for instance, was that such action would threaten a repeat of Korea and war with China.

A particular method of avoiding confrontation has been noninterference or giving way in each other's **sphere of influence**. Generally, the United States and the Soviet Union have avoided direct intervention in each other's spheres of influence (United States: Latin America/Caribbean; Soviet Union: Eastern Europe). The United States encouraged, but did nothing to help, dissidents in Hungary (1956), Czechoslovakia (1968), and Poland (1980). Similarly, U.S. anticommunist moves in the Dominican Republic (1965), Chile (1973), and Grenada (1983) occasioned only protests from the Soviets. The single direct confrontation between the powers (Cuba, 1962) resulted in a Soviet retreat in the American sphere.

As an evolving big power, China has not yet defined its sphere or had it tacitly accepted. Southeast Asia, however, will probably become in the future what it was in the past—an area of primary Chinese influence. Events such as the post-Vietnam withdrawal of American influence, Sino-Soviet rivalry in Indochina, and Sino-Vietnamese clashes are all part of that evolutionary process.

Escalation and Deescalation

The fact that limited wars are fought by rules of the game does not mean that sometimes those boundaries are not violated. **Escalation** occurs when the rules are changed and the level of combat increases. Conversely, *deescalation* is a decrease in the level of fighting.

The dynamics of combat change are truly complex, but we can basically say that they can be either irrational and destructive or positive and productive.[22] If we begin from the principle of fighting limited wars according to political rules, for political goals, and with an economy of force, then it follows that (de)escalation should be a deliberate, controlled strategy designed to signal a political message to the enemy. Accordingly, it is also important to send signals through diplomatic channels or public pronouncements so that the opponent will not misperceive the escalation as an angry spasm of violence or the deescalation as a weakening of resolve.

Escalation at its worst occurs when the pressures of military conflict careen beyond political control or when the opponent misperceives the message. In such cases, an action/reaction spiral is more likely to occur, leading to total, even nuclear, war.[23]

The object of (de)escalation should be to achieve peace by changing the rules to signal intent. (De)escalation requires careful conflict management and communication to emphasize its political rather than military meaning. It is a dangerous strategy, but when it is used skillfully, it can persuade an opponent that it is better to switch than fight.[24]

Limited Nuclear Warfare

Conflicts that use **tactical** (battlefield) and **theater** (extended area) **nuclear weapons** exist in a twilight zone between conventional and strategic nuclear war. We don't simply want to be able to categorize such conflicts. We want to understand them. Hence, to avoid controversy we can place limited nuclear warfare in its own category rather than consign it to either the conventional or the strategic nuclear category.

However, it is important to stress that although the limited use of nuclear weapons is certainly preferable to the strategic use of nuclear force, limited nuclear conflict is not simply an extension of conventional warfare with a quantitatively bigger bang. Tactical nuclear devices range from ¼ **kiloton (Kt)** and up, but many "small" tactical warheads are of Hiroshima size (12.5 Kt) and larger, and the United States alone possesses over 11,000 such devices. In addition, once the nuclear threshold is crossed, even with relatively low-yield weapons, two very important factors will change. First, just because the threshold will have been crossed, it will probably be psychologically easier to escalate from tactical to strategic weapons than it was to cross the line to begin with. Second, the mind-warping tensions that will occur once the nuclear threshold is crossed will significantly increase the chances for errors in judgment, even hysteria. In short, once the first mushroom cloud rises, no matter how small, the fate of the world will hang by a very thin thread indeed![25]

The Weapons

Theater and tactical nuclear forces range from artillery shells (less than 1, to 10 Kt) to short- and medium-range fighter-bombers (up to 1 **megaton**, or **Mt**) and short- and intermediate-range missiles. In short-range tactical weapons, NATO, with more than 6,000 warheads, outnumbers the Soviets by a 2:1 margin. That is offset by more than 1,100 Soviet medium-range ballistic missile (MRBM) warheads, a 2:1 advantage over NATO.[26] Comparisons, though, are always difficult, and the real import of these numbers is the awesome power of the weapons that face one another in Europe and elsewhere.

Use

The issues about when and how to use nuclear weapons have centered mainly on NATO strategy, although the problems are relevant to any area. At the heart of these controversies is not just the immediate impact of nuclear weapons but the very real possibility that use of such weapons could rapidly escalate to all-out nuclear war.[27]

first-strike

Timing: When to use nuclear weapons. One option is to use nuclear weapons early as a "shot across the bow." Proponents argue that this strategy would help break up a Soviet attack and would indicate a resolve that would deter the Soviets from further escalation. Opponents contend that it would be premature escalation and would prompt nuclear counterstrikes.

A second option is use as a final defense. Proponents favor this choice as avoiding nuclear war except as a last resort. Opponents counter that it would be too late and would require tactical strikes into NATO countries already overrun.

Current policy is subject to considerable debate. In November 1981, Secretary of State Haig indicated that NATO contingency plans included "demonstration" (early) nuclear warheads.[28] Others, including several former U.S. officials, have called on NATO to beef up its conventional forces and to adopt a "no first-use" doctrine.[29] That proposal, in turn, was condemned by Haig as requiring the United States to "reintroduce the draft, triple . . . its armed forces and put its economy on a wartime footing" and as "tantamount to making Europe safe for conventional [Soviet] aggression."[30]

Targeting. The **targeting** possibilities fall into three main categories: (1) tactical strikes against front-line troops, (2) tactical strikes against second-echelon military command and support facilities, and (3) strategic strikes against military and civilian targets deep within the opponent's heartland.

The strongest arguments for option 1, front-line strikes, are that it would have an immediate military impact and that it would be the step least likely to escalate to full-scale atomic warfare. The most negative aspect of this option is that oncoming Warsaw Pact forces would already be inside Western Europe. Therefore, nuclear strikes would be on one's own territory as well as on enemy troops.[31] This will be especially true if NATO abandons its current posture of holding a defensive line and adopts a strategy of maneuver, as is currently being proposed.[32]

Option 2, rear-echelon strikes, offers the possibility of avoiding attacks on NATO territory and of disrupting Soviet command and logistics functions that are considered vulnerable. It would also, however, be a mid-level escalation that would increase the risks of a cataclysmic nuclear spiral.

The third option, strategic strikes, is the most controversial. It is also the focus of the most recent strategy shift for NATO. It can be argued, on the one hand, that targeting missiles to strike deep within Soviet territory provides a high level of deterrence against either Soviet nuclear or conventional attack. It can also be argued, on the other hand, that a strategic capability carries a high probability of general nuclear war. The speed with which such missiles would strike also makes a preemptive strike more attractive and/or forces an opponent to adopt a "launch on warning" control system enhancing the chances of inadvertent nuclear war.[33]

Current strategy. The 1984 deployment in Europe of Pershing II MRBMs and Tomahawk cruise missiles is part of NATO's acquisition of an option 3 capability. That decision was made in 1979 in response to the Soviet deployment of SS-20 IRBMs in the western USSR and the increase in Soviet tactical weapons to parity with Western forces. The decision was also caused by the

The deployment of cruise and Pershing missiles, here being assembled in West Germany, increased NATO's ability to launch strikes against the Soviet Union.

relative equality of U.S. and USSR strategic forces and the resulting skepticism in Europe that the Americans would engage in a strategic exchange with the Soviets to defend Europe. Capability, however, does not necessarily mean intent, and current NATO strategy is flexible (or perhaps uncertain), with recent NATO military exercises practicing all three scenarios.

Strategic Nuclear War

The Bible's Book of Revelations speaks of an apocalyptic end to the world: A "hail of fire mixed with blood fell upon the earth; and . . . the earth was burnt up. . . . The sea became blood . . . and from the shaft rose smoke like the smoke of a great furnace and the sun and the air were darkened." Revelations continues, "Woe, woe, woe to those who dwell on earth," for many will die a fiery death, and the survivors "will seek death and will not find it; they will long to die, and death will fly from them."

Whatever your religious beliefs, the prophecy of the last book of the New Testament is unnerving. We now have the capability to sound "the blast of the trumpets" that will kill the living and make the living wish to die.

Can It Happen?

The simple answer to that question is "Yes." Humans have the *ability* to launch a nuclear war. Further, humans have the *will* to use nuclear weapons. Atomic weapons were dropped on Hiroshima and Nagasaki in 1945 and have been threatened on many occasions since. Finally, *proliferation* is increasing the likelihood of nuclear war. Six countries openly possess nuclear weapons, two others (Israel and South Africa) are strongly rumored to have them, and nearly thirty others have or are near the technological capability of building the bomb.

How It Might Start

For all its horror, nuclear war is well within the realm of possibility. Six possible scenarios for the onset of a nuclear exchange are (1) an accident, (2) an inadvertent error in judgment, (3) a fanatic, (4) escalation, (5) an unprovoked attack, and (6) a last gasp defense.[34]

Accident. A computer run wild brought the world to the edge of nuclear catastrophe in *War Games.* Chillingly, the 1983 movie's premise was not that far-fetched. It is possible that a technical malfunction or a human technical error could start a nuclear war. In recent years there have been several instances when U.S. computers warned of an incoming missile barrage.[35] Corrections were made, of course, but as response times shorten, the ability to verify computer warnings will decline. There have also been instances of "escaped" nuclear weapons, including the explosion of an ICBM in Arkansas that threw its warhead out of its silo.

Inadvertent. A second cause of nuclear war might be an error in judgment. In this scenario, misperception or misinformation plays a major role. False intelligence that a nuclear attack is imminent, for example, might cause a leader to strike first. In this case operational reality would have a devastating effect no matter what the reality was. Imagine you are the U.S. president and become convinced that the Soviets are about to launch an all-out strike. You can wait and pray, you can surrender, or you can strike first to destroy as many enemy missiles as possible and thus limit damage to your country. The temptation to strike first will be overwhelming.

Fanatic. What if Adolf Hitler had the bomb? Or the Ayatollah Khomeini? Control of nuclear weapons by a fanatical or even crazy leader is possible, and proliferation increases the chances. It could even happen in one of the superpowers. There is substantial evidence that Richard Nixon was under extreme psychological pressure at the time of his resignation, and there are hotly contested rumors that the secretary of defense instructed the military to ignore any presidential order to act unexpectedly.

Escalation. Any of the limited nuclear war strategies discussed in the previous section could easily and rapidly escalate to a full-scale, strategic exchange. Once even low-yield tactical nuclear weapons were used against oncoming front-echelon troops, the breakdown in communications and the psychological pressure on decision makers would make nuclear war likely.

Unprovoked attack. What if one side felt that it could successfully disable all or most of its opponent's strategic forces or that an attack combined with defensive measures would result in a victory with "acceptable" losses? A nuclear attack might then become a "rational" alternative. A nuclear attack against a nonnuclear country is also possible. Harry Truman, after all, did decide that atomizing two cities in Japan was preferable to a conventional invasion of the home islands.

Last gasp. This scenario might see a nuclear attack to fend off final conventional defeat. If Soviet forces had NATO trapped at Dunkirk, or if all Israel were about to fall to overpowering Arab invaders, beleaguered commanders might just order a last-gasp strike.

The Impact of Nuclear War

No one knows precisely what the impact of an all-out nuclear war would be. Some predict that it would end human existence on earth. Predictions have ranged from a modern ice age caused by the screening of the sun's rays by dust clouds to the earth being knocked off its axis and spinning wildly off into space.

The most popular image is similar to the carnage in the 1983 television movie *The Day After.* Let us assume a 1-megaton warhead, one-fiftieth the size of the Soviet's largest. Its detonation a mile above your city creates a huge fireball with temperatures in the range of 20 million degrees Fahrenheit. Within two and a half miles everything and everyone is set on fire. All is quickly snuffed out, however, by an atomizing blast. Death and destruction are total. In a second, two-mile ring, flesh is charred, blast winds reach 160 mph, and collapsing buildings and flying glass and metal crush and shred nearly everyone. Yet another two miles out, most homes are on fire, half the population is dead, the remainder probably lethally exposed to radiation. Still another four miles out, a third of the population is wounded, normal services are destroyed, and civil chaos threatens as panic sets in and people fight for medicine, food, and water. Those who survive will face uncertain futures of psychological trauma and devastated lifestyles. Only by stretching the imagination can they be called the lucky ones.[36]

There is another view of nuclear war that foresees neither the end of the world nor a society-shattering catastrophe. It makes two points. First, it argues that a nuclear attack may not be total and that a country must be ready to make "appropriate" nuclear responses to limited strategic strikes. Second, it claims that the development of defensive measures, such as antiballistic missile weapons and enhanced civil defense, would reduce deaths significantly. As one Reagan defense department official optimistically put it, "If there are enough shovels to go around, everyone's going to make it."[37]

It should be stressed that the debate over the impact of nuclear war is not meaningless speculation. Instead, it has an important impact on nuclear strategy. It is, to use the popular acronyms, a profound debate between the mutual assured destruction (MAD) theorists, who believe in deterrence, and the nuclear utilization theorists (NUTs), who believe you must plan to fight and win a nuclear war if necessary.

Deterrence

The doctrine of deterrence depends on one's ability to launch a major retaliatory "second strike" even after a massive first strike by an enemy. The premise, then, is that enemies will be deterred because even if they destroy you, they will, in turn, also be devastated. Deterrence has been the cornerstone of strategic policy for three decades. The exact nature of deterrence, however, is highly debatable because it is a nonevent. That is, it is successful only if nothing happens. But because of its nonhappening, you are never sure whether it was the deterrence or some other factor that prevented war.

With that caveat in mind, we can say that insofar as we assume it works,

deterrence is based on two factors: capability and credibility.[38]

Capability. Effective deterrence requires that you have the capacity to respond *after* an attack on your forces. This need has been the primary cause of what seems to be the "overkill" capacity of the superpowers. Figures on how many times over each nuclear arsenal can kill everyone are largely irrelevant. The issue is how many weapons will survive. As each power acquires more weapons, the other, it can be argued, must get more to ensure its capability of a retaliatory second strike. This, in turn, creates pressure on the first country to get yet more weapons, and the result is the arms spiral. This search for invulnerability based on numbers and types of weapons will be discussed more fully in the section on strategic posture options.

Credibility. It is also necessary for other states to believe that you will actually use your weapons. Here again, perception is a key factor, and some argue that the nuclear-freeze movement and other such causes run the risk

of deluding the Soviets into thinking the West might not have the will to respond before its capability was destroyed. That misperception could be more dangerous than the arms race.

Because of the two factors of capability and credibility, current deterrence strategy has centered on the MAD concept since the early 1960s. The basic idea is that both sides have the capacity to have some of their weapons survive a strike and the will to launch a response so painful that the other side is deterred.

Thinking the Unthinkable

There are those, the NUTs, who contend that deterrence theory is mad indeed. Strategist Colin Gray, for example, argues that any circumstances that would cause any form of war between the superpowers "are likely to be so desperate

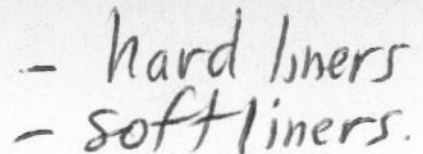

that there is no good reason to believe that deterrence would function."[39] Critics of deterrence theory also point out that more accurate, quicker weapons enhance the possibility of a disabling first strike. Finally, critics point out that deterrence theory relies on rationality and clear-sightedness when, in reality, decisions are often emotional and are based on misperception.[40]

Because nuclear utilization theorists believe deterrence will not always necessarily work, they argue that plans must be made to fight, survive, and win a nuclear war. The NUTs favor defensive measures such as ABMs and civil defense. They also favor developing contingency plans for fighting a protracted war involving a series of nuclear exchanges. Finally, they believe in building a first-strike capability and using highly accurate and explosive warheads that could, if necessary, disable the other side's ICBMs before they could strike. In short, they do not rule out first-strike preemptive war.[41]

Strategic Posture Options

The debate between advocates of MAD and NUT strategies creates many dilemmas in the structuring of a country's strategic posture. To review these options, we will examine choices in (1) the size of the nuclear force, (2) targeting, (3) control, and (4) types of delivery systems.

Size of Nuclear Force

Along a scale of nuclear strength, three key points are superiority, sufficiency, and minimum deterrence. The *superiority* option argues that you can be secure only when you can overwhelm your opponent. The problem with this line of thought is that superiority and absolute security for one side means inferiority and absolute insecurity for the other.[42] In reality, neither superpower has or is seriously trying to gain nuclear superiority, but perceptually both sides are convinced the other is trying to do just that. This perception drives the arms race and increases the chance of a preemptive nuclear strike by a country that perceives itself as faced with impending inferiority and vulnerability.

The doctrine of *sufficiency,* or enough forces to survive and strike back, is the announced doctrine of both superpowers and the basis of the MAD strategy. It also implies the willingness of each side to let the other achieve "essential equivalence" or "strategic parity." The difficulty is that, in the complex world of nuclear arms, equivalence is hard to measure and the chances of misperception are high.

The final nuclear force size option is *minimum deterrence.* This is the strategy of the "lesser" nuclear powers (France in particular). It relies on a small nuclear force and bases deterrence on the theory that even if you could not utterly destroy your opponent, the damage you could inflict would be so horrendous that no country would rationally risk it. This strategy has the positive point of restraining the arms spiral, limiting the budget drain of defense spending, and perhaps limiting nuclear war, should it occur, by convincing your opponent that it is not necessary to obliterate you. On the negative side, if a crisis does occur, your capability is limited, the temptation for a preemptive strike is high for the aggressor, and your credibility is doubtful. Would, for instance, France really use its weapons against the Soviet Union, knowing that utter destruction would end French civilization forever?

It should also be noted that various nonnuclear options are also possible. These will be discussed in the chapter on arms control and disarmament.

Targeting

Another area of controversy in nuclear strategy is what to attack or counterattack. The four basic options are (1) countervalue, (2) counterforce, (3) counterinfrastructure, and (4) countervailing.[43]

Countervalue. This option (also called countercity) was the underlying assumption of the MAD strategy through the early 1960s. It is based on the idea that, in retaliation for an attack on your forces or cities, their civilians would be countertargeted. Thus, it is inherently a second-strike strategy. It assumes that there may be few strategic military targets left worth hitting, since they already would have been launched against you and, further, that maximum terror, and therefore deterrence, is achieved by threatening to destroy your opponent's civilization. The drawback to this strategy is that it is a doomsday scenario, which abandons hope of containing damage and actually encourages an opponent to push all the proverbial buttons should it feel compelled to launch a nuclear strike.

Counterforce. A second option is primarily targeting your opponent's military forces. This policy gained an increasing number of advocates in the 1960s. Its strongest point is that it allows at least the chance that even a strategic exchange could be controlled. It also gives the option of a first strike to attempt to limit your damage by eliminating as much of your opponent's strategic capability as possible.

On the negative side, counterforce has some characteristics of shooting at the barn after the horses have run out. Although many military targets would remain, Soviet missile silos would be empty. Moreover, even if counterforce is designed as a second-strike, controlled response option, the weapons it relies on (very accurate and powerful "silo busting" missiles) are the same as those needed for a first-strike strategy. Deploying these systems dramatically increases the insecurity of an opponent by presenting the "use them or lose them" quandary once war threatens. And especially in the nuclear era, an insecure, nervous opponent increases the chance of inadvertent war.

Counterinfrastructure. A third option is to attack neither cities nor military forces as such. Rather, the goal is to threaten to destroy an opponent's economic and political infrastructure by targeting industry and control centers. Proponents argue that it maximally deters the Soviet Union by threatening to destroy what its leaders value most—political control. It also has

France's nuclear capability, such as this French ballistic missile nuclear submarine, is no match for the Soviets, but may be enough to deter the Soviets from nuclear or conventional attack.

some chance of limiting a nuclear exchange and avoids the futility and destabilizing aspect of counterforce strategy. The drawback of counterinfrastructure targeting is that industry and political control centers are mixed in with civilian population centers. From an opponent's point of view, the distinction between countercity and counterinfrastructure might be meaningless.

Countervailing. None of these doctrines is an absolute that rules out multiple targeting strategies. Indeed, American and Soviet strategy have moved toward a posture of flexible, countervailing force that would tailor and limit a nuclear response to the level of the initial strike by an opponent. The allure of flexibility and, thus, seeming rationality is strong, as is the possibility of limiting the exchange and damage. But there are also drawbacks. First, by implication, countervailing strategy means absorbing a first strike, since before launch or during flight you have little idea of what your opponent intends to destroy. Second, it assumes a level of postdetonation accurate information and rationality beyond the probable capability of any leader with nuclear weapons incinerating millions of his people. In short, it sounds good, but it may be beyond human ability.

Control

A third issue area of nuclear strategy is how tightly or loosely to control the release of weapons systems. *Tight control,* one with multiple authorizations needed before launch, has the advantage of minimizing the possibility of a nuclear war being started by an accident or by a fanatic.

Loose control, in contrast, lessens the chance that a country's retaliatory forces would be rendered inert by breakdown in the chain of command.[44] Such a disruption could result from the difficulty of evaluating a threat, deciding on a response, and launching your weapons systems all within as little as thirty minutes. One strategy is to attack your opponent's command, control, and communications (C^3) capability. This is sometimes called a "decapitation" strategy and would destroy the leadership and/or its ability to react. It is also possible that an initial strike could be aimed solely at communications systems. There has been speculation—and denial—that the *electromagnetic pulse* (EMP) from a single huge Soviet warhead could disable the U.S. communications and computer systems long enough to leave the country defenseless. It should finally be pointed out that the decreasing response time increases the critical nature of control mechanisms. A Pershing missile can reach the USSR from Germany in ten minutes, and the submarine missiles off the U.S. and Soviet coasts can strike in seven to ten minutes. The existence of such weapons pushes both countries ever closer to the necessity of launching-on-warning.

There is no such thing as a button that can launch nuclear war. Beyond that, however, launch procedures remain highly secret and controversial.

Types of Weapons Systems

Perhaps the most crucial decisions in nuclear strategy involve the types of long-range **strategic nuclear weapons** systems to be deployed. We will consider these options by examining the advantages and disadvantages of (1) land-based ballistic missiles, (2) cruise missiles, (3) sea-launched ballistic missiles, (4) manned bombers, (5) various types of warheads, and (6) weapons of the future.[45]

Land-based ballistic missiles. Ballistic missiles have long been the most numerous delivery vehicles in both the Soviet and the American arsenals. They have several *advantages.* One is accuracy. Soviet SS-18 ICBMs have a **circular error probability (CEP)** of .15 nautical mile, or about 900 feet. The Minuteman III has a CEP of .09 nautical mile, or 540 feet. This is especially important in attacking missile silos and other "hardened" military positions.[46] A second plus for ICBMs is that they are very powerful. The SS-18 can carry a single 25-megaton warhead or ten 2-megaton warheads. Third, ICBMs are relatively inexpensive (in defense terms), are easy to maintain, and require few support personnel.

The prime *disadvantage* of ICBMs is increasing vulnerability. As accuracy improves, and with MIRV (multiple independent reentry vehicle) missiles' ability to deliver multiple warheads, the survival probability for ICBMs decreases rapidly. Current estimates are that an attack of 500 SS-18s, each carrying three 5-megaton warheads, would destroy all or most U.S. ICBMs even though the silos are built to withstand a blast effect of 2,000 pounds per square inch. The United States has considered a variety of basing and maneuverability plans to increase ICBM survival rates, but to date each has proven technologically, politically, or financially unacceptable.

This enhanced kill probability increases nuclear instability because of the pressure on decision makers to "use them or lose them" if faced with a missile attack. Thus, a Soviet or American leader might be faced with either launching all his ICBMs or possibly having them destroyed before he knows the exact extent of an attack.

Cruise missiles. These are relatively slow (600 mph), low-flying (500 feet) missiles some of which have a range of 1,500 miles or more. They have two *advantages*. First, they are highly mobile and can be launched from the ground, from surface ships or submarines, or from aircraft. Thus they are highly versatile and have a degree of invulnerability. Second, cruise missiles are downright cheap ($1–2 million) by military standards.

There are, however, *disadvantages*. Cruise missiles are subject to defensive attack and have some accuracy problems. More important, they create significant arms control problems. Because they are small (20 feet long, 21 inches in diameter) and can be easily concealed, it will be extremely difficult to come up with a plan that assures each side that the other is not cheating.

Sea-launched ballistic missiles. Both superpowers and the British and French have a sea-launched ballistic missile (SLBM) capability. China is trying to develop a system. The primary *advantage* is invulnerability. U.S. nuclear ballistic missile submarines (SSBNs) are considered almost totally invulnerable despite advances in Soviet antisubmarine warfare (ASW). Soviet SSBNs, because of poorer technology and more sophisticated American ASW, are somewhat more vulnerable, but only in a limited sense. Given this relative invulnerability, SSBNs, especially American, are increasingly the guarantors of deterrence in an era when land-based ICBMs are becoming more vulnerable.

The main *disadvantage* of SSBNs and their SLBMs is cost. Currently, a fully equipped American SSBN costs well over $2 billion and is expensive to staff and maintain. Other SSBN/SLBM problems include missile accuracy and communications reliability, but recent advances are lessening these issues.

Manned bombers. Aircraft are still employed by all the nuclear powers. They have several *advantages*. They are flexible and are capable of tactical nuclear, strategic nuclear, or conventional attack. They can also be "called back" if there is a false alarm.

Vulnerability is the biggest *disadvantage* for manned bombers. Despite sophisticated defensive electronic gear and weapons systems, they are slow and subject to attack on the ground or by interceptors and surface-to-air missiles (SAMs). The ability to equip bombers with air-launched cruise missiles (ALCMs) gives aircraft a "stand-off" capability and will extend their utility. At that point, however, they become more missile platforms than bombers as such. Finally, there is a long-standing controversy over whether the United States should build a new generation of "penetrating" bombers (B-1, Stealth).

Warheads. The development of MIRV missiles, which carry several warheads that can independently strike separate targets, has had the *advantage* of greatly adding to Soviet and American firepower at relatively low cost. There are also *disadvantages,* mainly regarding nuclear stability. By increasing the threat to ICBM silos, MIRVs have increased the pressure to launch a retaliatory strike before enemy missiles hit or even to adopt a preemptive/first-strike strategy. MIRVs also complicate arms control because it is hard to detect how many warheads any given ICBM or SLBM is carrying.

Weapons of the future. Although they are not nuclear, it is necessary to mention a series of weapons systems that either have not been extensively used or exist on the drawing board: chemical, biological, and neutron weapons.

Chemical warfare has existed since 600 B.C., when the Athenians poisoned their enemy's water supply with a diarrhea-inducing substance. Today's chemical weapons are much more sophisticated and include mentally incapacitating psychochemicals. So far, international treaties, fear of retaliation, and world opinion have limited chemical use. The United States does not currently produce antipersonnel chemical weapons, but the Soviet Union does.[47] There have also been widespread reports that the Soviets have used chemicals in Laos, Cambodia, and Afghanistan[48] and that Iraq used poison gas against Iran in their war.

The use of *biological warfare* is also outlawed by treaty, but there are indications that both superpowers and others retain the technology to build biological weapons. The use of such a capacity could be devastating. During World War II, the British experimented with anthrax on a small island off their coast, and the lethal germs are still active two generations later.[49]

A *neutron weapon* is an enhanced radiation weapon that is produced by nuclear fusion (rather than fission). As such, it is technically a nuclear weapon, but it differs from most in that it produces a high radiation pulse but has a relatively limited blast effect. It would not extensively destroy buildings, but it would kill people, even in armored vehicles. Neutron weapons are designed for tactical use and have the advantage of killing troops while not physically destroying extensive areas beyond the immediate blast area. The danger of such a weapon is that the lack of physical destruction makes its use more "thinkable." Both superpowers probably have neutron technology, but because of tactical or political considerations, neither has deployed such weapons.[50]

Nuclear Defense

Though not a strategic option as such, the concept and possibility of nuclear defense plays an important role in today's nuclear arms planning and diplomacy. The thought of a true defensive system against nuclear attack, some sort of force field, perhaps, that would absolutely and forever shield us from enemy missiles, has considerable allure. As we shall see, however, the technical ability to construct an effective ballistic missile defense (BMD) system is highly speculative, and the attempt might have extreme negative consequences.

Ballistic Missile Defense

Development of an antiballistic missile (ABM) system was first attempted by both superpowers in the late 1960s. Although prototype systems were constructed, their high cost and unreliability led to a 1972 treaty that limited each superpower to only one ABM installation. (The U.S. system at Grand Forks, North Dakota, never went into operation; the Soviet system around Moscow is of limited value.)[51]

Star Wars—the Strategic Defense Initiative (SDI)

The idea of building a defense system against nuclear attack was rekindled by President Reagan in 1984 and has caused a major debate domestically and internationally.

The concept. The Star Wars concept is based on creating a "layered" defense system (see Figure 8-1) that would destroy attacking missiles during each of the flight phases during their 17,000-mile, thiry-minute flight from the Soviet Union to the United States. A missile's most vulnerable point is during its three- to five-minute "boost" phase, when it is rising straight and relatively slowly to the edge of space. During the next five minutes a "bus" detaches itself from the booster and maneuvers, releasing its MIRVed warheads and a large number of decoy warheads. These then speed through space for nearly twenty minutes and finally, in the last minute or two, plunge back through the atmosphere toward their American targets.

The proposed weapons. To create a layered defense, the Reagan administration is proposing to build a number of new weapons systems.[52] The administration claims that SDI research and development does not violate the letter of the ABM treaty (although the spirit is another matter). *Lasers* (light amplification by stimulated emission of radiation) are light beams powered by electrical, chemical, or nuclearly produced X-ray techniques. They travel at the speed of light and, basically, would burn holes through missiles and warheads. Laser generators could be stationed either on the ground or in space and would focus on and bounce their rays off a series of mirrors placed in orbit.[53]

Particle beam weapons would direct a charged particle (neutrons, electrons, protons) at missiles. These can travel at almost the speed of light, but since they are more affected by the atmosphere and gravity than lasers, they would be used to attack missiles in the postboost stage. *Kinetic energy* weapons, or "smart rocks," are small space- or ground-based projectiles equipped with homing sensors that could be fired at attacking missiles in all phases.

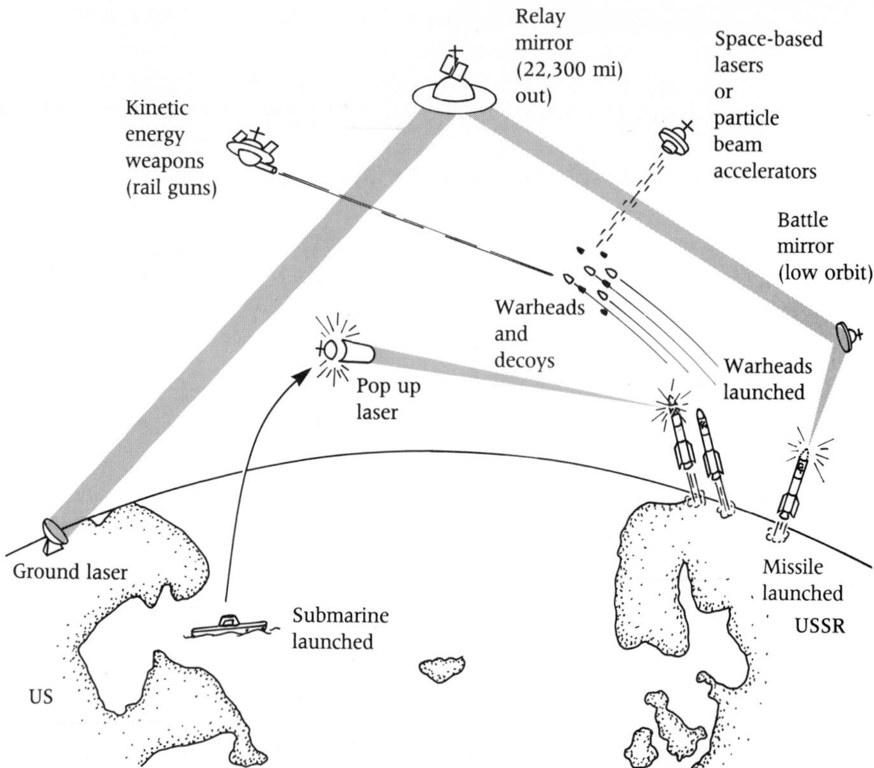

Figure 8-1. Various possible weapons systems for a layered strategic defense.

The argument for SDI. The Reagan administration claims that a strategic defense system could *rid the world of nuclear terror.* Reagan has even made an offer (with lots of qualifiers) to share the technology with the Soviets. If deterrence should fail, the theory goes, the world would be destroyed without a defensive system. The administration further argues that SDI would *enhance deterrence* by ensuring that much of the U.S. retaliatory capability would survive. SDI supporters are further confident that *science can overcome the monumental technological obstacles* to building a system that can detect and evaluate the tens of thousands of delivery vehicles, warheads, and decoys that would be involved in a massive nuclear attack. Finally, SDI advocates contend that the *cost* of developing and deploying such a system (guesses range from $100 billion to $1 trillion) *is worth it* if the result is an end to nuclear terror.

The arguments against SDI. Critics of SDI charge that it will cost too much, will not work, and is dangerous besides. The issue of the *tremendous price tag* for the system is as obvious as it is debatable. The contention that such a system *will not work* is more serious. Former Defense Secretary James Schlesinger has described the idea as "half Buck Rogers, half P. T. Barnum."[54] His comment typifies the doubts that many have that science can develop a system that (given extremely short decision times) can perform the equivalent of "hitting a bullet (traveling at perhaps 30,000 mph) with a bullet."

Most seriously, SDI opponents claim that trying to develop and deploy such a system would be dangerous. First, they say, it would militarize space. Some weapons would certainly be put in space, and an X-ray laser system would require placing up to 1,400 X-ray-generating nuclear devices into low orbit. Second, critics contend that the SDI will push the Soviets (as they have threatened) to develop a massive number of new nuclear delivery devices capable of overwhelming any defensive system. Some analysts even worry that the Soviets, rather than face a situation in which American missiles could attack them but their missiles could not counterattack, might decide to launch a preemptive first strike to avoid being put at such a decided disadvantage. It is also within the realm of possibility that an SDI would lull its possessor into a false sense of security, make the "unthinkable" a bit more "thinkable," and convince some future leader that a planned nuclear attack on an opponent was a rational choice. Finally, critics charge that pursuing the SDI program will further entangle the already horrendously complex nuclear disarmament problem, an issue discussed in Chapter 15.

What to believe. In the last analysis there is no "right" answer—or at least there is no right answer we can know for sure. The cost debate is largely a matter of subjective value, whatever number you pick. All that can be said for certain is that it will be huge. Whether the proposed weapons are technically feasible or Buck Rogers nonsense also depends on whom you listen to. Much of the proposal sounds beyond comprehension, but so, not long ago, did traveling in space. Virtually all great inventions have been laughed at before their time.

Finally, the safety or danger depends on a series of assumptions. Critics, most of whom are of the MAD school, argue that deterrence has worked and are willing to gamble that it will continue to work. They are unwilling to destabilize deterrence by provoking more Soviet offensive weapons and making the unthinkable thinkable. Proponents of the SDI program (generally NUT theorists) have their doubts about the (continued) effectiveness of deterrence.[55] They say a defensive system will both enhance deterrence and provide an alternative to certain destruction if deterrence does fail. Where you stand on these issues, in the last analysis, depends on what frightens you most.

Civil Defense

A second defensive possibility is the protection of people and industry. The Soviets spend an estimated $2 billion yearly on civil defense, but the United States has done little in that area since the late 1950s. The Reagan administration, however, has recently stepped up civil defense plans, including provisioned shelters and evacuation plans. Advocates contend that tens of millions of lives could be saved if a war did occur. Critics claim that evacuation plans would cause panic and could be frustrated by easily retargeted missiles. They also claim that shelters would "become crematoria in which people would be simultaneously dry-roasted and asphyxiated" and that even if large numbers survived, they would emerge to face a future of starvation and disease. Finally, critics of civil defense argue that it would create an illusion of safety, again making the unthinkable thinkable.[56]

Civil War

From the perspective of international politics, the primary concern with civil, or internal, war is that it will spread to involve outside countries. About 20 percent of all civil wars become internationalized,[57] and recent history is strewn with examples such as Vietnam, the Indo-Pakistani War over the revolt in East Pakistan (Bangladesh), and Lebanon.

Far from being minor, civil wars are lethal and, by most estimates, account for more battle deaths than international wars (especially if the two world wars are factored out). There is also evidence that internal violence is on the rise.[58] Between 1946 and 1977 some thirty-seven civil wars broke out, for an average of 1.2 per year, the highest in any period during the last century and a half.[59]

Given the high frequency of civil war and the fact that outside countries often support one or both sides, it follows that internal war is a concern of the international community. The search for peace must therefore address the causes of domestic as well as international violence.

Guerrilla Warfare and Terrorism

The last type of war we will examine is guerrilla warfare. Although this tactic is popularly associated with leftist insurgencies in the modern era, it is in fact an ancient art. The campaign of Joshua against the Kingdom of Ai in the Old Testament is a classic campaign of cunning overcoming superior strength. It should be also, and more contemporarily, noted that guerrilla warfare and the terror tactics often associated with it are not the exclusive domain of political leftists. That impression arose in the 1950s and 1960s, but in more recent years, as more established governments exist with socialist or communist policies, the number of rightist insurgent movements has increased. Left-leaning countries such as Nicaragua, Ethiopia, Afghanistan, and Angola are all beset by guerrilla forces. Many guerrilla movements and even terrorists, in fact, have little or nothing to do with left/right politics. The Irish Republican Army, the rebels of southern Sudan, the South West African People's Organization (SWAPO) in Namibia, and the occasional Kurdish uprisings in the

Middle East are best understood as flowing from nationalist aspirations and local causes rather than as part of the East/West conflict. In Cambodia, there

are even communist rebels (backed by communist China) trying to overthrow the communist government (backed by communist Vietnam)! The point is that guerrilla actions and terror tactics are widely found and not reserved to any particular ideological or political element.

Increase in Guerrilla Warfare

Most analysts agree that guerrilla warfare is becoming increasingly common. One cause is the growth of mass armies and military technology. In the days when armies were small and weapons were limited to swords or rifles, the difference in weaponry between government and rebel forces was limited. Today, governments use tanks, aircraft, and other sorts of sophisticated weapons unavailable to insurgents, who, therefore, increasingly must adopt guerrilla tactics. A second factor is that the advances in army strength and technology have a dangerous flaw: they make the military much more dependent on its supply lines, which are primary targets for guerrilla strikes.[60]

A third cause of the increased use of guerrilla tactics is that they avoid the label of aggression. Instead of directly trying to overthrow the Sandinistas in Nicaragua, for example, the United States supports the "contra" rebels. Even though the support is an open secret, it avoids the avalanche of criticism that an invasion would bring. A fourth factor in increased insurgency is the willingness of outside forces to supply rebels. In particular, this has been a trademark of the communist support of revolution.[61] Outside support is also spurred by the desire of the more established powers to fight "proxy" wars and avoid direct involvement, especially if there is a risk of confrontation with another major power. Soviet and Chinese support of the Viet Cong was an effective effort that temporarily weakened their prime international opponent, the United States. Similarly, Western aid is dispatched to the rebels in Afghanistan as a way of tormenting the Soviets.

Guerrillas and Terrorists

It is important to note that not all guerrillas are terrorists, nor are all terrorists guerrillas. *Guerrillas* are part of an organized force that uses "hit and run" tactics to attack a superior military force.[62] In a strict sense, any army can contain guerrilla elements (like the Green Berets in Vietnam), but in common usage, *guerrilla* usually refers to a rebel force that is using irregular tactics to try to bring down its country's government.

Terrorists, by contrast, are individuals or groups who use tactics such as assassination, kidnaping, and bombing to achieve a political goal. The goal may be as broad as the overthrow of a government or much more specific, as in recent terror tactics in Europe aimed at NATO in general and the Pershing II and cruise missiles in particular.

The confusion between guerrillas and terrorists comes because guerrillas sometimes use terror tactics as part of their campaigns. That is because both groups are faced with much the same problem—namely, defeating an opponent that is much stronger. To do that, it is necessary to attack opponents where they are weakest, rather than meeting their strength head on as in conventional warfare. Tactics include elements of both terror and propaganda, but the goal is the same: to break down an opponent's military and civilian morale and support.

Militarily, guerrillas and terrorists attack supply, communications, and transportation facilities. They also attack lightly defended outposts or patrols or individual members of the military/police. Guerrillas and terrorists also sometimes use random violence against civilians, either to get others to comply or to create a state of fear that will erode the public's faith in the ability of the government to protect them and, in turn, lead to a breakdown in governmental authority and control. In that sense, as noted earlier in this chapter, guerrilla and especially terror tactics depend heavily on the ability to hurt rather than the ability to defeat.

Propaganda is another key element of guerrilla activity. Mao Zedong once observed that in order to prosper, guerrillas needed to "swim" among the people like fish in the sea. Mao's point is that popular support will greatly strengthen guerrillas by providing intelligence, food and other supplies, and hiding places. Popular opposition will almost certainly doom a guerrilla movement. To achieve that support, guerrillas (at least successful ones) use propaganda methods to win popular support and undermine loyalty to the government.

Increasingly, guerrilla movements also use propaganda methods to win international support, which can be vital in gaining money and political support from outside governments. They distribute literature, make speakers available, hold press conferences for foreign journalists, and even invite reporters to join them and observe their (most commendable) activities. Dan Rather of CBS, for example, was spirited inside Afghanistan, darkened his face, donned the distinctive Afghan garb, and traveled with the guerrillas to bring back their story. It was, quite literally, a million-dollar press coup for the Afghan guerrillas.

Guerrilla War and Terrorism: How Effective?

Because of the success of Mao Zedong, Ho Chi Minh, Fidel Castro, and others, guerrilla warfare has gained a reputation as being unstoppable. That is a myth, although the nature of insurgent operations makes it very hard to defeat them decisively.[63] Like any other political movement, however, a successful insurgency must have the proper conditions for success. It needs to have a level of at least passive popular support and therefore is unlikely to gain ground in a society that strongly supports its government. Even more, an insurgency needs positive popular support to supply it with a variety of needs, not the least of which is recruits. A successful movement must also have sound organization and financing, a source of weapons, and leadership. It must be adaptive to the local situation. One reason that the various guerrilla organizations in Cam-

Guerrilla forces, whether leftist or rightist, such as these Nicaraguan contras, have become an increasingly common and effective factor in international relations.

bodia have suffered severe defeats at the hands of the Vietnamese is that the guerrillas tried to hold fixed positions, a violation of basic insurgency principles.

Terrorism similarly relies on a particular set of circumstances for success. It must be able to penetrate to its victims, it must have its acts given wide and sensational coverage by the media, and it must be able to win concessions from target governments. In the bombing of the Marine barracks in Lebanon by Moslem terrorists, all three elements were present, and that added to pressure that soon led to the withdrawal of American forces from that country.

It is extremely difficult to stop terrorism and perhaps impossible to stop it completely. As terrorism has grown, however, governments and individuals

have become more cautious and better able to counter it. Many embassies now resemble forts, bodyguards are common, metal detectors are everywhere, and approach roads are strewn with barricades. Many countries are also training specialized antiterrorist squads, and some, such as the Israelis', have had some spectacular successes. One disturbing side of this development, however, is that the tactics of the antiterrorists are sometimes as hair-raising as those of the terrorists.

Terrorist or Freedom Fighter: The Question of Morality

This question of tactics brings us to one final consideration, whether ends justify means. That question was raised in Chapter 5, but it is worth pondering again. Whether by intent or by circumstance, terror tactics kill unsuspecting civilians. But, then, so do conventional attacks by regular military forces. As noted earlier, World War II killed many more civilians than soldiers. A Palestinian guerrilla/terrorist might point out, for example, that the only difference between his bombs and Israeli bombs is that he delivers his by truck or hand while the Israelis deliver theirs by bomber. The Israelis might reply that the only reason they (are forced to) kill civilians is that the guerrillas operate among them.

Even for the majority who are unlikely to become terrorists, the question of justification is important. Many live in countries whose governments support guerrillas, and we need to make decisions about whether to support or oppose such operations. We may also be called on to give more direct aid to guerrillas/terrorists. In the absence of official aid, private American contributors have given substantial aid to the contra rebels in Nicaragua, and other Americans have given money to Noraid, an organization that almost certainly at least indirectly helps fund the weapons of the Irish Republican Army.

Summary

War is organized killing of other human beings. Virtually everyone is against that. Yet war continues to be a part of the human condition, and its incidence has not significantly abated.

Scholars, philosophers, and statesmen have tried to understand why wars occur in hopes of preventing them. To date, although much valuable research has been done, about the best we can do is to point out that war is a complex phenomenon that seems to have many causes. Some of these may stem from the nature of our species, some from the existence of nation-states, and some from the nature and dynamics of the world political system.

It is insufficient, though, merely to condemn war or to try to understand its origins. We must also understand how war is waged and its impact on international politics. As we have seen, force can be used, threatened, or merely exist as an unspoken possibility. However it is operationalized, its successful use requires planning and skill. (It is important to remember that if force is to be used, it must be employed as a means, or tool, rather than, as sometimes happens, as an end in itself.)

The nature of war is changing. Technology has enhanced killing power; nationalism has made war a patriotic cause; entire populaces, instead of just armies, have become engaged; and the power to hurt has equaled or supplanted the power to defeat as a goal of conflict.

War can be divided into five rough categories: limited (conventional), limited nuclear, strategic nuclear, civil, and guerrilla warfare. For each of these, we examined a variety of factors such as weapons, strategy, other options, and impact. We also saw that the ability to conduct war is continuing to change as new technology develops new weapons.

In short, the study of force involves several major questions. When and why does war occur? When it does happen, how effective is it, what conditions govern success or failure, and what options exist in structuring the use of force? The final question, discussed in Chapter 15, is how we can prevent war. That may be the most important question, but it is not the only question.

Terms

Circular error probability (CEP)—The radius within which there is a 50 percent chance that a warhead can be accurately delivered.

Escalation—Increasing the level of fighting.

Kiloton (Kt)—Explosive power equal to 1,000 tons of TNT.

Megaton (Mt)—Explosive power equal to 1 million tons of TNT.

Power to defeat—The ability to overcome in a traditional military sense—that is, to overcome enemy armies and capture and hold territory.

Power to hurt—The ability to inflict pain outside the immediate battle area; sometimes called coercive violence. It is often used against civilians and is a particular hallmark of terrorism and nuclear warfare.

Sphere of influence—A region which a big power claims is of special importance to its national interest and over which the big power exercises special influence.

Strategic nuclear weapons—Weapons that could be delivered intercontinentally, especially between the United States and the Soviet Union and/or China.

Tactical nuclear weapons—Relatively low-yield weapons used against enemy military forces.

Targeting—Selecting target options for nuclear weapons.

Theater nuclear weapons—Weapons with less than strategic range that can be used in a region, such as Europe, against an opponent's population, industrial, and command centers.

Notes

1. Emily Morison Beck, ed., *Bartlett's Familiar Quotations*, 15th ed. (Boston: Little, Brown, 1983) p. 972.
2. Melvin Small and J. David Singer, "Conflict in the International System, 1816–1977," in J. David Singer and associates, *Explaining War: Selected Papers from the Correlates of War Project* (Beverly Hills, Calif.: Sage, 1979), pp. 63, 68.
3. For a discussion, see Francis A. Beer, *Peace against War: The Ecology of International Violence* (San Francisco: W. H. Freeman, 1981), pp. 20–36.
4. Small and Singer, "Conflict in the International System," table 1, p. 63.
5. Ibid., table 4, p. 68. The 1946–1977 figure is an extrapolation.
6. Ibid., pp. 63, 68. The 1946–1977 figures are extrapolated.
7. Beer, *Peace against War,* pp. 37–38.
8. This scheme of causal division is suggested by the "three images" used by Kenneth N. Waltz in his classic *Man, the State and War: A Theoretical Analysis* (New York: Columbia University Press, 1959).
9. This discussion relies heavily on James E. Dougherty and Robert L. Pfaltzgraff, *Contending Theories of International Relations*, 2nd ed. (New York: Harper & Row, 1981), pp. 183–189, 215–218, 251–254, 302–324, 333, 342, 353–355, 373–377; and Lloyd Jensen, *Explaining Foreign Policy* (Englewood Cliffs, N.J.: Prentice-Hall, 1982), pp. 17–21, 61–68, 113, 152, 160–161, 181–189, 214–218, 254–258.
10. For such a view, see Karen A. Rasler and William Thompson, "Global War, Public Debts, and the Long Cycle," *World Politics* 35 (1983): 489–516.
11. For example, Bernice A. Carroll, Clinton F. Fisk, and Jane Mohraz, *Peace and War: A Guide to Bibliographies* (Santa Barbara, Calif.: ABC-Clio, 1983).
12. Jensen, *Explaining Foreign Policy,* p. 215; and Dougherty and Pfaltzgraff, *Contending Theories,* p. 339.

13. For a general discussion of costs and benefits, see Beer, *Peace against War,* pp. 118–130.
14. Alexander George, David Hall, and William Simons, *The Limits of Coercive Diplomacy,* (Boston: Little, Brown, 1971).
15. Barry Blechman and Stephen Kaplan, "U.S. Military Forces as a Political Instrument," *Political Science Quarterly* 94 (1979): 193–210.
16. Beer, *Peace against War,* p. 47.
17. Hans Morgenthau, *Politics among Nations,* p. 361.
18. Thomas C. Schelling, *Arms and Influence* (New Haven, Conn.: Yale University Press, 1966), pp. 1–34.
19. This section on goals relies on William V. O'Brien, *The Conduct of Just and Limited War* (New York: Praeger, 1981), pp. 234–237. Also see John Garnett, "Limited War," in John Baylis, Ken Booth, John Garnett, and Phil Williams, *Contemporary Strategy* (New York: Holmes & Meier, 1975), pp. 114–131.
20. O'Brien, *Conduct of Just and Limited War,* pp. 238–256.
21. Ibid., pp. 222–237.
22. This section relies heavily on Richard Smoke, *War: Controlling Escalation* (Cambridge, Mass.: Harvard University Press, 1977). Also see Robert E. Osgood, *Limited War Revisited* (Boulder, Colo.: Westview Press, 1979), especially pp. 15–32.
23. For some scenarios, see Herman Kahn, *On Escalation: Metaphors and Scenarios,* rev. ed. (Baltimore: Penguin, 1968).
24. For three case studies on the rules and (de)escalation, see Baylis, Booth, Garnett, and Williams, *Contemporary Strategy,* chaps. 10 (Korea), 11 (Vietnam), and 12 (Yom Kippur, 1973). On Vietnam, see Osgood, *Limited War,* pp. 33–52.
25. For a discussion of the issue of limited nuclear war, see Ian Clark, *Limited Nuclear War: Political Theory and War Conventions* (Princeton, N.J.: Princeton University Press, 1982). Tactical warhead estimates are from William Arkin, Thomas B. Cochran, and Melton M. Hoenig, "Resource Paper on the U.S. Nuclear Arsenal," *Bulletin of Atomic Scientists* 40 (September, 1984), table 4, p. 10S.
26. See Boleslaw Adam Boczek, "NATO and the Warsaw Pact: The Present and Future," in *The Warsaw Pact: Political Purpose and Military Means,* ed. Robert W. Clawson and Lawrence S. Kaplan (Wilmington, Del.: Scholarly Resources, 1982), p. 97. Also see T. B. Millar, *The East-West Strategic Balance* (London: Allen & Unwin, 1981), chap. 4, "The Military Equation in the European Theater," pp. 58–75.
27. For an overall view, see William R. Van Cleave and S. T. Cohen, *Tactical Nuclear Weapons* (New York: Crane, Russak, 1978).
28. *New York Times,* November 5, 1981, p. A1.
29. Robert McNamara, McGeorge Bundy, George Kennan, and Gerard Smith, "Nuclear Weapons and the Atlantic Alliance," *Foreign Affairs* 60 (1982): 753–768.
30. *Time,* April 29, 1982, p. 18.
31. *New York Times,* March 4, 1982, p. A6, and March 13, 1983, p. A12.
32. This section on targeting relies on David N. Schwartz, *NATO's Nuclear Dilemmas* (Washington, D.C.: Brookings Institution, 1983), especially chaps. 1 and 7. There are also several good readings in part 2: "Strategic and Military Problems of the Alliance," in *NATO: The Next Thirty Years,* ed. Kenneth A. Myers (Boulder, Colo.: Westview Press, 1980). Also see Paul Buterix, "NATO and Long-Range Theater Nuclear Weapons," in *The Crisis in Western Security,* ed. Lawrence S. Hagen (New York: St. Martin's Press, 1982), pp. 152–167.
33. Colin S. Gray, *Strategic Studies and Public Policy* (Lexington: University of Kentucky Press, 1982), pp. 102–107, 138–146.

34. Donald Frei, *Risks of Unintentional War* (Totowa, N.J.: Allanheld, Osum, 1983), p. 3.
35. U.S. Congress, Senate Committee on Armed Services, *Recent False Alerts from the Nation's Missile Attack Warning System,* A Report, 96th Cong., 2nd sess. (1980).
36. *Time,* March 29, 1983, p. 23, quoting "The Medical Consequences of Nuclear War" by the Physicians for Social Responsibility, published in March 1980.
37. Deputy Under Secretary of Defense Thomas K. Jones, quoted in Robert Scheer, *With Enough Shovels* (New York: Random House, 1982), p. 18. On the MAD/NUT debate, see Spurgeon M. Keeny, Jr., and Wolfgang Panofsky, "MAD versus NUT," in *The Nuclear Reader,* ed. Charles W. Kegley and Eugene R. Wittkopf (New York: St. Martin's Press, 1985), pp. 77–84.
38. Phil Williams, "Deterrence," in Baylis, Booth, Garnett, and Williams, *Contemporary Strategy,* p. 67.
39. Colin S. Gray, *Strategic Studies: A Critical Assessment* (Westport, Conn.: Greenwood Press, 1982), p. 87.
40. Dougherty and Pfaltzgraff, *Contending Theories,* p. 388.
41. *Time,* March 29, 1982, p. 22; *New York Times,* May 30, 1982, p. A1. Also see Gray, *Strategic Studies and Public Policy,* pp. 146–160.
42. This is derived from Henry Kissinger. See his early thoughts in *A World Restored—Europe after Napoleon* (New York: Grosset & Dunlap, 1964), pp. 1–4; and his later *White House Years* (Boston: Little, Brown, 1979), p. 232.
43. This section relies heavily on Gray, *Strategic Studies and Public Policy,* pp. 146–160; and Jerome H. Kahn, *Security in the Nuclear Age* (Washington, D.C.: Brookings Institution, 1975), pp. 166–169, 228–233.
44. Jonathan B. Tucker, "Strategic Command and Control Vulnerabilities," *Orbis* 26 (1983): 941–963.
45. This discussion relies heavily on Norman Polmar, *Strategic Weapons,* rev. ed. (New York: Crane, Russak, 1982).
46. Robert A. Hoover, *The MX Controversy* (Claremont, Calif.: Penguin Books, 1982), pp. 5, 30.
47. For a good overview, see U.S. Comptroller General, General Accounting Office, *Chemical Warfare: Many Unanswered Questions,* Report to the Committee on Foreign Affairs (GAO/IPE-83-6), April 29, 1983. The United States has, however, used chemicals, such as Agent Orange, that are indirectly injurious.
48. H. B. Schiefer, "The Possible Use of Chemical Warfare Agents in Southeast Asia," *Conflict Quarterly* 3 (1983): 32–41.
49. *Time,* November 9, 1981, p. 55.
50. Van Cleave and Cohen, *Tactical Nuclear Weapons,* pp. 33–42.
51. Ashton B. Carter and Davo N. Schwartz, eds., *Ballistic Missile Defense* (Washington, D.C.: Brookings Institution, 1984).
52. Donald M. Snow, "Laser, Charged-Particle Beams, and the Strategic Future," *Political Science Quarterly* 95 (1980): 277–294.
53. For general studies on these issues, see Thomas Karas, *The New High Ground* (New York: Simon & Schuster, 1983); and Curtis Peebles, *Battle for Space* (New York: Beaufort Books, 1983).
54. *Time,* March 11, 1985, p. 20.
55. Gray, *Strategic Studies,* p. 110.
56. John F. Troxell, "Soviet Civil Defense and the American Response," *Military Review* 63 (1983): 36–46; Carsten M. Haalard and Conrad V. Chester, "Will Technology

Make Shelters Obsolete?," *Orbis* 25 (1981): 771–798; *New York Times,* April 4, 1982, p. E6, and April 8, 1982, p. B8.

57. Small and Singer, "Conflicts in the International System," table 4, p. 68.
58. For the causes, see Dougherty and Pfaltzgraff, *Contending Theories of International Relations,* pp. 312–325.
59. Small and Singer, "Conflicts in the International System," table 4, p. 68. Also see Beer, *Peace against War,* pp. 31–36, 66.
60. Camille Rougeron, "The Historical Dimension of Guerrilla Warfare," in *Guerrilla Strategies,* ed. Gerard Chaliand (Berkeley: University of California Press, 1982), p. 40. Also Walter Thomas, *Guerrilla Warfare: Causes and Conflict* (Washington, D.C.: National Defense University Press, 1981).
61. William Pomeroy, ed., *Guerrilla Warfare and Marxism* (New York: International Publishers, 1968).
62. Walter Laqueur, *Guerrilla* (Boston: Little, Brown, 1976), pp. vii–xii, 3, 47, 326–409.
63. Douglas S. Blaufarb, *The Counterinsurgency Era* (New York: Free Press, 1977); and Theodore Shackley, *The Third Option: An American View of Counterinsurgency Operations* (New York: McGraw-Hill, 1981).

9

Diplomacy

The better part of valor is discretion.
Shakespeare, King Henry IV

And sheathed their swords for lack of argument.
Shakespeare, King Henry V

Blessed are the peacemakers on earth.
Shakespeare, King Henry VI

Diplomacy as Communication

We often think of diplomacy in stereotypic terms. There is an image of somber negotiations over green-felt-covered tables in ornate rooms. Modern diplomacy certainly includes such interactions, but it also extends much further. Indeed, diplomacy includes the entire range of communications between two or more governments.

As a *communications process,* diplomacy has two elements. The first element is *negotiation.* When two parties are talking with each other, either directly or through an intermediary, they are negotiating. The second aspect of diplomacy is *signaling*—saying or doing something with the intent of sending a message to another government. When leaders make bellicose or conciliatory speeches, when military forces are alerted or relaxed, when trade privileges are granted or sanctions invoked, or when diplomatic recognition is extended or relations are broken, these events are, or at least should be, signals. Indeed, the use of military power is a form of signaling. As Clausewitz said, war is not the end of diplomacy but a continuation. Military action can be designed as a signaling process to attain goals rather than to defeat enemies, and nonviolent signals and negotiation should continue during conflict.

The Evolution of Diplomacy

Diplomacy is as old as recorded history and almost certainly even predates it. Modern diplomacy has its origins in the practices of the Greek city-states, and this section will examine their contribution as well as the diplomatic practices of Rome, Byzantium, the Italian city-states, France, and nineteenth-century Europe. This historical review will bring us to about World War I, which marks the transition from the "old" diplomacy to the "new" diplomacy. Current diplomatic trends will then be discussed in the following section.[1]

Greece and Rome

It is in the writings of ancient Greece that we first encounter many of the terms (such as reconciliation, truce, alliance, and commercial treaty) used in modern diplomacy. Diplomatic missions are also described in the Homeric epics. Ambassadors were dispatched on an ad hoc (case by case) basis. Negotiations were conducted orally, but treaties were written. The Greeks also recognized neutrality, used arbitration, and had officials charged with furthering commercial relations. Rules concerning the declaration and conduct of war, maritime practice, the status of aliens, and other principles that remain important today were also evident in Greek practice.

Rome, which practiced conquest more than diplomacy, was important for organizational improvements on Greek practice. Ambassadorial appointments, instructions, and status became more formalized. Diplomatic immunity became more widely recognized, at least in theory. The Romans, with their penchant for laws, also stressed the sanctity of contracts, thus elevating the status of treaties.

Byzantium

The Byzantine Empire, which flourished after Rome's collapse, was noted for the beginnings of "professional" diplomacy. Diplomats were specifically trained as negotiators, and the first department of foreign affairs was established. In an age of chaos, and surrounded by powerful barbarian foes, the Byzantines also emphasized the darker sides of diplomacy, such as deceit and spying. They also created elaborate protocol procedures for military reviews and homage to the emperor designed to enhance beyond reality the image of Byzantine strength.

The Italian City-States

The diplomacy of the Italian states beginning in the fifteenth century is best known for its improvements on the Byzantine practices of cunning and artifice. The names Niccolò Machiavelli of Florence and Cosimo de' Medici, Duke of Florence, are synonymous with scheming conduct. Machiavelli counseled that it was best to be as powerful as a lion and as sly as a fox and summed up his estimation of human nature with the observation that one "must start with assuming that all men are bad and ever ready to display their vicious nature whenever they may find occasion for it."[2]

The Italian city-states also made more positive contributions to the evolution of diplomacy. They first established permanent diplomatic missions. Treaty making and protocol were improved. Summit meetings were also introduced as a diplomatic practice.

The French System

The direct predecessor of modern diplomacy is the French system, which is strongly identified with the contributions of Cardinal Richelieu in the seventeenth century. He was the first to see diplomacy as an ongoing process rather than a short-term expediency. He also began the practice of building public opinion support. Honoring treaties became an ethical as well as a pragmatic responsibility. Richelieu also insisted on precision in drafting agreements and consolidated all foreign affairs functions under one ministry.

Under Louis XIV, the minister of foreign affairs became a member of the king's cabinet, and permanent embassies were established in all the major capitals, with lesser-ranked missions in minor capitals. It was also during this era that the first diplomatic manual was written.[3]

Europe in the Nineteenth Century

The post-Napoleonic congresses at Vienna (1815) and Aix-la-Chapelle (1818) were important in codifying the status and functions of diplomatic agents. The nineteenth century was also both the height and the beginning of the end of the "old" style of diplomacy. Kings and emperors still held sway in a world dominated by Europe, but the American and French revolutions signaled the onset of the decline and fall of that system. Diplomacy of that day was characterized by Eurocentrism, great-power status, executive control, elite conduct, secrecy, and bilateral negotiations.[4]

Eurocentrism. In the 1800s, Europe was the center of the globe. America was isolated behind its oceans, and the rest of the world was either impotent or colonized.

Great-power status. The six great powers (Great Britain, France, Italy, Austria-Hungary, Prussia-Germany, and Russia) were considered to have both special status and special responsibilities.[5] Lesser states were bullied and sometimes divided up among the big six. Intervention and imperialism were common. The powers also had a special ability to maintain order, both by "policing" minor powers and colonial dependencies and by consulting and maintaining a balance of power among themselves. It was a system that worked reasonably well for a century before it catastrophically collapsed with World War I.

Executive control. Foreign policy making was dominated by the king. Louis XIV quite literally believed, "I am the state." Richelieu was concerned with public opinion, and legislatures were gaining power in Britain and America, but democracy was still the exception rather than the rule.

Elite conduct. The diplomatic corps was recruited exclusively from the nobility and gentry. It was an era when that class had similar values and members often were even related. Great Britain's King Edward VII, Germany's Kaiser Wilhelm II, and Russia's Czar Nicholas II were all cousins. Nationalism was developing, but to a substantial degree the elite diplomats were "men of Europe" who had as much loyalty, or more, to the "system" of elite and great-power dominance as to their national entities. In part, this elitism provided a common frame of reference and a mutual confidence that benefited negotiations.

Secrecy. Diplomats of the nineteenth century adhered to the belief that public negotiations caused undue posturing and a reluctance to compromise. Negotiations were almost always confidential and treaties were often secret.

Bilateral negotiations. Although there were a few noted multilateral conferences, such as the Congress of Vienna, **bilateral diplomacy** (direct negotiations between two countries) was the normal form of negotiation. Practitioners felt not only that conference diplomacy was slow and cumbersome but also that it confused the power relationships on which international relations hinged.

Modern Diplomacy

Although diplomatic practice has evolved slowly over the centuries, the years around World War I—symbolized by Woodrow Wilson's Fourteen Points—are generally recognized as a benchmark in the transition to modern diplomacy as part of the modern political era. The "Great War" was the beginning of the end of European world dominance. It also marked the fall of the German, Austrian, Ottoman, and Russian emperors. Nationalistic self-determination was on the rise in Europe and other parts of the world. New powers—the United States, Japan, and China—were beginning to rise and join or replace the declining European powers. The "old diplomacy" did not vanish, but it was substantially changed in the decades following the "war to end all wars." As will become clear, the "new diplomacy" is characterized by an expansion of geographic scope, multilateral diplomacy, parliamentarianism, democratization, open diplomacy, and summitry. Each of these new practices has been greeted as a "reform," but as we will see, the changes have not necessarily been for the better.

Expansion of Geographic Scope

The diplomacy of the twentieth century has been marked by expansion of its geographic scope. The two Hague peace conferences (1899, 1907), particularly the second, with its forty-four participants, included countries outside the European sphere. President Wilson's call for national self-determination foreshadowed a world of over 150 countries. Today, the United Nations, with its nearly universal membership, symbolizes the truly global scope of diplomacy.

Multilateral Diplomacy

Although conferences involving a number of nations occurred at times during the nineteenth century, that practice has expanded greatly in the modern era. The rise of **multilateral diplomacy** is symbolized by Woodrow Wilson's call for a League of Nations. There are now a number of permanent world and regional international organizations. Ad hoc conferences and treaties are also more apt to be multilateral. Before 1900, for example, the United States attended an average of one multilateral conference per year. Currently, American diplomats average more than one such conference per day.[6]

The United Nations General Assembly, pictured here, and other international bodies are the scene of parliamentary diplomacy involving general debate and voting.

Parliamentary Diplomacy

Parliamentary diplomacy, which includes debate and voting in international organizations, now sometimes supplants negotiation, compromise, and accord as the vehicle of diplomacy. Furthermore, with the decline of the legitimacy of great-power special status and responsibility, voting is often done on the basis of sovereign equality, China and Chad each casting one vote. The old system has not completely died out, however, and the UN Security Council, dominated by the five permanent members and their veto power, is the primary example (see Chapter 13).

Democratization

The elite and executive-dominant character of diplomacy has changed in a number of ways. One is that diplomats are drawn from a wider segment of each country's society. This has the advantage of making diplomats more representative of their nations and more sympathetic to the individuals therein. It also means, though, that diplomats have lost their common frame of reference and are apt to suffer from the antagonisms and misperceptions that nationalistic stereotyping causes.

A second democratic change is the rise of the roles of legislatures and public opinion in foreign policy making. Executive leadership still dominates that process, but it is no longer the exclusive domain of princes, presidents, and prime ministers. The rise in representative and popular power is certainly in accord with democratic theory, but it has its drawbacks. Democracy is too often impatient, crusading, and xenophobic, and executives have lost a degree of flexibility. Legislative and public opinion is also usually less well informed than the executive, although information and wise policy are far from synonymous.

Open Diplomacy

Of Wilson's Fourteen Points, his call for "open covenants, openly arrived at" is the best remembered. One advantage of **open diplomacy** is that it fits nicely with the idea of democracy. It also has the potential of avoiding perceptual errors that can occur if an opponent misjudges your commitments. Offsetting these advantages are several drawbacks. The majority of scholarly and practitioner commentary favors both open discussion of foreign policy goals and public treaties. It is the "openly arrived at," or negotiation, phase that is troublesome. Here, most analysts agree that confidentiality is important. Early disclosure of your bargaining strategy will compromise your ability to win concessions. Public negotiations are also more likely to lead diplomats to posture for public consumption. Concessions may be difficult to make amid popular criticism. In short, it is difficult to negotiate (or to play chess) with someone kibitzing over your shoulder.

Finally, it should be added that even secret treaties and understandings are not totally without merit. There are times when a desirable agreement cannot be made in public. The agreement ending the 1962 Cuban missile crisis included an oral pledge by the United States never to invade Cuba. President Kennedy would have found it difficult to give that assurance in public. U.S. involvement in the Vietnam War ended with North Vietnam's seeming to agree not to forcibly conquer the South in return for a pledge of over a billion capitalist dollars in U.S. foreign aid. Neither country could have made that agreement in public.

Summitry

Modern transportation has spawned an upsurge of high-level diplomacy. National leaders regularly hold bi- or multilateral summit conferences, and foreign ministers and other ranking diplomats jet between countries, conducting shuttle diplomacy. One hundred thirty years of American history passed before a president (Woodrow Wilson) traveled overseas while in office. Richard Nixon departed on his first state visit to Europe only thirty-three days after his inauguration. In early 1985 the funeral of Konstantin Chernenko occasioned the journey of the leaders of Britain, France, West Germany, India, Canada, and other countries to Moscow to meet his successor, Mikhail Gorbachev. Further, within three days of assuming power, Gorbachev had accepted invitations to visit Paris and Bonn and was considering a proposal by Reagan that he come to Washington. Indeed, given this century's transportation and communica-

After 30 years of hostility and war between their countries, Egypt's President Sadat and Israel's Prime Minister Begin were able to reach an accord at Camp David. Summits are risky but sometimes they pay off.

tions, national leaders have often become chief diplomats in practice as well as theory.

The advent of globe-trotting, leader-to-leader diplomacy, or **summitry**, is a mixed blessing. First among its *advantages* is that leaders can sometimes make dramatic breakthroughs. The Camp David accords were produced after President Carter, Egypt's president Anwar Sadat, and Israel's prime minister Menachem Begin isolated themselves at the presidential retreat in Maryland. Second, it can be argued that reciprocal visits help leaders gain firsthand impressions of their counterparts and their cultures. Lack of international contacts increases stereotyping and other misperceptions. A third advantage of personal contact among leaders is that mutual confidence or even friendship may develop. Henry Kissinger recalls that even though they were a "strange pair, Brezhnev and Nixon ultimately developed a modus vivendi because they came to understand the other's perception of his self-interest."[7]

Summit diplomacy also has strong *disadvantages.* The first is that it may lead to ill-conceived agreements. According to Kissinger, "Some of the debacles of our diplomatic history have been perpetrated by Presidents who fancied themselves negotiators."[8] Second, mistakes made by lower-ranking officials can be disavowed by their superiors. "When Presidents become negotiators no escape routes are left. . . . Concessions are irrevocable without dishonor."[9] Third, and again in Kissinger's words, leaders are afflicted with a "healthy dose of ego and "negotiations can rapidly deteriorate from intractability to confrontation."[10] In other words, contact may bring animosity instead of cordiality. Tensions between the United States and India during the early 1970s were heightened because "Nixon had no time for Mrs. Gandhi's condescending manner. Privately he scoffed at her moral pretensions, which he found all the more irritating because he suspected that . . . she had in fact fewer scruples than he."[11] Fourth, and finally, the failure of summitry can lead to increased tensions. High-level negotiations create hope; when they collapse, the resulting disappointment and mutual recriminations can leave matters worse than before. If a summit conference is the ultimate negotiation, then its failure makes it seem that no solution is possible. In such a case conflict may be the response.[12]

Diplomacy: A Game of Angels and Devils

Ambassador William Macomber has described diplomacy as "the angels' game."[13] That is in sharp contrast to Sir Henry Wooten's infamous characterization of a diplomat as an "honest man sent to lie for his country." In fact, neither characterization is true. Diplomacy is not the domain of the heavens or the darker regions. Nor is it as mysterious as bystanders and practitioners make it out to be. It is, in the last analysis, a combination of human interaction and state policy making. It is a necessary art that requires a breadth of vision and a precise mind. In the following sections we will explore diplomacy by looking at the functions of diplomats, the rules for effective diplomacy, diplomatic options, and conflict resolution.

Functions of Diplomacy

Diplomacy is carried on by a variety of officials with titles such as president, minister, ambassador, or special envoy, and it is worthwhile to explore the roles that those officials and other diplomats play.[14]

Observe and report. A primary diplomatic role has always been to gather information and impressions and to analyze and report these back to the home office.[15] This mostly includes routine activity, such as reading newspapers and reporting observations, but it also may involve espionage. As the next chapter indicates, many embassies contain a considerable covert element. Whatever the method, it is important for policy makers to know both the facts and the mood of foreign capitals, and the embassy is a primary source.

In some ways, the importance of the ambassador as an observer and reporter has declined. High-level policy makers are more likely to visit countries themselves, but they also bring back and share valuable insights and information. Countries are also far less isolated from one another, and there are many new information-gathering techniques. The result is that diplomatic

Leaders are symbols of their country. The attractiveness and charm of John and Jacqueline Kennedy, pictured here with French President de Gaulle, enhanced America's image.

reports compete with many other sources of information. This fact is offset, however, by the expansion of diplomatic focus. Diplomatic interest now includes economics and culture as well as politics as such, and thus there are many more facets of a foreign state to ascertain and analyze.

Negotiate. Diplomats also negotiate. Here the ambassadorial function has been partly supplanted by the globe-trotting diplomacy of presidents and foreign ministers. Still, there are many countries and many issues, and the ambassador is responsible for ironing out many major and minor issues with the host country.

Symbolically represent. Diplomats are, to a degree, the personification of their country. If ambassadors speak the language and respect the customs of the country to which they are accredited, and if they are intelligent, dignified, tactful, charming, and discreet and have integrity and patience, then they are apt to make a good impression. Diplomats, be they presidents or ambassadors, can be as winning as a fine wine, and "champagne is the lubricant of diplomacy."[16] The reverse characteristics can quickly alienate people. When, on a state visit to Mexico, President Carter was indisposed with diarrhea, and his condition was described as "Montezuma's revenge," it was roughly equivalent to telling a Polish joke in Warsaw. President Lopez-Portillo was not amused.

Certainly, with today's modern communications and transportation, there are many images of any one country that are projected. But day in and day out, the ambassador represents *the* official image of his or her country and society.

Intervene. Diplomats can sometimes tell a country what to do. Soviet representatives to some Eastern European countries combine the roles of diplomat and proconsul. They attempt to persuade, but they can also issue directives. American diplomats can also play that role in some weaker and/or dependent states. When South Vietnam resisted the U.S.-negotiated settlement, President Nixon cabled President Thieu that "all military and economic aid will be cut off . . . if an agreement is not reached" and that "I have . . . irrevocably decided to proceed . . . to sign [the agreement]. . . . I will do so, if necessary, alone . . . [and] explain that your government obstructs peace." As the United States' chief diplomat, Nixon was being distinctly undiplomatic. "Brutality is nothing," he told Kissinger. "You have never seen it if this son-of-a-bitch doesn't go along, believe me."[17] Thieu went along.

Propagandize. Diplomacy is also sometimes conducted for its propaganda value. Even where there is little hope for settlement, it may benefit a country's image to appear reasonable or to make opponents seem stubborn. As Nikita Khrushchev told a diplomat, "Never forget the appeal that the idea of disarmament has to the outside world. All you have to say is 'I'm in favor of it,' and it pays big dividends."[18]

The Rules of Effective Diplomacy

Diplomacy is an art. There is therefore no single formula for conducting successful negotiations and signaling. There are, however, a number of standards that can enhance the chances of effective diplomacy.[19]

Be realistic. It is important to have goals that match your ability to achieve them. As Kissinger has pointed out, "The test of a statesman . . . is his ability to recognize the real relationship of forces."[20] President Roosevelt has been criticized for "acquiescing" at Yalta (1945) to Soviet domination of Poland, but the fact is that the Red Army had already occupied the country, and only war would have dislodged the Soviets. Roosevelt wisely accommodated himself to the inevitable and concentrated on "winnable" points. "Dreaming the impossible dream" makes for a charming Don Quixote, but it is not effective diplomacy.

Avoid being dogmatic. A good negotiator shuns the temptation to think his or her position is morally superior. Crusading is better for rhetoric than for diplomacy. Almost any negotiation will involve some concessions, so it is important to maintain a degree of flexibility and not to slam the door on proposals before they are fully explored.

Understand the other side. Information about the facts, personality, and point of view of the other country is invaluable. It helps the diplomat know what his or her bargaining opponents may concede, what they will not, and what they have to back up their position. "Know thine enemy," as the old saying goes. As a corollary, it is also wise to make sure that thine enemy knows thee. Errors are a major cause of conflict, and they result from misperceptions based on cultural differences and the lack of or wrong information.[21]

Search for common interests. Unless you want war or unless you are willing to surrender to any demand to avoid conflict, it is necessary to search for common ground. This can include shared interests (such as avoiding war), compromises (on the half-a-loaf theory), or barters, in which each side trades concessions on different issues.

Compromise on nonvital issues. Most diplomats counsel that it is important to distinguish your central from your peripheral values. Intransigence over a minor point, when a concession can bring a counterconcession on an issue important to you, is folly. There is some research indicating that concessions, even unilateral ones, are likely to engender positive responses.[22]

Be patient. It is also important to bide your time. Being overly anxious can lead to concessions that are unwise and may convey weakness to an opponent.[23] As a corollary, it is poor practice to set deadlines, on yourself or others, unless you are in a very strong position or you do not really want an agreement.

Leave avenues of retreat open. It is said that even a rat will fight if you trap it in a corner. The same is true for countries. Call it honor, face, or prestige, it is important to leave yourself and your opponent an "out." "Either/or" ultimatums, especially public challenges, often lead to war. Austria's timed ultimatum to Serbia in 1914 led to World War I. By contrast, President Kennedy's care to allow the Soviets to withdraw their missiles gracefully from Cuba in 1962 averted World War III.

Options in Negotiation and Signaling

Although there are a few good rules to follow in diplomacy, the practice is more art than science. Effective diplomacy must tailor its approach to the situation and the opponent. In doing so, diplomats have to choose the channel, level, visibility, type of inducement, precision, method of communication, and extent of linkage that they will use.[24]

Channel: Direct or Indirect

One issue diplomats face is whether to negotiate directly with each other or indirectly, through an intermediary. *Direct negotiations* have the advantage of avoiding the misinterpretations that an intermediary third party might cause. As in the old game of "Gossip," messages can get garbled. Direct negotiations are also quicker. An additional plus is that they can act as a symbol. When, in

1969, the United States finally was ready to talk directly with China, Henry Kissinger instructed the U.S. ambassador to Poland (where periodic secret U.S./PRC meetings had been taking place) "to walk up to the Ambassador of the People's Republic at the next social function they both attended." It was a precedent-breaking move meant to signal not only China but also the Soviets of impending U.S./Chinese collaboration.[25] Also indicative of the heavy symbolism of the U.S. gesture was the Chinese ambassador's reaction. Ambassador Stoessel's chance to speak to the Chinese chargé finally came at a fashion show sponsored by the Yugoslav embassy. A model appeared wearing a see-through wedding dress, and the always decorous Chinese diplomat got up to leave. He was further unnerved to see Stoessel heading in his direction. "He looked scared and made for the stairs," the ambassador recalls. "He was running up the stairs and I was right behind him." Out the door they raced. "It was dark. It was snowing. It was cold. . . . I [finally] got him," Stoessel triumphantly concluded. Public Sino-American contact had begun.[26]

Indirect negotiations may also be advisable. Direct contact symbolizes a level of legitimacy that a country may not wish to convey. Israel, for instance, has refused to recognize or openly and directly negotiate with the Palestine Liberation Organization, because that would symbolize acceptance. It is well reported, however, that necessity has led to contact with the PLO, at times through intermediaries, to exchange prisoners and to explore other points.

Indirect diplomacy can also avoid the embarrassment of a public rebuff by the other side. During the opening moves between the United States and China, oral messages were sent through the "good offices" of Pakistan and Rumania, and written messages were exchanged on photocopy paper with no letterheads or signatures.[27]

Level of Contact: High or Low

The higher the level of contact, the more seriously a message will be taken. It implies a greater commitment, and there will be a greater reaction. Therefore, a diplomat must decide whether to communicate on a high or a low level.

A *high level of diplomacy* has its advantages. When a president, premier, or Communist Party leader speaks or writes, it is seriously noted in other capitals. Thus, when you wish your communication to be both immediately received and given great weight, it is best to have it issued from the highest level. When President Carter wanted to let Iran know that harming the hostages would cause a dangerous U.S. reaction, he said so himself and publicly.

There are other times when *low-level communications* are wiser. One attempt to negotiate with Iran during the hostage crisis involved sending two former U.S. officials to Teheran. Their mission collapsed, however, "due to the announcement that they were presidential emissaries." The Ayatollah Khomeini decreed that no Iranian official would meet with any American official. "It was a bad mistake," Secretary of State Cyrus Vance recalls. "Had their mission been kept unofficial and out of the spotlight, Khomeini might have received them."[28]

Low-level communications also avoid overreaction and maintain flexibility. Dire threats can be issued by generals and then, if later thought unwise, disavowed by higher political officers. Lower-level communications are also read as "trends in thinking" or "one viewpoint" rather than "official policy" and can be backed away from with no loss of face.

Visibility: Public or Private

Another diplomatic choice is whether to communicate in public or in private. *Public communications* have high symbolic value, just like direct communications. They increase credibility. During the U.S./PRC diplomatic dance, a major advance was achieved when the American ambassador to Warsaw was invited to the Chinese embassy there. He offered "to arrive discreetly at the rear door" but was told by the Chinese that "the main entrance was eminently suitable," presumably, Kissinger concludes, "to avoid any chance that Soviet intelligence might miss the occasion."[29]

Public communications also have the advantage of speed. During the Cuban missile crisis, urgent messages between Premier Khrushchev and President Kennedy were communicated at times via Radio Moscow and the Voice of America.

Private communications can also be useful. They may allow messages that, for diplomatic or domestic reasons, would be difficult to state publicly. In particular, they allow for the exploration of new and unpopular paths and avoid outbreaks of domestic or international opposition. It is also far easier to retreat from a position taken in private than one taken in public. Hence, when bluffing or uncertain, it is better to communicate confidentially.

Type of Inducement: Coercion or Reward

Yet another diplomatic choice is whether to use carrots or sticks. To induce an opponent to react as you wish, is it better to offer rewards or to threaten punishment?[30]

Coercive diplomacy, as we have seen, can be effective when you have the power, will, and credibility to back it up.[31] Such action can be directly communicated, with the 1962 blockade of Cuba a successful example. Coercion can also be communicated indirectly. In 1978, U.S. National Security Adviser Zbigniew Brzezinski told President Carter: "A President must not only be loved and respected, but also feared. I suggest that you try to dispel the impression that you . . . are too cerebral by picking some controversial subject and acting with anger and roughness to demonstrate that no one can pick a fight. If we do not do this soon, [foreign leaders] . . . will thumb their noses at us."[32]

At other times, *offers of rewards* may be a more powerful inducement. The alternative, coercion, may lead to war with high costs and uncertain results. It may also be possible to "buy" what you cannot "win." One song in *Mary Poppins* includes the wisdom that "a spoonful of sugar makes the medicine go down," and an increase in aid, a trade concession, a state visit, or some other tangible or symbolic reward may induce agreement. This is particularly true when dealing with allies or with stronger, hostile countries.[33]

Precision: Precise or Vague

Most diplomatic experts maintain that it is important to be precise when communicating. There are times, however, when purposeful vagueness may be in order.

Precision is a hallmark of diplomacy. Being precise when communicating and, especially, when negotiating agreements helps avoid later misunderstandings. Diplomats are often accused of wrangling over minute and seemingly inconsequential details, but those nuances may turn out to be very important. The seeming triumph of the 1978 Camp David accords on the Middle East was later tarnished by Israel's refusal to refrain from building new settlements in disputed Egyptian/Israeli territory. Because there was room for interpretation, each side felt it had been betrayed by the other.[34]

In some instances *vagueness* may be a better strategy. Such a tactic may "paper over" an irreconcilable difference. It is especially appropriate when, in a weak position, it allows retreat with honor, and/or when an agreement is more important than the details. The American/North Vietnamese peace accord called for the withdrawal of all "foreign" troops from the South. American troops were obviously foreign, but were North Vietnamese troops also foreign? That ambiguity allowed each side to do what it wanted. The United States left; North Vietnam stayed.

Method of Communication: Word or Deed

Diplomacy can communicate either by word or by action. Each has its advantages.

Oral and written communications are appropriate for negotiations and are often a good signaling strategy. They can establish position at a minimum cost and are more apt to maintain flexibility than active signaling.

Signaling by action also has its uses. It is often more dramatic than verbal signals. During the 1961 Berlin crisis, President Kennedy could have affirmed the U.S. commitment to that city while in Washington, but the fact that he *went* to Berlin was even more demonstrative. Verbal threats of military action are one thing; alerting forces, changing deployments, or actually committing to combat are even more persuasive. It must be remembered, however, that, hard as it is to take back words, it is even harder to "undo" deeds. And although actions indeed speak louder than words, they are also more likely to cause a strong counterreaction and intransigence by an opponent.

Linkage: Separate or Linked

A final question diplomats must decide is whether to "link" negotiations on one issue to the overall state of two countries' relations.

Proponents of **linkage diplomacy** contend that it is foolish to try to deal with another country outside the general framework of relations. Henry Kissinger, a champion of linkage diplomacy, explains that he and Nixon believed that "events in different parts of the world . . . were related to each other; . . . we proceeded from the premise that to separate them into distinct compartments would encourage the Soviet leaders to believe that they could use cooperation in one area as a safety valve while striving for unilateral advantages elsewhere. This was unacceptable."[35]

Opponents of linkage strongly disagree. They argue that if an agreement, such as an arms treaty, is in your national interest, you should sign it regardless of what the other side is up to elsewhere. If a treaty is not in your interest, you should not sign it no matter how generally well behaved your opponent is. Cyrus Vance told President Carter that "we should accept the fact of competition with the Soviets, and we should not link Soviet behavior in the Third World to issues . . . [as] fundamental . . . as SALT."[36] Indeed, linkage opponents are apt to argue that even in a time of bad will and worse behavior, an agreement on one issue may help create a positive climate that will allow settlement of other issues.

Crisis Management

A special area of diplomatic practice is crisis management. In many ways, the process is related to general negotiating and signaling, and the "rules" and "options" discussed above apply to crisis diplomacy as well as less perilous interactions. Skilled crisis management also involves sound decision making (Chapter 3), including a careful evaluation of one's national interest (Chapter 6) and power (Chapter 7).

A **crisis** is a situation in which (1) two or more countries have important national interests involved, (2) there is the possibility of war, and (3) there is a limited time to reach a solution.[37] The high national values, threat of war, and time constraints compress and intensify the diplomatic process and create a special set of considerations.[38]

Assuming that a realistic evaluation of interests and power has occurred and that decision makers are willing to engage in the perilous process of crisis diplomacy rather than immediately fighting or giving way, then there are three simultaneous strategies that can be employed. Two of these involve the power formula—namely, increasing your capabilities and increasing your credibility. The third approach is decreasing your opponent's stakes/values in the confrontation.

Increasing Capability

Military power is the asset that can be most readily increased in a crisis, given its limited time frame. *Assets* can be increased to some degree by speeding up production, calling up reserve forces, or taking equipment out of mothballs. Even if it is impossible to produce equipment or train troops fast enough to be used immediately, initiation of these moves may persuade an opponent that in a protracted conflict your power resources will prove superior.

Readiness is a second capability factor. Undertaking procedures to move your forces from peacetime status to a war footing increases your ability to respond quickly and effectively.

Given the relative nature of power, capability increases have the effect of raising the "net cost" the opponent will have to pay if war occurs. This strategy works best if you have greater potential than the other side. Even if you are weaker, though, it shows that victory will not come cheaply, and it may convince the opponent that victory is not worth the price.

Increasing Credibility

The second vital power element is credibility. Your opponent must be convinced not only that you can but that you *will* act. Your resolve can be demonstrated in several ways:

Proclaim willingness. Statements by leaders that war is better than retreat help create an air of resolve. President Carter's 1980 public proclamation that the United States would use force to keep the Persian Gulf open certainly put others on notice that America would act.

Invoke larger principles. Saying that the issue is linked to world peace, the communist (or capitalist) conspiracy, the domino theory, or other such transcendent values increases your apparent concern. Applying doctrines, such as Monroe's, or principles of behavior, such as the Munich syndrome's "You cannot appease aggression," also increases your apparent resolve.

Proclaim righteousness. Claiming that what you are doing is legitimate increases the perception that you will act. Invoking international law is one legitimizing technique. Obtaining a supportive vote in the United Nations or some other international organization is another. A third is getting "invited" in, as the United States was in Lebanon and the Soviet Union was in Afghanistan.

Invoke alliance obligations. Saying you must act because a solemn alliance leaves no choice increases credibility. The American pledge to defend Western Europe, nuclearly if necessary, is more credible because of the NATO treaty than it would be if it were just administration policy.

Invoke national honor. Resolve is enhanced by statements that you will be morally disgraced and/or will lose prestige if you shirk the challenge.

Claim you are losing control. Statements that domestic pressure is too great to resist or that subordinates may take things into their own hands up the ante.

Pretend irrationality. Hitler was particularly good at appearing crazily committed to war unless he got an immediate concession.

Engage in military demonstrations. Sending ships to a trouble area, having "practice" military maneuvers, or actually engaging in limited combat also increases perception of resolve. In recent years the United States has regularly conducted military maneuvers off the coast of or in countries near Nicaragua during times of tension.

Decreasing Your Opponent's Stakes

While you are increasing your power, and thus the perceived likelihood of conflict and the net cost to your opponent, it is also sound strategy to try to lower the other side's stakes, to make the issue seem less vital to your opponent. Whereas increasing power adds to the *costs* an opponent will have to pay, decreasing *stakes/values* is meant to make the conflict less important and not worth the cost. Tactics include the following:

Stress the limited nature of your goals. Statements that you do not want to threaten the existence or the basic position of your opponent are helpful. Saying that the issue is confined to a single country/area or that you will act only for a limited time is another approach. Saying that this is your "last demand" may also prove effective. Every time Hitler signed something, it was his "last" demand, and everyone believed him, until Poland.

Invoke community values. Call on your opponent to join you (by giving way) in preserving peace. If the two parties are in the same international/regional organization (such as the European Economic Community), highlight your common ties and interests. This is intended to make concessions appear to be a noble gesture instead of a retreat.

Provide avenues of retreat. As discussed earlier, it is important to leave an opponent room to retreat with dignity.

Minimize the extent of duress. Inasmuch as an opponent will find it hard to back down under threat, it is important to create the appearance of mediation, negotiation, and even mutual (if only symbolic) concessions.

Assert your basic goodwill. Treating the conflict as an unfortunate but singular event in otherwise nonhostile relations will help isolate the issue and diminish its value.

These points cover most of the main tactics of the three elements of crisis diplomacy, although others and numerous nuances could be added. Again, it must be stressed that the rules, options, and tactics described do not substitute for wisdom. They rely on accurate information and objective analysis of both your own and your opponent's power and goals. Success also depends on the native ability of decision makers and diplomats. Understanding how the game is played does not always make for successful diplomacy. As in any art, the fundamentals are important and must be mastered, but beyond that, individual skill is the essence of brilliance.

Summary

Diplomacy is a communication process that has two main elements. One is negotiating through direct or indirect discussions between two or more countries. The second element of diplomacy is signaling—that is, saying or doing something in order to transmit a message to the other side.

Diplomacy is an ancient art, and some of the historical functions of diplomacy are still important. Diplomacy, however, has also changed dramatically during this century, with such practices as summits, multilateral meetings, and parliamentary maneuvering as common now as they once were rare. These changes reflect the changes in the international system and have their benefits, but they are not all positive steps. At the very least, diplomacy has become more complex with the proliferation of actors and options. It has also become more vital given the possible consequences if it fails.

Diplomats, who now include presidents and prime ministers as well as foreign ministers and ambassadors, have many functions, such as reporting, negotiating, symbolically representing, and (sometimes) intervening. Good diplomacy is an art, but it is not totally freestyle, and there are general rules that increase the chances for diplomatic success.

There are also a wide variety of approaches or options in diplomacy. Whether contacts should be direct or indirect, the level of contact, whether communication should be public or private, the nature of rewards or coercion offered, how precise or vague messages should be, whether to communicate by message or deed, and whether issues should be linked or dealt with separately are all questions that require careful consideration.

Crises are a special type of international event characterized by high stakes, short decision times, and the possibility of conflict. Accordingly, their resolution includes special considerations, and there are a number of ways to communicate your resolve and to defuse your opponent's stakes and resolve. As with any aspect of diplomacy, these methods do not guarantee success, and there is no substitute for skilled practitioners.

Terms

Bilateral diplomacy—Negotiations between two countries.

Coercive diplomacy—Using threats or force as a diplomatic tactic.

Crisis—An international confrontation characterized by high stakes, a limited time to make decisions, and the possibility of conflict.

Linkage diplomacy—The practice of considering another country's general international behavior as well as the specifics of the question when deciding whether to reach an agreement on an issue.

Multilateral diplomacy—Negotiations among three or more countries.

Open diplomacy—The public conduct of negotiations and the publication of agreements.

Parliamentary diplomacy—Debate and voting in international organizations to settle diplomatic issues.

Summitry—Diplomatic negotiations between national leaders.

Notes

1. This section relies heavily on "Diplomacy and Negotiation in Historical Perspective," chap. 2 of U.S. Congress, House of Representatives, Committee on Foreign Affairs, *Soviet Diplomacy and Negotiating Behavior,* a study prepared by the Congressional Research Service (1979), pp. 11–26.
2. *The Prince* (New York: Random House, 1950), chap. 26.
3. François de Callierres, *Of the Manner of Negotiating with Sovereigns* (Paris, 1716), trans. A. F. Whyte (Boston: Houghton Mifflin, 1919).
4. In addition to House Committee on Foreign Affairs, *Soviet Diplomacy,* pp. 40–43, see Harold Nicholson, "Transition from the Old to the New Diplomacy," in *Modern Diplomacy: The Art and the Artisans,* ed. Elmer Plischke (Washington, D.C.: American Enterprise Institute, 1979), pp. 43–53.
5. Italy became a "great power" toward the end of the century. Spain was in a twilight zone, no longer a great power but to a degree living on past glory. Turkey was a power but declining and outside the confines of Europe. The United States was yet to assert itself.
6. Elmer Plischke, "The New Diplomacy," in *Modern Diplomacy: The Art and the Artisans,* ed. Elmer Plischke (Washington, D.C.: American Enterprise Institute, 1979), p. 54. The figure for 1973 was estimated at 475 annually.
7. Henry Kissinger, *The White House Years* (Boston: Little, Brown, 1979), p. 126.
8. Ibid., p. 142. For a general discussion, see Patrick Garrity, "The Dubious Promise of Summitry," *Journal of Contemporary Studies* 7 (1984): 71–79.
9. Ibid.
10. Ibid.
11. Ibid., p. 79.
12. For a critique of summit meetings, see J. Robert Schaetzel and H. B. Malmgren, "Talking Heads," *Foreign Policy,* no. 39 (1980): 130–142.
13. William Macomber, *The Angels' Game: A Handbook of Modern Diplomacy* (New York: Stein & Day, 1975).
14. This section relies on Macomber, *Angels' Game,* chaps. 1 through 6.
15. Kingdon B. Swayne, "The Reporting Function," in *Modern Diplomacy,* ed. Plischke, pp. 350–363.
16. Thomas A. Bailey, *The Art of Diplomacy* (New York: Appleton-Century-Crofts, 1968), pp. 35–43.
17. Kissinger, *White House Years,* pp. 1420, 1469.

18. Arkady Shevchenko, *Breaking with Moscow,* quoted in *Time,* February 11, 1985, p. 51.
19. These standards are to a substantial degree an amalgam of Hans Morgenthau's maxims in his *Politics among Nations,* 5th ed. (New York: Knopf, 1973); and Bailey, *Art of Diplomacy,* pp. 140–145.
20. Henry Kissinger, "The Just and the Possible," in U.S. Congress, Senate Committee on Government Operations, *Negotiation and Statecraft: A Selection of Readings,* 91st Cong., 2nd sess. (1970), p. 47.
21. For a discussion of the impact of misperception, see Joseph H. Rivera, *The Psychological Dimensions of Foreign Policy* (Columbus, Ohio: Charles E. Merrill, 1969), pp. 371–373, 391–401.
22. For a discussion of research, see Lloyd Jensen, *Explaining Foreign Policy* (Englewood Cliffs, N.J.: Prentice-Hall, 1982), p. 235.
23. Charles Lockhart, *Bargaining in International Conflicts* (New York: Columbia University Press, 1979), p. 125.
24. There are many excellent discussions. For one of the most recent, see I. William Zartman and Maureen Berman, *The Practical Negotiator* (New Haven, Conn.: Yale University Press, 1982). For a review of some of the formal models of bargaining, see Glen H. Snyder and Paul Diesing, *Conflict among Nations: Bargaining, Decision Making, and System Structure in International Crisis* (Princeton, N.J.: Princeton University Press, 1977), chap. 2, pp. 33–182.
25. Kissinger, *White House Years,* pp. 179, 188.
26. *New York Times,* September 24, 1982, p. A14.
27. Kissinger, *White House Years,* p. 701.
28. Cyrus Vance, *Hard Choices* (New York: Simon & Schuster, 1983), p. 276.
29. Kissinger, *White House Years,* p. 188.
30. Lockhart, *Bargaining in International Conflicts,* pp. 114–129, is excellent on this point.
31. On coercive bargaining, see Phil Williams, *Crisis Management* (New York: Wiley, 1976), pp. 135–191.
32. Zbigniew Brzezinski, *Power and Principle* (New York: Farrar, Straus, Giroux, 1983), p. 561.
33. Russell J. Lerg and Hugh G. Wheeler, "Influence Strategies, Success, and War," *Journal of Conflict Resolution* 23 (1979): 655–684.
34. Vance, *Hard Choices,* p. 229.
35. Kissinger, *White House Years,* p. 129.
36. Vance, *Hard Choices,* p. 102.
37. There are numerous definitions of *crisis.* This is the author's own. For a discussion, see Richard Ned Lebow, *Between Peace and War: The Nature of International Crisis* (Baltimore: Johns Hopkins University Press, 1981), pp. 7–12.
38. On crisis management, see Lockhart, *Bargaining in International Conflicts;* Williams, *Crisis Management;* Lebow, *Between Peace and War;* and Juergen Dedring, *Advances in Peace and Conflict Research* (Beverly Hills, Calif.: Sage, 1976). The following discussion has its primary origin in the constructs of Snyder and Diesing, *Conflicts among Nations,* especially pp. 198–203.

10

Penetration and Subversion

Rumor is a pipe
Blown by surmises, jealousies, conjectures,
And of so easy and so plain a stop
That the blunt monster with uncounted heads,
The still discordant wavering multitude
Can play on it.

Shakespeare, King Henry IV

States, as we saw in Chapter 3, are not black boxes. They are, instead, dynamic organizations composed of many sources of policy pressure. To a significant degree, international politics is a reflection of those pressures transmitted through foreign policy. Given the connection between a country's substructures (internal elements) and world politics, an increasingly important aspect of international interaction is penetration and subversion.

Penetration and Subversion Defined

Penetration and subversion is a process of *internal activity* in another state. Whereas diplomacy involves interaction *between* governments, penetration and subversion involves action by one government that interacts with another state's substructures. This relationship is shown in Figure 10-1.

Essentially, internal activity can be subdivided into two categories. The first is *information gathering*. This is part of the diplomatic function (Chapter 9) but is also carried out by an array of other organizations. The second type of activity is *manipulation*—that is, efforts to change the internal dynamics of another country's domestic process. Propaganda and terrorism are examples of techniques we will examine. As this chapter will show, aspects of penetration and subversion range from simple information gathering to attempts to topple governments. We will also see that such activity is on the rise and that it has an important part in the interplay of our world drama.

Spying, Subversion, Propaganda: Ancient Arts

Internal activity is as old as diplomacy and war. In ancient Greece, names such as Odysseus and Alexander the Great are closely identified with spying and propaganda. The Bible is also full of references to these activities. Joshua was an expert propagandist who sapped the morale of his enemies by spreading the news of his miraculous victories and the story that God had promised victory to the children of Israel. Moses, who sent twelve spies into the land of Canaan (Numbers 13:3), may have been the first spymaster, and Delilah used her charms to gain intelligence (Judges 16:9) and to neutralize Samson.

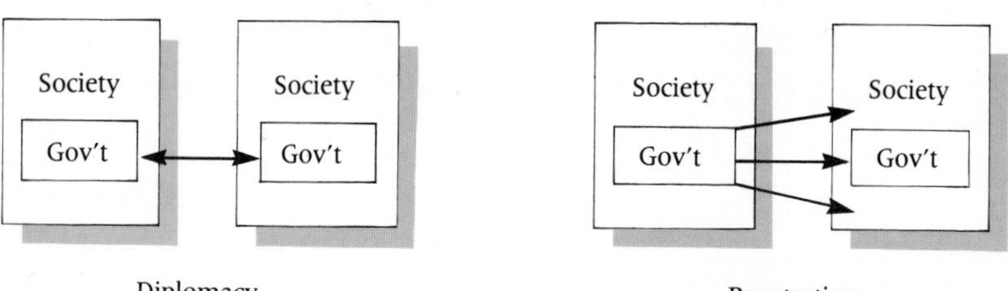

Figure 10-1. The difference between diplomacy and penetration.

For this she received eleven hundred pieces of silver from the Philistines, a magnificent sum, especially when compared with Judas Iscariot's mere thirty silver pieces.

The point here is that intelligence about an enemy, attempts to affect morale and opinion, and efforts to foment trouble in an opponent's camp have long been important tools of international politics. As Joshua learned, if you can crumble the enemy's resistance by blowing your horns, the victory can be just as sure as if you gain it by force, and less costly.[1]

Penetration and Subversion: Increasing Importance and Ability

If internal activity was important in antiquity, it has become even more vital in the twentieth century. Six factors have enhanced the role of intelligence. The *need to know* and the *ability to gather information* have both increased dramatically in this century. The *ability to manipulate* has also increased. The *expansion of contacts, increased role of public opinion,* and *tacit acceptance of some espionage* have also increased the importance and availability of intelligence and the ability to manipulate another country's internal situation.

The Need to Know

Intelligence about the assets and intentions of others has always been valuable. Recent world changes, including advances in technology and growth of interdependence, have made such information absolutely crucial.

Technology. Advanced technology has made information more important in two ways. First, the speed and destructiveness of modern weapons mean that the time to make defensive decisions may be extremely limited. Second, keeping up technologically with others has become essential. The technology gap between the Soviets and the Western allies is a matter of real concern for the Kremlin. A great deal of Soviet bloc espionage against the West is aimed at gaining computer technology and other electronic/industrial information.

Interdependence. World economic interdependence has also enhanced the importance of good intelligence. Governments use human and technical means to monitor allies and neutrals as well as enemies. Nigeria is pro-Western, but since that country is a major oil supplier, it is prudent for the United States to keep track of Nigerian developments. An upheaval, as occurred in January 1984, could threaten U.S. oil supplies, and it is vital that American policy makers know how to react. For each microfilm of a missile design that secret agents gather, thousands of pieces of data on Soviet wheat fields, Iranian oil production, and the Brazilian coffee crop are amassed and analyzed by intelligence agencies.

The Ability to Gather Information

Technology has vastly improved information-gathering techniques. Sensitive listening devices, high-resolution optics, infrared sensing equipment, computers that sort and assemble information, and a variety of other means have revolutionized the intelligence-gathering field. Electronic transmission of information has also opened advanced societies to penetration. Currently, in the United States, 70 percent of all domestic telecommunications and 60 percent of all traffic abroad is transmitted via satellites or microwave towers and is easily interceptible. Stories have even circulated in recent years that both the United States and the Soviet Union are experimenting with clairvoyance, extrasensory perception, and other psychic techniques to gather information.

The Ability to Manipulate

The third factor in the increasing importance of internal activity is the ability to manipulate. This aspect has been enhanced by advances in technology and a growing knowledge of psychology.

Technology. The advent of electronic media, first radio, then television, meant an inevitable lessening of the barrier that a national border can pose to the flow of information and propaganda. As we shall see, the major powers—and some lesser ones—spend billions of dollars broadcasting their views to the world.[2]

Psychology. There have also been advances in the understanding of social psychology. Especially since World War II, behavioral scientists have become involved in the design of propaganda. Persuasion will probably always be partly an art, but it is also very much a science.[3]

Increased Contacts

As previously discussed, advances in transportation and communication have greatly facilitated intercultural contacts. Even in "closed" countries, such as China, there is increasing foreign travel, which provides information about the country. Cultural contacts also provide propaganda opportunities.[4]

Related to this expansion in the level of contact is the increase in the size of diplomatic missions. Intelligence agents, with **diplomatic cover** titles, are an integral part of the missions of many countries. These agents are not only stationed in capital cities but also often placed in consular and other missions throughout the country. Soviet bloc countries have 2,100 diplomats in the United States (including those accredited to the UN), and between 600 and 850 of these are believed to be intelligence agents. These are supplemented by spies planted among tourists and immigrants and by agents recruited from among American citizens. This network is, in turn, countered by 2,000 U.S.

counterintelligence agents, a number that leaves the country "outmanned but not overwhelmed," according to one FBI official.[5]

Public Opinion

The importance of internal activity has also been enhanced by the rising role of public opinion in foreign policy. Morale has always been a target of propaganda, but the increased role of public opinion in foreign policy making (Chapter 3) has broadened opportunities to affect another country's policy. This is particularly true in more democratic countries, but it also has limited application in authoritarian political systems. When, in early 1984, the Syrians released a downed U.S. flyer to the Reverend Jesse Jackson, they showed a benign face that helped their image in the United States and increased pressure to pull the Marines out of Lebanon.

Tacit Acceptance of Spying

Finally, the availability of information is increased by the tacit acceptance of at least some spying. Both the Americans and the Soviets realize that accidental or inadvertent war can be prevented in part by letting the other side keep track of their activities. Neither side tries to interfere with many technical monitoring programs (e.g., satellites), diplomatic spies are tolerated as long as they are not too blatant, and NATO and the Warsaw Pact even invite each other to observe military maneuvers in Central Europe.

The Limits of Intelligence

Even though the ability to penetrate and subvert another country has increased, there are limits on the effectiveness of such activity.[6]

Target resistance. One limit stems from the ability of targets to frustrate intelligence efforts. All countries employ sophisticated coding of signals and other procedures to guard their secrets. Countries can also use double agents or other **disinformation** techniques to mislead an opponent. Additionally, all major governments have counterintelligence units designed to thwart penetration.

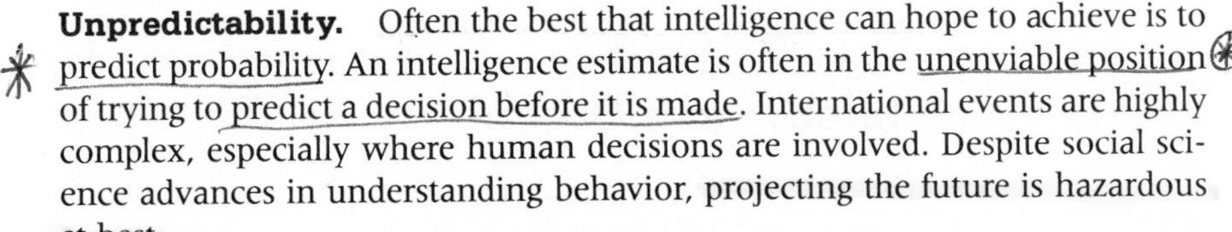

Unpredictability. Often the best that intelligence can hope to achieve is to predict probability. An intelligence estimate is often in the unenviable position of trying to predict a decision before it is made. International events are highly complex, especially where human decisions are involved. Despite social science advances in understanding behavior, projecting the future is hazardous at best.

Lack of resources. Even in the age of the computer, it is impossible to gather and analyze all relevant information. Intelligence agencies are also subject to budgetary and other domestic political pressures. The substantial reduction of the CIA's covert operations in the 1970s means that the agency is now short of agents in a number of skill areas. Lack of educational training has also left the American intelligence community short of analysts in such areas as Eastern Europe.

Self-imposed limits. Intelligence activity may be limited by a variety of ethical or political considerations. Later, for example, we will consider the morality of assassination. In the political realm, the United States was reluctant to cooperate with the antagonists of Iran's shah, a staunch ally, even after his regime began to crumble.

User limitations. A number of factors limit how well intelligence consumers utilize intelligence. Unexpected information or analysis that goes against "prevailing truths" may be perceptually rejected. There were, in the 1960s, estimates that the United States could not prevail militarily in Vietnam, but given American might and arrogance, they were too outlandish to believe. In short, despite the best evidence, decision makers often see and hear what they

want to.

Bureaucratic restraints. A last, and related, factor is organizational restraints. "Prevailing truths" also inhibit analysts from forwarding dissonant conclusions. Unusual analysis is often not applauded for its fresh approach. Rather, it is rejected as odd and misconceived, and the analyst's credibility is cast into doubt. Even if the analyst is brave enough to press an unusual idea, it will probably be suppressed at an intermediate level. Secretary of State Dean Acheson once unwisely opined: "You think Presidents should be warned. You're wrong. Presidents should be given confidence."[7] Finally, intelligence sometimes just falls through the bureaucratic cracks. A warning that Pearl Harbor might be bombed simply moved too slowly in 1941 to be of any use: it arrived after the Japanese attack. A last-minute alert was sent by Western Union rather than by military cable.

Organizing for Intelligence

Both the Soviet Union and the United States maintain extensive intelligence organizations.

U.S. Intelligence Organizations

Among American intelligence organizations, the *Central Intelligence Agency* (CIA) is the most well known. Formed in 1947, it employs about 15,000 people and has a budget of $1 billion, although the exact figure is secret and it may be the funnel to considerably greater funds. CIA activities range from routine monitoring of foreign publications through high-level analysis and policy recommendations. The director of the CIA is a regular adviser of the president. The CIA is also involved in a range of field operations through personnel stationed at American embassies and special operatives. The various types of activities will be detailed in the pages that follow.

The *National Security Agency* (NSA) is less well known than the CIA, but it is said to be a larger organization. It specializes in electronic intelligence and uses advanced technology to monitor the activities of the Soviet Union and others. There are also a variety of other intelligence agencies, including the Defense Intelligence Agency (in the Department of Defense), the Department of State Bureau of Intelligence and Research, and the Army, Navy, and Air Force operations.

Soviet Intelligence Organizations

Little is known for sure about the size and operations of the Soviet intelligence organizations. There are, however, two main organizations. The Committee for State Security, known as the *KGB* (its Russian equivalent letters), has responsibilities for both internal security and external intelligence gathering and operations. The activities of the KGB run the gamut from suppression of internal dissent, through intelligence gathering, to active measures such as subversion. Its agents are attached to all diplomatic missions, and they not only spy on their hosts, they also watch their own diplomatic personnel. The other main Soviet intelligence agency is the military's Chief Intelligence Directorate of the General Staff, known as the *GRU*. The GRU specializes mainly in military intelligence, and it also maintains specialized troops.

In sum, these organizations are probably considerably larger than their American counterparts, but it should be remembered that they carry out many domestic and paramilitary functions that are beyond the scope of the CIA and others.

Information Gathering, or Intelligence

Internal activity can be roughly divided into two categories: information gathering and manipulation. The techniques for these two types of activity can be further classified as open (or **overt**) and closed (or **covert**). In line with this division, we will examine the role and methods of overt and covert techniques of intelligence and manipulation.

Overt Intelligence

Despite popular stereotypes about cloak-and-dagger intelligence, the greatest volume of information, if not the most sensitive, is gathered through open methods. The two primary methods of overt intelligence gathering are (1) observation and the monitoring of public information and (2) the use of **national technical means** (NTM), such as satellites.

Observing and monitoring. A great deal of information can be gained through simple *observation*. The openness of the American system gives the Soviet Union an excellent chance to gather information. Between January 1980 and June 1981, 450 Soviet scientists and technicians visited the United States and attended conferences on such topics as lasers, optics, high-energy physics, computer software, engineering, and particle accelerators. Another 30 technical experts were associated with leading American scientific university programs through scholar exchange programs. Another Soviet delegation was given a tour of, and allowed to take pictures in, the Boeing Aircraft plant. In addition to their overt observation, they were also reported to have worn special shoes to pick up metal shavings to be analyzed for alloy compositions.[8]

Soviet operatives also regularly attend or watch American political events, just as U.S. observers never miss a May Day parade in Red Square. Soviet embassy officials regularly visit Capitol Hill offices, socialize with members of Congress and staff members, and attend committee meetings. The bits of information gained by such methods are seldom significant individually; they are more like pieces of a jigsaw puzzle. "They're looking for bits and pieces," one Senate source explained. "Every hearing on foreign relations, agriculture, or international economics the Soviets are going to cover. They're trying to see which way the decisions are going, what the thinking is."[9]

Monitoring public information is another major intelligence source. The vast majority of CIA professionals are involved in monitoring the print and broadcast media of other countries. They read journals, books, and whatever else they can obtain. *Red Star,* the leading Soviet military journal, is read with as much interest in Washington as in Moscow.

Here again, countries with closed political systems have an advantage over those with more open systems. The amount of technical, defense, and political information available in America through the press, professional journals and conferences, and public documents is immense. As many as ten Soviet embassy officials have signed up for reports and hearing transcripts issued by the Senate Armed Services Committee, and during the height of the MX-basing controversy, the FBI trailed two Soviet officials to Ely, Nevada (a potential MX site), where they were gathering data from the local library about the area.[10]

The problem of limiting the disclosure of sensitive information in a democratic system presents difficult issues. The Reagan administration has tried various methods to curb the flow, but any such attempt always threatens the freedoms guaranteed by the Constitution. It should also be noted that when divulging sensitive information has suited its purposes, the administration has itself done so. When, for example, President Reagan, in an attempt to build support, appeared on television and showed photos of Soviet arms in Nicaragua, the ability to gather such intelligence was compromised.[11] Similarly, disclosures that the Japanese and Americans could monitor Soviet air-ground

Keeping secrets in a democracy is difficult. Here, President Reagan gives one away and compromises the ability of U.S. intelligence experts to photograph foreign military bases.

communications during the 1983 downing of a Korean airliner alerted the Soviets to the breach of their military command system.

National technical means. Technological advances have created a new era in intelligence gathering. Sophisticated equipment can accomplish almost unbelievable feats, and to a substantial degree, NTM operates in the open and with tacit acceptance. The United States and the Soviet Union extensively use satellites that transmit photographic, computer-graphic, heat-sensitive, and other types of information back to earth. These technical spies crisscross the globe from 80 to 200 miles aloft or, even farther out (22,000 miles), travel at the same speed as earth and seem to hang motionless over the equator. The images they transmit are highly accurate, and some can even pick up the faint signals that leak from microwave phone communications. There are also a wide variety of high-flying spy planes and undersea and ground monitoring stations. One radar, the giant Great Dane, is reportedly able to spot a baseball at a range of 2,300 miles.[12]

Covert Intelligence

The area of covert intelligence is the stuff of John Le Carré novels such as *The Spy Who Came in from the Cold.*[13] Spy activities use either traditional **HUMINT** (human intelligence) or more technological methods, such as **SIGINT** (signal intelligence), which includes ELINT (electronic intelligence) and COMINT (communication intelligence).

HUMINT. Human intelligence (spies) includes both members of your own intelligence service and agents recruited from among the citizens of the country you are penetrating.

Foreign intelligence officers are normally stationed in another country under diplomatic cover. These officers ordinarily do not try to gather secret information directly. Instead they are involved with recruiting agents and receiving information from them. In 1983, Alexandr Mikheyev, of the Soviet UN mission, was expelled from the United States for trying to recruit a congressional staff member, and two other "diplomats" were also expelled for recruiting or actually receiving classified documents.[14]

Intelligence operatives are also sometimes sent under nondiplomatic cover. The danger, of course, is that they are not protected by diplomatic immunity and can be imprisoned. In late 1982, for instance, an executive of a Polish machinery corporation was charged with paying $100,000 to a Hughes Aircraft engineer for documents on weapons and radar systems.[15]

It is also possible to dispatch agents who may spend years, even decades, undercover as *legal or illegal immigrants* waiting for an assignment. In April 1981, a Hungarian who had come to the United States in 1956 was arrested for trying to buy information from a U.S. Army warrant officer. One KGB officer, Colonel Rudolf Hermann, illegally entered the United States from Canada, operated as a spymaster, and acted as a mole in case diplomatic agents were expelled. Hermann's son was enrolled in Georgetown University, a training ground for the U.S. Foreign Service, with the object of eventually entering U.S. government employment.[16]

Domestic spies are recruited by a variety of methods. In some cases, political reasons are involved. One of the classic spy rings in history, including the infamous Kim Philby, who worked for British intelligence, and Sir Anthony Blunt, who was the queen's art curator in Windsor Castle, was recruited by the Soviets at the beginning of World War II from among leftist students at Cambridge University. Another Soviet-recruited British spy, Sir Roger Hollis, actually headed his country's MI5 internal security service from 1958 to 1966. More recently, Arkady Shevchenko, a high-ranking Soviet diplomat serving as under secretary-general of the United Nations, worked for over two years as an American spy and then defected to the United States in 1978.[17]

Probably the most common method of recruiting spies is with money. California's "Silicon Valley," which houses 900 advanced technology companies and where life is hectic and expensive, has become a particular focus of espionage using the lure of dollars for secrets.[18] The 1984 film *The Falcon and the Snowman* tells the story of two such California-based spies, who, for a mix of money and idealism, sold secrets that Christopher Boyce got from his aerospace industry employer, TRW. Another method of recruiting spies is blackmail. If you can catch or trap your target in a sexual indiscretion or some other form of criminal or embarrassing activity, then you can threaten the individual with exposure.

Throughout history, spies have yielded some spectacular results. But HUMINT also has its drawbacks. Information from untrained contacts is often unreliable. "The level of emotion in [such] information is pretty high," one U.S. intelligence officer complained.[19] It is also possible that a contact may turn out to be a double agent, being used by the other side to trap your agents or to feed you false information.

SIGINT. Signal intelligence has become increasingly important as technology has improved. The ability of the Allies to crack the German code and monitor communication, for instance, significantly shortened World War II.[20] The dividing line between overt and covert technical means is at times vague and not overly important, but, essentially, covert means are those in which there is an attempt to mask their use from the target.

Eavesdropping on conversations is one type of technical intelligence gathering. The Soviets once planted a microphone ("bug") in the beak of the eagle in the Great Seal of the United States that hung in the U.S. ambassador's office. In more recent years, the U.S. embassy in Moscow has protested that the Soviets have bombarded it with (cancer-causing) microwaves in an attempt to intercept communications and to jam American listening devices.

The increase in use of microwaves for telephone communication has given both the Soviets and the Americans extensive access to each other's communications networks.  Soviet listening stations in Cuba, for example, monitor communications between U.S. financial institutions, businesses, and even government agencies. As one National Security Agency official put it, "They just sit down there with their huge vacuum cleaner and suck everything up."[21]

The use of computers for the transmission of all sorts of information has also vastly increased monitoring possibilities. Computers can also sort out and assemble vast quantities of information that previously would have been beyond human capacity to handle. These new capabilities have led to greater activity in the use of encrypted messages, jamming, and other countermeasures, but it is hard to be sure that a transmitted message or even a face-to-face conversation is not being monitored.[22]

Manipulation

Manipulation is the attempt to alter the internal, or domestic, situation of another country. Like intelligence activity, manipulation can be conducted overtly or covertly.

Overt Manipulation: Propaganda

Propaganda is the most common form of overt manipulation. Propaganda is an attempt to influence another country through emotional techniques rather than logical discussion or presentation of empirical evidence. It is, in short, a process of appealing to emotions rather than minds by creating fear, doubt, sympathy, anger, or a variety of other chemical responses. Although the use of propaganda is as old as history, increases in communication, democratization, and the understanding of psychology have made propaganda increasingly important. In essence, if you cannot persuade another country's leaders through force or diplomacy, you can try to persuade its people through propaganda. The United States spends over a billion dollars annually on propaganda, and there are estimates that the Soviets spend five times as much.[23]

Channels. There are a variety of propaganda channels. *Radio,* mostly via short wave, is a major thrust because it is rapid and receivers are commonly found even in poor and authoritarian countries. In 1980 the U.S.-sponsored Voice of America was broadcasting 891 hours a week in thirty-nine languages to an estimated 100 million listeners. Soviet broadcasting figures were 2,000 weekly hours and eighty-two languages. China broadcast 1,373 hours weekly, Egypt 1,065, and even Radio Tirana in Albania transmitted 1,000 hours weekly in sixty languages.[24]

Television is a second and rising propaganda channel.[25] Television's visual imagery has a higher impact than the printed or spoken word, and its potential is tremendous. For the present, the role of television as a propaganda medium is limited by the fact that many countries have few sets and because jamming is easy.

Still, the medium is receiving increased use. Both the United States and the Soviet Union have used it in their attempts to win the nuclear arms debate in Europe. In 1981, for example, a speech by President Reagan calling for arms control was broadcast live to Europe. Soviet leaders have also appeared on European television screens.[26]

Propaganda is also distributed by *printed material.* Millions of books, magazines, pamphlets, press releases, and leaflets are produced and distributed each year. One illustrative salvo in recent years saw the United States publish a ninety-nine-page analysis, "Soviet Military Power," detailing the Kremlin's ferocious forces and predatory purposes. Moscow's counterbarrage was entitled "Whence the Threat to Peace," a seventy-eight-page piece that, an American magazine judged, "could well have been produced on Madison Avenue."[27] There have also been instances in which foreign agents were able to penetrate a country's journalism establishment. The influential French journalist Pierre-Charles Pathé, for one, was a KGB agent from 1961 to 1979, and his writing subtly favored the Soviet cause.

Creating *events* is another propaganda ploy. Here the goal is not to broadcast a message directly but, rather, to create a media event that will make you look good. In 1983, for instance, Soviet leaders responded to a letter about peace from an American schoolgirl, Samantha Smith, by inviting her to the Soviet Union. It was "great press," showing how "hospitable and peace-loving" Soviets are.

Finally, *direct contact* has increasing possibilities in an age of high-speed communication and transportation. Nikita Khrushchev's tour of the United States in the late 1950s was designed to show the Soviet leader's benign face. When he kissed babies, munched corn at Iowa cookouts, and complained

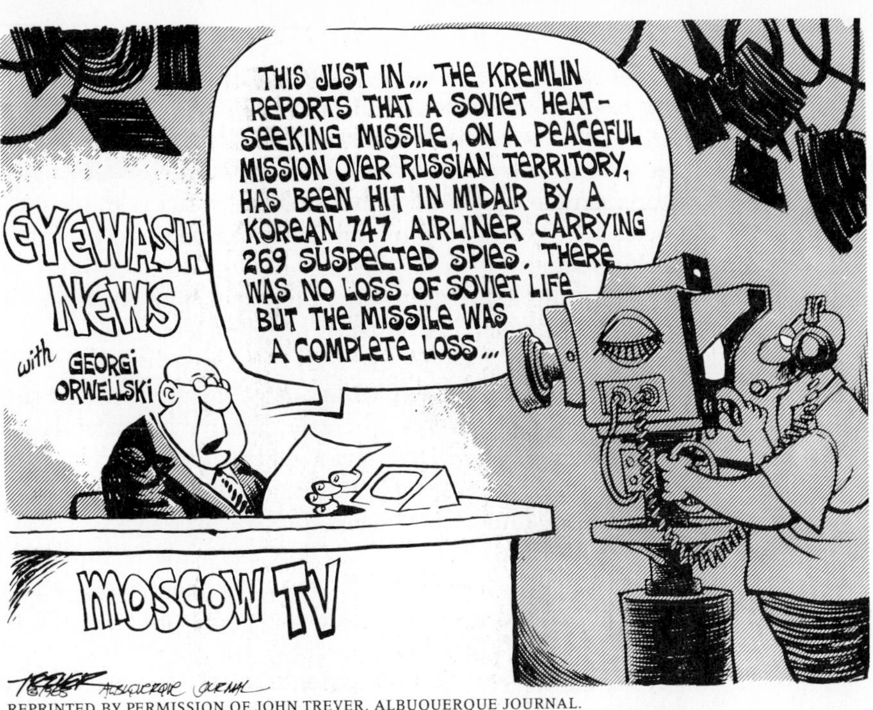

REPRINTED BY PERMISSION OF JOHN TREVER, ALBUQUERQUE JOURNAL.

when security considerations canceled his trip to Disneyland, who could still doubt his good nature? In more recent years, Soviet leaders have met with U.S. congressional delegations on several occasions, and Yuri Andropov wrote directly to West German legislators urging them to bar the stationing of Pershing missiles in their country.[28]

Techniques. There are a variety of techniques for projecting effective propaganda. One of these is *telling the truth.*[29] Sometimes the truth can be very damaging to the other side. The Soviets have regularly used reports and pictures of racial disturbances in the United States as propaganda in Africa. Similarly, when the Soviets shot down a Korean airliner in 1983, the United States reaped a propaganda windfall. On the positive side, images such as American astronauts standing on the moon require little doctoring to create a favorable impression.

Lying is another technique. Outright lies are not a common practice, perhaps because they are difficult to support and because they run the risk of being exposed. When that occurs, the former target can become the aggressor and try to embarrass you and attack your credibility. Still, lies, which are sometimes called "disinformation," play a role. After a terrorist attack on the Grand Mosque in Mecca (1979), Soviet propaganda alleged that the United States was behind the desecration. An increase in the use of forgery and other techniques to spread disinformation has become of such concern that the United States recently launched "Project Truth" to counter the Soviet campaign.[30]

Half-truths are the most common propaganda technique. One common ploy is to take a kernel of truth and project it as a general statement. The existence of some Soviet support of European peace activists has been used by the United States to try to discredit the entire movement as a communist front. Presenting controversial information as fact is another approach. There has been a degree of scientific doubt about alleged Soviet-backed chemical warfare in Southeast Asia, but that has not stopped the U.S. propaganda machine. A third half-truth technique is deliberate omission. In this case, the information presented is true but is not complete.

Rules for effective propaganda. As a last topic in this survey of propaganda, we can look at how to create effective propaganda. In many ways, these are the same sort of rules that would govern any advertising campaign.[31]

Keep it simple. Messages should be clear and easily understood. Mass audiences have little interest in long or complex messages.

Keep it active. Stories about action, particularly supported by pictures, attract and hold attention. Stories about Soviet terror attacks on villages in Moslem Afghanistan are better than a philosophical essay on "Marxism's Atheistic Threat to Islam."

Be relevant. Relate the message to the audience. Soviet pictures of Ku Klux Klanners on the march have a greater impact in Africa than in nonblack countries.

Be credible. Normally, as noted above, truths or half-truths are more effective than lies. If you have at least an element of truth, your "interpretations" are more believable and defensible. Even if you are going to lie, the message must at least be believable.

Be repetitive. A propaganda message is just one item in a bombardment of information that is projected daily. Repetition increases the chance of being "received" and also enhances the image of credibility.

Be emotional. The most effective propaganda appeals to emotions as well as minds. Fright, sympathy, resentment, and other emotions are powerful propaganda goals. The Soviets, for example, have tried to frighten Western Europeans over the possibility of nuclear war and to create resentment over the positioning of U.S. missiles in the region.

Covert Manipulation

The last of our four categories of internal activity is covert manipulation. This is by far the most controversial form of penetration. It involves both great reward potential and great risk. There are a number of manipulative techniques.

Subversion of decision makers. Recruiting officials to do your bidding is difficult but possible. There is substantial evidence, for instance, that the CIA attempted to coopt Iran's President Abolhassan Bani-Sadr in an effort to overthrow the Ayatollah Khomeini. That failed, but there were also charges of CIA

The Soviets used the visit of Samantha Smith as a propaganda opportunity to show their benign face to the world.

links to Khomeini's Foreign Minister Sadegh Ghotbzadeh, who was executed in 1982 for plotting to overthrow the Ayatollah.

Support of insurgencies. A much more common technique is the support of antigovernment guerrillas. There is no accurate estimate of the level of covert arms supplies and financial support, but the flow is extensive. In recent years, the United States has spent hundreds of millions of dollars supporting such causes as the "contra" rebels in Nicaragua and the anticommunist "mujahedin" in Afghanistan. The Soviets and Cubans also support antigovernment groups in El Salvador and Africa. China aids Cambodian rebels. Israel and

Syria pour weapons into the fratricidal conflict in Lebanon. In short, semi-secret gun running is a significant manipulative effort for many governments.

Support of terrorism. A third technique, terror, is increasing in incidence and importance. In 1983 there were almost 2,000 terrorist victims (of whom 387 were Americans) worldwide, more than ever before.[32] Terror tactics may be part of an insurgency or a separate effort. The Japanese Red Army, Italy's Red Brigade, Germany's Baader-Meinhof Gang are just a few of the notorious terrorist groups active in recent years.[33]

Terror tactics are aimed primarily at noncombatant targets, with only about 6 percent directed at military or police targets. The primary goal of terrorism as a form of manipulation is to destabilize the existing government or to exercise the "ability to hurt" in order to win political concessions. Ninety-five percent of all terrorist actions involve bombing, assassinations, armed attacks, kidnapings, hostages, or hijackings, with bombing (50 percent) and the taking of hostages (33 percent) the most common.[34]

Assassination. The widespread killing of government officials as part of a general campaign to destabilize the government might well be classified as terror, but the individual act of assassination against an individually targeted leader is a special case. Overall, assassination has been rapidly increasing. Between 1968 and 1980, there were 721 attempted assassinations worldwide, of which 454 were successful. These included 118 attempts (and 13 successes) against heads of state. The frequency of assassinations increased by over 400 percent during that period, from approximately 25 (1968) to 110 (1980).[35]

There have been allegations or proof of CIA-backed attempts on the life of foreign leaders such as Cuba's Fidel Castro, the Dominican Republic's Rafael Trujillo, and the Congo's (Zaire) Patrice Lumumba. More recently, Syria allegedly was involved in the assassination of Lebanon's President Bashir Gemayal, the Bulgarians and (less certainly) the Soviets were linked to the shooting of Pope John Paul II, and the CIA sponsored a manual that advocated the "neutralization" of Nicaragua's Sandinista leaders.

Summary

Not all of international relations is carried on between governments through accepted channels. Some interactions are carried on clandestinely and/or are aimed at changing the internal workings of another state. Spying, propaganda, and fomenting trouble among your opponents have long existed as tools of international relations. In recent years, however, penetration and subversion have become more important aspects of international relations than they once were. There is an increased need to monitor what other countries are doing. There have also been advances in the ability to gather information and the ability to manipulate the internal situation of others.

Internal activity can be roughly divided into information gathering and manipulation. Each of these can be carried out in the open (overtly) or in secret (covertly). Contrary to popular images, most information gathering is carried on through overt means, which range in sophistication from public media monitoring to the use of satellites and other national technical means. Covert information gathering, though a minority activity, is also important. Again, techniques range from traditional James Bondian spying to the use of highly sophisticated and secret technical devices.

Overt manipulation includes propaganda. Broadcasting information—some true, most altered—at a target audience has great potential because of new understanding of psychological factors, advanced techniques, and the greater impact of the people on policy in many countries. Covert manipulation is the most troubling aspect of intelligence work. It involves secret attempts to disrupt an opponent internally. Bribery, blackmail, assassination, and the support of guerrilla warfare and even terrorism are among its techniques. Few support such activities in the abstract, but when discussed relatively, as a choice among perhaps greater evils, such practices become more difficult to condemn (or support) absolutely.

Terms

Covert—Secret.

Diplomatic cover—Stationing intelligence agents in another country under the guise of diplomatic (and therefore protected) status.

Disinformation—False stories and information planted to embarrass or confuse another country.

HUMINT—Human intelligence; information gathered from your own agents or from agents recruited from the populace of another country.

National technical means—Satellites, listening stations, and other sophisticated devices used to gather information.

Overt—In the open.

SIGINT—Signal intelligence; information gathered by monitoring another country's communications and other transmissions.

Notes

1. On the history, see Chester G. Starr, *Political Intelligence in Classical Greece* (Leiden, The Netherlands: E. J. Brill, 1974); and Richard Wilmer Rowan with Robert G. Deinborfer, *Secret Service: Thirty Three Centuries of Espionage* (New York: Hawthorn Books, 1967). More general but comprehensive is the three-volume study edited by Harold D. Lasswell, Daniel Lerner, and Hans Speier, *Propaganda and Communication in World History* (Honolulu: University Press of Hawaii, 1979).
2. Bryant Wedge, "International Propaganda and Statecraft," *Annals of the American Academy of Political and Social Science* 398 (1971): 37.

3. Yasumasa Tanaka, "Psychological Factors in International Persuasion," pp. 50–60, and W. Phillip Davidson, "Some Trends in International Propaganda," p. 10; both in *Annals of the American Academy of Political and Social Science* 398 (1971).
4. Arthur Goodfriend, "The Dilemma of Cultural Propaganda," *Annals of the American Academy of Political and Social Science* 398 (1971): 104–126.
5. *U.S. News and World Report,* April 18, 1983, p. 32.
6. This section draws heavily on Michael Handel, "Avoiding Political and Technological Surprise in the 1980s," in *Intelligence Requirements for the 1980s,* vol. 2, *Analysis and Estimates* (Washington, D.C.: National Strategy Information Center, 1980), pp. 85–111; and Richard K. Betts, "Analysis, War, and Decision: Why Intelligence Failures Are Inevitable," *World Politics* 31 (1978): 61–89.
7. Quoted in Betts, "Analysis, War, and Decision," p. 77.
8. Michael Satchel, "How We Give Away Our Secrets," *Parade,* September 6, 1981, p. 9. Also see *New York Times,* January 10, 1983, p. A21.
9. "'Friendly' Soviet Intelligence Agents Target Capitol Hill," *Hartford* [Conn.] *Courant,* March 28, 1981, p. A20.
10. *Hartford Courant,* January 10, 1982, p. A12, and March 20, 1982, p. A20.
11. *New York Times,* March 5, 1982, p. A12.
12. *U.S. News and World Report,* September 12, 1983, p. 24. *Newsweek,* September 12, 1983, p. 25, and January 31, 1983, p. 20.
13. For a bibliographic guide, see Paul W. Blackstock and Frank L. Schaf, Jr., eds., *Intelligence, Espionage, Counterespionage, and Covert Operations: A Guide to Information Sources* (Detroit: Gala Research, 1978).
14. *Time,* May 2, 1983, p. 24.
15. *New York Times,* October 15, 1982, p. B14.
16. Herbert Romerstein, "Soviet Intelligence in the United States," in *Intelligence Requirements for the 1980s: Counterintelligence,* ed. Rob Godson (Washington, D.C.: National Security Information Center, 1980), p. 188.
17. Kim Philby, *My Silent War* (New York: Grove Press, 1968). *Hartford Courant,* November 22, 1981, p. A10. On Shevchenko, see his *Breaking with Moscow* (New York: Knopf, 1985).
18. *New York Times,* October 23, 1983, p. E20.
19. *Time,* March 22, 1982, p. 22.
20. Frederick W. Winterbotham, *The Ultra Secret* (New York: Harper & Row, 1976).
21. Quoted in *Time,* October 29, 1984, p. 38.
22. David Kahn, "Cryptology Goes Public," *Foreign Affairs* 58 (1979): 141–159. James Bamford, *The Puzzle Palace: A Report on America's Most Secret Agency* (Boston: Houghton Mifflin, 1982), especially chaps. 5 and 6, is a fascinating look at the U.S. National Security Agency.
23. Kenneth L. Adelman, "Speaking of America: Public Diplomacy in Our Time," *Foreign Affairs* 59 (1981): 719.
24. Ibid., p. 718.
25. Bernard Rubin, "International Film and Television Propaganda," *Annals of the American Academy of Political and Social Science* 398 (1971): 81–92.
26. *New York Times,* November 19, 1981, p. A1.
27. *Time,* March 22, 1982, p. 23.
28. *New York Times,* September 21, 1983, p. A9.
29. This section is based on Ralph K. White, "Propaganda: Morally Questionable and Morally Unquestionable Techniques," *Annals of the American Academy of Political and Social Science* 398 (1971): 26–35.

30. U.S. Congress, House of Representatives Permanent Select Committee on Intelligence, *Soviet Covert Action,* Hearings before the Subcommittee on Oversight, 96th Cong., 2nd sess. (1980). *New York Times,* November 4, 1981, p. A15.
31. This section is based on White, "Propaganda," and on Norman J. Padelford, George A. Lincoln, and Lee D. Ovey, *The Dynamics of International Politics,* 3rd ed. (New York: Macmillan, 1976), p. 355.
32. Robert Sayre, "International Terrorism: A Long Twilight Struggle," *Department of State Bulletin* 84 (October 1984): 48.
33. For an excellent bibliography, see Myron J. Smith, Jr., ed., *The Secret Wars: A Guide to Sources in English,* vol. 3, *International Terrorism, 1968–1980* (Santa Barbara, Calif.: ABC-Clio, 1980). Also see Marius H. Livingston, ed., with Lee Bruce Kress and Marie G. Wanek, *International Terrorism in the Contemporary World* (Westport, Conn.: Greenwood Press, 1978); and Edward F. Mickolus, *Transnational Terrorism: A Chronology of Events, 1968–1979* (Westport, Conn.: Greenwood Press, 1980).
34. For an excellent survey of the causes, tactics, and consequences of terrorism, see the entire 463rd volume of the *Annals of the American Academy of Political and Social Science* (1982). The specific information in this paragraph is drawn from Brian M. Jenkins, "Statements about Terrorism," in that volume. Also see Edward Mickolus, "Trends in Terrorism," in Livingston, *International Terrorism,* table 1, p. 48.
35. Thomas H. Snitch, "Terrorism and Political Assassinations: A Transnational Assessment, 1968–80," in Livingston, *International Terrorism,* pp. 54–68, especially figure 1, p. 58, and tables 1 and 2, pp. 60–61.

11

Economics: The North

So far as my coin would stretch;
and where it would not,
I have used my credit.
Shakespeare, King John III

In your college or university, the study of politics and economics is probably divided into two separate departments. The distinction between these two subjects is not so precise in the real world, however. Indeed, to a significant extent economics is politics, and vice versa. As Chapter 7 has already shown, a country's domestic economic situation, its natural resources, its industrial strength, and its agriculture are key factors in determining national power. Further, economics can be used as a diplomatic weapon. The granting of trade concessions or the imposition of trade restrictions can be used to reward or punish other countries. Disputes over trade can also affect political relations. For example, U.S. relations with both Japan and Western Europe have recently been strained by economic issues.

Other financial and monetary issues and politics also intertwine. Foreign aid is often given for political rather than developmental reasons. The role of multinational corporations can also cause tensions, as when the death in 1984 of thousands of Indians caused by a lethal gas leak from a Union Carbide plant in Bhopal further damaged already strained U.S./Indian relations. The imbalance between the American dollar and other world currencies has created some harsh international disputes as an avalanche of imports has caused a serious U.S. trade deficit. This and the loss of jobs to foreign competition have created domestic pressures to protect American industry at the expense of foreign suppliers.

The list of interrelations between economics and politics could go on for pages, and, to be sure, we will see many more in the chapters to follow. The point is that economics is a vital and inseparable part of the world's political structure and interchange.

The two chapters that follow will continue our examination of the impact of economic circumstance and policy. As we shall see, economic factors are not only an asset; they can be used as a tool. To further explore the status and use of economic factors, this chapter will focus on the current situation of the "North," or developed countries. The next chapter will center on the "South," or less developed countries. Still later, Chapter 16 will further discuss trade, monetary relations, and development and the attempts to promote economic cooperation within and between the two poles of the North/South axis. Finally, before beginning here, it would be worthwhile for the reader to review the role of economics in society and the North/South dimension of world politics as discussed in Chapter 1.

International Economics and History

In world politics, economics is a means of influence as well as a power asset. As such, it is also a potential target for one's foes. While it is true that in the modern era economic factors have become ever more important, their role extends far back into history. The Old Testament book of Exodus records what may have been the first attack on a country's economic (and social) infrastructure in order to overthrow imperial domination. Attempting to persuade the pharaoh to release the Israelites from their Egyptian captivity, Moses (with God's help) turned the Nile "to blood. . . . And all the fishes died; and the Nile became foul so that the Egyptians could not drink water." When that failed, Moses dispatched successive plagues of frogs, gnats, and flies to bedevil the Egyptians. Still they persisted. Next a plague was visited on their livestock, and all the Egyptians were infected with boils. Despite these travails, a very stubborn pharaoh refused to give in. Discretion would have been the better part of valor. At Moses' command, "thunder and hail and fire . . . rained upon the land of Egypt" and struck down every man, beast, plant, and tree of the fields. Adding to the Egyptians' misery, Moses then dispatched a swarm of locusts that "covered the face of the land" and "ate all the plants in the land and all the fruits on the trees . . . not a green thing remained." Enough was enough. The locusts plus three solid days of darkness convinced the Egyptians, and the Hebrews were delivered from their captivity (Exodus 10:11).

With more historic certainty, economics is also known to have affected other areas of ancient international relations. Trading records extend back to almost 3000 B.C., and there is other evidence of trade into the Neolithic age. The earliest human records reveal warfare for plunder, resources, and other economic gain. Trade wars were also known early. The Phoenicians allied themselves with King David of Israel to crush their economic rivals, the Philistines. The Greek city-states also engaged in economic strife, and the Punic Wars between Rome and Carthage were also partly rooted in economics.[1]

The Increasing Role of Economics

Whatever its earlier role, economics is becoming a more important aspect of international relations, as shown by increasing trade, interdependence, and domestic impact.

Increasing Trade

Trade is booming in the twentieth century, and the international flow of goods and money is a vital concern to all world states. Only a little more than seventy years ago, in 1913, the entire flow of goods in world commerce totaled only \$20 billion. By 1982, world trade stood at \$1.8 trillion. Even considering inflation, this represents a tremendous jump in world commerce. Figure 11-1, using 1963 (= 100) as a base, depicts the rise in the volume of trade. Trade growth has been especially rapid during the post–World War II era of significant tariff reductions. During the 1913 to 1948 period of world wars, depression, and trade protectionism, the volume of trade increased at an annual rate of only 0.6 percent. The postwar period has seen annual increases at a rate of approximately 9.6 percent.

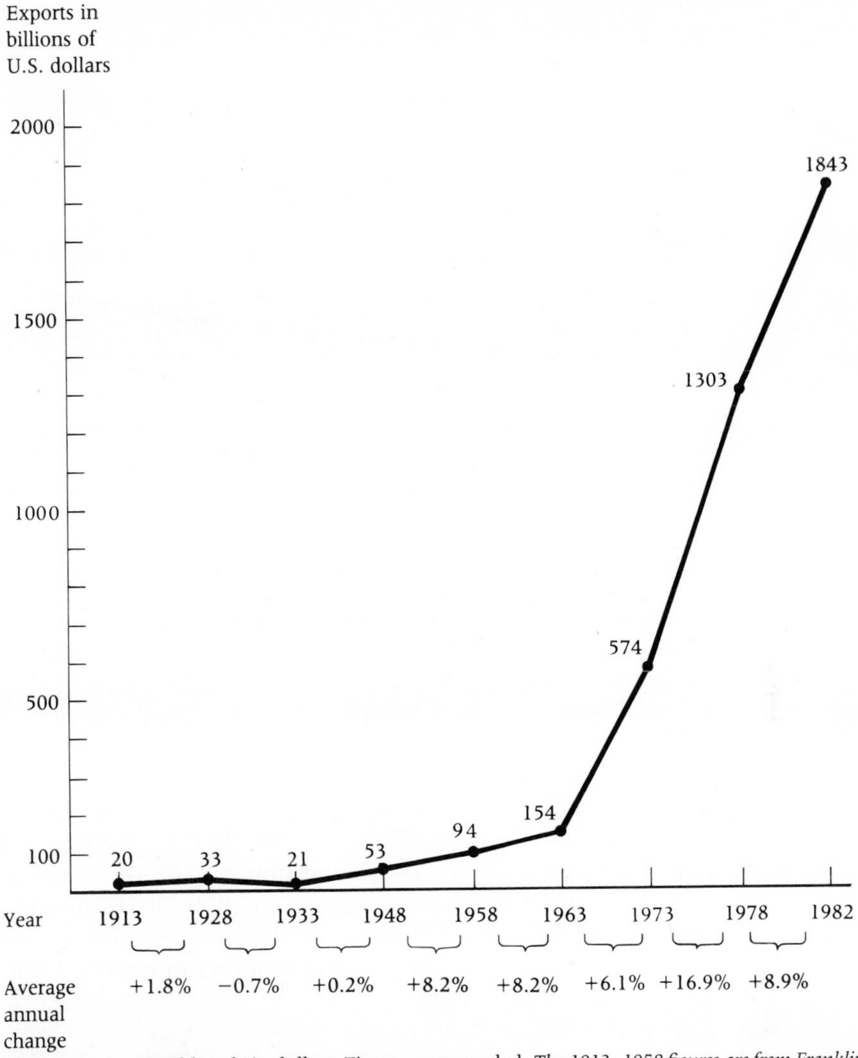

Exports in billions of U.S. dollars

2000

1500

1000

500

100

1843

1303

574

154

94

53

20 33 21

Year 1913 1928 1933 1948 1958 1963 1973 1978 1982

Average annual change +1.8% −0.7% +0.2% +8.2% +8.2% +6.1% +16.9% +8.9%

Figure 11-1. World trade in dollars. Figures are rounded. *The 1913–1958 figures are from Franklin R. Root,* International Trade and Investment, *3rd ed. (Cincinnati: South-Western Publishing, 1973), p. 24. The 1963–1982 figures are from General Agreement on Tariffs and Trade,* International Trade, 1982/83 *(Geneva: General Agreement on Tariffs and Trade, 1983), appendix, table A1.*

The rapid growth of trade has been caused by a number of factors, including productive technology, resource requirements, materialism, transportation, and free-trade philosophy.

Productive technology. The industrial revolution, which began in eighteenth-century Europe, is one factor behind increased trade. As productive efficiency increased, the supply of goods increased. From 1705 to 1885 world

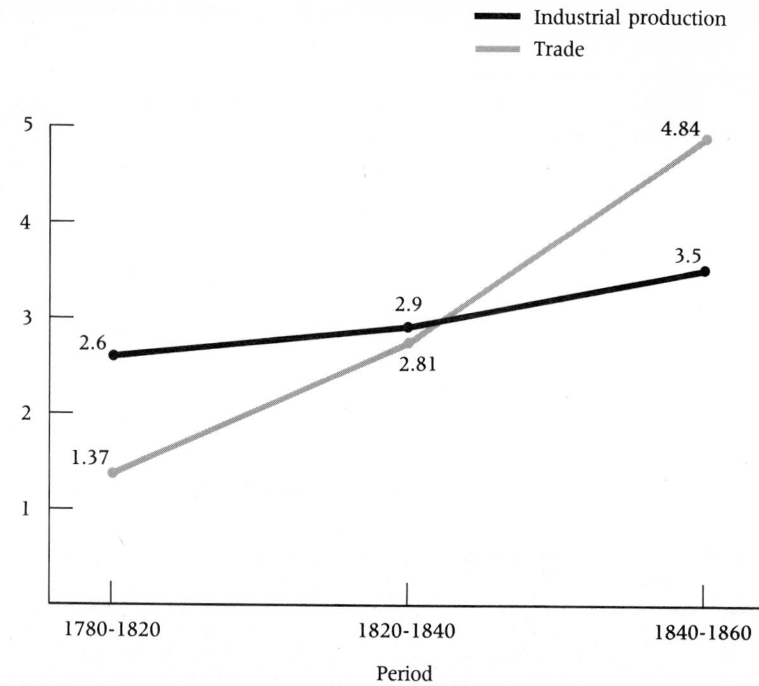

Figure 11-2. World industrial production and trade, 1780–1860. *Data from Walt Whitman Rostow,* The World Economy *(Austin: University of Texas Press, 1978), p. 67.*

industrial production increased at an annual rate of only 1.5 percent, and trade increased at only about 1 percent a year. In the years that followed, however, productivity rapidly increased, and the volume of trade followed suit. Figure 11-2 shows this relationship.

In the simplest terms, the age of machine production of goods such as textiles meant that more manufactured products were available and that they were available at lower prices. These manufactures, then, formed the "supply" side of trade development.[2]

Resource requirements. Industrialization and other technological advances also affected the "demand" side of international trade. During the nineteenth century and through World War II, importation of raw materials by the industrialized European countries was a primary force in trade as manufacturing needs both increased demand and outstripped domestic resource availability. During the late 1800s, for example, raw material accounted for 97 percent of all French and 89 percent of all German imports.

In the postwar world economy, manufactured goods have become a more significant percentage of the total imports of industrialized countries, and raw materials have become relatively less important in trade. Still, in absolute terms, they have continued to expand on a nearly 1-to-1 ratio with the growth of trade, and the demand for resources is strong, if often unstable.[3]

Materialism. The rise in the world's standard of living, especially in the industrialized countries, has also contributed to "demand" pressure on international trade. More workers were brought into the wage-producing sector, and their "real" (after inflation) wages went up. The real wages of English craftspersons held relatively steady between 1300 and 1800, for instance, but then more than doubled by the 1950s.[4] In short, more people had more money to buy things.

Transportation. Technology has also increased our ability to transport goods. The development of railroads and improvements in maritime shipping were particular spurs to trade. They both increased the volume of possible trade and decreased per unit transportation costs. Imagine if automobiles still had to be brought from Japan by sailing ships and distributed by wagon train! The famous clipper ship *Flying Cloud* (1851) weighed only 1,782 tons, and the "immense" *Great Eastern* (1858) weighed 22,000 tons and could carry 15,000 tons of cargo. By contrast, the modern tanker *Seawise Giant* is 1,500 feet long (five football fields, almost one-third mile) and carries over one-half million tons of oil.

Free-trade philosophy. The 1930s and early 1940s were a period of global trauma, marked first by a great economic depression, then by World War II. One cause for these successive miseries, it was said, was the high tariffs that had restricted trade and divided nations. To avoid a recurrence, the victorious United States took the lead in reducing barriers to international trade.[5] The General Agreement on Tariffs and Trade (GATT) came into being in 1947 when countries accounting for 80 percent of world commerce agreed to work to reduce barriers to international trade. As a result of this and a series of related efforts, world tariff barriers dropped dramatically. American import duties, for example, currently average under 11 percent, or about one-fourth of their mean level in the 1930s.

Increased Economic Interdependence

As we saw in Chapter 1, world economics have become increasingly intertwined. Domestic economics, including employment, inflation, and overall growth, is heavily dependent on foreign markets, imports of resources, currency exchange rates, and a variety of international economic factors. The rise in trade is both a cause and a result of this increased international economic **interdependence.** Increased trade stimulated economies and *caused* new demands for, and dependencies on, foreign products and resources. This, in turn, *resulted* in even greater trade, because stimulated production and consumption needed even more trade to supply them. Thus, there is a circular relationship among interdependence, trade, and economic growth. The discussions of economics in Chapters 1 and 7 detailed some specific statistics relating to interdependence. Even without such statistics, one can easily understand that a world in which Russians eat American wheat, Japanese export cars to Americans but import oil from the Arabs to fuel their own cars, and the French watch televisions built in Asia and ship wine everywhere is highly interdependent. The idea of **autarky**, of any country's being truly economically independent, has long since ceased to be a realistic concept.

Increased Domestic Impact: A Two-Way Street

Another aspect of increased world economic relations is the escalating interrelationship between domestic and international economics. Every country's economic health, to a greater or lesser degree, is affected by the world economy. As Figure 11-3 shows, between 1950 and 1970 trade grew much faster than other key economic indicators.

To reiterate an earlier point, it is extremely important to understand the impact of world trade and monetary relations on domestic economies. Millions of jobs and entire industries can be created or destroyed by foreign sales or competition. Inflation can be accelerated or eased by currency exchange rates. Oil and other vital resources can flow in vast quantity or can be subject to rationing and long lines. In short, you and the world economy are more intimately linked than you probably imagine.

It should also be stressed that the interrelationship between international economics and domestic economics works in both directions. Domestic economics and politics affect the international scene just as world factors affect

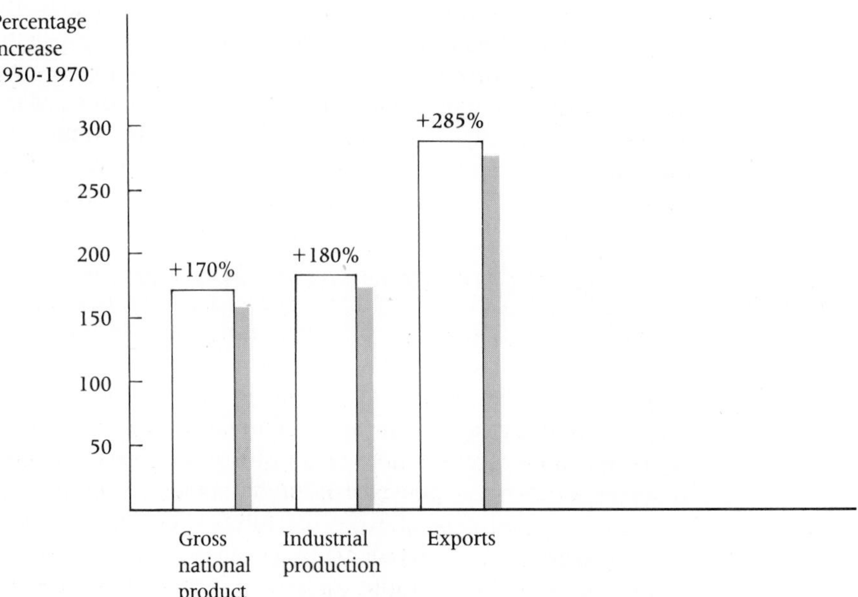

Figure 11-3. Growth in world economics and trade, 1950–1970. *Data from Andre Gunder Frank,* Crisis in the World Economy *(New York: Holmes & Meier, 1980), p. 3.*

the national situation. American inflation, as we shall see, helped cause a financial crisis in world banking during the early 1980s. The U.S. deficit is also a major concern to world economic leaders.

Further, domestic politics and international politics are strongly linked. The global economic downturn of the last decade has caused intense domestic pressure to raise tariffs and take other actions to protect domestic jobs and industries. Presidents and prime ministers may fancy themselves world leaders, but in the last analysis, they are elected by domestic voters.

Patterns of Trade

In addition to the level of world trade, it is important to consider the patterns of international commerce. Three facts stand out. First, trade is overwhelmingly dominated by the North, the developed countries. The percentage of world trade shared by less developed countries is both small and relatively static. In fact, if the oil-producing nations are considered separately, the less developed countries (LDCs) have lost ground slightly. Figure 11-4 shows the percentage of world trade in 1963, 1975, and 1982 held by various classes of states.

A second, and related, pattern of world trade is that little commerce occurs among less developed nations. North/North trade accounts for 55.2 percent of all world commerce, North/South trade 37.4 percent, and South/South trade a scant 7.4 percent.[6]

A third important trade pattern involves types of exports. Developed countries predominantly export manufactured and processed products. LDCs mostly export primary products (food, minerals, etc.). This is discussed in greater detail in the next chapter, but we can note here that this pattern leaves the LDCs in a disadvantaged position because the prices of primary products expand more slowly than those of manufactured goods and because world demand for primary products is highly volatile.

Issues in Trade

Although tariffs have tumbled during the past decades, and trade has boomed, all is not well. Several aspects of international commerce are major issues on the world stage, and we will examine these in the following pages: first, the renewed debate over the wisdom of relatively free trade; second, the growth and power of multinational corporations; and third, the prickly issue of East/West trade. There are still other issues, such as the formation of cartels (international trading blocs) and the nature of the North's responsibility for the economic development of the South, but these will be discussed in the next chapter. To set the stage for all these issues, however, we must first consider the current political/economic situation and also types of trade barriers.

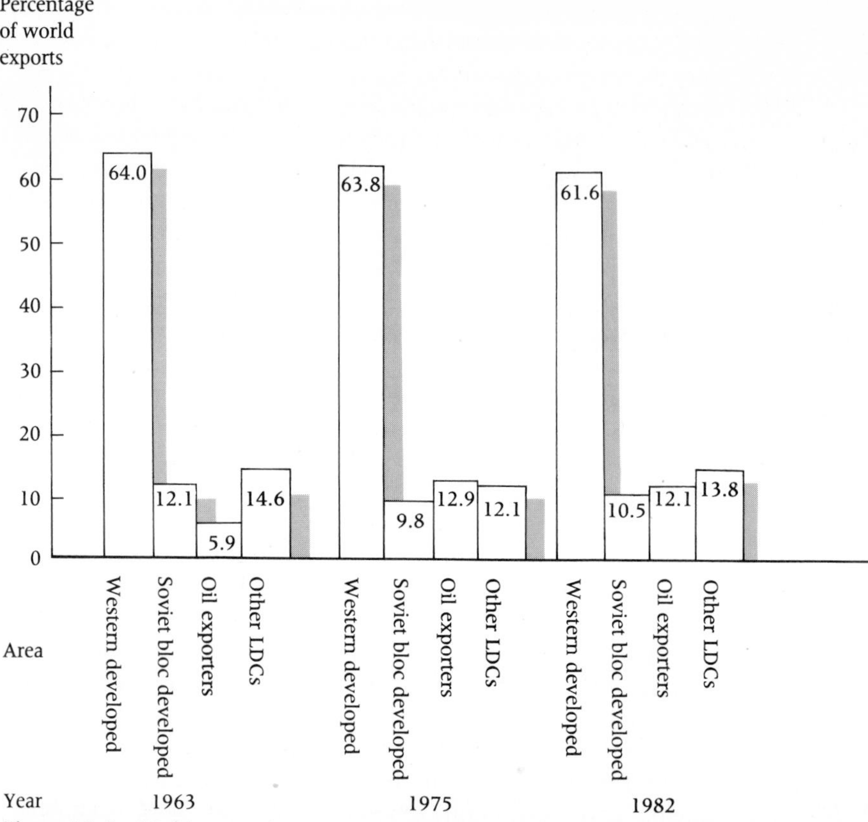

Figure 11-4. World exports by major area. Totals may not equal 100 percent because of rounding. *Data from General Agreement on Tariffs and Trade,* International Trade, 1982/83 *(Geneva: General Agreement on Tariffs and Trade, 1983), appendix, table A3.*

Troubled Trade

So far in examining world commerce, we have seen that trade and the economies of the industrialized nations are expanding at a vigorous rate. That is true in the long view, but in the shorter run there are disturbing signs. Whereas between 1963 and 1972 trade volume expanded at an annual average rate of 8.5 percent, during the next ten years it met or exceeded that figure only twice. In six of the years, trade increased less than 5 percent, and by the beginning of the 1980s expansion was at 2.0 percent (1980), 0.5 percent (1981), and −2.5 percent (1982).[7] The growth of industrial production also slowed, and the Western industrialized nations were bedeviled by unusually high rates of unemployment and inflation.[8]

The debate over the causes of this downturn and whether it represents a short-term cyclical recession or a more serious long-term crisis is beyond our discussion here. Whatever its causes and future, the economic difficulties of the 1970s and early 1980s have dramatically increased the pressure to restrict trade. As one symbol of this pressure, the 1982 GATT conference was unable to make any new progress in trade. At best, according to the *New York Times*, the conferees were able to reach only a "fragile consensus" to avoid an outbreak of protectionism.[9]

Trade Barriers

If the economic war that looms does break out, its weapons will be trade barriers. **Tariffs** are the most familiar trade barrier. At present, tariff barriers are generally low, but they are high selectively. In 1983, in an effort to protect Harley-Davidson, the last American motorcycle company, the Reagan administration hiked by 1,000 percent the import duty on heavy-weight motorcycles from Japan.[10] Still, although it is possible that a sudden escalation of tariff rates could occur, the complex series of international agreements governing their level makes such an event unlikely.

A lesser-known but important way of restricting trade is by **nontariff barriers** (NTBs). Reminiscent of a Paul Simon song, one team of economic analysts said, "There must be 50 ways to restrict foreign trade without using a tariff."[11] Import or export *quotas* are one NTB. These limit the number of units that can be shipped, as in the case of Japanese cars to the United States. The early 1980s *embargo* on the shipment of U.S. grain to the Soviet Union illustrates another type of barrier. *Technical restrictions* such as health and safety regulations are another barrier. The Japanese export 6 million vehicles and import only 38,000. One reason is that safety changes and strict inspections drive the cost of a Buick up over $24,000 and a Cadillac over $40,000. Governments can also *subsidize* industries either directly or indirectly through tax breaks. Subsidization allows a domestic company to undersell foreign competition at home. *Dumping* is yet another (and illegal) practice that disrupts normal trade flow. In this case, economic incentives allow a company to sell its product more cheaply abroad than at home. In the early 1970s, for instance, Japanese televisions were selling for $333 in Japan and for only $180 in the United States! It was a great deal—unless, of course, you were an American television manufacturer or plant worker. A final type of trade barrier is a *boycott*. This is a refusal to trade with a particular company or buy a particular product. Arab countries, for one, will not do business with companies that use blacklisted ships, banks, or goods of Israeli origin. U.S. Commerce Department figures show that in 1980 American businesses complied with 60 percent of all Arab boycott requests, for $7 billion in trade restrictions.[12]

This issue of NTBs is highly contentious. Japan is a master of using these techniques, but protests have been growing. Relations between that country and others, particularly the United States, could be damaged by the lopsided **trade balance** in favor of Japan.

It is also likely that any new trade restrictions will take place in the form of NTBs. Within the range of NTBs, some types, such as subsidies, are more subtle, and less subject to the charge of protectionism. Other types, like quotas, have a more immediate effect, and in all cases, NTBs avoid violating the postwar norm of keeping tariffs low.

Free Trade: Pro and Con

During the economic prosperity of the 1950s and 1960s, **free trade** advocates far outnumbered protectionists. The lean times of more recent years have changed that, and protectionism has been resurrected. It is important to remember that, in the last analysis, trade policy is based primarily on *political* forces. Economic theory makes many valuable contributions, but in the end it is the political leaders who decide. Thus, international economic policy and the various positions on trade are based on a combination of *systems-level economic realities* such as energy needs and *state-level domestic pressures* from interest groups, legislatures, consumers, and others.

Free Trade: Pro

Advocates of free trade argue from a series of economic and political propositions. These include the benefits of specialization, the promotion of competition, the ability of trade to promote world cooperation, and the conflict-inhibiting effect of commerce.

Benefits of specialization. The most basic economic idea supporting free trade is the image of each country efficiently doing what it can do best. In the early nineteenth century, the economist David Ricardo formulated the **law of comparative advantage**, which holds that all countries can benefit from specializing.[13] Consider the following example: Germany produces iron at $50 a ton and wheat at $70 a ton. France produces iron at $90 a ton and wheat at $30 a ton. Even given transportation costs of $10 per ton, France can save money by purchasing German iron, and Germany can save money if it buys French wheat. Figure 11-5 shows this relationship.

This example is, of course, simplistic. Many more sophisticated modifications of the theory have been formulated, and economists adjust their thinking to real-world exigencies. Still, the vision of world prosperity inspired by specialization has been a powerful concept. As one American economic official recently declared, "Neither the United States nor the [European Economic Community] has exhausted the potential for gain in terms of growth and more and better jobs from specialization, innovation, competition, and economies of scale."[14]

Promotion of competition. A second economic free-trade argument focuses on competition. Without foreign competition, domestic manufacturers have a captive market. Especially if one corporation dominates its field or if there is

	IRON		WHEAT	
	Germany	France	Germany	France
Production cost	$50	$90	$70	$30
Transportation	+10	+ 0	+ 0	+10
Total cost and direction of trade	$60 ⟶	$90	$70 ⟵	$40

Figure 11-5. An example of the law of comparative advantage.

monopolistic collusion among supposed competitors, a variety of ill effects, from price fixing to lack of innovation, may occur. Many observers believe that the Detroit automakers were stuck in a big-car rut until pressure from foreign competition forced them to reform their product and their production techniques.

World cooperation. A third, and this time political, argument claims that free trade promotes world cooperation. *Functionalism* (to be discussed extensively in the chapter on international organization) argues that cooperating in certain specific functions, such as trade, can lead to habits of cooperation that can be transferred to other, more potentially conflictive areas. If countries can trade together in peace, the interactions will bring greater contact and understanding. Cooperation will then become the rule rather than the exception, and this, it is thought, will lead to political cooperation and interaction. The move toward the political integration of Europe, which began with economic cooperation, is the most frequently cited example.[15]

Conflict inhibition. A fourth, and again political, argument for free trade is that it restrains conflict. Trade not only promotes functional cooperation, advocates claim, it also leads to interdependence, which makes fighting more difficult. The theory here is that if countries become highly dependent on each other for vital resources and products, then the cutoff of those supplies would dissuade or even prevent them from fighting. If oil and iron are necessary to fight, and if Country A supplies Country B's oil, and B supplies A's iron, then they are too enmeshed to go to war.

In reality, of course, a very high level of specialization and integration would be required to make this idea work perfectly. Indeed, dependency can cause conflict in some cases. The United States has repeatedly threatened military action to protect its Middle East oil supplies. Still, to take such action might lead to destruction of the oil fields themselves or further alienation of the Arab states, and so a level of restraint is achieved. Like many theories, then, conflict inhibition is simple on the surface but highly complex in its application.

Free Trade: Con

There are also several political and economic arguments for protectionism. These include protecting the domestic economy, diversification, compensating for existing distortions, national security, and using protectionism as a policy tool.[16]

Protecting the domestic economy. The need for trade barriers to protect the domestic economy is a favorite theme of domestic interest groups. Threatened industries and associated labor unions seek protection from competition. They argue that domestic business will suffer and domestic workers will be unemployed while foreign companies and workers reap the profits. Whatever the objective truth of this argument—and most economists dismiss it—the political pressure for protectionism is intense. An associated argument seeks protection for "infant industry." This is an especially common contention in LDCs trying to industrialize but is also heard worldwide. Many economists give the idea of such protection some credibility but argue that supposedly "temporary" protection too often becomes permanent.[17]

Diversification. A closely related argument holds that economic diversification should be encouraged. Specialization, it is said, will make a country too dependent on a few resources or products. If demand for those products falls, then economic catastrophe will result. In reality, of course, no modern, complex economy will become that specialized, but the argument does have a simplistic appeal.

Compensating for existing distortions. Yet another protectionist argument is that in the real world many trade distortions exist that are unaccounted for by pure economic theory. Factors including persistent trade barriers, government-managed economies, and state-directed trading have created an imperfect economic world. If the oil-producing countries set prices, if communist governments act as state traders, if France continues to leave video recorders sitting on the dock while "awaiting inspection," then, the argument goes, nice-guy free-traders will finish last.

The answer to some of these distortions is to correct them rather than retaliate. Others, however, such as state trading, are a long-term reality, and as one recent analyst observed, "During the 1970s . . . the premises on which the free trade ideal had been founded were no longer applicable to large segments of industrialized economies."[18]

National security. A fourth, and very political, protectionist argument involves national defense. The contention here is somewhat the reverse of the "conflict inhibition" pro–free trade argument above. Protectionists stress that their country must not become so dependent on foreign sources that it will be unable to defend itself. In recent years, the U.S. government has acted to protect industries ranging from speciality steels to basic textiles partly in response to warnings that the country was losing its ability to produce weapons systems

The benefits of free trade have not impressed this auto worker who lost his job because of foreign imports.

and uniforms.[19] Although it is improbable that a protracted global war that could threaten supplies will occur, and even though major dependencies already exist, the national security argument does have some very selective validity. More important, it has a powerful emotional appeal when it is used by a threatened industry that is even remotely connected to defense needs. A related argument, reviewed under "East/West Trade," below, is that you should not send a potential opponent goods that have military applications.

Policy tool. The final protectionist argument looks at foreign trade as a source of political power. The Arab oil embargo, the Arabs' boycott of companies doing business with Israel, the U.S. grain embargo against the Soviet Union, and growing trade and financial pressure on South Africa are all recent examples of trying to use economic means to achieve political ends.[20] The historical evidence does not indicate that, in general, the use of trade is an effective political tool. However, the idea has a powerful attraction for policy makers, both economically and as a diplomatic signaling device, and it will continue to be a factor in international relations.

Free Trade and the Future

There is no good guess about the future balance between the forces of free trade and protectionism. It is unthinkable that the world will return to the high-tariff, trade-restricted policies of the 1930s. A level of independence may be desirable, but autarky is neither desirable nor possible. Still, free-traders are worried.[21] As Ronald Reagan has warned, "When governments get too involved in [hampering] trade, economic costs increase and disputes multiply. Peace is threatened."[22]

Some easing of protectionist pressures will probably occur as the industrialized economies adjust to and recover from the economic shocks of the 1970s. But the intertwining of domestic and foreign economic sectors, the competitive rise of at least a few Third World countries, and other structural changes in the world economy make it likely that protectionism will remain a strong force in the foreseeable future.[23]

Multinational Corporations

Another series of related economic issues revolves around the growth and practices of the world's **multinational corporations** (MNCs).[24] In this section, we will focus on international business in general terms and then on its role in the economic interchange of the industrialized nations. Later sections in this chapter will also refer to MNCs and East/West trade and to the role of international banking. The following chapter will deal with the interaction between MNCs and the Third World.

MNCs: Past and Present

A multinational corporation is a private enterprise that includes subsidiaries operating in more than one state. This means more than merely international trading. Rather, it implies ownership of manufacturing plants and/or resource extraction and processing operations in a variety of countries. Many therefore contend that MNCs are transnational organizations whose operations transcend national boundaries. Whether this is true and to what degree is, as we shall see, a highly controversial issue.

Historical roots. The idea of multinational enterprise is not new. Some have traced the roots of modern MNCs to Europe's great trading companies, beginning with the Dutch East India Trading Company in 1689.[25] The level of multinational enterprise expanded in the nineteenth century and into the twentieth. It was not long after Henry Ford began building Model Ts that his corporation had its first subsidiary in Europe. Indeed, as early as 1902 one British author wrote a book, *The American Invaders,* warning against the takeover of the European economy by such American predators as Singer Sewing Machine, Otis Elevator, and General Electric.[26]

Not until after World War II, however, did the development of MNCs truly accelerate. Between 1945 and 1968 direct private investment in international ventures increased 10 percent annually.[27]

REPRINTED BY PERMISSION OF TRIBUNE MEDIA SERVICES.

MNCs today: economic goliaths. As fast as trade and other forms of international commerce have grown, MNCs have expanded even more rapidly. To get some idea of the size and continuing rate of MNC expansion, consider some of the following statistics:[28]

- There are about 2,000 large (operating in six or more countries) and over 8,000 smaller MNCs.
- By 1990 the 300 largest MNCs will account for over three fourths of the world's GNP and employ 20 percent of its work force.
- In 1982 the top fifty MNCs had combined foreign and domestic sales of $1.24 trillion and a profit of $39 billion.
- Of the top fifty, 42 percent are U.S.-based, 38 percent are European, and 14 percent are Japanese. Only three of the top fifty are based outside the **trilateral countries** (United States, Japan, Western Europe), and all of those three are oil companies (in Mexico, Venezuela, and Brazil).

If we consider Ford Motor Company again for a moment—and it ranks only seventh in world sales—it has grown from its one original division to a point where, by the late 1960s, it was a network of sixty corporations. Forty of these were foreign, and they accounted for nearly $3 billion in invested assets.[29]

Finally, it is instructive to measure companies against countries. There is, of course, no comparison in coercive power between any corporation and a state, but corporations do wield considerable economic muscle. Table 11-1 compares the MNCs' gross corporate product (GCP), sales, with the **gross national product** (GNP), goods and services produced, of a number of coun-

Table 11-1. Corporations and Countries, 1982 (figures in billions of dollars).

Corporations (rank, GCP)	*Countries (GNP)*
Exxon (1, $97.2)	
	East Germany ($89.1)
	Czechoslovakia ($77)
	Nigeria ($77)
	Austria ($76.3)
	Argentina ($61.5)
General Motors (3, $60.0)	
	South Korea ($59.1)
	Norway ($57.3)
	Finland ($50.1)
	Greece ($43.8)
	Taiwan ($40.2)
	Poland ($35.2)
IBM (8, $34.4)	
	Iraq ($31)
	Algeria ($29)
	Egypt ($26)
	Israel ($19.9)
	Chile ($19.8)
Nissan (25, $16.5)	
	Hungary ($16.4)
VW (36, $15.4)	
	Bulgaria ($14.4)
	Cuba ($13.9)
	Syria ($9.4)
	Vietnam ($7.6)
	Bolivia ($6.1)

Source: Fortune, August 22, 1983, p. 170. GNP drawn from *World Almanac, 1984* (New York: Newspaper Enterprise Association, 1983).

tries. According to these standards, if companies were countries, forty of the top one hundred world economic powers would be corporations.

MNCs: Pro and Con

The growth and practices of giant, global MNCs have provoked heated controversy over whether they are assets or liabilities.

The case for MNCs. Several economic and political arguments can be made on behalf of MNCs.[30]

MNCs reflect a complex and interdependent world. In an era when national boundaries are becoming increasingly permeable and when a whole range of transnational organizations and relationships are developing, the MNC is a "natural" development.

MNCs provide host countries with technical advantages. Supporters argue that MNCs can best engage in the "expensive business" of developing "new productive knowledge, both technological and managerial."[31] These benefits can then be transferred to a host country. This argument is made with particular reference to the role of MNCs in LDCs, but it is also applicable to benefits for industrialized countries. A recent surge of ties between American and Japanese auto manufacturers partly involves the transfer of Japanese technology and managerial techniques to the lethargic U.S. auto industry.

MNCs provide host countries with needed capital. As discussed more fully in the next chapter, MNCs are one source of capital in developing countries. It should be noted here, though, that the vast bulk of MNC investment is in industrialized countries. In addition, while private investment in LDCs increased from $35.1 billion in 1967 to $84.4 billion in 1976, its relative impact dropped from 13.0 percent to 8.9 percent of those countries' domestic economies.[32]

MNCs provide jobs. Investment in host countries sometimes creates jobs, and employment opportunities have expanded in both developed and less developed countries. Two important caveats should be noted, however. One is that MNCs also export jobs. The AFL-CIO estimates that 90,000 American jobs were lost between 1966 and 1971 as a result of the expansion of U.S. multinationals abroad. Second, there are questions about the quality of employment created by MNCs. Often host-country workers are trained for only the least skilled jobs.[33]

MNCs are part of the growth of transnational cooperation. This final argument for MNCs is more political than economic. Those who take this approach see MNCs as part of the functionalist growth toward higher stages of international cooperation.[34]

The case against MNCs. There are also a variety of charges leveled against global enterprises.

MNCs drain host countries' capital. Critics charge that MNCs take more capital out in profits than they put in through investments. One illustrative study found that during one three-year period U.S. firms invested $1.1 billion in Latin America but extracted $5.4 billion in profits.[35]

MNCs exploit host countries' labor. The multinationals pay lower wages than they would in their home country. It is also true, though, that they pay more than locally owned companies.[36] Further, some manufacturing that uses technology-intensive techniques, for example, may actually lead to a decline in employment.[37]

MNCs deplete host countries' resources. As we have seen, LDC exports are often centered on primary products and natural resources. Some manufacturing is introduced, but to a substantial extent resources are still extracted and sent to an already industrialized country for processing.

MNCs engage in political manipulation and other unethical activities. Critics view MNCs as self-interested actors who, too often, operate outside the boundaries of ethical behavior. MNCs are indicted for political meddling (such as the involvement of International Telephone and Telegraph in the 1973 overthrow of Chile's President Allende), for violating human rights (trading with and investing in repressive nations), and for bribery and other illegal payments (such as Lockheed's $1.6 million bribe to Japanese Prime Minister Kakuei Tanaka, who was convicted in 1981).[38]

MNCs engage in unethical activities that are not permitted in their home country.

There are many related charges in this area. U.S. (and other) drug companies, for example, sell many products in other countries, sometimes without prescription, that are banned as hazardous in the United States. MNCs also engage in unacceptable industrial processes. In 1980, for example, a U.S.-owned chemical plant in Nicaragua was found to have one third of its workers suffering from mercury poisoning, and the region's entire population was threatened by the discharge of forty tons of mercury waste into Lake Managua, a major source of drinking water for the nation's capital.

Yet another charge against MNCs is that they also operate against the interest of the home country. In the estimate of one study, "The goal of corporate diplomacy is nothing less than the replacement of national loyalty with corporate loyalty."[39] Charges range from exporting jobs to cheap labor markets and avoiding taxes by shifting profits to low-tax countries to cooperating with international opponents of the home country. In 1973, for example, the Philippine subsidiary of Exxon refused to sell oil to the U.S. Navy at its Subic Bay base because the company was adhering to the Arab oil boycott of the United States.[40]

The final anti-MNC charge somewhat contradicts the immediately preceding point: *MNCs can be used by their home country for imperialistic bullying of host countries.* As one study put it, "Fears in a host government . . . arise . . . because of [both] conscious interference by a foreign government through the parent company . . . [and] also . . . unconscious interference—of domination by inadvertence."[41]

MNCs: a temperate perspective. As the above pro and con arguments over the role of MNCs indicate, these giant enterprises are of mixed value. On the positive side, they do facilitate the transfer of capital, technology, and management techniques. They also play a role in economic integration that functionalists claim will lead to a higher world order.

Some of the critics' points are also well taken, however. Global corporations have caused some economic dislocation in both home and host countries. MNCs have also sometimes taken excessive profits, depleted resources, and added little to the development of host countries. MNCs have also pursued their own interests, sometimes in contradiction to the interests of home or host governments. Finally, the addition of any new set of powerful, self-interested actors to an already quasi-anarchistic world is a troubling development.

The appropriate response to this mixture of assets and liabilities is better *regulation*. Given the state of the world economy, the elimination of MNCs is neither probable nor desirable. Instead, both national and international standards should be strengthened. On the *national* level, both home and host countries are "catching up" in the governance of MNCs.[42] Many host countries, for instance, are establishing limits on profit-taking and are decreeing that domestic investors must own a majority of any corporation operating in the state.

There are also several *international* efforts to set standards. The United Nations has established the Center on Transnational Corporations. The Inter-

In 1984, a chemical leak at a Union Carbide plant in Bhopal, India, killed, blinded, and injured thousands. Many critics charge that multinational corporations fail to apply the same safety standards in foreign countries as they do in their home countries.

national Labor Organization monitors related labor issues, and the industrialized North, through the Organization for Economic Cooperation and Development (OECD), has established a Committee on International Investment and Multinational Enterprises.[43]

The issue, then, is not whether to continue or disband MNCs but how to harness them. Given their economic power and their ability to escape regulation, that will be a difficult task, but it is possible and it has begun.

East/West Trade

Along with the issues of free trade versus protectionism and the role of MNCs, the question of East/West trade is a major source of tension among the North's industrialized states. The basic issue is whether trade between the Western states and the Soviet bloc is both good business and good politics or whether it amounts to trading with the enemy.

A Growing Interchange

Whatever its wisdom, trade between the trilateral countries (United States, Japan, Western Europe) and the Soviet bloc, represented by the Council for Mutual Economic Assistance (CMEA), has increased steadily, as Table 11-2 illustrates.

Table 11-2. East/West Trade, 1963 and 1982.

	1963		1982	
	Dollar value (billions)	Percentage of all exports	Dollar value (billions)	Percentage of all exports
Exports from West to East	4.0	4.0	52	4.6
Exports from East to West	4.0	21.1	59	30.1

Data from General Agreement on Tariffs and Trade, *International Trade, 1982/83* (Geneva: General Agreement on Tariffs and Trade, 1983), appendix, table A3.

Within the general context of expanding trade, two points should be noted. First, East/West trade is, in general, more important to the CMEA than to the trilateral powers. For the Soviet Union and its allies, trade with the West represents a substantial part of their export total. Second, imports of high-technology items are extremely important to the economies of the CMEA countries.

Western Restraints: Growing Conflict

In the years after World War II, the trilateral countries cooperated in maintaining a list of militarily applicable items that could not be exported to communist countries.[44] The United States was the leading advocate of extensive restrictions, and in an era of cold-war hostility and U.S. dominance, a long list of embargoed items was maintained.

Policies diverge. In the 1960s and 1970s, Western unity began to fall apart. The United States was beset by many political and economic problems and lost some of its leadership status. Western Europe and Japan became more assertive, detente eased tensions, and the economic slowdown of the late 1970s increased pressure to trade.

The result was that trade with the Soviet bloc expanded, the Western Europeans and the Japanese leading the way and the Americans trailing behind. By 1980, 6.5 percent of German and Japanese exports, 4 percent of French exports, and 3.5 percent of Italian exports but only 1.7 percent of U.S. exports went to CMEA countries. This trade is particularly important to the developing technical segment of the Western European economies and, according to some sources, supports some 200,000 jobs in West Germany alone.[45]

The pipeline imbroglio. The policy divergence between the United States and the other trilateral countries grew to real strain in the early 1980s. First, after Afghanistan, President Carter imposed economic sanctions on the USSR and tried to line up cooperation by the NATO allies. Then, with the inauguration of Ronald Reagan, the American attitude hardened even more. Finally, a real rift developed between the United States and Western Europe in 1981–1982 over a deal that proposed a 3,000-mile pipeline between the Soviet

Union's natural gas fields and the energy-hungry countries of Western Europe. The European countries agreed to supply the Soviets with much of the equipment and technological support as well as $5 billion in loans needed to build the pipeline. In return, Europe would receive 40 billion cubic meters of gas annually at a cost of $10 to $20 billion in hard currency. For the economically lagging, energy-short Europeans and for the technology- and hard-currency-deficient Soviets, it was a mutually sweet deal.

Everyone was happy—except the United States government. The Reagan administration launched a campaign to block the agreement by pressuring its allies and by forbidding U.S.-based MNCs to allow their Western European subsidiaries to cooperate. The Europeans were outraged. They charged that the United States was not only ignoring the economic plight of European countries (such as 9 percent unemployment) but also violating their sovereignty. "France," proclaimed Premier Pierre Mauroy, "cannot accept unilateral measures by the United States."[46] The American president was also pressured by his own domestic business groups, which wanted to be involved in the lucrative contracts. It was, in the end, the Reagan administration that retreated, but the gas-line flare-up is an indication of the ongoing debate over what and how much to trade with the CMEA countries.

East/West Trade: Pro and Con

Arguments against Extensive Trade

No Western political leader argues for a complete trade embargo against the CMEA, but those who favor strict limits make several points.[47]

Trade supplies technology. For the United States and many of its developed-nation allies, the export of technology is an important source of revenue. In 1983 alone, U.S. firms earned $7.6 billion just by licensing the foreign production of high-tech equipment. This is certainly financially desirable. The point here is that the West's greatest advantage over its Eastern-bloc rivals is advanced technology, and some argue that the West is selling its advantage to the communists. In April 1984, for example, a U.S. Defense Department official testified before Congress that an Apple II personal computer could be used to target nuclear weapons. The Defense Department has resisted the sale of a long list of technological items and information and reviews such transfers not only to communist countries but to countries that are apt to "reexport" them, such as Sweden, Finland, India, Iraq, Syria, and Libya. The dilemma, then, is that although trade is good for Western business, the export of technology, from truck plants to computers, both saves international opponents billions of dollars in research and development costs and helps their economies expand more quickly than would otherwise be possible.

Trade supplies military capacity. Trade critics also say the West is supplying its enemies with military potential. Direct military supplies are, of course, embargoed, but the line between military and civilian is often imprecise. The giant Kama Truck Works in the Soviet Union was built (1971–1975) by over 150 Western MNCs for over $1 billion. It has over 50,000 machine tools and 180 miles of assembly lines and can turn out 150,000 heavy-duty trucks and 250,000 diesel engines annually. Whether these trucks will always carry potatoes to Soviet vodka distilleries or whether they might someday carry ammunition to the Western front is unknowable.[48]

Trade encourages dangerous dependency. A third antitrade argument is that it is perilous to become dependent on an adversary. The Reagan administration stressed this point during the pipeline controversy. Washington claimed that the Soviets had cut off gas supplies to China, Israel, and Yugoslavia in the past and might try to politically pressure Europe in the future.[49]

Trade supplies cash. A final charge is that if you buy Soviet natural gas or too much of anything from communist countries, you supply them with much-needed hard currency to build up their economy. As President Reagan fulminated, "They do not have the cash for [their] purposes the way they once did . . . [but the pipeline] will give them $10 billion to $20 billion a year in cold, hard cash."[50]

Arguments against Restraints

Proponents of expanded East/West trade make a series of counterpoints. It is something of an irony that many of the strongest proponents of trade with the communists are the supposedly ultracapitalist captains of the MNCs.[51]

Economic pressure doesn't work. Trade proponents cite the failure of the trade pressures on the USSR, Iran, and others as examples of futility. They further argue that such pressure can be counterproductive, forcing the other side into a stubborn defense of its sovereignty.

Trade restraints hurt you more than them. The argument here is that because of loss of sales or perhaps loss of supplies, trade embargoes or other restraints may be equivalent to cutting off your own nose. American farmers lost billions of dollars during the 1980–1982 grain embargo, and even after it ended, they recaptured only a small part of the previous market.

The losses to business in the embargoing country and the political futility of restraints are most pronounced where there are alternative suppliers. Other countries, such as Argentina, were only too happy to sell wheat to the Soviets. The Carter administration's post-Afghanistan economic boycott also cost U.S. industrial firms well over a billion dollars in lost contracts, which went instead to French and German firms.[52]

Trade promotes peace. A final argument, which we have seen before in a more general context, is that trade has the functional impact of encouraging cooperation and restraining aggression through interdependency. Regarding

Reagan's "dangerously dependent" argument above, one French official countered, "Moscow needs the hard currency more than we need the gas."[53] In short, the Soviets might not be able to afford blackmailing, much less attacking, Western Europe.

A Right Answer?

The issue again is not whether to trade but what and how much. Although there is no absolute right answer, several points do stand out. First, using economics as a political weapon is very risky. Not only is its impact uncertain, but it often costs you more than the target country. Second, it is particularly ineffective when there is disunity among the supplying countries. The Soviets quickly found alternative grain sources in 1981; the only big losers were American farmers. Third, trying to impose unity may cause political discord among allies, as the pipeline controversy shows.

None of this means that economic pressure can't work. Nor does it dismiss the need for restrictions on the transfer of clearly military-application technology. Rather, the evidence suggests that even if the theory of using economics as a political tool seems attractive, in practice the odds of success are slim.

International Monetary Relations

Of all the facets of international economic relations, the importance of the ebb and flow of the world's currencies is the least understood. Periodically we hear news reports, for example, that the American dollar is stronger against the Japanese yen, British pound, or German mark, and our reaction is "Good!" But is it good? That depends. If you are traveling to Japan or planning to buy a BMW, you are in luck. Your American dollar will buy more. If, however, you are an American exporter trying to sell overseas or if your product competes with foreign imports, then the news isn't good at all.

Money, you must remember, has no intrinsic value. We accept it in exchange for other goods and services only because we are confident that others will, in turn, accept it for goods or services we ourselves want. This principle is true on an international as well as a personal scale. Therefore, the stability of world **monetary relations** is vital to global economic well-being. This has always been true, but as trade and other economic relations have expanded, the importance of monetary interchange has increased proportionately.

In the rest of this chapter, we will look at the nature of exchange rates, the history of monetary regulations, current issues including balance of payments and lending practices, and attempts to reform the monetary system. The financial position of LDCs and attempts at financial cooperation are also discussed in Chapters 13 and 14, respectively.

Exchange rates are, very simply, the values of two currencies vis-à-vis each other—how many dollars per yen and vice versa.

The exchange rate is important because it affects several aspects of the balance of payments and domestic economics (see below). Trade, for example, is partly governed by how much foreign imports cost relative to domestic supplies. Consider the following:

- An auto costs 50,000 yen to make in Japan.
- An auto costs 10,000 dollars to make in the United States.
- The exchange rate is 5 yen = 1 dollar.
- Thus, the cost of a car is about the same in the two countries, and, given transportation costs and tariffs, the countries will exchange equal numbers of cars.
- If the dollar gets "stronger," and the yen "declines" to an exchange rate of 7.5 yen = 1 dollar, then the U.S. car will cost 75,000 yen (plus transportation and shipping) in Japan, compared with 50,000 yen for a Japanese model. U.S. car exports will decline. The Japanese cars will sell for only $6,667 (50,000/7.5) in the United States. Japanese car exports will boom; U.S. manufacturers will lose part of their domestic market.

Before you advocate "weakening" the dollar, it is important to remember that there are negative consequences. If you depreciate the dollar or appreciate the foreign currencies, things you need or want to buy from abroad, such as oil, are going to be more expensive. Since we rely on many foreign supplies, domestic inflation will increase. Further, the strong dollar has encouraged the foreign buying of more U.S. government securities, thus helping to finance the huge budget deficits. Less foreign investment capital will drive up interest rates. Foreign travel will also cost more. In short, the message is that currencies need to be in a balance that reflects their real supply/demand relationship in order for the international economy to stay in balance.

Monetary Relations since World War II

The Bretton Woods System

As part of postwar planning, the Western allies met in 1944 at Bretton Woods, New Hampshire, to establish a new monetary order. The **Bretton Woods system** operated on the principle of "fixed convertibility into gold." At its root, the system depended heavily on the strength of the American dollar, which was set at a rate of $35 per ounce of gold. As long as the American economy was strong, international confidence remained high and countries accepted and held dollars on a basis of "as good as gold."

In addition to this system of convertibility, Bretton Woods established several institutions to help promote and regulate the world economy. For our discussion here, the most important of these is the *International Monetary Fund* (IMF). The primary function of the IMF is short-term lending to countries with international balance-of-payments problems. If a country is spending more than it is taking in, it can draw on IMF funds to help buy back its own currency, thus maintaining exchange-rate stability.

The End of Bretton Woods

The Bretton Woods system lasted for twenty-five years, and it worked reasonably well as long as the American economy dominated the world and the dollar remained strong. Beginning in the 1960s and accelerating in the early 1970s, the foundation of the Bretton Woods system collapsed. The basic cause was the growing U.S. trade deficit and the resulting run on the dollar. The growth of world competition, the costs of American foreign policy (especially Vietnam), the astronomical rise in oil prices, domestic spending and inflation, and other factors further lowered confidence in the dollar. Countries were less willing to hold dollars and increasingly asked the United States to buy them back at the $35 = 1 ounce gold rate. The crisis year was 1971. Unable to continue under the old system, the United States took a series of steps that took the country off the gold standard. In place of fixed convertibility, a new system, one of "free floating" currency relations, was established. Here, the value of a country's currency was basically left to supply and demand.[54]

The Current Situation

Despite the appeal of its economic simplicity, the free-floating system has not worked well. One problem is that large interest rates in the United States plus its political stability have kept the demand for American dollars high despite large U.S. trade deficits. Another is that the Japanese government has acted to keep the yen artificially low in order to boost trade. These and other factors have caused strong calls for another round of monetary reforms, but to date no plan has been found acceptable.

Current Monetary Issues

Issues facing the world monetary system include instability, balance-of-payments problems, and lending practices.

Instability

As mentioned above, one current monetary difficulty is based on the wide fluctuations of currencies and the fact that political considerations have distorted economic adjustments. The U.S./Japanese situation is a prime example. Even though the United States runs a huge trade deficit vis-à-vis Japan, which should weaken the dollar, the yen depreciated 50 percent against the dollar between 1978 and 1982. This gives the Japanese an "unnatural" advantage and further aggravates the trade imbalance. In general, the dollar is estimated at 15–20 percent too high against foreign currencies.[55] As one analyst put it, "The wild swings in currency rates have turned financial theory upside down. Instead of having trade patterns influence currency rates, those rates now affect trade patterns."[56]

Balance-of-Payments Imbalances

If all the economic theories worked perfectly, the flow of money between countries would remain in a state of near equilibrium. Because of the intervention of politics, major imbalances occur.

The **balance of payments** is a figure that represents the entire flow of money into and out of a country—that is, credits less debits.[57]

Credits (plus items)	Debits (minus items)
1. Exports	1. Imports
2. Foreign travel of others to your country (military, tourists)	2. Your citizens' travel in other countries
3. Foreign purchases of your services (e.g., consulting)	3. Your purchase of foreign services
4. Gifts and other transfers from abroad (foreign aid, charity)	4. Gifts to those abroad
5. Capital imports (loans to, investments in your country)	5. Capital exports
6. Profits, interest from foreign investments	6. Profits, interest paid to foreign investors
7. Government receipts from foreign activity	7. Government overseas expenditures

During the 1970s, the balance of payments of many industrialized countries suffered because of high oil import costs. By 1982, however, the situation was at least stabilized. In that year the balance of payments for the Western industrialized countries was −$28.2 billion, but that was considerably below the astronomical −$62.6 billion 1980 figure. The United States, however, remains an area of concern. Massive deficits in trade and official overseas spending more than offset gains from sale of services and investments return and leave the United States in an overall deficit position. In 1984, for the first time, monthly deficits exceeded $10 billion and the annual deficit topped $100 billion.[58]

Although these imbalances are of concern, they pale when compared with the problems experienced by the non-oil-exporting LDCs. These will be examined in the following chapter.

Lending Practices

The final issue of international monetary policy that we will explore is lending. Because of the increasing cost of oil to LDCs, a surplus of OPEC funds in Western banks, and other factors, the level of international lending grew wildly during the 1970s. By the early 1980s, debtor nations owed nearly $700 billion to creditor institutions.[59] Even beyond this figure, the total of all foreign lending to private as well as public recipients is estimated at over $2 trillion.[60] Nearly half of this is owed to private banks, and that, combined with general global economic difficulty, has raised concern that a series of loan defaults could bankrupt many Western lending institutions, leading to a financial crisis. In many cases, the extent of foreign loans exceeds total shareholder equity in a bank, meaning that if the international borrowers could not pay, the bank would be bankrupt.

Economic ramifications. A combination of high debt levels and international economic problems has created a lending crisis that threatens domestic financial institutions and international monetary stability. In addition to early unwise borrowing and lending and some poor investment decisions, the strong U.S. dollar has created repayment problems as interest rates were hiked to offset the declining value of foreign currencies and also to reflect the U.S. interest rate (which was at a record peacetime high in the late 1970s and early 1980s). By the end of 1982, LDCs were $18 billion in arrears. As the payment of loans and interest became increasingly burdensome to borrower countries, a number of such countries threatened to default on their loans.[61] As Brazil's finance minister warned, "The U.S. is playing with fire."[62]

The debt crisis has had a number of negative impacts. The development of LDCs has been hampered as they struggle to at least meet interest payments. The debt crisis has also caused an erosion in the confidence on which banks rest. Some officials have warned that widespread payment defaults could lead to a major crisis in the world banking system, and, at least in some part because of the erosion in confidence in bank solvency, forty-eight U.S. banks went out of business in 1983, the most in forty-four years.

Political ramifications. In addition to the economic impact of the immense level of international debt, there are political perils. One is that the unmet or difficult debt repayments cause strains between the lending and borrowing nations. It is all too easy for Americans to disparage Latin American irresponsibility and for Latin Americans to become outraged at what might be seen as just one more form of Yankee imperialism.

Further, debt can influence individual policy choices. There is an old saying that "if you owe a banker a dollar, he controls you, but if you owe a banker a million dollars, you control him." That axiom was applied during the Polish labor/political crisis of the early 1980s. The West was restrained from tougher economic sanctions against Poland in part because of the reality that the country might default on its $26 billion in debts to Western governments and banks.

For the immediate future, Western financial institutions are weathering the crisis. Factors such as a pickup in the world economy, lower interest rates, stable oil prices, and new borrowing and lending prudence eased the immediate crisis by late 1984. The industrialized nations have also substantially increased the reserves available to the IMF. This organization, in turn, has used its new capacity to help LDCs refinance their debts. Renewed lending or political and/or economic turmoil could, however, provoke a global financial crisis.

Summary

Economics and politics are closely intertwined aspects of international relations. Each is a part of and affects the other. This interrelationship has always been true, but it has become even more important in recent history. Economics has become more important internationally because of dramatically increased trade levels, ever-tightening economic interdependence between countries, and the growing impact of international economics on domestic economics. The stronger role played by international economics means that relations between countries have increasingly been influenced by economic relations. Currently, for example, the most significant question in U.S./Japanese relations is the trade imbalance (in Japan's favor) between the two allies. Conversely, politics also significantly affects economic relations. Domestic political pressures are important determinants of tariff policies and other trade regulations. Trade can also be used as a diplomatic tool. The U.S. grain embargo against the Soviet Union in response to the invasion of Afghanistan is one example.

Our discussion of international relations is divided into three parts. This chapter discussed economic issues that are centered primarily in the developed countries (North). The next chapter discusses the economic situation of the less developed countries (South). Chapter 16 discusses the world's efforts to achieve greater economic cooperation, coordination, stability, and equity.

This chapter has focused mainly on questions of trade and on questions of monetary relations. Trade, as noted, has become an increasingly more important part of world politics. The increases in trade have brought many benefits, but there are also problems. The patterns of trade are one problem. Overall, the North, which produces manufactured goods, has a considerable advantage over the South, which produces mostly primary products (agricultural products and raw materials). There are also problems in bilateral trade patterns. The gross imbalance in exports and imports between Japan and the United States is a previously mentioned example. Another troublesome trade issue is the continued existence of a wide variety of barriers to trade. In part, these are based on tariffs, but nontariff barriers are more important. There are significant arguments on both sides of the question of eliminating trade restrictions. Free-traders argue that trade results in greater efficiency and lower costs because of the law of comparative advantage. Free-trade advocates also contend that international commerce promotes world cooperation and inhibits conflict. Those who reject complete free trade argue that trade barriers are needed to protect domestic industry. They further maintain that overreliance on other countries is dangerous for national security reasons and that trade can be a valuable policy tool to reward friends and punish enemies.

The wisdom of trade between the Western allies and the communist countries is a very special trade question. There is a good deal of dispute within the West about what level and what type of trade with the communists is appropriate. Some consider trade between East and West both good business and a method of promoting cooperation between the two camps. Opponents of unrestricted trade, strongly including the United States during the past few years, argue that trade too often supplies opponents with technology and goods that increase their strength and that it encourages dangerous dependency on an enemy for needed resources and products.

The question of the status and role of multinational corporations is another issue related to foreign commerce. Today, commerce is heavily influenced by huge corporations that conduct business worldwide. In purely economic terms, some MNCs rival small countries in their output. MNCs are highly controversial. Some argue that they are a necessary part of today's complex international economic structure and that they provide many benefits in the form of transferring technical ability, capital, and jobs. Critics of MNCs charge them with exploiting host countries, interfering with their politics, and engaging in unethical economic and social practices.

International monetary relations is a very important but little-understood part of international economics and politics. With the collapse of most of the post–World War II Bretton Woods economic system, monetary relations have become unsettled and troublesome during the last decade and a half. Exchange rates, which supposedly float relatively freely and adjust according to market conditions, are sometimes out of balance. The mid-1980s strength of the American dollar, partly artificial, caused numerous problems, including a massive U.S. trade deficit. Another major issue in current monetary relations is international lending practices. During the 1970s, the rate of lending by private banks to foreign countries, especially in the Third World, increased dramatically. By the early 1980s, owing to a number of economic factors, a crisis existed. Debtor countries were unable to meet payments and threatened to default on loans. This, in turn, threatened the viability of the lending institutions, many of them American banks, and carried the potential of serious economic consequences domestically for the banking institutions and their depositors and supporting governments and internationally for the entire monetary structure. As of this writing, the crisis had eased somewhat but was far from being resolved.

Terms

Autarky—Economic independence from external sources.

Balance of payments—A figure that represents the net flow of money into and out of a country due to trade, tourist expenditures, sale of services (e.g., consulting), foreign aid, profits, and so forth.

Bretton Woods system—The international monetary system that existed from the end of World War II until the early 1970s; named for an international economic conference held in Bretton Woods, New Hampshire, in 1944.

Exchange rate—The values of two currencies relative to each other—for example, how many yen equal a dollar or how many lire equal a pound.

Free trade—The international movement of goods unrestricted by tariffs or nontariff barriers.

Gross national product—A figure that represents all the goods and services a country produces; a common standard for measuring a country's economic strength.

Interdependence (economic)—The close interrelationship and mutual dependence of two or more domestic economies on each other.

Law of comparative advantage—The assertion that all countries can benefit from specializing in producing and exporting what they produce most efficiently and cheaply while importing what other countries can produce more efficiently and cheaply.

Monetary relations—The entire scope of international money issues, such as exchange rates, interest rates, loan policies, balance of payments, and regulating institutions (e.g., the International Monetary Fund).

Multinational corporations—A private enterprise that has production subsidiaries or branches in more than one country.

Nontariff barrier—A nonmonetary restriction on trade, such as quotas, technical specifications, or unnecessarily lengthy quarantine and inspection procedures.

Tariff—A tax, usually based on percentage of value, that importers must pay on items purchased abroad; also known as an import tax or import duty.

Trade balance—A figure that represents the difference between the value of imported and exported goods.

Trilateral countries—The United States, Japan, and Western Europe.

Notes

1. Fritz M. Heichelheim, *An Ancient Economic History* (Leiden, The Netherlands: A. W. Sitjthoff's Uitgeversmaatschappij N.V., 1958), pp. 116–129, 222–248. Also see Moses I. Finley, ed., *Second International Conference on Economic History, 1962,* vol. 1, *Trade and Politics in the Ancient World* (New York: Arno Press, 1979).
2. R. L. Major, "Recent Trends in World Trade in Manufactures," in R. A. Bachelor, R. L. Major, and A. D. Morgan, *Industrialization and the Basis for Trade* (Cambridge: Cambridge University Press, 1980), pp. 16–32. Also see various readings in Raymond Bernon, ed., *The Technology Factors in International Trade* (New York: National Bureau of Economic Research, 1970).
3. Arthur Lewis, "The Rate of Growth of World Trade, 1830–1973," in *The World Economic Order,* ed. Sven Grassman and Erik Lundberg (New York: St. Martin's Press, 1981), pp. 15–19. Also see Andre Gunder Frank, *Latin America: Underdevelopment or Revolution* (New York: Monthly Review Press, 1969), and Samir Amin, *Accumulation on a World Scale* (New York: Monthly Review Press, 1974).
4. Walt Whitman Rostow, *The World Economy: History and Prospect* (Austin: University of Texas Press, 1978), chart II-6, p. 85, and table III-28, p. 182, for other industrial countries.
5. Joyce Kolko and Gabriel Kolko, *The Limits of Power* (New York: Harper & Row, 1972), pp. 11–28.

6. General Agreement on Tariffs and Trade, *International Trade, 1982/83* (Geneva: General Agreement on Tariffs and Trade), appendix, table A3.
7. International Monetary Fund *Survey,* September 19, 1983, p. 275.
8. Organization for Economic Cooperation and Development, *Historical Statistics, 1960–1980* (Paris: Organization for Economic Cooperation and Development, 1982), various tables. For a crisis view, see Andre Gunder Frank, *Crisis in the World Economy* (New York: Holmes & Meier, 1980). A bit more evenhanded is Michael Beenstock, *The World Economy in Transition* (London: Allen & Unwin, 1983), pp. 1–57.
9. *New York Times,* November 29, 1982, p. A1.
10. *New York Times,* April 24, 1983, p. E3.
11. Peter H. Lindert and Charles P. Kindleberger, *International Economics,* 7th ed. (Homewood, Ill.: Irwin, 1982), pp. 153–174.
12. *New York Times,* October 22, 1981, p. D1; Dan S. Chill, *The Arab Boycott of Israel* (New York: Praeger, 1976).
13. Free-trade theory goes back even further. See [Edward Misselden], *Free Trade or the Means to Make Trade Florish* [sic], originally published in 1622 (New York: Augustus M. Kelley, 1971).
14. Statement of Robert Hormats, Assistant Secretary of State for Economic and Business Affairs, in U.S. Department of State *Bulletin,* March 1982, p. 34.
15. For an excellent short discussion, see Bruce Russett and Harvey Starr, *World Politics* (San Francisco: W. H. Freeman, 1981), pp. 414–419.
16. The economic protectionist arguments are evaluated in Franklin R. Root, *International Trade and Investment,* 3rd ed. (Cincinnati: South-Western Publishing, 1973), pp. 303–323.
17. For a discussion of the impact of trade, see Robert Z. Lawrence, "Is Trade Deindustrializing America?" and comments and discussion in Brookings (Institute) Papers on *Economic Activity,* no. 1 (1983): 129–171.
18. Robert B. Reich, "Beyond Free Trade," *Foreign Affairs* 61 (1983): 780. Also, on current distortions, see John Zysman and Stephen Cohen, "Double or Nothing: Open Trade and Competitive Industry," *Foreign Affairs* 61 (1983): 117–129. For a topical debate involving EEC policy, see Wolfgang Hager, "Protectionism and Autonomy: How to Preserve Free Trade in Europe," *International Affairs* (London) 58 (1982): 413–427; and reply by Brian Hindley, "Protectionism and Autonomy: A Comment on Hager," *International Affairs* 59 (1983): 77–86.
19. Reich, "Beyond Free Trade," p. 787.
20. Margaret Doxey, "Sanctions against the Soviet Union: The Afghan Experience," in *The Year Book of World Affairs* (London: Institute of World Affairs, 1983), pp. 63–80. Also see James Mayall, "The Sanctions Problem in International Economic Relations," *International Affairs* 60 (1984): 631–642.
21. "Protectionism," an editorial, *Finance and Development* 29 (March 1983): 2–5.
22. *Time,* February 6, 1982, p. 31.
23. On possible adjustments, see Reich, "Beyond Free Trade"; Zysman and Cohen, "Double or Nothing"; and Albert Bressard, "Mastering the World Economy," *Foreign Affairs* 61 (1983): 745–772.
24. For a bibliography, see Helga Hernes, *The Multinational Corporation: A Guide to Information Sources* (Detroit: Gala Research, 1977). Also see Richard J. Barnet and Ronald E. Muller, *Global Reach: The Power of Multinational Corporations* (New York: Simon & Schuster, 1974).
25. Abdul A. Said and Luiz R. Simmons, "The Politics of Transition," in *The New*

Sovereigns: Multinational Corporations as World Powers, ed. Abdul A. Said and Luiz R. Simmons (Englewood Cliffs, N.J.: Prentice-Hall, 1975), p. 7.

26. Ibid. Also Eugene V. Rostow and George W. Ball, "The Genesis of the Multinational Corporation," in *Global Companies,* ed. Eugene V. Rostow and George W. Ball, published for the American Assembly, Columbia University (Englewood Cliffs, N.J.: Prentice-Hall, 1975), p. 6. *The American Invaders* is by Fayelle A. Mackensie (London: Grant Richards, 1902).
27. Said and Simmons, "The Politics of Transition," p. 9.
28. Based on figures in *Fortune,* August 22, 1983, p. 170. Also see Werner Feld, *International Relations: A Transnational Approach* (Sherman Oaks, Calif.: Alfred, 1979). For a view that MNCs are not taking over, see George Modelski, "Multinational Business," *International Studies Quarterly* 16 (1982): 411.
29. Said and Simmons, "The Politics of Transition," p. 10.
30. A good brief summary of the pros, cons, and recent evidence is in Robert Cohen and Jeffry Fieden, "The Impact of Multinational Corporations on Developing Nations," in *The Challenge of the New International Economic Order,* ed. Edwin P. Reubens (Boulder, Colo.: Westview Press, 1981), pp. 158–168.
31. Henry Johnson, "Economic Benefits of the Multinational Enterprise," in *Nationalism and Multinational Enterprise,* ed. H. R. Halho, J. Graham Smith, and Richard W. Wright (Dobbs Ferry, N.Y.: Oceana, 1973), p. 169.
32. Beenstock, *The World Economy in Transition,* table 3.8, p. 86.
33. On the employment issue, see Duncan C. Campbell and Richard L. Rowan, *Multinational Enterprises and the OECD Industrial Guidelines* (Philadelphia: University of Pennsylvania Press, 1983), pp. 17–23.
34. Joseph S. Nye, "Multinational Enterprises and Prospects for Regional and Global Political Integration," *Annals of the American Academy of Political and Social Science* 403 (1972): 118.
35. Gerard Chaliand, *Revolution in the Third World,* quoted in L. S. Stavrianos, *Global Rift: The Third World Comes of Age* (New York: William Morrow, 1981).
36. Melvyn B. Krauss, *Development without Aid* (New York: New Press, 1983), p. 132.
37. Eric Kierans, "The Cosmocorporation: An Unsympathetic View," in Halho et al., eds., *Nationalism and Multinational Enterprise,* p. 179.
38. Thomas N. Gladwin and Ingo Walter, *Multinationals under Fire* (New York: Wiley, 1980), chaps. 5, 6, and 9. Also see Neil H. Jacoby, Peter Nehemkis, and Richard Eells, *Bribery and Extortion in World Business* (New York: Macmillan, 1977).
39. Barnet and Muller, *Global Reach,* p. 89.
40. Ibid., p. 78.
41. Jack N. Behrman, *National Interests and the Multinational Enterprise: Tensions among the North Atlantic Countries* (Englewood Cliffs, N.J.: Prentice-Hall, 1970), p. 9. Also see Robert Gilpin, *U.S. Power and the Multinational Corporation* (New York: Basic Books, 1975).
42. For U.S. issues and policy, see C. Fred Bengsten, Thomas Horst, and Theodore H. Moran, *American Multinationals and American Interests* (Washington, D.C.: Brookings Institution, 1978), especially chaps. 2, 12, and 13.
43. Campbell and Rowan, *Multinational Enterprises,* p. 4; Ehrenfried Pausenberger, "How Powerful Are Multinational Corporations?," *Intereconomics* 3 (May/June 1983): 131; and Raymond J. Waldmann, *Regulating International Business through Codes of Conduct* (Washington, D.C.: American Enterprise Institute, 1981).
44. This and the following sections rely on Robert V. Roosa, Armin Gutowski, and

Michiya Matsukawa, *East-West Trade at the Crossroads,* a Task Force Report to the Trilateral Commission (New York: New York University Press, 1982), pp. 1–35; also, Morris Bornstein, "Issues in East-West Economic Relations," in *East-West Economic Relations and the Future of Europe,* ed. Morris Bornstein and William Zimmerman (London: Allen & Unwin, 1981), pp. 51–55.

45. General Agreement on Tariffs and Trade, *International Trade, 1982/83,* appendix A9; *New York Times,* January 17, 1982; and Organization for Economic Cooperation and Development, *Historical Statistics, 1960–1980* (Paris: Organization for Economic Cooperation and Development, 1982), section 13, pp. 108–111.
46. *Time,* August 2, 1982, p. 30.
47. These and the pro arguments rely on a discussion in U.S. Senate Committee on Foreign Relations, *The Premises of East-West Commercial Relations,* a Workshop, 97th Cong., 2nd sess. (1983). The pros and cons are also discussed in *Business Week,* September 12, 1983, pp. 68–69.
48. On this point and the entire issue of MNC relations with the East bloc, see J. Wilczynski, *The Multinationals and East-West Relations* (Boulder, Colo.: Westview Press, 1976), pp. 56–58 and *passim.*
49. *Time,* December 7, 1981, p. 31.
50. Ibid.
51. These are best seen in Senate Committee on Foreign Relations, *Premises of East-West Commercial Relations.*
52. Ibid., p. 115.
53. *Time,* August 2, 1982, p. 31.
54. J. Carter Murphy, *The International Monetary System: Beyond the First Stage of Reform* (Washington, D.C.: American Enterprise Institute, 1979), pp. 2–25; Lindert and Kindleberger, *International Economics,* pp. 391–397.
55. *New York Times,* April 26, 1982, p. A1.
56. *New York Times,* May 8, 1983, p. A1.
57. List based on Leland B. Yeager, *International Monetary Relations: Theory, History, and Policy,* 2nd ed. (New York: Harper & Row, 1976).
58. For figures, see International Monetary Fund, *Annual Report, 1983* (Washington, D.C.: International Monetary Fund, 1983), tables 4 and 8, pp. 18, 22.
59. IMF *Survey,* March 21, 1983, p. 82; *Time,* May 28, 1981, p. 6.
60. *New York Times,* May 19, 1982, p. A12.
61. *Time,* October 1, 1984, p. 46.
62. Ibid.

12

Economics: The South

Having nothing, nothing can he lose.
Shakespeare, Henry VI

How apt the poor are to be proud.
Shakespeare, Twelfth Night

Our chapter on the economics of the industrialized countries (the North) dealt with strength. Surely the North has problems, but they pale when compared with the position of the less developed South. This chapter will examine the reality of economic deprivation that grips most of the globe. It will detail the massive disparity between North and South and also look at the increasingly insistent demands of the South that the North share its wealth. Then it will take up the most critical need, development capital, and look at its possible sources—trade, loans, private investment, and foreign aid. As we shall see, however, none of these sources is proving adequate. Thus, our chapter will end, as it begins, on a gloomy note. The beginnings of the international response to world poverty will be dealt with in the later chapter on economic and social cooperation.

Existing Patterns

The South: The Harvest of Poverty

Sensationalism is not the aim of this book, but it is hard to recount conditions of impoverishment in neutral, academic terms. Some of the relative North/South figures have already been presented in Chapter 1, but they bear repeating here. Fully three fourths of the world population lives in **less developed countries** (LDCs), yet they account for only 21 percent of the world's GNP, 25 percent of its export earnings, and 9 percent of its public health expenditures. On average, if you live in an LDC, you will (compared with a Northern fellow human):

- Earn only 9 percent of a Northern citizen's income.
- Die sixteen years earlier.
- Be 5.3 times more likely to have your baby die. For those who live, malnutrition will often retard normal physical and mental growth.
- Have only 5 percent of the doctors per capita and 18 percent of the hospital beds per capita of your Northern neighbor.
- Be twice as likely to be illiterate.
- Have 73 percent of the caloric and 32 percent of the animal protein nourishment.

Indeed, for most who read this book, the state of life for many in the South is beyond comprehension. Lack of adequate nutrition, medical care, and education creates a debilitating cycle.

Finally, it should be noted that, at least in relative (to the North) terms, the socioeconomic plight is not improving. It is true that some indicators, such as literacy, physicians per capita, and life expectancy, show advances in Third World conditions. Still, the general economic gap between North and South is widening. Over the past thirty years, the average per capita income in LDCs has increased only $125, compared with a jump of $2,950 for the Western industrialized countries. Thus, the poverty gap, which stood at 10:1 in 1950, increased to approximately 13:1 in 1980. Relatively, then, the rich are getting richer, and the poor are getting poorer.[1]

Development: In the Eye of the Beholder

The goal of LDCs is, of course, "development." Yet that term is an uncertain one. Traditionally, development has been measured by quantitative indexes such as gross national product. There are, however, alternative views. One, which might be termed "liberal economic," contends that true development should be measured by reduced unemployment and poverty and a rise and equalization in the living conditions of those in LDCs, taking into account *both* the conditions within the LDC and the gap between those in the North and those in the South. In short, liberal economists argue that even if GNP skyrockets, there is inadequate development if gross economic disparity persists within LDCs or between North and South.[2]

A related perspective has been labeled the **dependencia school**. It argues that GNP rates and other such indexes of growth are secondary to the patterns of production and trade. Advocates of this view contend that while *classic imperialism* (direct control and exploitation of colonies) has declined, indirect control and exploitation continue through capitalist control driven by the need of capitalism for external markets, profitable investment opportunities, and cheap labor. What results, they say, is *new imperialism*, without colonies but imperial nonetheless. Dependence theorists contend that the capitalist North has imperially continued economic colonial relations with the South, which produces low-cost, low-profit **primary products** (agricultural products, raw materials) while the North produces high-price, high-profit manufactured goods. It is, therefore, in the interest of the capitalist exploiters to keep LDCs dependent and to support local elites who work in the interest of the North rather than their own people.[3]

As we shall see, the traditional approach to development looks to integrate LDCs into the current world economic system while maintaining basic order and stability. Those who believe in and disapprove of dependencia want to change the system's basic nature and create economic equality within and among nations. Whatever one's perspective, however, it is hard to avoid the fact that "progress" has been uneven and has not been an unmitigated blessing for the LDCs.

Modernization: A Mixed Blessing

In addition to its more "traditional" woes, the Third World also suffers many negative side effects from the process of modernization. Medical advances have decreased infant mortality and increased longevity, but that has added to *explosive population growth*. Sub-Saharan Africa, for instance, nearly dou-

Life for most of the people in the Third World means poverty, illiteracy, ill health, and an early death.

bled its population from 210 million in 1960 to 393 million in the early 1980s. At its current annual growth rate of 2.9 percent, it is the world's most rapidly expanding population.

Economic change has also brought *rapid urbanization* with a host of incumbent difficulties. In 1950 there were only three cities in Africa with populations over 500,000; now there are twenty-nine. In the urbanization process, older tribal and family loyalties are being destroyed, with few new offsetting value systems to take their place. The result is social and political instability. The cities are also often swamps characterized by unemployment, poor sewage facilities, and shanty housing.

Poor planning has too often led to the misdirection of attempts to improve conditions. "Spectacular" development projects such as steel mills or "symbolic" projects such as airports have been built at the expense of slower, less obvious efforts to build an economic infrastructure and tailor it to local needs. One has to wonder, for example, about the UN-backed decision to build a $75 million conference center in Ethiopia (or that country's lavish expenditures to celebrate the tenth anniversary of its Marxist revolution) at the same time that a worldwide relief effort was underway for a country where 300,000 people had already died of starvation.

Finally, development has brought *industrial and environmental dangers.* Within a few weeks of each other, a gas explosion at a plant in Mexico City burned hundreds to death and a gas leak in Bhopal, India, killed thousands. Numerous other more general, but no less worrisome, hazards such as air and water pollution have too often accompanied economic "progress."

Third World Development: A Mixed Pattern

In our survey of Third World development, we should also take note of the mixed pattern of development. First, within individual countries there is a wide disparity between a few in the wealthy and middle classes and the many poor. Second, within the Third World, a few countries are beginning to make progress. Most countries, however, continue to stagger under crushing economic limitations.

Internal disparity. Within the Third World there are cities with sparkling skyscrapers and luxuriant suburbs populated by well-to-do local entrepreneurs who drive Mercedes and splash in marble pools. For each such scene, there are many more of open sewers, contaminated drinking water, distended bellies, and other symptoms of rural and urban human blight. In short, whatever economic benefits have accrued are not evenly distributed. Figure 12-1 shows the percentage of income earned by the highest-income 10 percent of the population in six Third World countries. For example, in Honduras the top 10 percent accounts for half of all personal income.

A few newly industrializing countries. A second pattern of uneven economic growth in the Third World is the disparity between countries. It is possible to show, for example, that for LDCs, manufacturing efforts, GNP, and other positive factors expanded considerably in the 1970s.[4] This progress was confined, however, to a relative few **newly industrializing countries** (NICs) such as Taiwan, South Korea, Hong Kong, Singapore, Brazil, Mexico, Argentina, and India. In 1978 fully 75 percent of all Third World manufacturing was produced in just ten of its countries, with 40 percent coming from just three countries.[5] Thus, figures for the Third World can be deceptive. There are a few relative success stories, but for most countries, and for most of the people within the countries, the economic picture is bleak.

Capital Needs and Development

In order to catch up, the countries of the Third World need massive amounts of capital to supplement their own internal efforts to improve socioeconomic conditions. Many things can be accomplished with domestic resources and drive, but these **capital needs** require outside resources as well.

In obtaining those resources, LDCs are constrained by the limited amount of financial reserves, or **hard currency**, that they possess. Most private and many public investors and traders are selective in the currencies they will accept. American dollars are the standard currency of exchange. Others, such as British pounds, German marks, Swiss or French francs, and Japanese yen, are also widely convertible. Guatemalan quetzals, Iraqi dinars, Malaysian ringgitos, Nigerian nairas, and Seychelles rupees are another story. They and most

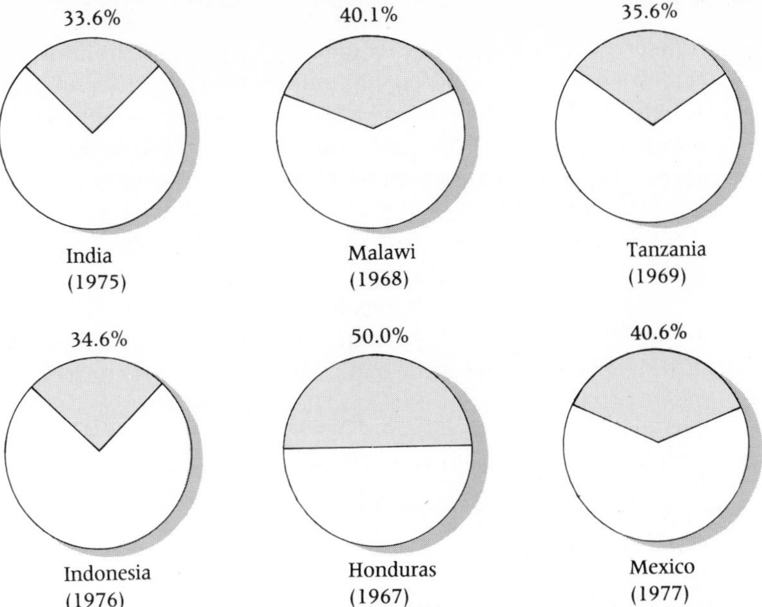

Figure 12-1. Income distribution. Shaded area is percentage of all personal income earned by the richest 10 percent of the population. *Figures from The World Bank.* World Development Report, 1981 *(Washington, D.C.: International Bank for Reconstruction and Development, 1981), table 25, pp. 182–183.*

world currencies are generally not acceptable in international economic transactions. Further, these countries have small reserves of acceptable trading currencies. In 1979 some 77 percent of all hard-currency reserves were concentrated in the industrialized and oil-producing countries.[6]

A primary issue for LDCs, then, is the acquisition of hard-currency development funds. Four main sources of convertible currencies are available: loans, investment, trade, and aid. Unfortunately, as we shall see in our discussion of these sources, there are limitations and drawbacks to each, and no single source is sufficient to meet the Third World's enormous and complex needs.

Loans

One source of hard currency is loans granted by private or government sources. Loans can involve direct cash transfers, credits to buy goods in the lending country, or government guarantees of private transactions. As noted in the previous chapter, the level of international borrowing expanded dramatically in the 1970s and reached nearly $700 billion by the early 1980s.

The *advantage* of borrowing is that it gives the recipient country control over its own development. Funds can usually be used as the LDC sees fit. Loans are also "businesslike" and in accord with national pride.

The *disadvantage* of loans is that they create a false impression of capital flow and must be paid back. It is too easy to overmortgage the future to pay for today's project, and figures indicate that that has indeed happened. Even if the loan is for a necessary and valuable purpose, if it does not increase the LDC's exports and, thus, capital inflow, then it may cause deep financial difficulties because it did not generate the hard-currency funds to meet debt payments. In the 1970s many countries borrowed heavily to finance development. In particular, a number of oil-producing countries borrowed against future oil sales. The downturn in the oil market in the early 1980s brought many of these countries close to ruin. Box 12-1 gives some of the disturbing figures for Third World debt.

The upshot of these figures is that borrowing has reached and exceeded the limits of responsibility for many countries. Through the intervention of the IMF and national central banks, and through debt restructuring, the repayment crises of the early 1980s have been somewhat abated. The basic problems have not been solved, though, and the immense debt precludes further borrowing for many countries as a large-scale source of development capital.

Investment

A second source of capital for LDCs is investment by private interests. The amount of investment capital available worldwide is staggering, yet the vast majority of it is invested in industrialized countries, and what does go into the Third World is concentrated in the few oil exporters or the newly industrializing countries.

Box 12-1. Facts about Third World Debt.

- Annual borrowing increased from \$11.4 billion in 1973 to \$54.6 billion in 1982.
- Debt of all countries increased approximately 16 percent between 1973 and 1982; for the LDCs it increased over 50 percent.
- In 1982 LDC debt equaled 120 percent of exported goods and services. For Latin America, the figure was 246 percent. In other words, many countries owe more internationally than they earn internationally.
- For LDCs, debt as a percentage of GNP rose from 12.4 percent in 1970 to 21.5 percent in 1979.
- For LDCs, the cost of servicing the debt (payments plus interest) rose from 11.7 percent of all income in 1970 to 16.4 percent in 1979.

Sources: George Kurian, *Encyclopedia of the Third World*, rev. ed., vol. 3 (New York: Facts on File, 1982), appendix III, table 11, p. 2035. World Bank, *World Development Report, 1981* (Washington, D.C.: International Bank for Reconstruction and Development, 1981), table 13, p. 158. International Monetary Fund, *Annual Report 1983* (Washington, D.C.: International Monetary Fund, 1983), pp. 30–31.

The Reagan administration has particularly pushed the idea of private investment as a source of development capital. Many Third World countries also court private investors. The overall impact of direct investment is, however, both limited and troublesome. It is *limited* in the sense that investments are essentially conservative and flow to already industrialized countries. It must also be remembered that investors take profits out, so that *net* private investment flow (new investments minus profit taking) is the key figure. In 1980 that figure accounted for a net inflow of only $4.3 billion to LDCs. Of that figure, only a trickle ($200 million) went into the poorest LDCs. Overall, in the 1970s, private investment constituted only 20 percent of the net capital flow to LDCs and, in the second half of that decade, was declining in terms of uninflated dollars.[7]

Private investment is also a *troublesome* source of capital. The investments are made primarily by the huge multinational corporations (MNCs) discussed in the previous chapter. These investments create at least the potential for the malpractices discussed earlier. Thus, for many countries, the prospect of heavy foreign investment presents the dilemma of being caught between the Scylla of poverty and the Charybdis of foreign intervention.

Trade

A third possible source of development capital is export earnings. Yet this avenue is a source of weakness rather than strength for most LDCs.

LDC trade weakness. There are several sources of LDC trade weakness. First, non-oil-exporting LDCs command only about 13 percent of the world export market, a figure that has been relatively static for two decades.

Second, in 1982 these countries had a net trade deficit of $61 billion (exports $255 billion, imports $316 billion). That figure has been in constant deficit since the oil-price hikes of the mid-1970s.[8]

A third contributing factor to LDC trade weakness is that these countries are heavily dependent on the export of primary products, including foodstuffs, minerals, fibers, and other raw materials. Figure 12-2 shows the 1982 trade in primary and manufactured products for various areas of the world. Even the percentages in Figure 12-2 do not fully tell the story, because many LDCs are trade-dependent on the export of one or a few primary products. Figure 12-3 shows the dependency of a number of LDCs.

Dependency on primary products leaves the LDCs disadvantaged in terms of market weakness and relative pricing.

Market weakness is common for primary products. A number of factors, such as damage to a crop or a downturn in world demand, can quickly disrupt markets and devastate earnings. During the past decades, world trade in products such as cotton, sisal, jute, wool, and other fibers has been harmed by the development of synthetics. Natural-rubber sales have been drastically reduced

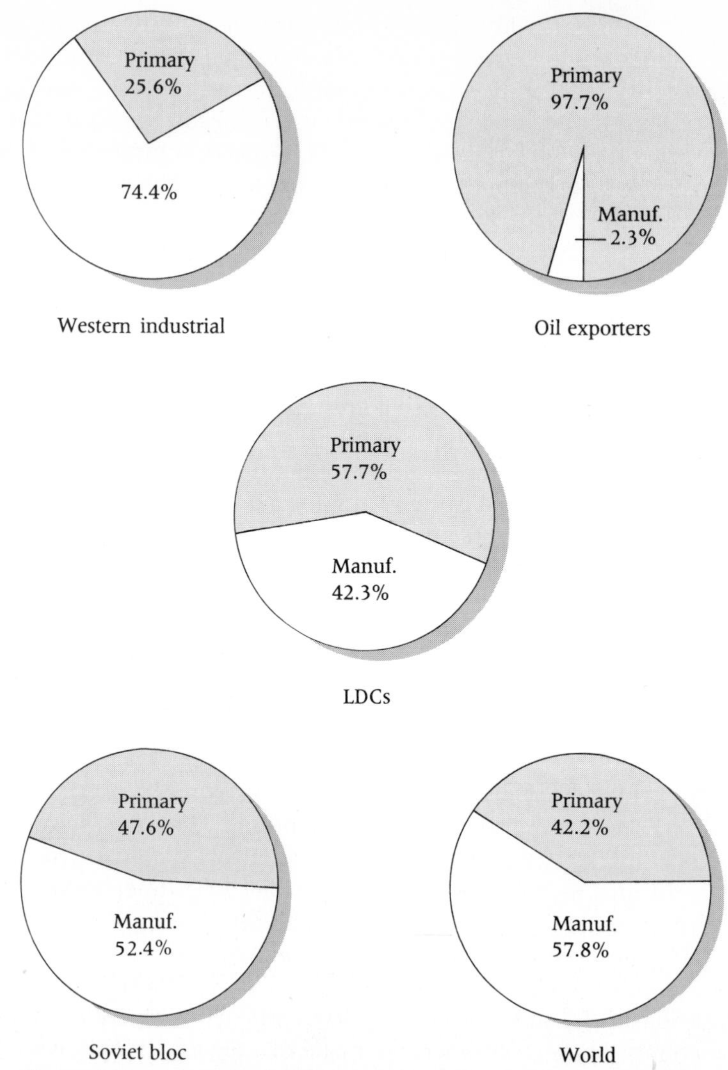

Figure 12-2. Primary and manufactured exports, 1982. *Data from General Agreement on Tariffs and Trade,* International Trade, 1982/83 *(Geneva: General Agreement on Tariffs and Trade, 1983), appendix, table A22.*

by synthetic substitutes. Sugar sales have been harmed by synthetics and dietary changes. Minerals such as tin and lead have also experienced market declines.

Prices are also weaker for primary products. During the decade between 1973 and 1982, the price of primary products exported by non-oil-producing LDCs grew at an annual average of 6.2 percent, while the world price of manufactured products grew at an average of 9.4 percent annually. Thus, it takes increasingly more of a given unit of a primary product to buy a unit of manufactured product.[9]

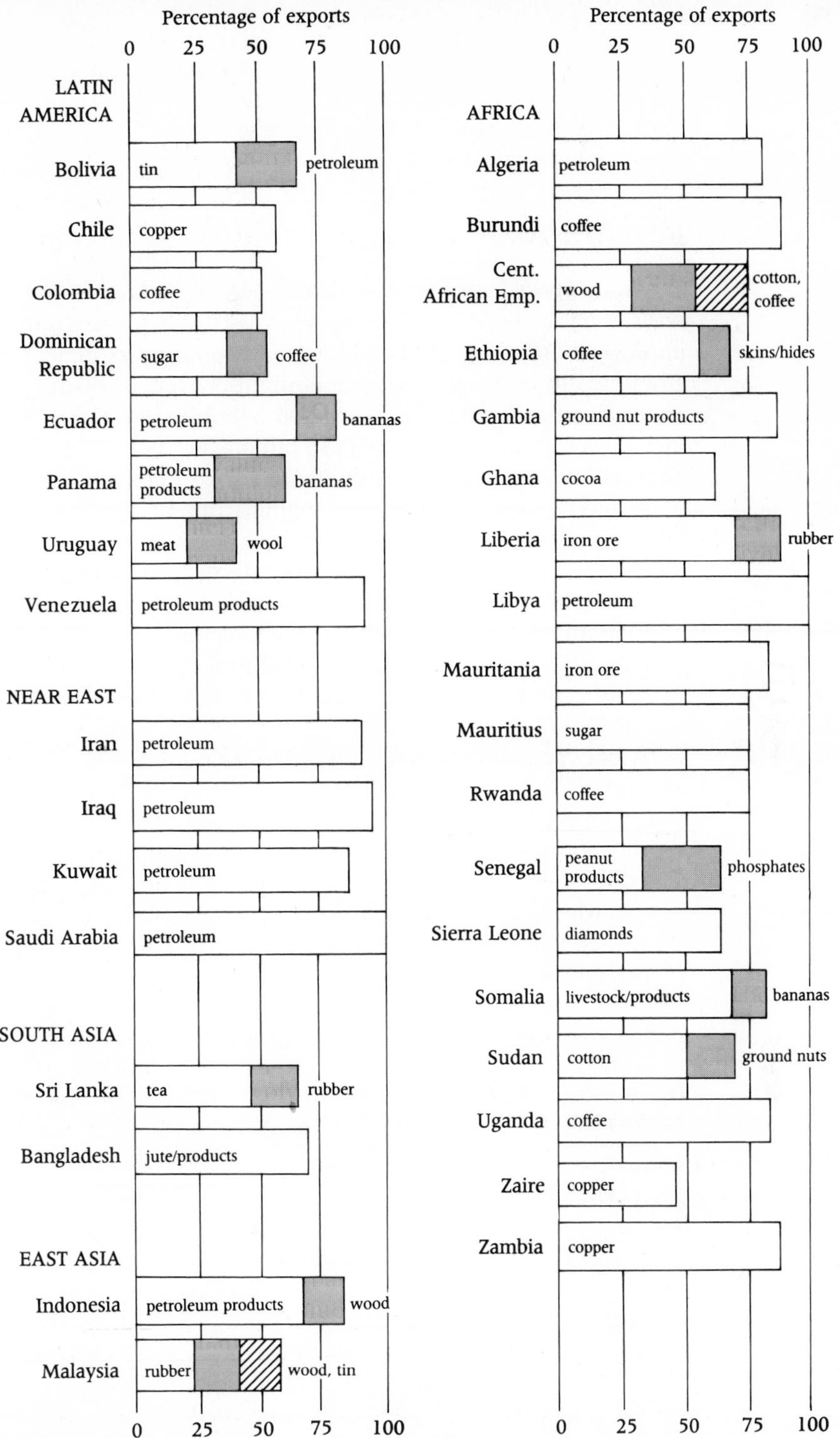

Figure 12-3. Primary-product trade dependency. *Source: U.S. Department of State,* The Trade Debate *(Washington, D.C.: U.S. Government Printing Office, 1979), p. 29.*

The use of trade, then, to acquire capital and improve economic conditions has not been highly effective. The pattern of LDC exports of primary products, balance-of-payments deficits, and market and pricing weakness all have the LDCs disadvantaged vis-à-vis the industrialized countries.[10]

Foreign Aid

The fourth possible external source of capital for LDCs is foreign aid. In some ways, the flow of official development assistance to the Third World has been impressive. Between 1970 and 1980, economic development from all sources amounted to more than $250 billion.[11] Between 1949 and 1979, the United States alone accounted for over $200 billion in aid. Other major aid sources include communist countries ($86 billion, 1955–1979), international financial institutions such as the World Bank (approximately $84 billion, 1968–1979), other industrialized countries (ranging from $3.8 billion in 1970 to $19.6 billion in 1980), and the oil-exporting countries (average approximately $6 billion, 1975–1980). Table 12-1 shows recent aid figures.

Further analysis of the figures, however, shows that aid is neither a story of undisguised generosity nor one of unblemished success. Factors that tend to reduce the impact of aid include political considerations, military content, recipient per capita aid, donor aid relative to wealth, and aid application.

Political considerations. One factor that limits the effectiveness of aid is its political direction. **Bilateral aid**, given directly from one country to another, makes up the bulk of aid, and many such aid decisions are based heavily on considerations of political impact rather than economic need. About 50 percent of U.S. economic aid is allocated to the Economic Support Fund (ESF), which provides aid to promote economic and political stability in areas where the United States has special security interests. Food aid accounts for another 20 percent of the U.S. aid total, and development aid is only just over 30 percent. This allocation created a 1984–1985 distribution that saw tiny El Salvador as the largest U.S. aid recipient in Latin America. Israel received

Table 12-1. Foreign Aid by Source (billions of U.S. dollars), 1980–1983.

Source	*1980*	*1981*	*1982*	*1983*
Western industrial countries	18.11	18.29	18.53	18.50
OPEC countries	8.63	7.67	4.58	4.34
Communist countries	2.66	2.98	2.86	2.93
Other countries	0.31	0.41	0.36	0.35
Multilateral agencies	7.79	7.93	7.51	7.50
Private agencies	2.31	2.02	2.31	2.20
Total	39.81	39.30	36.15	35.82

Source: IMF Survey, August 6, 1984, p. 229.

more aid than all of Africa, and Egypt and Israel together received over 25 percent of all U.S. economic aid.[12]

The Soviets follow the same pattern of distributing aid according to political priorities. Of the 4,216 Soviet foreign aid projects funded between 1945 and 1981, 3,006, or 71 percent, were in socialist countries. Of the projects in developing countries, 678, or 56 percent, were concentrated in just six friendly or politically important countries.[13]

Military content. The extent of aid is also often inflated by the inclusion of military assistance. Whatever their political value, arms at best have no development value and at worst provide the tools of economic destruction. Of total U.S. aid in 1979, for example, about $6.5 billion, or just under 50 percent, was military aid. Of the $86 billion in aid given by communist countries to LDCs between 1955 and 1979, military aid amounted to $53 billion, or 61.6 percent of the total.

Recipient per capita aid. In evaluating the flow of aid, it is also important not to be overly impressed by gross numbers. Viewed either as recipient per capita aid or as donor aid relative to wealth, economic assistance is modest.

Recipient per capita aid in 1979 amounted to only $11.16. The poorest (−$371 per capita GNP) LDCs received only $6.80 per inhabitant and the slightly less impoverished LDCs received approximately $14 per capita.[14]

It should be further noted that when the few largest aid recipients are eliminated, these figures decline considerably. Israel received $263 per person; others, as Table 12-2 shows, received much less.

Table 12-2. Average Regional and Country Per Capita Aid Receipts, 1978–1980.

Region *Country*	*Aid (millions of U.S. dollars)*	*Per Capita (dollars)*
Africa	9,238	21.30
Angola	177	7.00
Egypt	1,597	100.80
Ethiopia	172	5.40
Liberia	68	52.00
Zimbabwe	56	7.80
Latin America/Caribbean	3,961	11.30
Brazil	437	3.60
Colombia	188	7.20
Mexico	481	7.10
Peru	265	15.30
Asia	9,367	7.00
Bangladesh	1,114	12.80
India	1,114	2.50
Sri Lanka	342	23.30

Source: United Nations, *1981 Statistical Yearbook* (New York: United Nations, 1983), table 75, pp. 468–469. Includes aid from industrial countries and multilateral organizations. China is not included in Asia estimate.

Donor aid relative to wealth. Another analytical approach that lessens the seeming significance of aid figures is dollars given in comparison to wealth. Particularly in the United States, there is a myth that the country is some sort of Daddy Warbucks and that foreign aid is a massive giveaway that unmercifully burdens the taxpayer. Like most folk tales, it is far from the truth. In 1980, the United States spent $7.1 billion for economic aid. Although it is true that this was more than Americans spent on flowers, seeds, and potted plants ($4.5 billion) or even going to movies or sports events ($6.9 billion), it was only 35 percent of tobacco expenses ($20.4 billion) and only 17 percent of alcohol expenditures ($42.7 billion). Furthermore, while aid as a percentage of the Western industrialized countries' GNP has been steady (from 1965 through 1980) at about 0.4 percent, the U.S. effort has declined from almost 0.5 percent in 1965 to about 0.25 percent in the late 1970s and early1980s.[15] Table 12-3 shows the relative aid giving of Western industrialized countries in 1970 and 1980. Note that in 1980 the United States ranked eleventh of fourteen Western aid donors. If, in 1980, the United States had been as generous as the Dutch, U.S. aid would have totaled almost $26 billion and would have increased Western aid by about 70 percent. Another interesting note is that in 1980 the OPEC countries gave $6.9 billion in aid, which equaled 1.35 percent of their GNP.[16]

Table 12-3. Economic Aid.

	Contribution (millions of $)		***Per Capita Contrib. ($)***		***Contribution as a Percentage of GNP***	
Country	***1970***	***1980***	***1970***	***1980***	***1970***	***1980***
Netherlands	196	1,577	15.04	111.50	.61	.99
Norway	37	473	9.54	115.73	.32	.82
Sweden	117	923	14.54	111.00	.38	.76
Denmark	59	468	11.97	91.32	.38	.72
France	971	4,044	19.13	75.29	.66	.62
Belgium	120	581	12.45	58.98	.46	.49
West Germany	599	3,517	9.88	57.13	.32	.43
Britain	447	1,781	8.05	31.83	.36	.34
Japan	458	3,304	4.43	28.29	.23	.32
United States	3,046	7,138	14.87	32.04	.31	.27
Switzerland	30	246	4.79	38.60	.15	.29
Austria	11	174	1.48	23.17	.07	.23
Finland	7	106	1.52	22.18	.07	.22
Italy	147	672	2.74	11.78	.16	.17
Total	6,245	25,004	10.92	39.97	.34	.37

Source: Roger D. Hansen and Contributors, *U.S. Foreign Policy and the Third World: Agenda 1982,* published for the Overseas Development Council (New York: Praeger, 1982), table F-8 p. 234. Reprinted with permission. (Table adapted.)

Aid application. A final factor that limits the impact of aid is its application. Too often in the past aid has been used to fund highly symbolic but economically unwise projects such as airports, sports arenas, or grandiose government buildings. Inefficiency and corruption have also sometimes drained off aid from its intended applications. Aid critics also charge that some countries have used aid to allow other budget funds to be shunted or reallocated to nondevelopmental uses, including arms purchases.[17] The level of Third World military expenditures is of particular concern. In 1978, LDC military expenses equaled $69.9 billion, or 260 percent of all foreign aid.

These points must be kept in perspective, however. Third World countries do have legitimate defense needs, and at times symbolic projects enhance national pride and legitimacy. Aid, it must be remembered, has also had many outstanding applications and has, for example, helped turn India, which once suffered under the constant threat of famine, into a country that can now meet many of its own food needs.[18]

Third World Response to Economic Disadvantage

As we have seen on several occasions, the North/South axis of international politics has become increasingly important and contentious. The poor countries of the Third World are increasingly asserting that they have a "right" to share in the world's economic wealth. They have acted on a number of fronts to enhance their own economic situations and to pressure the industrialized countries to redistribute part of their wealth. Some of these development efforts fall within the realm of comparative domestic politics and are beyond our scope here.[19] There are, however, a number of aspects of development that are directly related to our study, and we will examine these in terms of Third World expectations, demands, and actions and also development of the Third World movement.

Rising Expectations in the Third World

One of the most important developments of the post-1945 world has been the independence movement among Third World countries. Dozens of former colonial dependencies in Africa and Asia demanded and won political sovereignty. Attaining political independence did not complete the revolution, however. The Afro-Asian states and countries of Latin America remained in an economically subservient and disadvantaged position vis-à-vis the dominant industrialized states, many of which were their former colonial masters.[20]

As early as the mid-1950s it became clear that the emerging Third World states would not docilely accept continued manipulation. A number of forces were present, emerged, or intensified in the 1960s and 1970s that acted to promote increasing Third World demands and solidarity.

Nationalism is one factor. Third World leaders recognize that true sovereignty cannot exist without economic independence.

Relative deprivation is another factor. The rapid increase of communications technology has brought the image of the North's relative richness to the South. Whether or not their objective lot has improved, the impoverished people of the South are more aware of their relative deprivation and therefore are more discontent.

Increased moral/cooperative rhetoric is another factor that has promoted Third World assertiveness. From the time of the League of Nations and accelerating during and after World War II, there has been increased lip service to the idea of international cooperation and responsibility to promote peace, economic well-being, and human rights. This rhetoric is symbolized by chapters IX and X of the United Nations charter, which dedicate that organization to cooperative principles and establish the Economic and Social Council.[21] Whatever the sincerity of the North in these fine phrases, the South takes them seriously and is demanding that the industrialized states practice what they have so nobly preached.

Transnational ideology has also contributed to the Third World's assertiveness. Whether or not they have adopted Marxism, few Third World leaders have not heard the communist and socialist camps' condemnation of continuing capitalist/imperialist exploitation of the South. Given Third World economic conditions and North/South economic relations, it is a message that strikes a sympathetic note.

Economic turmoil is a factor motivating the South. A variety of related and destabilizing economic events, including the breakup of the Bretton Woods monetary system, the worldwide economic downturn in the 1970s, and exploding energy costs, occurred during the past two decades. Conditions in the South went from bad to worse, and the affected countries responded with a series of declarations of economic rights and responsibilities, detailed in the following sections.

Development of the Third World Movement

The developing identity of the Third World first took the form of *political nonalignment.* In 1955 twenty-nine African and Asian countries convened the Bandung Conference. They discussed ways to hasten the independence of colonial territories and also rejected the idea that they had to be associated with either of the superpower blocs in the East/West conflict. Instead, many embraced the principle of nonalignment, which stressed a distinctive Third World political identity. As part of that identity, the South's states would not be passively neutral in world affairs. Indeed, they would be active, but they rejected alignment with either bloc. This political movement has continued, meeting in Belgrade (1961), Cairo (1964), Lusaka (1970), Algiers (1973), Havana (1979), and New Delhi (1983).

It should be pointed out that the nonalignment movement is more symbol than unified reality. Of the ninety countries attending the Havana conference, about half, including the host country, Cuba, distinctly leaned toward one or the other of the superpowers. Further, some Third World countries did not attend because of the attempts by Cuban President Fidel Castro to turn the conference into an anti-American forum. Still, the nonaligned movement has had a powerful influence on Third World consciousness and has helped promote the related economic movement.

The Third World has also been the scene of a growing economic movement. Nonalignment provided a role model for similar economic assertiveness. A coalition of disadvantaged countries, the "Group of 77," emerged and called for the first United Nations Conference on Trade and Development (UNCTAD), which met in Geneva (1964). That conference and the Group of 77 (now over 120 countries) evolved into an ongoing UNCTAD organization that has met in New Delhi (1968), Santiago (1972), Nairobi (1976), Manila (1979), and Buenos Aires (1983). UNCTAD has served as a vehicle for the LDCs to discuss their needs and to press demands on the North.

UNCTAD and the Group of 77 have also promoted many other discussions of the Third World's economic position. The most significant of these was a 1981 meeting at Cancún, Mexico, between North and South. Fourteen states representing the Group of 77 met with eight Western industrialized states representing the Organization for Economic Cooperation and Development (OECD), a twenty-four-member organization that serves to promote economic coordination among the Western industrialized countries.[22] (We will explore the level of North/South economic cooperation more fully in Chapter 16.) Although little of substantive importance was accomplished at Cancún, the meeting did serve as a symbolic admission by the North that it has a stake in the South and that North/South economic relations are subject to negotiation between the two spheres.

Third World Demands

The development of Third World consciousness and assertiveness has led to a series of demands on the industrialized North. These calls for reform are collectively known as the **New International Economic Order** (NIEO). More than any other single document, the Declaration on the Establishment of a New International Economic Order outlines and symbolizes the Third World's view of, and its calls for reform of, the "old" international economic order. This declaration, adopted as a resolution by the UN General Assembly in 1974,[23] begins by protesting the North's domination of the existing economic structure and the maldistribution of wealth. To remedy this situation, the NIEO declaration calls for a number of reforms.

Trade reforms. The NIEO envisions improved and stabilized markets for primary products. This would include removal of trade barriers and the regulation of prices and supplies.

Monetary reforms. Reforms in monetary relations include stabilization of inflation and exchange rates and increased funding from the IMF, and other international monetary agencies. The NIEO also includes demands for greater LDC participation in the decision making of the IMF and other such international agencies.

Industrialization. The 1974 resolution also calls on the North to assist the South in gaining technology and increasing industrial production.

Economic sovereignty. Additionally, the Third World asserts its right to control its own resources and to regulate the activities of multinational corporations.

Economic aid. Finally, the Third World has called on the developed countries to extend economic aid at a level at least equivalent to 0.7 percent of the GNP of each. Only four industrialized countries are currently at or above this level (see Table 12-3), and if that standard were met, it would almost double aid (from the 1980 figure) to over $50 billion.[24] There are also calls for more nonpolitical **multilateral aid** to be given through the World Bank and other such institutions. These calls for reform have been supplemented and detailed in the periodic UNCTAD meetings and other Third World forums.

Third World Action

The countries of the South have not passively waited for the North to respond to their demands. They have instead taken action on a number of fronts. Not all these moves have succeeded, but they are marks of the South's growing assertiveness. Areas of action include cartel formation, nationalization and control of MNCs, and protection of developing industry.

Cartels.

A **cartel** is an international trading agreement among producers who hope to control the supply and price of a primary product. The first cartel was established in 1933 to regulate tea, but of the current nineteen cartels, all but the tea organization were formed after 1960. In their importance to the world economy, cartels range from the Organization of Petroleum Exporting Countries (OPEC) to the Asian and Pacific Coconut Community.[25]

The rise of OPEC and its subsequent decline illustrate many of the strengths and weaknesses of cartels. This thirteen-member organization (which includes both Middle Eastern states and others such as Mexico, Venezuela, and Nigeria) was founded in 1960 but did not immediately have a major impact. In 1970 the price of oil was still only $1.35 per barrel (bbl), or 3.2 cents per gallon. Within a few years, however, a number of factors, including increased energy needs in the North and stagnant oil production in the United States, strengthened the economic hand of OPEC. Many members nationalized production,

Cartel - internat. trading agreement among producers who hope to control the supply + price of a primary product.

Between 1970 and 1981 OPEC was able to raise the price of oil 2,500 percent. Since that time, both the price of oil and its power has declined markedly.

and they also dramatically hiked prices. The North's economy convulsed, but with OPEC members producing 68 percent of all supplies (1976) and with world supply short of demand, OPEC was in the driver's seat. By 1981 the price of OPEC oil had risen almost 2,500 percent, to $34 per bbl. Money poured into the OPEC treasuries as black gold flowed out. During the 1970s, more than a trillion dollars was accumulated, and the OPEC countries' balance-of-payment surplus peaked at an annual $109 billion in 1980.

The decline of OPEC began to be obvious in the early 1980s, although its causes were paradoxically contained in the glittering success of the seventies. The humbling of OPEC was rooted in the changing balance of production, declining demand, declining price, and intra-OPEC competition.

The changing balance of production. OPEC never contained all the major oil producers. Important producing countries like the United States and the Soviet Union were not involved. Furthermore, the steep rise in oil prices spurred oil exploration and the development of previously uneconomical oil supplies such as shale and low-capacity wells. Offshore drilling was particularly important; major fields were being developed by Britain and others in the North Sea and by the United States off its coasts. By 1980, non-OPEC oil production was over 40 percent of the world total, and in 1982 the balance shifted: non-OPEC countries were producing 54 percent of all oil. That meant not only that some countries could meet more of their energy needs, it also meant new competition for OPEC. Britain, for instance, not only has moved from oil importer to oil exporter but is not in OPEC and sells its oil below OPEC prices.

Declining demand. A second cause of OPEC's decline is the drop in demand experienced in the 1980s. The high oil prices of the 1970s caused a worldwide effort to conserve energy and to develop alternative supplies. As a result, oil consumption outside the communist countries dropped from 52.4 million bbl/day in 1979 to 45.5 million bbl/day in early 1983, thus creating a sea of surplus oil.[26]

Declining price. In classic economic fashion the demand decline was followed by a drop in price. The 1981 OPEC price of $34 per bbl had, by late 1984, dropped to $29 per bbl, and oil could be bought on the spot market and from non-OPEC countries in the $26-per-bbl range.[27]

Intra-OPEC competition. Finally, the individual economic needs of the OPEC countries have created competition within the cartel. Many cartel members, such as Nigeria and Mexico, borrowed billions of dollars to finance various projects. When demand slumped, export revenues fell, and these countries began to struggle to sell enough oil to pay off the principal and interest on their debts. The demand decline meant that the crude-oil imports of the Western industrialized states dropped 32.3 percent between 1979 and 1983. OPEC production also declined, dropping almost 5 percent annually between 1979 and 1982, and in late 1984 was at 17.5 million bbl/day, or 50 percent of capacity. The net result is that the annual balance of payments for OPEC countries plummeted from a $109 billion surplus in 1980 to an $18 billion deficit in 1982.[28] This income decline eroded OPEC internal cohesion as some revenue-desperate members began to "cheat" on production quotas and prices. By 1984, then, OPEC was barely surviving the tremendous economic pressure on its members.

The lesson of OPEC for cartels is that when a cartel can act *with unity* to control the bulk of world production of a *vital resource,* then the cartel can be a success. Most cartels, however, are not so lucky, even for a short time. They are subject to demand variations, competition from nonmembers, development/expansion of substitutes, conservation/decline in demand, and intra-cartel competition. The result is that cartels have not proved to be a significant technique for Third World development.

Nationalization and Control of MNCs

A second area of action to accomplish the NIEO program has involved Third World countries' taking closer control of their domestic economics. One route has been **nationalization** of foreign-owned companies. This process requires that at least a majority of any company be owned by the host country or its citizens. Between 1960 and 1976, seventy-one countries nationalized 1,369 enterprises at an accelerating rate, as Table 12-4 indicates.

Although nationalization is an effective method to gain control of production, it does have its drawbacks. Nationalizations have caused some international squabbles as MNCs have looked to their home countries for support

Table 12-4. Nationalizations, 1960–1976.

Years	*Total*	*Average per Year*
1960–1969	455	45.5
1970–1976	914	131.0
1960–1976	1,369	80.5

Data from George Thomas Kurian, *Encyclopedia of the Third World,* rev. ed., vol. 3 (New York: Facts on File, 1982), table 7(ii), p. 2060.

over compensation disagreements with the nationalizing country. The potential for nationalization has also inhibited foreign investment. MNCs are less willing to risk their money, thus limiting one source of capital inflow for LDCs.

As discussed in the previous chapter, recent years have seen many host countries establish rules that limit profit taking, require local processing and capital reinvestment, and mandate training and other personnel policies. But even here, progress has been slow and uneven. The pressure to attract investment capital is so strong that some LDCs are actually easing restrictions on MNCs. Thus the struggle between the desire for economic sovereignty and the need for investment capital continues unabated.

Protection of Developing Industry

A third thrust of Third World activity has been an attempt to protect developing industries from foreign competition. China is one of the most recent developing economies to fly the protectionist flag. The temptation and domestic political pressure for developing countries to use tariffs and nontariff barriers to protect infant industries are strong and may, in the earliest stages, even have some merit. Protectionist policies work against the theory of comparative advantage, however, and also invite retaliation by more economically powerful states. Most important, there is evidence that LDC protectionism doesn't work. As one analyst concluded, "Empirically, the record shows that those countries that have followed low tariff policies and eschewed quantitative restrictions . . . all have outstanding export performance records. On the other hand, the rate of export growth of countries following high protectionist policies . . . has been well below par."[29]

The Response of the North

Some of the goals of the NIEO can be furthered by the individual and collective policies of the countries of the Third World. These actions can go only so far, though, in promoting greater economic equality. A pivotal part, then, in advancing the NIEO is the cooperation of the North. Thus far that cooperation has been limited. It is true that there have been important advances in international economic cooperation. Some of this progress has included improvements in North/South cooperation, and these will be discussed in Chapter 16.

The recalcitrant rich. Overall, though, the North has been slow to respond. There are those who contend, with a good deal of logic and evidence, that because of economic interdependence and other factors, the North has a vital stake in the South's development. Whatever the truth of this global view, it has occasioned only a limited response in the North. Traditional narrow self-interest has been strengthened by the economic turmoil of the recent past. Given the vastly superior economic and political strength of the North, its reluctance to cooperate has meant that, so far, the NIEO remains a series of conscience-disturbing demands rather than a developing program.[30]

The Soviet response. So far our discussion of the North/South axis has focused mainly on the Western industrialized states. The Soviet Union and its Eastern European allies have followed policies akin to their capitalist counterparts. We have seen that Moscow's foreign aid is highly politicized and militarized. Further, although the Soviet Union has rhetorically encouraged NIEO demands, it has also, according to one study, "stubbornly resisted attempts to redefine the world economic order in any fashion that might imply . . . Soviet responsibility as an affluent nation to aid less developed countries."[31]

The Future of the South

The future development of the South remains uncertain. Even assuming that the future can be projected from the recent past, your predictions for the future depend on whether you're an optimist or a pessimist.

On the positive side, there is progress on many fronts. A few newly industrializing countries now export a diversity of manufactured products and have robustly expanding GNPs. Many social indicators also show improvement. The population explosion is beginning to ease, new agricultural techniques give hope of feeding the hungry, life expectancy has improved, and illiteracy has declined. There is also at least a genesis of recognition in the North of its interest in and responsibility for the development of the South. In short, for many, things are better than they were, and for a few, things are much better.

More negatively, the South has long suffered under a heavy burden of socioeconomic/political problems. Economically, it continues to be disadvantaged, dependent, and exploited. Socially, many parts of the Third World are handicapped by overpopulation, illiteracy, hunger, disease, and the breakdown of traditional societal structures. Politically, LDCs are often inexperienced, internally divided, and subject to coups and countercoups as well as outside interference.

Despite some of the hopeful signs, the prospects for the future are at least troubling. The world population recently hurtled through the 5 billion mark, environmental problems threaten coming generations, and there is a resurgence of protectionism and other forms of shortsighted economic self-interest. There are few signs that the North will radically reform its trade, aid, investment, monetary, or political policies. In sum, we have improved on the past, and in the future we may well improve on the present. But progress is painfully slow. It is, at best, an evolution rather than a revolution, and there are many who seriously question whether the world can progress far enough, fast enough to avoid apocalypse.

Summary

The economic issues facing the North and those facing the South are, in most respects, fundamentally different. The North is concerned with preserving and expanding its economic prosperity. In the South the major issue is survival, in economic terms and, all too often, in human terms. For many in the world's less developed countries, life is a struggle against starvation, disease, illiteracy, and death.

Measuring "progress" in LDCs is controversial. In absolute terms, there [illegible]ve been some advances. Relative to the North, however, the South is falling [illegible]er behind. Modernization has also brought some negative consequences, [illegible]g explosive population growth, destructive urbanization, and poor [illegible]

[illegible] also be noted that *South* is a word that somewhat hides the wide [illegible] Third World. A few newly industrializing countries have ex[illegible]trializing economies. There is also, in most LDCs, a wealthy class [illegible]t Third World countries, however, and for most of the citizens [illegible] prosperity—even comfort—is only a hope, and a dim one at [illegible]

Capital is [illegible]of the LDCs. They need hard currency to buy the goods and ser[illegible]w them to develop their economies. There are four basic source[illegible]: trade, loans, foreign aid, and foreign investment. In each of t[illegible]ever, the LDCs face difficult problems. The catch-22 of trade is tha[illegible]ary products that LDCs mainly produce do not earn them enough capi[illegible] found industries to produce manufactured goods that would earn more money. Loans are unsatisfactory because of high repayment costs and because they have largely dried up in recent years. Foreign aid is minor compared with world needs and is often given on the basis of political expediency rather than economic necessity. Investment capital flows least into the most needy countries and is often accompanied by unacceptable practices by multinational corporate investors.

In recent years, the countries of the Third World have begun to make greater demands for economic equity and have increasingly come together to press those demands on the North. These demands for fundamental economic reform are collectively referred to as the New International Economic Order. The LDCs have also taken actions such as the founding of international trading agreements called cartels. OPEC is the most well known and successful of these. Most cartels, however, have not worked well because of the disadvantages that primary-product producers face vis-à-vis the industrialized countries. The LDCs have also acted to protect developing industries and to nationalize MNCs. Each of these steps, though, has its drawbacks as well as its advantages. So far, the response of the North to the demands of the South has been extremely limited.

The economic and social future of the South is far from cheerful. There are some good signs, such as expanding literacy, but there are also many troubling omens. The massive starvation in Ethiopia and other countries in Africa and the epidemic economic, social, and political unrest on a global basis are very possibly Scrooge-like glimpses into Christmas future. In Chapter 16 we will examine attempts to work together for economic betterment and equity, but they are too little and may very well come too late to avoid repeated and greater catastrophes.

Terms

Bilateral (foreign) aid—Foreign aid given by one country directly to another.

Capital needs—The requirements of all countries, and LDCs in particular, for money to expand their economies.

Cartel—An international agreement among producers of a commodity that attempts to control the production and pricing of that commodity.

Dependencia school—The belief that the industrialized North has created a neocolonial relationship with the South in which the LDCs are dependent on and disadvantaged by their economic relations with the capitalist, industrial countries.

Hard currency—Currencies, such as dollars, marks, francs, and yen, that are acceptable in private channels of international economics.

Less developed countries—Countries, located mainly in Africa, Asia, and Latin America, with economies that rely heavily on the production of agriculture and raw material and whose per capita GNP and standard of living are substantially below Western standards.

Multilateral (foreign) aid—Foreign aid distributed by international organizations such as the United Nations.

Nationalization—The process of a country's taking over control of a previously foreign-owned multinational corporation.

New International Economic Order—A term that refers to the goals and demands of the Third World for basic reforms in the international economic system.

Newly industrializing countries—The few Third World countries which are successfully moving from primary-product to manufactured-goods production and whose GNPs and standards of living are improving at a rate above average.

Primary products—Agricultural products and raw materials, such as minerals.

Notes

1. Herbert Sperber, "The Efficiency Reducing Effects of Official Development Aid," *Intereconomics,* March/April 1983, p. 84. A good general study of international economics in a political world is Joan Edelman Spero, *The Politics of International Economic Relations* (New York: St. Martin's Press, 1981).
2. On development and approaches, see Ian M. D. Little, *Economic Development* (New York: Basic Books, 1982), pp. 3–15, and R. M. Sundrum, *Development Economics* (New York: Wiley, 1983), pp. 63–79.
3. Little, *Economic Development,* pp. 218–266, discusses dependencies.
4. For a treatment of NICs, see Colin I. Bradford, "The Rise of NICs as Exporters on a Global Scale," in *The Newly Industrializing Countries: Trade and Adjustment,* ed. Louis Turner and Neil McMullen (London: Allen & Unwin, 1982), pp. 7–26; also, Bela Balassa, *The Newly Industrializing Countries in the World Economy* (New York: Pergamon Press, 1981).
5. World Bank, *World Development Report, 1981* (Washington, D.C.: International Bank for Reconstruction and Development, 1981), p. 24.
6. *Encyclopedia of the Third World,* rev. ed., vol. 3 (New York: Facts on File, 1982), appendix III, table 6, p. 2032.
7. World Bank, *World Development Report, 1981,* p. 50. Also see Michael Beenstock, *World Economy in Transition* (London: Allen & Unwin, 1983), p. 86.
8. General Agreement on Tariffs and Trade, *International Trade 1982/83* (Geneva: General Agreement on Tariffs and Trade, 1983), appendix, table A3.
9. Ibid., tables 6 and 7, pp. 23, 25.
10. For a discussion, see Committee for Economic Development, *Transnational Corporations in Developing Countries* (New York: Committee for Economic Development, 1981).
11. Sperber, "Efficiency Reducing Effects," p. 84.
12. U.S. General Accounting Office, *Political and Economic Factors Influencing Economic Support Fund Programs,* GAO ID 83-43, April 18, 1984. Also see U.S. Department of State, *International Security and Development Cooperation Program,* Special Report 108; and Robert D. Hansen and contributors, *U.S. Foreign Policy and the Third World: Agenda 1982,* prepared for the Overseas Development Council (New York: Praeger, 1982), table F-16, p. 242.
13. John L. Scherer, *USSR Facts and Figures Annual,* vol. 7 (Gulf Breeze, Fla.: Academic International Press, 1983), pp. 224–225.
14. World Bank, *World Development Report, 1981,* p. 56. These figures are for economic aid. They exclude aid from communist countries and do not include China as a potential recipient. If China were added, per capita would drop to $7.88.
15. Hansen, *Agenda 1982,* table F-18, p. 244.
16. On OPEC aid, see Ibrahim F. I. Shihata, *The Other Face of OPEC: Financial Assistance to the Third World* (New York: Longman, 1982).
17. Sperber, "Efficiency Reducing Effects," p. 85.
18. For a supporting view, see World Bank, *World Development Report, 1981,* p. 56.
19. There is a host of books on development. For one, see Benjamin Higgins and Jean Downing Higgins, *Economic Development of a Small Planet* (New York: Norton, 1979).
20. This section on the growth of the New International Economic Order movement relies heavily on Jyoti Shankar Singh, *A New International Economic Order* (New

York: Praeger, 1977), pp. 1–10; Jagdish N. Bhagwati, ed., *The New International Economic Order* (Cambridge, Mass.: M.I.T. Press, 1977), pp. 1–21; Robert K. Olson, *U.S. Foreign Policy and the New International Economic Order* (Boulder, Colo.: Westview Press, 1981), pp. 1–17; Higgins and Higgins, *Economic Development*; and D. H. N. Johnson, "The New International Economic Order," in *The Year Book of World Affairs, 1983* (London: Stevens & Sons), pp. 204–223.

21. For this development and earlier genesis, see Robert E. Asher, Walter M. Kotschnig, William Adams Brown, Jr., and associates, *The United Nations and Economic and Social Cooperation* (Washington, D.C.: Brookings Institution, 1957), pp. 9–55.
22. In addition to most Western European countries, OECD includes the United States, Canada, Australia, Japan, Turkey, and New Zealand.
23. For an extended discussion, see Ervin Laszlo, Robert Baler, Jr., Eliot Eisenberg, and Venkata Raman, *The Objectives of the New International Economic Order* (New York: Pergamon Press, 1980).
24. Higgins and Higgins, *Economic Development*, pp. 269–271, especially boxes 10.1 and 10.2.
25. *Encyclopedia of the Third World*, appendix IX, p. 2067.
26. *Time*, February 7, 1983, p. 43.
27. *Time*, October 29, 1984, p. 68.
28. General Agreement on Tariffs and Trade, *International Trade*, table 9, p. 72. *Time*, February 7, 1983, p. 43.
29. Melvyn B. Krauss, *Development without Aid* (New York: McGraw-Hill, 1983), pp. 52–53. Bela Balassa and associates, *The Structure of Protectionism in Developing Countries* (Baltimore: Johns Hopkins Press, 1971), part I, pp. 3–102. This view is also voiced in World Bank, *World Development Report, 1981*, pp. 25–26.
30. Helge Ole Bergensen, Hans Henrik Holm, and Robert D. McKinlay, *The Recalcitrant Rich: A Comparative Analysis of the Northern Response to the Demands for a New International Economic Order* (New York: St. Martin's Press, 1982), especially pp. 223–250. Also see Philip Taylor, "Third World Policies and Preservative Adaptation," in *Third World Policies of Industrialized Nations*, ed. Philip Taylor and Gregory A. Raymond (Westport, Conn.: Greenwood Press, 1980), pp. 253–270.
31. Donald R. Kelley, "The Soviet Union and the Third World: The East-South Connection," in Taylor and Raymond, eds., *Third World Policies*, p. 240.

13

International Organization

Friendly counsel cuts off many foes.
Shakespeare, Henry VI

He that is giddy thinks the world turns round.
Shakespeare, The Taming of the Shrew

A Prologue to Chapters 13–16

This text began with a literary analogy between international relations and Shakespeare's belief that "all the world's a stage, And all the men and women . . . players." The world drama, as we have followed it to this point—its actors, its plot, its action—has been a troubled tale. The actors, if not always villains, have too often been convinced of their own righteousness and have pursued their interests at the expense of others. Discord has time and again triumphed over harmony. The specters of hunger and disease continue to stalk the world, yet the rich nations content themselves with little more than expressions of pity.

Still, the world survives and has a future. It is that future, rather than a gloomy contemplation of the past, that should consume our intellects. Indeed, a major thrust of this text is to enable its readers not only to understand what has been and what is but also to contemplate what might be. As the Bard of Avon tells us in *Hamlet,* "We know what we are, but not what we can be." Another, more contemporary analogy drawn earlier was between our world drama and *The French Lieutenant's Woman.* That novel has two endings, one of love and peace, the other of conflict and tragedy. It may well be that the fate of humankind similarly hangs in the balance of the world drama.

One possible path is akin to Shakespeare's dictum that "what is past is prologue" (*The Tempest*). If that is true, then the divisions, self-interest, and conflict that have often characterized the past will continue into the future. To continue, however, does not necessarily mean that we can survive as before. The nuclear arms race, the flood of world population, modernization's threat to our ecological survival, and the seething demands of the poor, no longer silent, world majority all carry apocalyptic potential.

Catastrophe is not certain, and, indeed, we may continue to muddle through, but it is also possible, as *Hamlet* tells us, that we may

> ***Unfold* [*a tale*] *whose lightest word***
> ***Would harrow up thy soul, freeze thy young blood,***
> ***Make thy two eyes, like stars, start from their spheres,***
> ***Thy knotted and combined locks to part,***
> ***And each particular hair to stand on end,***
> ***Like quills upon the fretful porpentine.***

There *is* an alternative, more salutary future that is possible. It involves a world that the idealists urge upon us as discussed in Chapter 2. Analysts of this school would have us follow the counsel offered in *King Henry VI:* "Now join hands, and with your hands your hearts."

The final four chapters of this book are about the world's effort to find a new order. They are an exploration of the movement toward international cooperation. The placement of these chapters at the end of the text sadly reflects the significance of cooperation past and present. It does not, however, symbolize the importance of cooperation for the future.

The author of this text firmly believes that there are many signs that we, as global citizens, are beginning to see our mutual stake in one another and that we are beginning, however uncertainly, to move toward a process of accommodation rather than competition. The author is even more convinced that such efforts are crucial for the future. Each of the final four chapters explores one aspect of cooperative behavior. Chapter 13 addresses international organization as it is and as it might be. Next, Chapter 14 discusses the concept and practice of international law. Then, in Chapter 15, the painfully slow struggle to find a basis for arms control or disarmament is analyzed. Finally, Chapter 16 details the growth of economic and social cooperation in the world.

The issue that faces us all is which of the alternative endings to adopt. The time left for decision is uncertain, but pressing problems make it clear that procrastination is perilous. To end, as we began, with a thought from Shakespeare,

> ***There is a tide in the affairs of men,***
> ***Which taken at the flood, leads on to fortune;***
> ***Omitted, all the voyage of their life***
> ***Is bound in shallows and in miseries.***
>
> **Julius Caesar**

Introduction

The nation-state has, for the past several centuries, been the primary actor in world politics. Indeed, as discussed in the chapter on nationalism, it is hard to conceive of any other form of organization. Yet alternatives do exist.

International organization is one of these alternatives. Many established agencies are currently involved in promoting political, economic, and social cooperation. Many observers contend that such efforts are the hope of the future. They may be right. It is just possible that ongoing organizations will serve as prototypes or building blocks for a future, higher form of political loyalty and activity.

There are also those who dismiss the notion of international organization as idealistic dreaming. But there was also a time when we believed that the world was the center of the universe. We now know that the sun does not turn around the earth; perhaps we can learn that the nation-state need not be the center of the political cosmos.

Types of International Organization

The term *international organization* tends to bring *United Nations* to mind. There are many more, however, and for our purposes they can be divided into general, regional, and specialized types of international organizations. One commonality among some of them is that their memberships consist of national governments. Therefore, they are termed **international governmental organizations (IGOs)**. There are also a significant and growing number of **international nongovernmental organizations** (**NGOs** or sometimes **INGOs**), which are made up of private organizations and individuals instead of member states.[1]

We have already addressed some international organization types and activities under such headings as intergovernmental organization and nongovernmental organizations (Chapter 3), alliances (Chapter 9), and cartels (Chapter 12). We will, further, in the next three chapters, examine organizations that focus on promoting cooperation in law, disarmament, and socioeconomic endeavors. Thus, although many of the organizations discussed in this chapter have a variety of purposes, our primary focus will be their impact on the world's political order.

A *universal intergovernmental organization* is one that draws its membership from all areas of the world. The United Nations is the most obvious example, but there are many others, such as the World Health Organization.

Regional intergovernmental organizations are those that draw their membership from one geographic region. Some regional organizations, such as the Organization of American States (OAS), are multipurpose, much like the UN. Others are somewhat active in a variety of areas but concentrate on one. The European Economic Community (EEC) is an example of a primarily economic regional organization, and the Organization of African Unity (OAU) devotes most of its energy to political affairs. Additionally, there are a host of single-purpose regional organizations. Most regional military alliances would fall in this category, as would regional economic organizations such as the Economic Community of West African States.

A *general intergovernmental organization* is one that is active in a number of areas such as political, economic, and social development and/or cooperation. The United Nations is, again, an example, as is the British Commonwealth. Of all the types of international organizations, those with general functions are the rarest.

Specialized intergovernmental organizations are single-purpose, or functional, organizations. A vast array of these specialized agencies exists, and they deal with almost every conceivable subject from health through postal regulations (Universal Postal Union, headquarters, Berne, Switzerland) to air travel (International Civil Aviation Organization, headquarters, Montreal, Canada).

Nongovernmental organizations is our final category. As mentioned, NGOs are different from IGOs in that they are not made up of member states. Some NGOs, such as the Catholic church, are active in several geographic and policy areas. Most NGOs, however, are limited-purpose (Red Cross, Amnesty International, Socialist International, and so on) and/or are limited geographically (African Football Confederation, for example).

Finally, as may be clear, this typology of organizations is not mutually exclusive, as Table 13-1 shows.

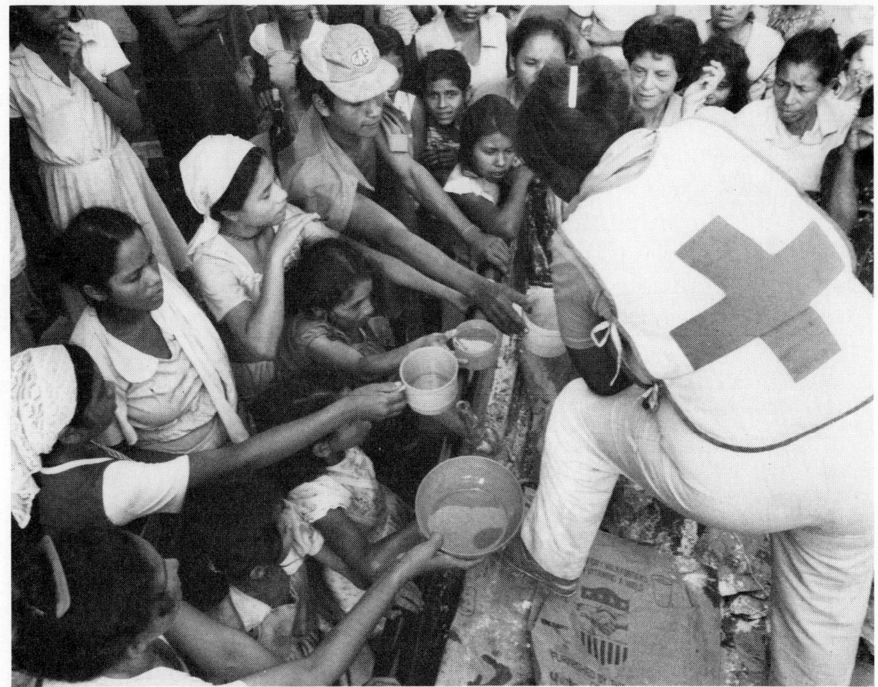

The Red Cross, shown here working in El Salvador, is one example of the growing number of nongovernmental organizations active on the world stage.

The Roots of International Organization

International organization is primarily a modern phenomenon, but extend far back in history. Three main root systems have nourished t growth.

Universal Concern for the Condition of Human

Philosophy. The first branch of the root system is the universalis ception of humankind. Confucius (551–479 B.C.) deplored violen Erasmus (1466–1536) rejected war as brutal, wicked, wasteful, and stupid.

Table 13-1. Types and Examples of International Organizations.

	Purpose			
	General		*Specialized*	
Geography	***IGO***	***NGO***	***IGO***	***NGO***
Universal	United Nations	Catholic Church	International Monetary Fund	Red Cross, Amnesty International
Regional	Organization of American States	European People's Party	European Economic Community	African Football Confederation

Other early philosophers agreed that all persons shared a responsibility for one another's welfare.[2] Still other philosophers, including William Penn, the Abbé de Sainte-Parme, and Immanuel Kant, argued that the way to accomplish these ends was through general international organizations.

Organization. The first example of an organization based on these principles was the *Hague system,* named for the 1899 and 1907 peace conferences held at that city in the Netherlands. The 1907 conference was more comprehensive, with forty-four European, North American, and Latin American states participating.

Organizationally, the Hague system included a rudimentary general assembly and a judicial system. The conferences also adopted a series of standards to limit the conduct of war. World War I destroyed the plans for a third Hague conference in 1915, but the move toward universal organization was underway.

The next step along the path was creation of the **League of Nations** after World War I. The league was intended mainly as a peacekeeping organization, although it did have some elements aimed at social and economic cooperation. Despite the hopes with which it was founded, the league could not survive some of its own organizational inadequacies, the unstable post–World War I peace, the Great Depression, and the rise of militant fascism. After only two decades of frustrated existence, it died in the rubble of World War II.

The *United Nations* is the latest, and most advanced, developmental stage of universal concern with the human condition. Like the League of Nations, it was established mainly to maintain peace, but it has increasingly become involved in socioeconomic issues. In addition, as we shall see, the UN and its predecessor, the league, represent the coming together of all the root systems of international organization. They are more properly seen as the emergent saplings of extensive cooperation and integration.

Big-Power Peacekeeping

The second branch of the root system is the idea that the big powers have a special responsibility to cooperate and preserve peace. The Roman Peace, enforced by the imperial power of Rome, was viewed by Dante and others with nostalgia amid the turmoil of the Middle Ages. As early as 1625, Hugo Grotius, the "father of international law," suggested that the "Christian powers" confer to "settle the disputes of others" or even "compel parties to accept peace on fair terms."[3]

This idea took on substance with the Congress of Vienna. That conference and three others between 1815 and 1822 led to the Concert of Europe. This informal coalition of the major European powers and the following balance of (big) power diplomacy managed generally to keep the peace for the century between the fall of Napoleon and the outbreak of World War I.

The persistence of the philosophy of big-power responsibility (and authority) was evident in the Council of the League of Nations. The council was granted authority (Covenant Article 4) to deal "with any matter within the sphere of activity of the League or affecting the peace of the world." Significantly, five of the nine seats on the council were permanently assigned to principal victorious allies of World War I. The council was thus the concert continued.

Finally, the special status and responsibilities of the big powers are reflected in the United Nations Security Council. Like its predecessor, the Security Council is the main peacekeeping organ and includes permanent membership for the big five powers (U.S., USSR, China, Britain, and France). Additionally, each of the major powers can cast a veto that, as a lone vote, can block Security Council action. We will further explore these issues, but for now we should notice that a descendant of the Concert of Europe is alive and well in New York.

Functional Cooperation

The third branch of our root system lies in the specialized agencies designed to deal with specific, generally nonpolitical economic and social problems. The six-member Central Commission for the Navigation of the Rhine, established in 1815, is the oldest surviving IGO, and the International Telegraphic (now Telecommunications) Union (1865) and the Universal Postal Union (1874) are the oldest surviving IGOs with global membership. As detailed below, the growth of these specialized IGOs and NGOs has been phenomenal. This aspect of international activity is also reflected in the UN through the eighteen specialized agencies associated with the world body.

Growth of IGOs and NGOs

An important phenomenon of the twentieth century is the rapid growth in the number, activities, and importance of IGOs and NGOs.

Quantitative Growth

This century has seen rapid growth in the number of all types of international organizations. Table 13-2, as well as some discussion in Chapter 1, highlights this rapid expansion. As the table indicates, there are now about ten times as many IGOs and thirty-five times as many NGOs as in 1900. Further, both the average number of IGO memberships of any single country and the ratio of IGOs to countries has approximately doubled. Thus, there are not only more IGOs absolutely and relative to the number of countries, but the level of participation has dramatically increased.

Reasons for Growth

This century's rapid growth of international organizations, both in number and in scope of activity, is the result of a number of forces.[4]

Table 13-2. Expansion of International Organizations, 1900–1980.

	Year		
Category	*1900*	*1945*	*1980*
No. of IGOs	30	123	292
No. of NGOs	69	795	2,427
No. of countries	38	65	181
Memberships	412	2,284	6,432
Avg. no. of IGOs per country	0.7	1.9	1.6
Avg. no. of NGO memberships per country	9.6	30.5	38.2

Data from Werner J. Feld and Robert S. Jordan with Leon Hurwitz, *International Organizations* (New York: Praeger, 1983), table 1.1, pp. 16–17, and figure 1.3, p. 19. (Figures are approximate.)

Increased international contact. The revolutions in communications and transportation technologies have brought the states of the world into much closer contact. These interchanges need to be routinized and regulated. The Universal Postal Union and the International Telegraphic Union, founded in the 1800s, have been joined in more modern times by the International Air Transport Association, the Intergovernmental Maritime Association, and almost 300 others.

Increased interdependence. The world's increased interdependence, particularly in the economic sphere, has fostered a variety of IGOs designed to deal with this phenomenon. The International Monetary Fund and the World Bank are just two examples. Regional trade and monetary organizations, cartels, and (to a degree) multinational corporations are other examples.

Transnational issues. More than ever before, many of the world's problems affect many states and require solutions that are beyond the resources of any single state. One such issue (and its responsible international organization) is nuclear proliferation (International Atomic Energy Agency).

Inadequacy of state-centered systems. A fourth incentive for the expansion of international organization is the failure of the current nationalism-focused system. The agony of two world wars, for instance, convinced many that peace was not safe in the hands of nation-states. The League of Nations and then the United Nations were successive attempts to organize for the preservation of peace. The continuing problems in health, food, human rights, and other areas have also spurred the organization of IGOs and NGOs.

Transnational political movements. Political movements increasingly extend beyond the borders of a single state. The monarchist Concert of Europe of the 1800s has given way to the Communist International, the Socialist

International, and the World Anti-Communist League. The British Commonwealth and the even more loosely knit French Community would also fall within this motivational category.

Concentration of power. The concentration of military power in the two superpowers and the concentration of economic power in the industrialized states have led less powerful actors to join coalitions in an attempt to influence events. "Vulnerability" has, thus, motivated the nonaligned movement, the peace movement, the New International Economic Order, and their associated organizations.

Role models. Finally, the existence and successes of international organizations have generated still other IGOs and NGOs. People and countries have, in short, learned that they can sometimes work together internationally, and that has encouraged them to try new ventures in international organization and cooperation.

Purposes of International Organization

The concept of international organization is complex, and its advocates are divided on proper goals and roles. These differing aims include world government, comprehensive cooperation, functional cooperation, and/or political advantage.

World Government

Vision. Some proponents of international organization envision a day when there will be one **world government.** They argue for a "top down," revolutionary approach to solving world problems. According to this approach, the current national states would give up most of their sovereignty to a new, supranational organization, which would have central lawmaking, enforcing, and adjudicating authority. Within this general goal, there are several approaches that vary according to how hierarchical the organization would be. That structure could range from a *unitary* world government with subunits serving only administrative purposes, through *federalism,* in which a central authority and member units share power, to *confederalism,* in which the members are highly interdependent but retain all or most of their sovereign authority.[5]

There is also dispute about the proper locus of supranational government(s). Some argue for a single, world system, while others propose regional supranational structures.

Critique. The image of a peaceful and cooperative world is highly attractive, but there are many who doubt that world government can be attained.[6] These skeptics argue that, first, there are *practical barriers* to world government. The assumption here is that nationalism has too strong a hold and that neither political leaders nor masses would be willing to surrender independence to a universal body. In short, are we ready to "pledge allegiance to the United States of the World"?

Critics of the world government movement also pose *theoretical objections*. They worry about the concentration of power that would be necessary even to begin enforcing international law and addressing the world's monumental economic and social problems. Critics further doubt that any such government, even given unprecedented power, could succeed in solving world problems any better than less (potentially) authoritarian alternatives. Finally, some skeptics argue that centralization would inevitably diminish desirable cultural diversity and political experimentation in the world. A last criticism of the world government movement is that it diverts attention from more reasonable avenues of international cooperation such as the United Nations and other existing international organizations.

Comprehensive Cooperation

Most supporters of international organization advocate a more limited role for IGOs. This school of thought believes that IGOs can best serve as vehicles to promote cooperation among states rather than through the subordination of states to a global authority.

The United Nations and some regional organizations are designed to advance international cooperative efforts to maintain peace, better economic conditions, protect the environment, and, in general, improve the human condition. Insofar as IGOs play an "independent" role, proponents of this approach argue that it should be one mainly of mediation and conciliation rather than coercion. The object here is to teach and allow, not to force, national states to work together.

Functionalism

An even more limited approach to international organization is **functionalism**. As noted above and in Chapter 11, functionalists favor a "bottom up," evolutionary approach to international cooperation. They argue that by cooperating in specific, usually nonpolitical areas, we can learn to trust one another. This, in turn, will lead to broader and higher levels of cooperation.

The best-known proponent of functionalism, David Mitrany, argues, for example, that "sovereignty cannot be transferred effectively through a formula, [but] only through a function." Mitrany then argues that in time "the accumulation of such partial transfers" of sovereignty will "overlay political divisions with a spreading web of international activities" that will promote world peace and integration.[7]

A recent extension of functional cooperation is the creation of *international regimes* that deal with particular issue areas. A regime is not so much a single organization as a complex of international organizations and generally accepted rules of behavior in areas such as monetary relations, trade, health, or air traffic control. In short, regimes represent an advance from national cooperation through one functional organization on one issue to cooperation through a complex of related organizations on a complex of issues.

Political Advantage

Finally, it should be noted that many approach international organization as a tool to further their self-interested concept of the "correct" international order. This approach is rarely stated openly, but it is obvious in the struggles within the UN and other IGOs. The East/West, North/South, and other struggles are waged with vengeance. This seemingly contradictory use of supposedly integrative international organizations to gain national advantage is part of the world's struggle between the forces of order and the forces of anarchy.

Evaluating International Organization

Thus far this chapter has been introducing the concept of international organization and laying the groundwork for addressing the most vital questions: How do IGOs work and how successful are they? This second question, the matter of evaluation, is by far the most difficult, and it is well to stop here and consider our standards.

In the following sections (and the remaining chapters), we will spend considerable time looking at global, regional, and specialized IGOs and NGOs. We will especially focus on the United Nations, both as a generalized study of international organization and as a specific study of the world's most important IGO.

The "bottom line" of this analysis will be "How well does it work?" In responding to that question, we will consider several possible *standards.* One of these is *successes and failures.* Where has the UN (or any IGO or NGO) succeeded and where has it failed? It will be important to maintain balance in this approach to evaluation. Those who optimistically support international integration are prone to emphasize progress, to see the glass half full. Cynics—and there are many—who dismiss the UN as impotent are apt to see the glass half empty. It is important to maintain balanced objectivity in evaluation of international organizations.

This observation brings us to the second standard, which involves *ideals versus what is possible.* The UN was founded in the anguished aftermath of World War II. As a result, the rhetoric that surrounded its creation and the language found in its charter (constitution) are full of idealistic hope. Article One of the charter symbolically proclaims that it is the purpose of the UN "To maintain international peace and security . . . To develop friendly relations among nations . . . [and] to achieve international cooperation in solving international [economic, social, cultural, and humanitarian] problems."

Obviously, we have not yet come close to attaining those goals. Does that mean the UN has failed? Perhaps from the ideal perspective it has, but that is an impossible standard. It is more realistic to evaluate the UN in accordance with what is possible. As we will see, the UN and other international organizations are substantially limited by the willingness of member states to cooperate or to surrender sovereignty. Thus, to a substantial degree, the UN does not always work because we will not let it. In the words of the classic comic character Pogo, "We have met the enemy and they are us."

When evaluating IGOs, then, keep their limitations and the sources of those restrictions in mind. Judge them according to what it is possible for them to accomplish rather than by an artificially idealistic standard.[8]

International Organization: Structure and Issues

One important aspect of international organization is structure and related issues. Constitutions, rules of procedure, finance, organization charts, and other administrative details are often dismissed as inconsequential by the political novice. They are not! To the contrary, such "nitty-gritty" items are often extremely important in determining political outcomes. In the following discussion of the structure of international organization and the issues related to that structure, we will examine membership, representative bodies, administrative structure, and financial arrangements. As will rapidly become obvious, the discussion will focus on the UN, both as the leading IGO and as an example of the structural issues facing all attempts to organize internationally.[9]

Membership

Theoretically, membership in most international organizations is open to any state which falls within the geographic and/or functional scope of that organization *and* which subscribes to the principles and practices of that organization. In practice, politics often becomes heavily involved in membership questions.

Admitting members. Most IGOs have procedures for admitting new members. From 1945 to 1955 in the UN, membership was a cold-war issue, the United States and the Soviet Union each blocking the membership of states sympathetic to the other superpower. Then, in a compromise, sixteen new members were admitted all at once.

Today the UN has nearly universal membership, although a few gaps and problems remain. Switzerland has never joined because of its absolute neutrality. North and South Korea have not been admitted. There is also the issue of possible Palestinian representation, but U.S. opposition has blocked any serious consideration.

Expulsion and withdrawal. There are also issues related to members leaving international organizations. At times members have voluntarily withdrawn, usually for political reasons. Indonesia announced withdrawal from the UN in 1965 but never followed through. Countries can also be expelled from the UN. Nationalist China was effectively, if not technically, expelled from the UN when the seat was transferred to the mainland. There was also an unsuccessful attempt to expel South Africa for violating the UN Charter.

Membership, then, can be an important issue. It is advantageous to have all appropriate states as members. They should, however, follow the principles and rules, and that "qualification" sometimes opens up the issue to politics.

Representative Bodies

Types: plenary and limited membership. Almost all IGOs have some form of **plenary** (all members) **representative body**. The theoretical basis for plenary bodies is the collective and equal responsibility of all members for the concerns and policies of the organization.

In the United Nations, the plenary organ is called the **General Assembly**, but in other IGOs it may be termed a council, conference, commission, or even a parliament. These plenary bodies normally have the authority to involve themselves in virtually all aspects of their organization and, thus, in theory, are the most powerful element of their organizations. In practice, however, the plenary organization may be secondary to the administrative structure or some other element of the organization.

A second type of representative body is based on *limited membership*. The theory here is that some members have a greater stake, responsibility, or capacity in a particular area of concern. The United Nations' peacekeeping **Security Council** has fifteen members. Ten are chosen by the General Assembly for limited terms, but five are permanent members. These five (United States, Great Britain, Soviet Union, China, and France) were the five leading victorious powers at the end of World War II and were thought to have a special peacekeeping role to play.

Limited-membership bodies have *advantages*. First, smaller bodies function more efficiently. Second, a strong case can be made for focusing responsibility on those members with the greatest concern.

Limited membership also has *disadvantages*. One is that it detracts from the concept of mutual responsibility. It can be argued, for instance, that in an increasingly interactive world there is little of significance that does not concern everyone. Another problem is that the existing membership may become outmoded. The "big five" of the Security Council were something of a fiction in 1945, when, for instance, a chaotic China was seated at the insistence of the United States. After the Chinese Communist takeover in 1949, the situation became even more unrealistic, the rump Nationalist government on Taiwan occupying China's seat until 1971 (at which time the seat was transferred to the Beijing government).

Further, the current Security Council structure does not reflect the changes in the bases of power or the strength of states that have occurred during the last four decades. The United States and the Soviet Union certainly remain *the* powers, but if France and Britain are powers, what about Japan, West Germany, India, Brazil, Saudi Arabia, and Nigeria? In short, ought there be permanent members, and, if so, who should they be?

Voting issues. One of the difficult issues to face any international organization is the *formula for allocating votes.*[10] Three major alternatives as they exist today are majoritarianism, weighted voting, and unilateral negative voting.

The most common voting formula used in IGOs is **majoritarianism**. This system has two main components: (1) each member casts one equal vote, and (2) the issue is carried by either a simple majority (50 percent plus one vote) or, in some cases, an extraordinary majority (commonly two thirds).

The theory of majoritarianism springs from the concept of sovereign equality and the democratic notion that the will of the majority should prevail.[11] The UN General Assembly and most other UN bodies operate on this principle. There is, however, as discussed in Chapter 1, substantial difficulty with the concept of sovereign equality. Although this idea has a level of philosophical appeal, it does not reflect reality. Should Costa Rica, with no army, cast an equal vote with the powerful United States or Soviet Union? Should Nauru, with a population of thousands, cast the same vote as China, with its billion people? It might be noted, for example, that in the General Assembly states with less than 15 percent of the world's population account for two thirds of the vote.[12]

An alternative to majoritarianism is **weighted voting**, or a system that allocates unequal voting power on the basis of a formula. Two possible criteria are population and wealth. The European Parliament is, for example, based in part on population. Voting in the Council of Ministers of the European Communities is based on a mixture of size and strength, with votes ranging from ten (e.g., West Germany) to two (Luxembourg). Finally, a number of international monetary organizations base voting on financial contributions. The United States, for instance, casts 20.6 percent of the vote in the World Bank, 29.5 percent in the International Finance Corporation, and 20.01 percent in the International Monetary Fund.

The desirability of weighted voting depends on your perspective. A good philosophical case can be made for population, and most domestic representative institutions are based on that factor. Americans might well agree that their country should outvote Mexico four to one, but would the same Americans be as willing to be outvoted by China by a similar four-to-one margin? The financial contribution standard also makes some pragmatic sense, but as we have seen (Chapter 12), many Third World states contend that "wealth weighted" voting continues the system of imperial domination by the industrialized countries. Weighted voting, in short, is most attractive when the balance is in your favor.

The UN Security Council is a limited membership body and also allows any of its five permanent members to unilaterally veto council actions.

A third voting scheme is *unilateral* **negative voting**, in which a member can unilaterally block action. The most common variation is a requirement for *unanimity.* The Organization for Economic Cooperation and Development, the Arab League, and others operate on that principle. Unanimity preserves the concept of sovereignty but can easily lead to stalemate and inaction.

A second variation is the **veto**, most prominently found in the UN Security Council. Following the theory of major-power responsibility, any of the five permanent members can, by its single vote, veto a policy statement or action favored by the other fourteen members. Since 1945 the veto has been cast well over one hundred times, each of the members using its special prerogative to protect its interests. Whatever arguments might be made for or against such a system, its existence in the UN is unlikely to change because of power realities and because of the difficulty of revising the charter.

Administration

In addition to representative/legislative bodies, most international organizations have an administrative structure. We will not be concerned with the details of organization and procedure but will concern ourselves with the appointment, allegiance, and role of international bureaucracies.[13] In the UN, the administrative structure is called the "**secretariat**," and the "secretary-general" is the chief administrator; our discussion will use those terms in reference to all IGO bureaucracies.

Appointment. In the UN, the secretary-general is nominated by the Security Council, then elected by the General Assembly for a five-year term. The secretary-general then appoints his principal deputies and other members of the secretariat.[14]

These simple facts do not, however, adequately emphasize the political considerations that govern the appointment of administrators. Because nomination of the UN secretary-general is subject to veto in the Security Council, that position has been one of intense struggle. The current secretary-general, Javier Perez de Cuellar, was named only after a protracted stalemate, and in the early 1960s the Soviet Union even proposed a "troika" plan that would have had three secretaries-general.

Politics also heavily influences the appointment of the understaff. Several of the principal deputy positions are, by tradition, reserved for and, in practice, named by one big power or another. There has also been pressure by Third World countries to distribute secretariat positions on a geographical basis.

Allegiance. A second administrative issue is the proper allegiance of UN officials. The issue is where their primary loyalty lies. Are they UN officials? Or are they representatives of their home governments? Most international organizations subscribe to the principle that their administrative officers should be free from nationalistic influence and, in particular, ought not to take direction from their home governments.

In practice, however, ignoring one's home government's preferences, especially if one expects to return home someday, is difficult. At the very least, administrators may subconsciously possess an orientation based on their national heritage and loyalties that affects their decisions. Whatever the theory, the contest in the UN and other IGOs over the appointment of administrators indicates that a pure international perspective has not fully evolved.

Role: Restraint versus activism. A final administrative issue is the proper role of an international secretariat. The possibilities range along a scale from a relatively restrained concentration on administrative matters to activist political leadership.

The change in role of the UN secretary-general gives a capsule view of the possible positions along the restraint/activism scale. The UN secretariat is, symbolically, the last major organ discussed in the charter, and it was originally conceived as largely administrative, although the secretary-general could bring peace-threatening situations to the attention of the Security Council.

The first secretary-general, Trygve Lie of Norway (1946–1953), and his successor, Dag Hammarskjöld of Sweden (1953–1961), were activists who steadily expanded the role of their office. Hammarskjöld was especially assertive, broadly interpreting his powers to include taking the initiative to uphold the principles of the charter even when the General Assembly and Security Council would not or could not act. The height of Hammarskjöld's power came during the Congo (Zaire) crisis in the early 1960s. The secretary-general used UN forces to try to avert outside intervention and to establish domestic peace during the postindependence turmoil in that African country. It is somehow symbolically fitting, if tragic, that he was killed when his plane crashed during a personal mission to the area in 1961.

Hammarskjöld's independence was not appreciated by all the big powers, however, and it caused a Soviet attempt to drive him from office and water down the position. He fended off that threat, but after his death his successors have had to take a more careful path, although each has been active in areas of quiet diplomacy.

International Organization: Roles and Issues

At the heart of the value of any international organization is the question of the roles it can or should play. In essence, we have to ask ourselves: What is it that we want international organizations to do, and how well are they to do it? In the following pages we will examine their wide scope of activity. The discussion will particularly emphasize the political roles (conflict avoidance and peacekeeping). Other roles will also be noted but will be discussed more fully in later chapters.

Political Roles

The United Nations and many other IGOs play a variety of political roles that focus on trying to prevent international conflict or on restoring the peace when violence occurs.

Maintaining peace. International organizations play both a passive and an active role in avoiding conflict.

One role for IGOs is the *passive* one of a forum in which members publicly air their points of view and privately negotiate their differences. The UN is thus like a theater or set where the world drama can be played out without some of the dire consequences if another "shooting locale" is chosen. This *public debate* aspect involves denouncing your opponents, defending your actions, trying to influence world opinion, and winning symbolic victories. One scholar has termed this function the "Grand Debate Approach to Peace."[15] In this role the UN serves as a sort of safety valve that allows the venting of frustrations in a controlled environment. (See Figure 13-1 for a look at the structure of the UN.)

The UN also serves as a basis for *diplomatic discussion* among members. In addition to the diplomatic interchange that occurs within the main organs, the UN sponsors many other conferences that address specific problems such as arms control.

International organizations also regularly play a more *active* role in resolving political disputes. They perform the following functions:

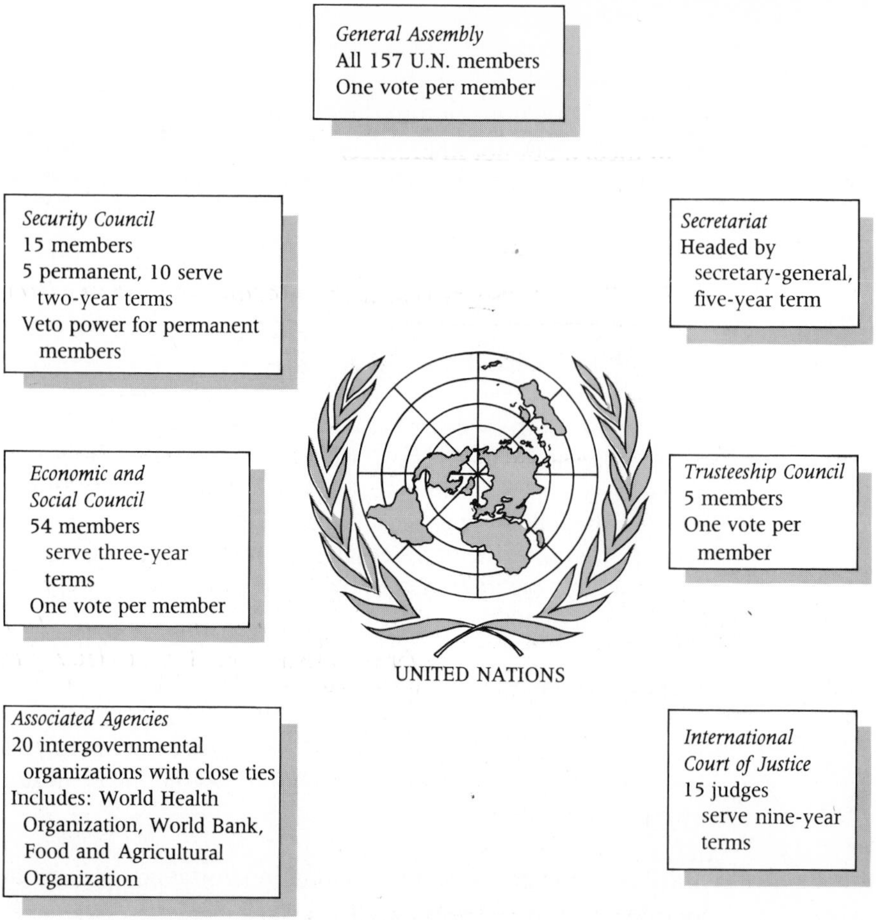

General Assembly
All 157 U.N. members
One vote per member

Security Council
15 members
5 permanent, 10 serve two-year terms
Veto power for permanent members

Secretariat
Headed by secretary-general, five-year term

Economic and Social Council
54 members serve three-year terms
One vote per member

Trusteeship Council
5 members
One vote per member

UNITED NATIONS

Associated Agencies
20 intergovernmental organizations with close ties
Includes: World Health Organization, World Bank, Food and Agricultural Organization

International Court of Justice
15 judges serve nine-year terms

Figure 13-1. The structure of the United Nations.

1. *Inquiry*—factfinding by neutral investigators.
2. *Good offices*—encouraging parties to negotiate; acting as a neutral setting for negotiations.
3. *Mediation*—making suggestions about possible solutions.
4. *Arbitration*—using a special panel to find a solution that all parties agree in advance to accept.
5. *Adjudication*—submitting disputes to an international court.

These activities do not often capture the headlines, but they are a vital part of conflict avoidance. For example, in studying the effectiveness of the UN in this area, one scholar found that, of over 130 disputes considered by the UN from 1946 to 1977, all but a dozen were settled successfully.[16]

Restoring the peace. In addition to its diplomatic resources, the United Nations has at least a limited ability to intervene militarily in a dispute. There is also a limited history of other organizations, such as the Organization of

American States, undertaking collective military action. In the UN, this process is often called "peacekeeping." It is normally conducted under the auspices of the Security Council, although the General Assembly has sometimes authorized action.[17]

In theory, but not in practice, the peacekeeping function of international organization rests on the concept of **collective security**. This idea was first embodied in the covenant of the League of Nations and is also reflected in the charter of the United Nations. Its basic tenets are these:

1. All countries forswear the use of force except in self-defense.
2. All agree that the peace is indivisible. An attack on one is an attack on all.
3. Everyone pledges to join together to halt aggression and restore the peace, and all agree to supply whatever material or personnel resources are necessary to that end.
4. The peacekeeping force will be under the control of an international organization.

If you think about it, this theory is something like the theory that governs domestic law enforcement. First, acts of violence are considered a transgression against the collective. If you assault someone in California, the case is not the victim versus you but *California* versus you. Second, except in self-defense, we cannot resort to violence to settle domestic disputes. Third, we rely on a collective security force, the police, and jointly support that force through taxes.

Collective security, then, is not only an appealing idea but one that works—domestically. It has not, however, been a success on the international scene. There are a number of problems of specific application, such as how to tell the aggressor from the victim in some cases. But these uncertainties also exist domestically and are resolved. The real breakdown in collective security is the unwillingness of countries to subordinate their sovereignty to collective action. Thus far, governments have generally maintained their right to view conflict in terms of their national interests and to support or oppose UN action on the basis of their nationalistic points of view. The Soviet Union, for example, has refused to pay its assessed dues to support earlier UN operations in the Middle East or in the Congo. Thus, collective security exists only as a goal, not as a practice.

Despite the theoretical ideal of collective security, in practice the UN has been able to take only limited action in a limited number of armed conflicts. Between 1945 and 1980, the UN mounted fifteen operations that utilized armed units and eight military observation missions.[18]

Several characteristics of these missions can be noted. First, most have occurred in Third World locations, such as the Middle East, Cyprus, the Congo, the India/Pakistan border, Yemen, and Indonesia. Second, UN forces have generally utilized military contingents from smaller or nonaligned powers. Canada, the Scandinavian countries, Ireland, and India are some of the most frequent contributors. Third, UN forces have generally acted as buffers between the conflicting parties, and with the exception of Korea and the Congo, UN forces have not conducted active military operations. Instead they have positioned themselves between the combatants. At times this provides an "excuse" to stop fighting, and at other times, given the status of UN personnel, it provides an inhibiting effect.

United Nations peacekeeping, then, is not a process of a stern international enforcer smiting aggressors with powerful blows. Few are willing to invest any international organization with that much power and independence. Rather, UN peacekeeping is a "coming between," a positioning of a neutral force that creates space and is intended to help defuse an explosive situation. That in no way should lessen the at times valuable role the UN has played. In the early 1960s, UN troops kept the Congo from exploding into a cold-war battlefield, and UN forces were an important factor allowing the disengagement of Egyptian and Israeli troops in 1973.

Other Roles

In addition to maintaining and restoring the peace, international organizations engage in a wide variety of other activities. We will briefly note these roles here and then examine most of them more fully in the following three chapters.

Law promotion. An important and expanding role of international organizations is their contribution to international law. As discussed more fully in the next chapter, the signatories of the UN charter and other constitutions incur obligations to obey the principles therein. International organizations also sponsor multilateral treaties, which may establish a presumption of law. The resolutions of international representative bodies such as the General Assembly also contribute to the growth of law. Finally, tribunals such as the International Court of Justice help establish legal precedent.

Promoting arms control and disarmament. International organizations are not only involved in individual conflicts, they are concerned with conflict in general. Consequently, they are active on a number of fronts trying to regulate or eliminate the weapons of war, as we shall see in Chapter 15.

Promoting the quality of human existence. Perhaps the most significant contribution of international organizations to date has been in the area of individual human betterment. A wide variety of IGOs and NGOs devote their energies to problems of the environment, humanitarian causes, economic progress, and social concerns such as health, nutrition, and literacy. As we shall see in Chapter 16, the need is staggering, but a start has been made.

Promoting self-government. Yet another role of the UN and other IGOs is to encourage national self-determination. The UN Trusteeship Council once oversaw the status of a large number of colonial dependencies, but with the wave of independence in recent decades, only one trust territory, Micronesia,

United Nations troops, pictured here in Lebanon, often try to act as a buffer between antagonists.

remains under its direct auspices. There are, however, a number of related issues that come before the UN. One is the case of Namibia (South West Africa). South Africa originally governed this territory on a mandate from the League of Nations and has refused to give up its hold despite UN and Organization of African Unity demands. The question of the Palestinian people is another issue of national status that the UN (and the Arab League) has considered, and some countries have tried to introduce the status of Puerto Rico into the UN debate.

Promoting international organization and integration. A final role of the UN that deserves mention is its promotion of other international organizations. The United Nations not only operates in association with a variety of other regional and specialized IGOs, it also grants consultive status to nearly 700 NGOs. Thus, international organizations of all types cooperate to encourage and strengthen one another.[19]

The Status of the UN: Above, Apart, in the Middle

A final major issue of international organization is its status in relation to its member states. Three basic positions are possible. One is **supranationalism**, which means that the international organization has authority over its members, which, therefore, are subordinate units. A second possibility is *indepen-*

dence. In this case, the international body follows its own initiative in determining its action and policy. A third and final position is that of *interactive arena.* Here the organization is the scene of cooperation and conflict among states, each striving to better its own position. Further, the policy of the organization is determined by the outcome of that self-interested struggle. As we shall see, the reality of international organization is that it is a mix of all three positions.

Supranationalism

The least developed status of international organizations is supranationalism. Few states are willing to concede any significant part of their sovereignty to any international body. But there are limited signs that the dogged independence of nation-states is giving way to limited acceptance of international authority. In the next chapter, for instance, we will see that countries normally abide by some aspects of international law, even at times when it conflicts with domestic law.

The European Parliament also has supranationalist stirrings. In recent years it has made several "binding" decisions, including banning the importation of seal skins.[20] Such actions may seem trivial in a world of nationalism, but they are a start and are virtually unparalleled in international political history.[21]

Independence

A second and more developed position is organizational independence. Here the organization is a self-directed actor in world politics. International bodies, like any organization, develop their own norms of behavior, expectations, and policy preferences. These characteristics are especially centered in the secretariats, or administrative structures.[22]

Although no IGO is completely, or even mostly, independent of its membership's wishes, many have developed a degree of actor status and personality. We often hear, for example, that "the UN should do something" about a situation, and at times it does.

To a degree, organizational independence is intended and established in the charter of various IGOs. The European Coal and Steel Community's High Authority was created to act independently, as was the International Court of Justice. The UN charter directs that the secretary-general or any of his staff "shall not seek or receive instructions from any government or from any other authority external to the organization." And the popularly elected European Parliament is a unique example of an IGO assembly whose representatives are popularly elected rather than appointed and directed by national governments.

Independence is also a product of the assertiveness of the international bureaucracies. We earlier noted the sometimes self-directed activity of the UN secretary-general and, in particular, the ideas of Dag Hammarskjöld, who argued that he had a "responsibility" to maintain peace "irrespective of the views and wishes of the various Member Governments."[23] As we also saw, however, independence can be a perilous path. It brought Hammarskjöld and his office under severe attack and led to the tacit pruning of the powers of his successors.

Independence, then, while more developed than supranationalism, is not the basic trait of international organizations. It is, instead, a growing, albeit secondary, phenomenon that is the source of struggle between the perceptions and preferences of national and international leaders.

Interactive Arena

The most common status of IGOs is still that of an interactive arena in which member states pursue their individual national interests. The arena itself is technically neutral, but members or coalitions of members often try to use the organization as an instrument to further their goals.[24] The Arab states, for one, have used the UN to condemn Israel for "Zionist imperialism."

To examine the "use" of the UN and other IGOs, we will briefly explore the interaction between the UN and the United States, the Soviet Union, China, and the Third World states.

The United States and the UN

United States policy in and toward the United Nations has been marked by a desire to dominate the organization and to use it as far as possible as a vehicle for furthering American policy objectives. When this has not been possible, the United States has minimized its willingness to participate in and acquiesce to the turbulence and uncertainty of worldwide multilateral diplomacy and decision making.

For the first twenty years of the UN's existence, the United States was generally able to dominate the organization. The world body was primarily the scene of East/West cold-war struggle, and the Western bloc and its followers heavily outnumbered the Soviet Union and its sympathizers in all the UN's major organs. During the 1945–1965 period, this pro–United States balance of power was reflected in the fact that the Soviet Union cast 103 (95 percent) of the 109 vetoes in the Security Council.[25] The United States cast none. During the first two decades, American policy also encouraged expansion of General Assembly authority in order to circumvent the Soviet veto in the Security Council.

In the 1960s and 1970s, rapid expansion of UN membership ended U.S. dominance of the UN. The new Third World members were not willing to follow U.S. leadership, and some old allies, such as Latin American countries, showed greater independence. The net result was that, with nonaligned countries supporting the U.S. position only 19 percent of the time, it became necessary for the United States to use its veto in the Security Council, and the American position began to lose in the General Assembly and other organs. The loss of control in the General Assembly caused the United States to revert to an emphasis on the Security Council. The United States has also attempted to use its financial muscle to gain influence by threatening to reduce its support of the UN budget.[26]

Today the United States is both a mainstay and a troubled member of the United Nations. As a *supporter,* the United States is the largest contributor (25 percent) to the UN budget. The UN is also headquartered in New York City, and, with a few exceptions, the United States has not attempted to use that geographic fact to manipulate UN proceedings. Third, despite grumblings, the United States has generally participated in most UN activities. Both official policy and public opinion strongly support continued UN membership.[27]

There are *frustrations,* however. Primarily, these result from a combination of "inflated expectations and the trauma of rejection."[28] The inflated expectations are mirrored in American public opinion. Although most Americans support UN membership, only a minority (30 percent in 1980) feel the UN is doing a good job. Belief that the UN is ineffective is the most common reason given for negative attitudes.[29]

The trauma of rejection is reflected in U.S. reaction to loss of control in the voting organs of the UN. At one point in 1983, a second-level member of the American UN delegation suggested that the UN move its headquarters, saying, "We will be at dockside bidding you a fond farewell as you set off into the sunset."[30] American frustration can also be seen in its 1982 warning that if Israel was expelled from the UN, it "would have serious consequences for continued U.S. participation in and [financial] support for the UN." Finally, and most seriously, in late 1983, the Reagan administration withdrew from the 161-member United Nations Educational, Scientific, and Cultural Organization (UNESCO). Other countries also threatened to follow the American departure. The U.S. State Department charged that UNESCO had become a forum for Third World criticism of the United States, had "extraneously politicized virtually every subject it deals with," and had "exhibited hostility toward the basic institutions of a free society."[31] The U.S. withdrawal may not be permanent, however. Some years earlier, the United States also withdrew from the International Labor Organization (ILO), complaining that the ILO ignored labor conditions in communist countries. When, as a result, the ILO addressed that issue, the United States resumed its membership. On the negative side, though, Poland withdrew because of ILO criticism of its suppression of the Solidarity labor movement. United Nations criticism of oneself, of course, always smacks of politicization, while criticism of one's opponents is equally always the epitome of objective justice.

On balance, it should be noted that U.S. frustrations do not reflect a situation in which American preferences and interests are regularly ravaged at the hands of an anti-American, irresponsible United Nations. The United States is far too powerful in the organization, and in the world, for that. Indeed, the evidence shows that the United States is still the most influential member of the world organization. One UN study, for example, found the United States in the majority on 70 percent of all UN votes,[32] and another survey concluded that on most important issues "there has been rather close correlation between UN policies and American preferences."[33]

The Soviet Union and the UN

The Soviet view of international organization has been shaped by the mutually reinforcing factors of political reality and communist ideology. First, in terms of *political reality,* the Soviet Union, like its Western rival, has approached the UN primarily as a political instrument. Unlike the Americans, however, the Soviets have never had the luxury of dominating the world organization. Especially during the UN's first decades, the Soviets and their supporters were a minority in the UN, a fact that accounts for at least some of their extensive use of the veto, their refusal to pay all of their assessed obligation to the UN budget, and other forms of seeming intransigence. Second, *communist ideology* tends to support the feeling of being in a minority and, therefore, in a defensive position. The Soviets see the UN as an arena for struggle and one that has been dominated by the bourgeois interests of Western capitalism.[34]

The policy orientations that result from the real and ideologically perceived minority status in the UN have caused the cautious Soviets to avoid expansion of UN activity and have resulted in several distinct Soviet principles of international organization participation.[35] First, the Soviets reject the idea of the UN as an independent actor. Secretary-General Dag Hammarskjöld's assertiveness sparked an intense Soviet reaction. Soviet writers dismiss the idea of the UN as a supranational organization both as impractical and as a violation of the principle of sovereignty. They argue, for example, against any "attempt to infer that decisions taken by IGOs are of a legally binding nature."[36]

Second, the Soviets back the power principle in decision making. They distinguish between the "juridical equality" of all IGO members and the "actual inequality" based on power. Given this view, the Soviets stress the role of the Security Council, where they have a veto. Indeed, one Soviet theorist has characterized the veto as "the key principle of the Charter."[37]

Third, the Soviets view the UN as primarily a political institution. They view as secondary the organization's social and economic functions. Because the Soviets perceive the UN as dominated by the Western powers, they also see UN socioeconomic activity as an attempt to "strengthen [capitalist] influence in the countries of the Third World."[38]

The shift in power in the UN has not revolutionized Soviet attitudes, but there has been some impact. The loss of Western control and the increase of Third World demands have given the Soviets an opportunity to exploit the situation. They have, for example, used the issues of anticolonialism, Zionism, and racism to attack and rhetorically embarrass the Western allies. This has led to some rethinking and ambiguity about the power of the UN. While rejecting UN legal authority, the Soviets can complain that "over 100 resolutions against the South African racists . . . are non-effective."[39]

Still, the loss of Western control does not signal a gain in Soviet strength in the UN. Instead, neither power can easily dominate the Afro-Asian majority.

As a result, the Soviets basically adhere to their restricted view of the UN. Among other factors, the Third World powers classify the industrialized Soviet bloc along with the Western powers as part of the developed North. As such, the New International Economic Order demands are leveled against communists as well as capitalists, and the Soviets implicitly recognize that along the North/South axis they may increasingly find themselves allied with the Western bloc in resisting the South's demand for a real redistribution of economic resources.[40]

China and the UN

China's orientation toward the United Nations is based on a mixture of ideology, nationalism, and self-identification with the Third World.[41] These are a sometimes incompatible set of orientations that give a cautious mark to Chinese policy. Beijing's actions in the UN have also been restrained because during most of the 1970s the newly admitted country adopted a "learning" attitude, gaining experience without generally asserting itself.

For a quarter century, China was excluded from the UN by U.S. opposition. The U.S. Congress, for one, declared that "to seat such aggressors [as China] . . . would mean moral bankruptcy for the United Nations and destroy every last vestige of its effectiveness."[42] For its part, a spurned China condemned the UN as a "dirty international stock exchange in the grip of a few big powers" and declared that "speaking frankly, the Chinese people are not at all interested in sitting in the United Nations."[43]

Neither the American opposition nor Chinese reluctance prevailed in the long run; in October 1971 reality prevailed, and China took its proper place in the UN. It was a time of dancing in the aisles by some Third World representatives and dire predictions of disruption and disaster by some in the West. The question was, how would China behave?

Overall, China's UN activity has followed a course safely between earlier Pollyanna and Cassandra expectations.[44]

Caution has been one mark of Chinese behavior. During its first five years, the Beijing delegation was reluctant to strike out boldly. In the General Assembly, it was active on only a dozen of more than one hundred agenda items. China was similarly cautious in the Security Council, casting in 1971–1976 only two vetoes, the least of any permanent member (United States, 17; United Kingdom, 9; Soviet Union, 5; France, 4).

Nonparticipation is a related distinguishing characteristic of Chinese voting in the UN. Four possible positions are available on UN votes: for, against, abstaining (present, not voting), or not participating. In the Security Council, for example, the PRC did not participate (in 1971–1976) in 29.1 percent of the votes, compared with 0.6 percent nonparticipation for the Soviet Union and France and 0 percent for the United States and England. The big five's respective records were similar in the General Assembly.[45]

This nonparticipation is partly a result of China's early caution. It also stems from China's attempt to steer between its principled stands based on

Despite dire predictions to the contrary, the Chinese have played a responsible, even cautious role at the UN. Shown here is the Chinese delegation on the day of its seating in 1971.

ideology and its *Realpolitik* desire to support some capitalist, First World–oriented measures.

Third World orientation is a third trait of Chinese activity in the UN. One study analyzed Beijing's voting in terms of agreement with the votes cast by the Western, communist, and Third World countries.[46] It found that China was most supportive of the Third World and least favorable to the West, with the PRC/U.S. relationship the lowest of all. Support of the Soviet Union fell about midway between the two extremes, with Moscow and Beijing in agreement just slightly over half the time.

Responsibility is a last Chinese characteristic we will note. Contrary to some predictions, China has not wrecked the UN. China ideologically favors revolutionary disorder, and it also tends to view the UN as dominated by, and thus preserving, superpower hegemony. Therefore, in principle, China opposes the use of UN peacekeeping forces. Yet it has not used its veto to derail those forces in the Middle East and elsewhere. In general, observers of the UN give China high marks for integrity and nonobstructiveness in its dealings.

The cautious role that China has played in the UN will almost certainly change as China's confidence, experience, and power grow. In fact, there are already indications of that trend. China's Third World orientation led it to support Mexico's Luis Echeverria Alvarez for secretary-general over Austria's Kurt Waldheim in 1971. When it found itself alone, however, China gave way, as it did again in 1976 at the time of Waldheim's reelection.

In 1981 the story was different. China was determined to block a third term for the European and supported, instead, Tanzania's Salim A. Salim. In a Security Council deadlock that lasted five weeks and sixteen ballots, China repeatedly vetoed Waldheim, and the United States blocked Salim. The result was the compromise nomination of Peru's Javier Perez de Cuellar. It was an example of a new Chinese assertiveness that will probably increasingly mark its UN role.[47]

The Third World and the UN

Given the influx of Third World countries into the UN and their rise in power in that body, it is important to consider their view of and role in the world organization and other IGOs. Third World commentators, like Marxists, are apt to portray the UN, at least historically, as a vehicle for neocolonial Western domination. Thus the UN and, in particular, the veto-dominated Security Council were and are suspect.[48]

The growing assertiveness of the less developed countries (LDCs) and the changing balance of power in their favor in the General Assembly, in the Economic and Social Council, and elsewhere have led to a changing orientation. Now the UN and other IGOs are increasingly being used by the LDCs to band together and assert their demands for political, social, and economic equity. In a generally power-politic world, the United Nations and other IGOs provide a ready forum for Third World complaints against the larger powers, and, insofar as there is majoritarian voting, give the collective Third World a vehicle for giving substance, in terms of passed resolutions, to its proposals and criticisms. As such, IGOs are a primary arena of the North/South struggle.

The South has pushed, for one, to restructure the UN Charter, the International Monetary Fund Articles of Agreement, and other IGO constitutions, which they view as documents drawn by and for the superpowers. The LDCs have also promoted the United Nations Conference on Trade and Development (UNCTAD) and other such IGO subunits in order to press their demands for the New International Economic Order. It is this challenge to the established order in UNESCO that led to the United States' withdrawal. The South has also used other organizations, such as cartels, to gain collective strength. Thus the future of the UN and many other IGOs promises to be one in which the traditional patterns of dominance are challenged, and the East/West political rivalry will have to share the stage with the economic demands of the South on the North.

International Organization and the Future

International organization has many critics. It is all too easy to view the continued conflict in the world and the ongoing economic and social misery and dismiss international organization as inadequate, misguided, and impossibly idealistic. Even the recently retired United Nations secretary-general, Kurt Waldheim, seemed pretty discouraged in an article he wrote to commemorate the UN's fortieth anniversary. According to the secretary-general, it is "perfectly clear" in the area of peacekeeping that "the habit of international security is waning." Waldheim's assessment of UN activity in economic and social areas was equally distressed as he saw the organization approaching "zones of sensitivity that sharply pit members of different backgrounds against one another."[49]

The alternative is—what? Can the warring, uncaring world persist in the face of nuclear weapons, persistent poverty, exploding population, mass starvation, resource depletion, and potential environmental catastrophe? No, it cannot! That reality leads Waldheim to a sort of optimism that, in the face of these monumental **transnational** issues, the countries of the world will find that it is in their "enlightened self-interest" to work toward a "single great world community . . . a single global village."[50]

One can only hope that Waldheim is right. What is certain is that we face problems that cannot be handled in the same old ways. Those ways haven't been very successful in the past, and they carry the potential of cataclysmic disaster for the future. It is also clear in the rapid growth of international organizations during this century that the world has begun to try to reform its political system to meet the new challenges. What is unclear is whether old, no longer relevant attitudes can be changed quickly enough. It is also clear that critics of international organization are too often just that, only negative, and they disparage the organization without noting its contributions or suggesting improvements. International organization holds one hope for the future, and for those who would disparage that effort, the answer is to make other, positive suggestions rather than implicitly advocating a maintenance of the status quo.

Summary

One of the clearest signs of the changing nature of the international system is this century's rapid rise in the number of international organizations. There are many classifications of international organizations, the most basic distinction being between international governmental organizations, which are made up of member countries, and international nongovernmental organizations, which are made up of private organizations and individuals.

Current international organization is the product of three lines of development. One is the idea that humans constitute a single people and should live in peace and mutual support rather than in conflict and self-interested pursuit. A second is the idea that the "big powers" have a special responsiblity for maintaining order. A third is the growth of specialized international organization to deal with narrow, nonpolitical issues. This century's rapid growth of all types of international organization stems from increased international contact among states and people, increased economic interdependency, the growing importance of transnational issues and political movements, and the

increasingly apparent inadequacy of the state-centered system for dealing with world problems.

There are significant differences among views on the best role for international organizations. Some favor moving toward a system of supranational organization, in which some form of world government would replace or substantially modify the present state-centered system. Others argue that international organizations are best suited to promoting cooperation among states rather than trying to replace the state-centered system. Still others contend that international organization should concentrate on performing limited functional activities with the hope of building a habit of cooperation and trust that can later be built on. Finally, at least in practice, many view international organizations as vehicles that should be manipulated, if possible, toward gaining your country's individual political goals.

However one defines the best purpose of international organization, it is important to be careful of standards of evaluation. The most fruitful standard is judging an organization by what is possible, rather than setting inevitably frustrating ideal goals.

There are a number of important issues related to the structure of international organizations. One group of questions relates to membership: how and when to admit new members and when to expel members. Whether representative bodies should have plenary or limited membership is a related issue, as is the voting scheme to be used in such bodies. Current international organizations use a variety of voting schemes that include majority voting, weighted voting, and negative voting. Another group of structural questions concerns the administration of international organizations: How should administrative officers be appointed, to whom do they owe allegiance, and what are their proper role and power?

There are also a number of significant issues that relate to the general role of international organization. Peacekeeping is one important role, and international organizations help maintain or restore peace through a variety of diplomatic methods. They sometimes also intervene militarily. The idea of collective security still exists in theory, but in fact the self-interest of UN members has meant that UN peacekeeping operations have been limited in scope and have relied on smaller, usually nonaligned countries for the bulk of their forces. Other roles for the UN and other international organizations include promoting international law, promoting arms control, bettering the human condition, promoting self-government, and furthering international cooperation.

Currently, international organizations operate on three planes. The least common is the supranational level, at which IGOs have authority over nation-states. International organizations also act independently. That is, they have a will of their own, apart from the collective wishes of their members. Finally, international organization serves as an interactive arena in which members pursue their self-interest. The brief studies of the policies of the United States, the Soviet Union, China, and the Third World provide illustrations of this interactive utilization.

Terms

Collective security—The original theory behind UN peacekeeping. It holds that aggression against one state is aggression against all and should be defeated by the collective action of all.

Functionalism—International cooperation in specific areas such as communications, trade, travel, health, or environmental protection activity. Often symbolized by the specialized agencies, such as the World Health Organization, associated with the United Nations.

General Assembly—The main representative body of the United Nations, composed of all member states.

International governmental organizations (IGOs)—International organizations whose membership consists of national governments.

International nongovernmental organizations (NGOs or INGOs)—International organizations whose membership consists of private organizations and individuals.

League of Nations—The first true general international organization. It existed between the end of World War I and the beginning of World War II and was the immediate predecessor of the United Nations.

Majoritarianism—One voting scheme used in international organizations; based on one vote for each member, with most issues decided by majority vote.

Negative voting—A voting scheme whereby a single negative vote can block action. See *veto* for one example.

Plenary representative body—An assembly, such as the UN's General Assembly, that consists of all members of the main organization.

Secretariat—The administrative organ of the United Nations, headed by the secretary-general. In general, the administrative element of any IGO, headed by a secretary-general.

Security Council—The main peacekeeping organ of the United Nations. The Security Council has fifteen members, including five permanent members.

Supranationalism—The idea that international organizations can or should have authority higher than individual states and that those states should be subordinate to the supranational organization.

Transnational—Extending beyond the borders of a single country; applied to a political movement, issue, or other phenomenon.

Veto—A negative vote cast in the Security Council by one of the five permanent members; has the effect of defeating the issue being voted on.

Weighted voting—A voting scheme that gives some members more votes than others, based on population, wealth, or some other factor.

World government—The concept of a supranational world authority to which current countries would surrender some or all of their sovereign authority.

Notes

1. There are many scholarly schemes for classifying such organizations as well as differences in definition and terminology. There is also disagreement over whether some organizations, such as alliances, are properly international organizations at all. One recent discussion of many of these points is Werner J. Feld and Robert S. Jordan with Leon Hurwitz, *International Organizations: A Comparative Approach* (New York: Praeger, 1983), especially pp. 1–40. Also see Anthony J. N. Judge, "International Institutions: Diversity, Borderline Cases, Functional Substitutes, and Possible Alternatives," in *International Organization: A Conceptual Approach*, ed. Paul Taylor and A. J. R. Groom (London: Francis Printer, 1978), pp. 28–83; and Clive Archer, *International Organizations* (London: Allen & Unwin, 1983), pp. 36–67. For an exhaustive catalogue, see *Yearbook of International Organizations* (Brussels: Union of International Associations, published annually). The 1981 edition indexed 14,784 organizations.
2. A. LeRoy Bennett, *International Organizations: Principles and Issues*, 2nd ed. (Englewood Cliffs, N.J.: Prentice-Hall, 1980), pp. 9–17.
3. Quoted in Inis L. Claude, Jr., *Swords into Plowshares: The Problems and Progress on International Organization*, 4th ed. (New York: Random House, 1971), p. 25. Claude discusses the origins of international organization, and his concept of "three streams" is influential but somewhat different from that used here.
4. This section is loosely based on Feld, Jordan, and Hurwitz, *International Organizations*, pp. 1–80. Another, related concept of international organization is "regimes," which are norms, rules, and organizations that coordinate a particular functional area. See the entire issue of *International Organization* 36 (1982), especially Robert O. Keohane, "The Demand for International Regimes," pp. 325–356.
5. See Paul Taylor, "Confederalism: The Case of the European Communities," pp. 317–335, and George A. Codding, Jr., "Federalism: The Conceptual Setting," pp. 326–344, both in Taylor and Groom, *International Organization*.
6. This discussion relies on Claude, *Swords into Plowshares*, pp. 411–432.
7. David Mitrany, *A Working Peace System* (Chicago: Quadrangle Books, 1966), pp. 31, 38. For an overview of functionalism, see Paul Taylor, "Functionalism: The Theory of David Mitrany," in Taylor and Groom, *International Organization*, pp. 236–252. For specific areas of cooperation, see Evan Luard, *International Agencies: The Emerging Framework of Interdependence* (London: Macmillan, 1977).
8. This view is also taken by Edward C. Luck, "The U.N. at 40: A Supporter's Lament," *Foreign Policy* 57 (Winter 1984–1985): 143–159.
9. For an overview of the United Nations, see *Everyone's United Nations*, 9th ed. (New York: United Nations, 1979).
10. For two studies, see W. J. Dixon, "Evaluation of Weighted Voting Schemes for the United Nations General Assembly," *International Studies Quarterly* 27 (Fall 1983): 295–314; and Ebere Osieke, "Majority Voting Systems in the International Labour Organization and the International Monetary Fund," *International and Comparative Law Quarterly* 33 (1984): 381–408.
11. Claude, *Swords into Plowshares*, pp. 120–140, discusses this point.
12. Bennett, *International Organizations*, p. 91.
13. Feld, Jordan, and Hurwitz, *International Organizations*, pp. 85–128. Also see Mihaly Simai, "Some Problems of International Secretariats," in Taylor and Groom, *Inter-*

national Organization, pp. 111–117; and Bennett, *International Organizations*, p. 405.

14. T. Weiss, "International Bureaucracy: Myth and Reality of the International Civil Service," *International Affairs* 58 (1982): 286–306.
15. Claude, *Swords into Plowshares*, pp. 335–348.
16. Bennett, *International Organizations*, pp. 112–119, 141.
17. Based on John F. Murphy, *The United Nations and the Control of International Violence* (Totowa, N.J.: Allanheld, Osmun, 1982); and Bennett, *International Organizations*, pp. 143–181.
18. Bennett, *International Organizations*, p. 157.
19. Ibid., p. 442. Also see Chiang Pei-heng, *Non-Governmental Organizations at the United Nations* (New York: Praeger, 1981). It should be noted that, as with all political organizations, there can be rivalry and conflict among international organizations.
20. *New York Times*, March 22, 1982, p. A12.
21. Paul Taylor, "Elements of Supranationalism: The Power and Authority of International Institutions," in Taylor and Groom, *International Organization*, pp. 216–235.
22. Leon Gordenker and Paul R. Saunders, "Organization Theory and International Organization," in Taylor and Groom, *International Organization*, pp. 84–107.
23. Quoted in Archer, *International Organizations*, p. 148. Pages 141–159 deal with the general issue of independence.
24. See Archer, *International Organizations*, pp. 136–141, on this point. Also see Feld, Jordan, and Hurwitz, *International Organizations*, pp. 151–155.
25. John G. Stoessinger, *The United Nations and the Superpowers* (New York: Random House, 1965), p. ix. Stoessinger has a good discussion of this general issue. The nonaligned countries and the Soviet Union voted together on approximately 80 percent of all votes.
26. Robert Meager, "United States Financing of the United Nations," in *The U.S., the U.N., and the Management of Global Change*, ed. Toby Trister Gati (New York: New York University Press, 1983), pp. 101–128. Also see *Time*, March 26, 1984, p. 27.
27. Paul D. Martin, "U.S. Public Opinion and the U.N.," in Gati, *Management of Global Change*, p. 295.
28. Richard Bissell, "U.S. Participation in the U.N. System," in Gati, *Management of Global Change*, p. 99. Also see U.S. Department of State, "What's Wrong with the United Nations and What's Right," *Current Policy*, no. 49 (December 1978).
29. Martin, "Public Opinion," pp. 288, 291.
30. *Facts on File*, 1983: 717.
31. *Editorial Reports*, 1983: 976.
32. *Time*, March 26, 1984, p. 27.
33. Donald J. Puchala, "U.S. National Interest and the United Nations," in Gati, *Management of Global Change*, p. 350.
34. See Archer, *International Organizations*, pp. 102–112, on the Marxist and Soviet view.
35. This section is based on Archer, *International Organizations;* Luard, *International Agencies*, pp. 140–142; Stoessinger, *Superpowers, passim;* and Gregorii Morozov, "The Socialist Conception of International Organization," in *The Concept of International Organization*, ed. Georges Abi-Saab (Paris: UNESCO, 1981), pp. 173–193.
36. Morozov, "Socialist Conception," p. 179.
37. Ibid., p. 181.

38. Ibid., p. 184.
39. Ibid., p. 182.
40. Gati, *Management of Global Change,* p. 59.
41. On ideology, see Archer, *International Organizations,* pp. 114–116. Also see William R. Reeney, "Chinese Global Politics in the United Nations General Assembly," in *China and the Global Community,* ed. James C. Hsuing and Samuel S. Kim (New York: Praeger, 1980), p. 141.
42. Quoted in Samuel S. Kim, *China, the United Nations, and World Order* (Princeton, N.J.: Princeton University Press, 1979), p. 105.
43. Quoted in Kim, *China,* pp. 100, 191.
44. The following section depends heavily on Kim, *China,* pp. 97–241 and *passim.*
45. Ibid., table 3.6, p. 124, and table 4.3, p. 210.
46. Trong R. Chai, "Chinese Policy toward the Third World and the Superpowers in the U.N. General Assembly, 1971–1977: A Voting Analysis," *International Organization* 33 (1979): 391–403.
47. *New York Times,* October 26, 1981, and January 4, 1982.
48. This section relies on Mahammed Bedjaoui, "A Third World View of International Organizations," in Abi-Saab, *Concept of International Organization,* pp. 206–245; and Archer, *International Organizations,* pp. 117–122. Another good short discussion of the Third World's perspective and positions is Kurt Waldheim's "The United Nations: The Tarnished Image," *Foreign Affairs* 63 (1984): 93–107.
49. Waldheim, "The United Nations," p. 107.
50. Ibid.

14

International Law

The law hath not been dead, though it hath slept.
***Shakespeare,* Hamlet**

Two decades ago, when the author of this text took "Introduction to International Relations," the professor came to our point here, the study of international law. He dramatically paused, looked around the room, flared his nostrils, shot his eyebrows skyward, and snorted a guttural "Bah!" Then, in a few short sentences, he dismissed the idea of international law as a fiction in a world of war, human-rights violations, and economic inequity.

It was, for a man who was a refugee from the ravages of World War II Europe, an understandably cynical view. It was also, however, wrong. International law is not a fiction. True, it has sometimes slept, but it is far from dead. Indeed, as we shall see in this chapter, it is not only alive, it is growing at a healthy pace.

The Nature of Law

Any law, whether international or of the more familiar domestic variety, is a combination of expectations, rules, and practices that help govern behavior. First, as we shall see, all law systems are dynamic, continually evolving systems. Second, no law system is perfect. Even in the most law-abiding societies, rules are broken and the guilty sometimes escape punishment. Third, law both reflects and directs a society. In other words, to a substantial degree, law is a mirror of the norms of a society. We legalize what we do in practice. Law, however, can also lead a society to change its behavior by enacting philosophical principles into required standards of conduct. Fourth, and finally, law depends on a mixture of voluntary compliance and coercion to maintain order.

The Dynamics of Law

A system of law is not something that just happens. It grows. Similarly, a political system does not just happen. It also grows, advancing from a primitive level to ever more sophisticated levels of organization. This concept, that of a *primitive but evolving legal system* in an evolving political system, is important to understanding international law.

Primitive Nature of International Law

A primitive society has a number of features that we also find in international law and relations. First, there is no formal rulemaking, or legislative, process. Instead, codes of behavior are derived from custom or from explicit agreements among two or more societal members or groups. Second, there is little or no authority in any formal government to judge or punish violations of law. Primitive tribes have no police or courts. Third, a primitive society is often made up of self-defined units (such as kinship groups), is territorially based, primarily governs itself, and resorts to violent "self-help" in relations with other groups.[1]

In its current state, international law is very akin to a primitive political system. As discussed more fully below, there is at best a rudimentary legislative system. Further, the enforcement and adjudication systems are extremely limited. In addition, international law exists within a system of sovereign, nationalistic, territorial states that often clash in pursuit of their self-defined interests. If we accept this analogy, then we can conceive of international law as a primitive legal system. This view allows us to be encouraged by the thought that international law and its society may evolve to a higher order rather than to be discouraged by its current lack of sophistication.

Growth of International Law

Just as our "primitive but dynamic" concept would predict, international law is a growing phenomenon.

Early growth. The beginnings of modern international law coincide with the origins of nationalism as discussed in Chapter 4. As sovereign, territorial states arose, there was a need to define and protect their status and to order their relations. Gradually, as this political system emerged, elements of ancient Jewish, Greek, and Roman practice combined with newer Christian concepts and also with custom and practice to form the rudiments of international law.[2]

This early development was given voice and encouraged by a number of important theorists. The most famous of these was the Dutch thinker Hugo Grotius (1583–1645), whose study *De Jure Belli ac Pacis (On the Law of War and Peace)* earned him the title "father of international law." Grotius and others discussed and debated the sources of international law as well as its application to specific circumstances such as the conduct of and justification of war, the treatment of subjugated peoples, and the relations of states.

During the late eighteenth and the nineteenth centuries, international law expanded and changed. As the international system became more complex, the scope of international law grew to cover many new areas of commercial and social interchange. Older areas of law were also refined; for example, the rules of diplomacy were substantially formalized during the immediate post-Napoleonic period. As the political focus of power shifted from rulers to the national state, the concept of the state, rather than the individual monarch, as the subject of law evolved.

The twentieth century. The current century has seen a significant expansion of both concern with and practice of international law. As already discussed in a number of places, ever-increasing international interaction and interdependence have rapidly increased the need for rules to govern a host of functional areas such as trade, finance, travel, and communications. The ever more apocalyptic consequences of war have encouraged the formation of conventions governing the conduct of war and have also promoted an increasingly accepted ethic against aggressive war.

These needs and reactions have been evident in a variety of forms. First, the Hague conferences, followed by the League of Nations, and now the United Nations have been founded on and have incorporated principles of international law. Second, these international organizations and others have also included the beginnings of institutions that resemble the legislative, enforcement, and judicial elements of a developed domestic legal system. A third element of growth is the increase of multilateral "lawmaking" treaties governing such subjects as genocide, atmospheric nuclear testing, proliferation, use of the oceans, and human rights. These treaty-established norms of conduct have not always been followed, but their violation has drawn increasing condemnation. This point leads to the fourth factor in current growth, which is raised expectations. The increased rhetorical emphasis on law plus enhanced communications means that world opinion is more likely to be aware of and to condemn violations of the norms of international conduct. What were once "splendid little wars," fought out of sight in remote places, now are apt to appear gruesomely on the seven o'clock news and to be condemned as violations of the UN charter. All these elements are reflected in a fifth factor, which is the increased need felt by national leaders to justify actions in terms of international law and even, on occasion, to give way to the pressure of law.

Effectiveness of Law

One of the charges used to discredit the existence of international law is that it exists only in theory and not in practice. As evidence, critics cite the continuing presence of war, imperialism, and other forms of "lawlessness" that exist today.

The flaw in this argument is that it does not prove its point. In the first place, international law *is* effective in many areas. Besides, the fact that law does not cover *all* problem areas and that it is not *always* followed does not disprove its existence. There is, after all, a substantial crime rate in the United States, but does that mean there is no law?

International law is *most effective* in governing functional international relations. In line with our earlier discussion of functionalism (Chapter 13), cooperation in and regulation of **functional relations**—that is, those in "nonpolitical" areas—have been rapidly increasing. This has been marked by the growth of what some scholars have termed international "regimes"—organizations and laws that regulate various functional areas.

International law is *least effective* when applied to the vital interests of sovereign states. When important political interests are involved, governments still regularly bend international law to justify their actions rather than alter their actions to conform to the law.

That does not mean, however, that the law never influences political decisions. To the contrary, there is a growing sensitivity to legal standards. During the 1962 Cuban missile crisis, an American air strike was deferred in part because of Robert Kennedy's reluctance to be remembered as a General Tojo

The injustices of war and other aspects of international relations led Hugo Grotius to look for a more humane way to conduct international politics, earning him the title of father of international law.

(convicted at the Tokyo war-crime trials). The Soviets were also greatly tempted to invade Poland in the early 1980s, but world reaction, based on the norm of sovereignty, would have been outraged, and the Soviets were dissuaded. Thus, even where it works the least, international law works some of the time and works more often than before.

The International Law System

International law, like any legal system, can be divided into three essential elements: lawmaking, adherence to the law, and adjudication of the law.

Lawmaking

The sources of any system of law can be divided into considerations of philosophy and practice.

The Philosophical Roots of Law

Where do laws come from? There are two basic sources. One of these is *external* to the society. Here the idea is that some "higher" metaphysical standard of conduct should govern the affairs of humankind. An important ramification of this position is that there is or ought to be one single system of law that governs all people. The second source possibility is that law is derived from factors *internal* to the society. This school of thought sees law as reflecting the will and practices of each individual society.

External roots. The external source can be further subdivided into two schools. One relies on *divine principle,* or a theological basis. Many of the early Western proponents of international law relied on Christian doctrine as a foundation for law. There are also elements of long-standing Islamic, Confucianist, and Buddhist law and scholarship that can be cited as forming a basis of international conduct.

A second school of external-source thought is that based on the *nature of humankind.* **Naturalists** believe that humans, by nature, have certain rights and obligations. Examples of rights would include life and security; obligations would include not stealing or murdering. Since states are collectives of individuals, and the world community is a collective of states and individuals, nature's individual rights and obligations also apply to the global stage and form the basis for international law.

Internal roots. Some legal scholars reject the idea of divine or naturalist roots and, instead, focus on the *customs and practices* of society.[3] This is the **positivist** approach. Positivists believe that law reflects society and the way people want that society to operate. Therefore, law is and ought to be the product of the codification or formalization of a society's standards and practices.

Critics condemn this approach as "amoral," and cynics argue that it legitimizes immoral, albeit common, practice. It should be carefully noted here, though, that widespread practice, such as aggressive war, does not necessarily imply legitimacy. In the first place, peace is the statistical norm in practice. And, second, international society condemns aggression in theory. Thus, despite frequent misbehavior, aggression is a lawless act.

Current Sources

Modern international law is drawn from a number of sources, with an emphasis on the positivist approach. These sources are best summarized in the Statute of the International Court of Justice (ICJ).[4]

International treaties. Agreements between and among states are binding according to the doctrine of ***pacta sunt servanda*** ("the treaty must be served/carried out"). All treaties are lawmaking for their signatories, but it is possible to argue that some treaties are even applicable to nonsignatories. The 1948 Convention on the Prevention and Punishment of the Crime of Genocide, for one, has been ratified by over eighty states. Some would argue, therefore, that it is "recognized" and "codified" practice and therefore is binding even on those states (including the United States) that have not formally agreed to it.

International custom. Norms are the second most important source of international law. The old, and now supplanted, rule that territorial waters extended three miles from the shore grew from the distance a cannon could fire. If you were outside the range of land-based artillery, then you were in international waters. Maritime rules of the road and diplomatic practice are two other important areas of law that grew out of custom. Finally, it might be noted that treaties (e.g., the Vienna Convention on Diplomatic Relations, 1961) often are established to formalize long-standing custom.

General principles of law. According to this standard, the ICJ applies "the general principles of law recognized by civilized nations." Although such language is vague, it does have its benefits. It allows "external" sources of law, such as "morality," to be considered. The principle of "equity," what is fair when no legal standard exists, also has some application under general principles.[5]

Judicial decisions and scholarly writing. In many domestic systems, the legal interpretations of the courts set *precedent* according to the doctrine of *stare decisis* ("let the decision stand").[6] Similarly, the rulings of the ICJ, other international tribunals, and even domestic courts when they apply international law, help shape the body of law that exists. Additionally, the work of legal scholars is sometimes considered by courts in their deliberations.

Characteristics of Lawmaking

Two additional points should be made about current international lawmaking. First, it is *nonlegislative*. That means that there is no legislative authority. The General Assembly cannot legislate international law. United Nations decisions do, however, theoretically bind members, and overwhelming resolutions may be construed as reflecting "custom" and/or "general principle," and therefore may subtly enter into the stream of international law. We may, then, be seeing the beginnings of legislated international law, but, at best, it is in its fetal stages.

Second, international lawmaking is *decentralized*. There is no single institutional, geographical, or intellectual source of law, and no central place to **codify**, or write down, the law. This fact creates difficulties as differing rules, practices, and interpretations clash, and they will be discussed further below. Decentralization does not mean, however, that international law is a meaningless hodgepodge. Consider **domestic law** in the United States, which contains over 80,000 municipal, state, and federal rulemaking authorities that adopt a blizzard of often contradictory standards! The American system of reconciling these differences is, of course, more established than the international law process, but in both the alignment process is usually slow and is a result of politics and compromise.

Adherence to the Law

Adherence to the law is a second essential element of any legal system. Any legal system is based on (1) what makes people comply and when noncompliance occurs, (2) how the law is enforced.

Compliance. Obedience in any legal system, be it international or domestic, primitive or sophisticated, is based on a combination of voluntary acceptance and coercion.

Voluntary compliance occurs when the subjects obey the law because they accept its legitimacy (for example, accept the authority) and/or agree that it is necessary to the reasonable conduct of society. *Coercion* is the process of gaining compliance through threats of violence, imprisonment, economic sanction, or other punishment.

Any society's legal system could be placed along a scale between complete reliance on voluntary compliance and complete reliance on coercion (Figure 14-1). No society exists at either extreme, and while most rely mainly on voluntary compliance, the mixture of legitimacy and authoritarianism varies widely. Most Americans, for example, obey the law voluntarily, whereas the black majority in South Africa are obedient primarily under duress.

Enforcement. In all legal systems enforcement relies on a combination of *enforcing authorities* and *self-help,* with mediation a midpoint. Here again a scale can be drawn with the two extremes (authority, self-help) at its end points, as shown in Figure 14-1. In more sophisticated legal systems, most enforcement relies on a central authority such as the police. Still, even the most sophisticated legal system continues to recognize the legitimacy of such self-help doctrines as self-defense.

Primitive societies rely primarily on self-help and mediation to enforce laws and norms. Central authorities develop slowly and are used only in extreme circumstances.[7] Yet no society that has progressed beyond the most primitive has a complete absence of enforcement authority, and it is here that we can place international law.

International law: Primitive adherence. Because the international legal system is still primitive, enforcement and compliance reflects that stage.

Enforcement, in particular, has been slow to develop. Collective security has remained a theory, economic sanctions have been generally unsuccessful, and international law continues to rely mainly on self-help to enforce adherence, as reflected in the UN charter's recognition of national self-defense. There have been, however, a few examples of enforcement. War criminals were punished after World War II, economic sanctions had some impact in loosening the white grip on the black majority of Zimbabwe (Rhodesia), and UN actions in Korea, in the Congo, and elsewhere did contain some elements of enforcement.

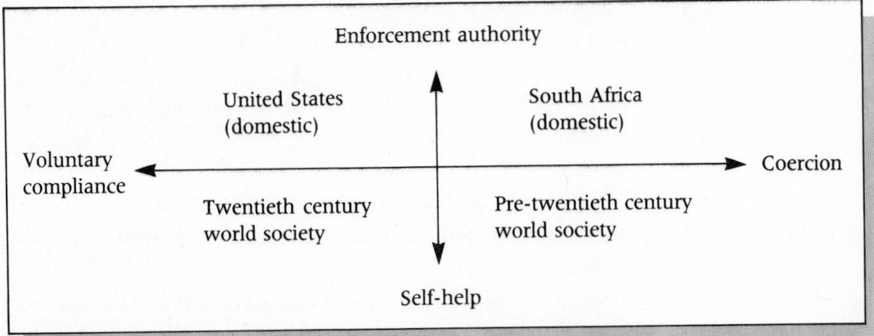

Figure 14-1. Factors in adherence to the law, with examples.

The element of voluntary *compliance* has grown more quickly than that of enforcement authority in international law. As we saw above, under "Growth of International Law," functional international law has expanded rapidly because of the need to regulate complex international interactions in trade, finance, communications, diplomacy, and other areas. In addition, as noted, there is a growing nexus of concepts that also restrains actions in more political areas. Aggression, violation of human rights, and other unacceptable practices still occur, but they increasingly meet with widespread condemnation.

Thus, in the area of adherence, international law is a primitive but developing legal system. It is slowly moving out of the lower right quadrant of Figure 14-1 and, one hopes, toward the upper left quadrant.

Adjudication of the Law

The mechanisms and processes to judge the law are the third essential element of any legal system. As primitive law systems develop into more sophisticated ones, the method of settling disputes evolves from (1) primary reliance on bargaining between disputing parties, through (2) mediation/conciliation by neutral parties, to (3) **adjudication** by neutral parties.[8]

The international law system is in the early stages of this developmental process and is just now developing the institutions and attitudes necessary for adjudication.

Institutions of adjudication. There are a number of long existent international courts in the world today. The genesis of these tribunals extends back less than a century to the Permanent Court of International Arbitration established by the Hague Conference at the turn of the century. In 1922 the Permanent Court of International Justice (PCIJ) was created as part of the League of Nations, and in 1946 the current **International Court of Justice** (ICJ), which is associated with the UN, evolved from the PCIJ. The ICJ sits in The Hague, Netherlands, and consists of fifteen judges who are elected to nine-year terms through a complex voting system in the UN. In addition to the ICJ, there are a few other regional courts of varying activity, including the Court of Justice of the European Communities, the European Court of Human Rights, the Inter-American Court of Human Rights, the Central American Court of Justice, and the Community Tribunal of the Economic Community of West African States.

Attitudes toward adjudication. Although the creation of international tribunals during the twentieth century indicates progress, the concept of sovereignty remains a potent barrier to adjudication.[9]

In theory, the authority of the ICJ extends to all international legal disputes. In reality, the court is limited by the reluctance of states to submit to its jurisdiction. States must not only agree to be subject to the ICJ, they may also make "reservations" to that acceptance. The United States, for example, rejects ICJ jurisdiction in any "domestic matter . . . as determined by the United States." This is an extremely broad disclaimer and, in effect, means the United States can reject ICJ jurisdiction on virtually any issue.

Third World attitudes are influenced by the sovereignty issue and by the fact that many countries' legal systems rely more on mediation than on adjudication. Courts were also often instruments of white colonial oppression and are therefore viewed with suspicion.

Use and effectiveness of adjudication. The result of these attitudes is that use of the ICJ has been sporadic. During its history, it has dealt with only approximately fifty contentious cases and another twenty advisory opinion cases on issues submitted by organs of the UN. This is a rate of less than two cases per year.[10] Furthermore, the rate of submission is declining from 3.4 cases per year in the 1950s to 1.1 per year in the 1970s.

There are some signs of hope, however, to counter this trend. The 1980s have seen several significant cases submitted to the ICJ. The United States and Canada turned to the court in 1984 to settle fishing rights on the resource-rich Georges Bank off New England and Nova Scotia. Also in 1984, Nicaragua asked the ICJ to hear its complaint against U.S. aid to guerrillas. The Reagan administration rejected the court's jurisdiction, arguing that the issue was "political," but at least it argued the jurisdictional issue before the court rather than just ignoring it. In December 1984, in a significant move, the court agreed to hear the case over U.S. objections, putting the United States in the uncomfortable position of either arguing its case (and probably losing) or refusing to participate and suffering from widespread criticism for failing to live up to its professed support of international law and the ICJ.

Beyond the ICJ, there has been evidence that some of the other international courts, especially in Europe, have had some effect.[11] The "half full" standard must also be applied here. The international judicial system is still primitive, but each of the 128 opinions issued by the PCIJ and ICJ in this century is one more than the zero instances of international adjudication in the last century.

International Law and Cultural Perspective

As primitive political systems evolve and expand to incorporate diverse peoples, one problem that legal systems have encountered is the "fit" between differing, culturally based concepts of law and equity. International law, in an evolving world, faces the same difficulty. Most of the law and process that currently exist are based on European and American concepts and practices, and the newly assertive states of Africa, Asia, and Latin America question and sometimes reject law based on the "white man's" culture.

Differing Perspectives

The culture and international status of the Western countries, the Soviet Union, China, and the Third World each engender some differences in interpretation of international law.

The Western view. The Euro-American view of law is based on principles designed to protect the power position of the long-dominant states of this bloc. *Order* is a primary point, as is *sovereignty.* Closely related is the theory of *property,* which holds that individuals (and states) have a "right" to accumulate and maintain property (wealth). This is a major philosophical underpinning of capitalism. Western law also relies heavily on the *process* and *substance* of law rather than on equity. Thus, there is an emphasis on courts and what the law is rather than on what is fair.

The Soviet view. Law looks somewhat different from a Soviet-Marxist perspective. The Soviets view much of existing law as a vehicle for *imperialist exploitation.* They also divide international law into categories. They believe, for example, that the superpower blocs should not interfere with each other's sovereignty. Within the socialist camp, however, the Soviets hold that *interference to maintain socialism* is legitimate. This is exemplified by the Soviet invasion of Czechoslovakia in 1968 and the enunciation of the Brezhnev Doctrine, which held that socialist states had a right and obligation to intervene in other socialist states to prevent their system from being subverted by capitalist/reactionary forces. The Soviets also hold that at least *indirect intervention* through support of revolution in the exploited Third World is legitimate. Finally, they rhetorically support Third World demands to restructure international economic law on the basis of equity, although they claim that since they did not create the inequity, they should not be required to redistribute their own resources.[12]

The Chinese view. China's perspective on international law is based on its Marxist ideology and its history of being imperialistically exploited. Current international law is viewed as a product of imperialism. The Chinese reject *pacta sunt servanda,* the obligation to uphold treaties, when the treaty was imperialistically imposed. The Chinese hold that treaties based on coercion can simply be renounced. In practice, however, they sometimes tacitly recognize the status quo or are willing to negotiate revisions, as the recent agreement with Britain on the future of Hong Kong illustrates. The Chinese also reject the Soviet concept of legitimate interference to maintain socialism, and they condemn the Czechoslovakian invasion as Soviet-style imperialism. The Chinese also stress equity, or the idea that the law should benefit all parties. This view places them solidly within the Third World in its demand for a New International Economic Order.[13]

The Third World view. The Third World's view of international law is influenced by its history of exploitation and its "newness" as a collection of sovereign states, as well as its cultural traditions and current status. The new nations claim that, at the point of their independence, they enter the system of sovereign states with a *clean slate.* That is, they are not bound by preexisting agreements or practices that work to their disadvantage. These countries support sovereignty and reject aspects of international law that they claim are imperialistic abridgments of their sovereignty. They insist on *noninterference.* They support, for example, the "Calvo clause," by which Western-based multinational corporations agree that their home governments have no right to interfere in host countries to protect the MNCs' property. The Third World also *rejects weighted decision-making schemes,* such as those in the Security Council and the International Monetary Fund, that favor the rich and powerful. Finally, Third World countries emphasize *equity* over the substance and process of law. For them, the bottom line is fairness, especially in terms of economic maldistribution.[14]

Can There Be "One" Law?

Given the differences in perspective we have just noted, the question arises: Can the world arrive at one system of law? The answer is "Yes!" or, at least, "It is possible, if not certain."

Some scholars have presented a rather pessimistic view of the chances for accommodating divergent legal values within a universal law.[15] Others, however, have argued persuasively that striking similarities exist between cultures. International legal scholars of this persuasion tend to distinguish between *abstract principles of law* based on theory, religion, morality, and philosophy and *pragmatic principles of law* based on practice governed by national interest.[16] They contend that almost all cultural and legal systems support concepts such as human dignity and oppose violence and exploitation. The optimistic view can, for instance, point to the statement of Japanese Justice Kontro Tanaka that "nine years of experience on the International Court of Justice have led me to conclude that a common basis of jurisprudence . . . exists . . . in spite of . . . different religious, racial, and cultural backgrounds."[17]

What needs to change, the optimists contend, is some of the practices of law which no longer serve the system and which are particularly disadvantageous to the Third World. This change and the accompanying stresses, they point out, are a normal part of any dynamic system, if perhaps accentuated by the rapid shifts the world is undergoing. In the long run, they are confident that if adjustments and compromises are made in the enlightened self-interest of all parties, then universally accepted concepts of law can and will prevail.

Issues in Law

As a developing legal system in a dynamic world political system, international law is anything but "settled." There are many unresolved issues, and in this section we will examine some of the "frontiers" of international law. For analytical purposes, the discussion will be divided between two rough categories: (1) issues between states and (2) individuals and international law.

Issues between States

The state has been the traditional focus of international law. The state has been the *subject* of international law—the law has applied to its conduct. A great deal of international law also addresses the status of states, thus making the state the *object* of international law.

Sovereignty. Independence and equality continue to be a cornerstone of the contemporary state system, but they are no longer legal absolutes. The concept of sovereignty was extensively discussed in Chapter 1, but one can add here that it is being chipped away by a growing number of law-creating treaties that limit action. Sovereignty is also ever so slowly being restricted by a growing body of general principles that govern human rights and other aspects of the relations between a state and individuals within its borders.

War. Most of the earliest writing in international law was concerned with the law of war, and that issue has continued to be a primary focus of development. In addition to issues of traditional "state versus state" warfare, international law is now attempting to regulate the related subjects of revolutionary and internal warfare and terrorism.

First let's consider *traditional warfare.* When a war is "just" has long been a concern of international law. Today, *aggression* is outlawed by the UN charter, and the only legitimate reasons to resort to violence are (1) in self-defense and (2) as part of a UN or regional peacekeeping effort. There have also been extensive efforts to regulate the *conduct* of warfare. These have included such aspects as prohibiting the use of certain types of weapons (such as poison gas), standards for the treatment of prisoners of war, and restrictions against unnecessary attacks on noncombatants. The *status of neutrals,* their rights and obligations, is a third area of concern. All these areas are sources of great difficulty because of the high political stakes involved and also because changes in the nature of conflict (technology, mass warfare) create new problems and extend beyond traditional concepts. In addition to some early discussions (Chapter 13), the next chapter will address several of these issues.[18]

Increasing concern with revolutionary/internal warfare and terrorism has also brought attempts to deal with these types of violence within the context of international law. To a degree, wars of liberation have been affirmed by the General Assembly's 1974 "recognition of the legitimacy of the struggle of the peoples under colonial or alien domination to exercise their right of self-determination and independence by all necessary means at their disposal."[19] This does not mean acceptance of outside intervention on behalf of wars of liberation, although non-Western legal thought is more likely to accept such acts as legitimate.

There are also considerable efforts to agree on ways to deal with issues of terrorism, including hostages, violence against civilians, and the prosecution and extradition of terrorists. A greal deal remains to be done, but progress is being made in some areas such as skyjacking, which is increasingly defined as illegitimate by almost all members of the international community.[20]

Law of the sea. The status of the world oceans is another long-standing subject of international law. The international rules of the road for maritime shipping have long had general acceptance. The extension of a state's territorial limits to three miles into the ocean was another widely acknowledged standard.

In more recent years, the resource value of the seas and harvesting and extraction technology have created uncertainty and change. Undersea oil exploration, in particular, is the source of serious dispute between a number of countries. As early as 1945, the United States claimed control of the resources on or under its continental shelf. In 1960 the Soviet Union proclaimed the extension of its territorial waters out to twelve miles, a policy that has been imitated by others. Several Latin American countries claim a 200-mile territorial zone, and the United States not only established a 200-mile "conservation zone" in 1977 to control fishing but in 1983 extended that control to all economic resources within the 200-mile limit.

In an ambitious attempt to settle and regulate many of these issues, the Law of the Sea Convention (1982) seeks to define coastal zones, establish an International Seabed Authority to regulate nonterritorial seabed mining, and provide for the sharing of revenue from such efforts. Although the vast majority of the world's states signed the accord, its effectiveness has been cast in doubt by the opposition of the United States and a few other states. U.S. objections particularly focus on what the United States sees as a (hostile, socialist) Third World attempt to control deep-sea mining in a way detrimental to its interests, and at this writing, negotiations to resolve differences were continuing.[21]

Air and space. Twentieth-century technology has created the need to regulate the use of air and space. The airspace above a country is recognized by the 1944 Chicago Convention of International Civil Aviation. There have, however, been concerns with enforcement procedures, especially during accidental, innocent passage, as in the 1983 Soviet downing of a Korean airliner in Soviet airspace. There are also disputes over the dividing line between air and space, and they will escalate as satellites and space vehicles maintain positions over the territory of states. Other aspects of developing space law include agreements to ban nuclear weapons in space and to prevent countries from claiming exclusive jurisdiction over areas in space or on celestial bodies, such as the moon. As travel, military, and resource development technologies improve, space is likely to become an increasing source of conflict with need of legal regulation.[22]

Antarctic. Regulation of the Antarctic region has been governed by agreements among fourteen countries with long-standing activity in the region. Agreements include a 1959 treaty pledging to use the area only for peaceful purposes. Recent interest in resource development and attempts by some states to have the UN regulate the area have caused new and continuing negotiation.

Environment. Protection of the environment is another of the technology-related legal issues of the twentieth century. Growing concerns with the drift of acid rain and air pollution over borders, the contamination of border lakes and international rivers, and deep-sea dumping are the subjects of disputes and efforts to define the responsibilities and liabilities of states.[23] These issues will be covered more extensively in the final chapter.

Individuals and International Law

In addition to states, international law is increasingly concerned with individuals. This concern has long included the treatment of individuals by states. More recently, international law has expanded to include responsibility of individuals for their acts.

Prisoners of war. The 1949 Geneva Convention established generally accepted rules on the treatment of POWs despite some later violations. A remaining problem is how to distinguish a POW from a criminal. The Palestine Liberation Organization claims that its fighters who infiltrate Israel and are captured are POWs. Israel treats them as terrorist murderers.

Aliens. In general, aliens are governed by the domestic law of the country in which they are residing or traveling. Americans, for example, do not carry their constitutional rights abroad with them. Home states therefore do not ordinarily have the right to intervene, although they sometimes do when acts against their nationals are politically motivated or do not meet rudimentary standards of justice. With increased travel, migratory labor, and international movement of investment capital, the treatment of aliens and their property remains a developing legal area.[24]

Human rights. International law is developing affirmatively in the area of defining human rights. The UN charter supports basic rights in a number of provisions, as do many international instruments, such as the Universal Declaration of Human Rights (1948). The 1975 International Covenant on Civil and Political Rights and the 1975 International Covenant on Economic, Social, and Cultural Rights both expanded the recognized definitions. There are also many limited pacts, such as the 1977 Helsinki accords, that address European human rights.

Much, however, remains to be done. The two 1975 covenants have been ratified by only about half the world's states. The United States, for one, has not, because of fears that these agreements might be used as platforms for interfering in domestic civil rights issues or as vehicles for demanding international resource redistribution under the NIEO. Additionally, there are efforts to further refine and extend agreed rights to women, children, refugees, and other classes of people. Finally, the enforcement of human rights remains largely in the hands of individual states, although world opinion is making violations less acceptable.[25]

Individual responsibility. Traditionally, individuals were *objects* rather than subjects of international law. That means that international law governed their treatment but not their responsibilities. A series of precedents in this century have begun to change that concept. In the Nuremberg and Tokyo war trials after World War II, German and Japanese military and civilian leaders were tried, convicted, imprisoned, and, in some cases, executed for waging aggressive war, for war crimes, and for crimes against humanity. The trial (and execution) of Japanese General Tomoyuki Yamashita further established the precedent that commanders were responsible for the actions of their troops.[26] This precedent has not been expanded, although there were some calls to apply the rules to U.S. commanders for the My Lai massacre and other actions by U.S. troops in Vietnam.[27] In recent years, the French arrested Klaus Barbie for crimes during the Nazi occupation, and there were extensive efforts to apprehend Josef Mengele, the Nazi concentration camp doctor who cruelly experimented on prisoners, before it was confirmed that he had drowned in Brazil.

International Law and the Future

As noted in the beginning of this chapter, the often anarchic and inequitable world has made it easy for some to dismiss talk of international law as idealistic prattling. That was probably never valid and certainly is not valid now. An

The Nuremberg war crimes trials established the principle that aggressive war and inhuman actions are punishable crimes under international law.

irreversible trend in world affairs is the rapid acceleration of states and people interacting in almost all areas of endeavor. As these interactions have grown, so has the need for regularized behavior and rules to prescribe that behavior. The growth of these rules in functional international interactions has been on the leading edge of the development of international law. Advances in political/military areas have been slower, but here too there has been progress. Thus, as with the United Nations, the pessimist may decry the glass as only half full, whereas, in reality, it is encouraging that there is more and more water in the previously nearly empty glass.

All the signs point to increasing respect for international law. As a general rule, even enemies at their worst moments still respect many aspects of that law, and departures from the law draw increasing criticism from the world community. It is likely, therefore, that international law will continue to develop and to expand its areas of application. There will certainly be areas where growth is painfully slow, and there will also be law violators who sometimes get away with their unlawful acts. But, just as surely, there will be progress.

Summary

International law can be best understood as a primitive system of law rather than in comparison with much more developed domestic law. There are only the most rudimentary procedures and institutions for making, adjudicating, and enforcing international law. That does not mean, however, that international law is impotent, only that it is in an earlier stage of development than domestic law.

As a developing phenomenon, international law is dynamic and has been growing since the earliest periods of civilization. This growth has accelerated in the twentieth century because the increasing level of international interaction and interdependence requires many new rules to govern and regularize contacts in trade, finance, travel, communication, and other areas. The possible consequences of war have also spurred the development of international law.

Thus far, international law is most effective when it governs functional international relations. International law works least well in areas that touch on the vital interests of the sovereign states. Even in those areas, though, international law is gradually becoming more effective.

The international law system has three essential elements: lawmaking, adherence, and adjudication. Regarding lawmaking, international law can be argued to spring from a number of sources, including divine principle, the nature of humankind, societal custom and practices, and lawmaking documents passed or agreed to by states. As in most primitive legal systems, international lawmaking is still heavily nonlegislative and decentralized, but it is slowly taking on those more advanced characteristics. Regarding adherence, international law, again like primitive law, relies mainly on voluntary compliance and self-help. Here again, though, there are early and still uncertain examples of enforcement by third parties, a feature that characterizes more advanced systems. The third essential element of a law system, adjudication, is also in the primitive stage in international law. But the application of international law by domestic courts and, even more important, the existence of the International Court of Justice, the Court of Justice of the European Communities, and other such international judicial bodies represent an increasing sophistication of international law in this area as well.

As a developing system in a still culturally diverse world, international law has encountered problems of fit with different cultures. Most current international law is based on European and American ideas and practices, and many states from the Third World and other groups take objection to certain aspects of international law as it exists.

The changes in the world system in this century have created a number of important issues related to international law. Among these are the validity and status of sovereignty, the legality of war and the conduct of war, rules for governing the surface, subsurface, and floors of the world's international seas, the regulation of air and space, and protection of the environment. In general, international law has been interpreted as applying to states, but it is also increasingly concerned with individuals. Primarily it applies to the treatment of individuals by states, but it also has some application to the actions of individuals. Thus people, as well as countries, are coming to have obligations, as well as rights, under international law.

Terms

Adjudication—The legal process of deciding an issue through the courts.
Codify—To write down a law in formal language.
Domestic law—Law that applies within a state.
Functional relations—Relations that include interaction in such usually nonpolitical areas as communication, travel, trade, and finances.
International Court of Justice—The world court which sits in The Hague with fifteen judges and which is associated with the United Nations.
Naturalists—Those who believe that law springs from the rights and obligations that humans have by nature.
Pacta sunt servanda—Translates as "the treaty must be served/carried out" and means that agreements between states are binding.
Positivists—Those who believe that law reflects society and the way that people want the society to operate.

Notes

1. The comparison of primitive societies and international relations/law is based on Roger D. Masters, "World Politics as a Primitive Political System," in *International Politics and Foreign Policy,* ed. James N. Rosenau (New York: Free Press, 1969), pp. 104–118. As Masters points out, the comparison between the two can be carried only so far.
2. This section relies on Werner Levi, *Contemporary International Law* (Boulder, Colo.: Westview Press, 1979), pp. 7–14.
3. Werner Levi, *Law and Politics in the International Society* (Beverly Hills, Calif.: Sage, 1976), pp. 15–19.
4. A good general source is Clive Parry, *The Sources and Evidences of International Law* (Manchester, U.K.: Manchester University Press, 1965).
5. Levi, *Contemporary International Law,* pp. 43–45, is good on this point.
6. *Stare decisis* is specifically rejected in Article 59 of the Statute of the ICJ, but as Werner Levi points out, "The fact is that all courts . . . rely upon and cite each other abundantly in their decisions," ibid., p. 53.
7. In addition to Masters, "Primitive Political System," see Michael Barkum, *Law without Sanctions* (New Haven, Conn.: Yale University Press, 1968).
8. There are technical differences between arbitration and adjudication, but they are treated alike for our purposes here. For a discussion, see Levi, *Contemporary International Law,* pp. 298–299.
9. This section relies on Levi, *Contemporary International Law,* pp. 299–301; Frederick Hartmann, *The Relations of Nations,* 6th ed. (New York: Macmillan, 1983), pp. 115–124; and Edward McWhenney, *The World Court and the Contemporary International Law-Making Process* (Alphen aan den Rijn, The Netherlands: Sijthoff & Noordhoff, 1979).
10. For a list, see International Court of Justice, *Yearbook, 1982–1983* (The Hague: ICJ, 1983), pp. 3–5.

11. Benjamin B. Ferencz, *Enforcing International Law: A Way to World Peace* (London: Oceana, 1983), p. 483.
12. For a view emphasizing practice, see Kazimierz Crzybowski, *Soviet Public International Law* (Leyden, The Netherlands: Sijthoff, 1970); and Grigory I. Tunkin, *Theory of International Law,* trans. W. E. Butler (Cambridge, Mass.: Harvard University Press, 1974).
13. Jerome A. Cohen and Hungdah Chiu, *China and International Law* (Princeton, N.J.: Princeton University Press, 1974).
14. Daniel C. Papp, *Contemporary International Relations* (New York: Macmillan, 1984), p. 409.
15. Adda Bozeman, *The Future of Law in a Multiculture World* (Princeton, N.J.: Princeton University Press, 1971).
16. Wolfgang Friedmann, *The Changing Structure of International Law* (New York: Columbia University Press, 1964).
17. Quoted in Levi, *Law and Politics,* p. 138.
18. Geoffrey Best, *Humanity in Warfare* (New York: Columbia University Press, 1980); and Myres S. McDougal and W. Michael Reisman, eds., *International Law in Contemporary Perspective* (Mineola, N.Y.: Foundation Press, 1981), pp. 964–997, 1003–1017.
19. Quoted in Levi, *Contemporary International Law,* p. 322.
20. Yonah Alexande, Marjorie Ann Browne, and Allan S. Nanes, eds., *Control of Terrorism International Documents* (New York: Crane Russak, 1979), is a compilation of treaties and UN and other IGO resolutions in this area. Also see Alona E. Evans and John F. Murphy, eds., *Legal Aspects of International Terrorism* (Lexington, Mass.: Heath, 1978).
21. *Issues before the 38th General Assembly of the United Nations, 1983–1984* (n.p.: United Nations Association of the United States of America, 1983), pp. 103–107. For a general treatment, see D. P. O'Connell with I. A. Shearer, eds., *The International Law of the Sea,* 2 vols. (Oxford: Clarendon Press, 1982); and McDougal and Reisman, *International Law,* pp. 511–609.
22. There is a growing literature on space law. See Delbert D. Smith, *Space Stations: International Law and Policy* (Boulder, Colo.: Westview Press, 1979); also "The Moon Treaty: Should the United States Become a Party," a discussion in American Society of International Law, *Proceedings* of the 74th annual meeting, Washington, D.C., April 17–19, 1980, pp. 152–174.
23. See Gunter Handl, "The Environment: International Rights and Responsibilities," discussion in American Society of International Law, *Proceedings,* pp. 223–248.
24. Levi, *Contemporary International Law,* pp. 175–192.
25. McDougal and Reisman, *International Law,* pp. 940–942. Also see a symposium, "Perspectives on Enforcement of Human Rights," in American Society of International Law, *Proceedings,* pp. 1–29; and William T. R. Fox, "Human Freedom in a World of States," in American Society of International Law, *Proceedings* of the 75th annual meeting, Washington, D.C., April 23–25, 1981.
26. Richard Lael, *The Yamashita Precedent* (Wilmington, Del.: Scholarly Resources, 1982).
27. Jay W. Baird, ed., *From Nuremberg to My Lai* (Lexington, Mass.: Heath, 1972).

15

Disarmament and Arms Control

He's mad that trusts in the tameness of a wolf.
Shakespeare, King Lear

Lord, what fools these mortals be.
Shakespeare, A Midsummer Night's Dream

I would give all my fame for a pot of ale and safety.
Shakespeare, Henry V

An Improbable Parable

The Opening Scene

It was a fine and sunny, yet somehow foreboding, autumn day many millennia ago. Og, a caveman, was searching for food near the cave of his not-too-distant neighbor Ug. It had not been a good season for hunting game or for berry and root gathering, and Og's stomach grumbled and his mind fretted about the coming winter and his family.

The same snows would come to Ug's cave, but Ug had been luckier. He had just killed a large antelope, grown fat from the summer's rich grazing. Ug, then, was feeling prosperous as he prepared to clean his kill in the clearing in the forest.

At that moment Og, hunting spear in hand, happened out of the forest and came upon Ug, who was grasping his gutting knife. They had met before, and though not friends, they had lived in peace. Indeed, it was a time when everyone lived in peace. It was not a matter of philosophy, really. It was just that life was hard, and a person's energy and weapons were devoted to hunting and to fending off the ever-marauding jackals. War had not been invented yet—but the arms race was about to begin.

Both Og and Ug were startled by their sudden meeting, but they exchanged the customary greetings of the day. Still, Ug was troubled by Og's lean and hungry look. Unconsciously, he grasped his knife more tightly. The tensing of Ug's ample muscles alarmed Og. Equally unconsciously, Og's spear point dropped to a defensive position. Fear was the common denominator. By this time, each wanted to escape the confrontation, but they were trapped. Their disengagement negotiation went something like this (translated):

Ug: You are pointing your spear at me.

Og: And your knife glints menacingly in the sunlight. But this is crazy, Ug. I mean you no harm, your antelope is yours.

Ug: Good, Og, and of course we are friends. I'll even give you a little meat. But first, why don't you put down your spear so we can talk better?

Og: A fine idea, Ug, and I'll be glad to put down my spear, but why don't you lay down that fearful knife first? Then we can be friends again.

Ug: Spears can fly through the air farther. . . . *You should be first.*

Og: Knives can strike more quickly. . . . *You should be first.*

And so the conversation in the clearing went on, with Og and Ug equally unsure of the other's intention, each proclaiming his peaceful purpose, and both unable to agree on how their weapons could be laid aside.

The Continuing Drama

In one form or another that dialogue has continued since the days of our prehistoric ancestors. Popes and princes, peons and philosophers, presidents and presidium heads have all proclaimed for peace and damned the weapons of war. We could survey the entire history of these utterings, but it will be sufficient here to consider the urgings of two recent world leaders.

Ronald Reagan: Why don't we reduce our arsenals? And if we start down that road of reducing, for heaven's sake, why don't we rid the world of these weapons? Why do we keep them? Here's a world today whose principal armaments would wipe out civilians in the tens and hundreds of millions. Let's get back to being civilized.[1]

Mikhail Gorbachev: Never before has so terrible a threat loomed so large and dark over mankind. . . . [We must] advance toward the cherished goal, the complete elimination and prohibition of nuclear weapons for good, toward the complete removal of the threat of nuclear war. This is our firm conviction.[2]

Both President Reagan and General Secretary Gorbachev, then, are for peace and love—just like Og and Ug. If only the other side would trust them and put down its weapons first, then . . .

Armaments: The Complex Debate

The debate over arms is one of the most complex and important in our time. More than most subjects, trying to reduce it to proportions suitable for an introductory text without rendering the discussion superficial presents a considerable challenge to an author. To help resolve that difficulty, the reader can do several things. One is to review the discussion of types of arms in Chapter 8. This will help clarify the discussion of types of weapons and such concepts as deterrence. A second good idea is to review the terms at the end of this chapter. The literature on arms is especially full of acronyms, and the chapter end guide will help you keep things straight.

Third, the reader should understand that there are many subtleties beyond the scope of this chapter. The following discussion on the case for and the case against arms must be read with the understanding that there are many intermediate points. Few favor unlimited armaments or absolute disarmament. This chapter also, to a degree, treats arms as a singular phenomenon. It is surely true that conventional and nuclear arms are substantially different and raise varying problems, but it is also true, in a sense, that all arms come from the same impulses, that they have the same ultimate destructive end, and that their control is bedeviled by many of the same barriers. There are also many variations concerning which types of arms are more destabilizing, what is offensive and what is defensive, and a host of other questions. We will certainly delve into some of these, but this chapter, and indeed all the chapters, should be seen as a starting place, rather than a comprehensive end, to your studies.

The Case against Arms

The historical refrain against the ever-escalating buildup of arms condemns weapons because of their cost, the dynamic and spiraling arms race, their promotion of war, and their destructiveness.

Arms Are Expensive

It is a truism that arms are very expensive and therefore represent a *budget burden*. World military expenditures will exceed $1 trillion in 1985 and are expected to rise to $1 trillion, 600 billion by the year 2000. It also goes without saying that if these swords could truly be converted into plowshares, that if arms dollars could be redirected into schools, hospitals, economic development, and other peaceful purposes, then the human condition would improve. In particular, the cost of arms weighs heavily on less developed countries (LDCs). Between 1972 and 1982, military expenditures increased at a real growth rate of 5 percent in LDCs, compared with 2.4 percent in developed countries.[3]

There is also some evidence that, in addition to consuming scarce resources, excessive arms spending can have a negative effect on a country's general economic health.

For one thing, arms spending may have a suboptimal effect on *employment*. Because military expenditures are in capital-intensive industries (28,000 jobs per billion dollars in the United States), they create fewer jobs than expenditures in more labor-intensive areas such as public transit (32,000 jobs per billion dollars) or education (71,000 jobs per billion dollars).

There is also some evidence that high arms expenditures can cause *economic dislocation*. A tremendous percentage of the Soviet Union's most talented minds are, for example, channeled into technical careers in the Soviets' military-industrial complex and therefore are unavailable in people-oriented areas such as civil engineering, the social sciences, law, and medicine.

In addition to consuming limited talent, military expenditures consume limited natural resources (such as oil), limited products (electronic equipment), and limited skills (machinists). The result is that even if there is a demand for certain products and the money to buy them, they may be unavailable because they or the resources and labor needed to make them have been preempted by military consumption.

There is also some relationship between defense expenditures and *inflation*, especially when massive budget deficits are used to help finance arms expenditures.[4]

Each of the above arguments about the negative impact of arms has its advocates and each has an element of truth, but they should be accepted only with caution. The relationship between defense spending and economics is extremely complex, and scholars differ widely on specific impacts. First, there is no clear evidence that lower defense expenditures will necessarily lead to a reallocation of "available" budget money to nondefense categories. Nor is it always true that increased defense expenditures directly and necessarily reduce nondefense outlays. Certainly there is a relationship between guns and butter, but it is not a constant or one-to-one variance.[5]

Second, inasmuch as defense and nondefense expenditures are not always directly related, the associated job issue is complex. The loss of a billion defense dollars (28,000 jobs) might mean a net loss of jobs, particularly in the short run, because of no, partial, or slow reallocation of those funds into more labor-intensive economic areas (transportation, education).

Third, many argue that there is a "spillover" effect between military and civilian economic development. While it is true, for instance, that at least 60 percent of all American aeronautical engineers work primarily on national defense, the technologies they develop benefit the commercial aircraft industry. Military technology is often useful only for defense, but there are some transferred benefits.

Fourth, inflation is a multicausal phenomenon. Defense expenditures are only a part of budgets, and budgets are only part of the cause of inflation. A review of the research leads to the conclusion that defense expenditures have contributed to inflation only sometimes, under some conditions, in some countries.[6]

Arms Bring More Arms

Another indictment of military spending is that it creates fear in other countries, causing them to buy more arms, thus setting off an arms race. This contention seems "obvious," and, indeed, there is some evidence that, in some specific cases, it is true. Further, the level of the other side's arms expenditures can be used as a powerful political argument to increase military spending, even if it is not the direct cause.

As an overall phenomenon, however, the arms-race model has not been supported by social science research. Technological changes, bureaucratic pressures, domestic politics, economic trends, and a variety of other factors are related to the level of arms expenditures.[7]

Arms Cause War

A third argument against arms is that they cause war by increasing tension (Theory A). There can be little doubt that arms both create a possibility of war and help create a climate of hostility and anxiety that is fertile ground for war. But, here again, the relationship is complex. Arms may instead be amassed because of war-producing tension. Thus, both arms and war may be the result of tension (Theory B). These varying relationships can be seen in Figure 15-1.

What we can say, then, is that tension, arms, and violent conflict are interrelated. No one would deny that arms races are dangerous and that they might sometimes lead to war, but there is also no good evidence that arms directly and consistently cause wars.[8] Instead, arms, tension, and wars all promote one another, as seen in Figure 15-2.

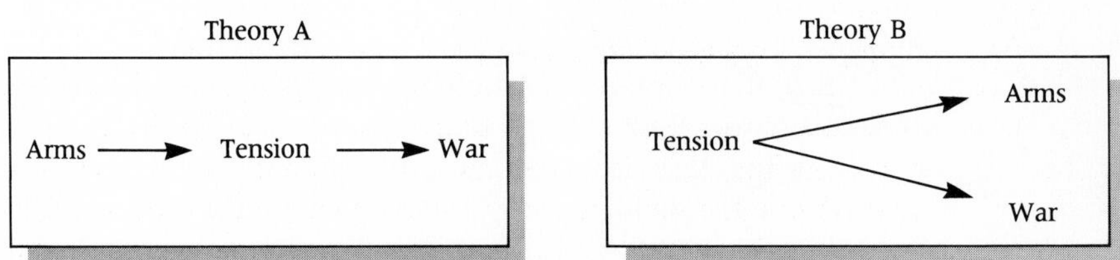

Figure 15-1. Two theories of the relationship of arms, tension, and war.

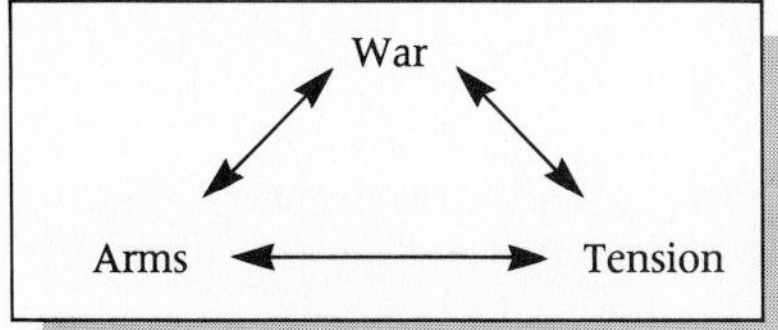

Figure 15-2. Interrelationship of arms, tension, and war.

Arms Are Destructive

The final indictment of arms is that they kill people and animals, destroy property, and damage the environment. It is important to keep that in mind. Chapter 8 detailed the destructiveness of war and the horrifying realities need not be recounted here. Suffice it to reiterate that the wars of yesterday may well pale in comparison with the life-ending, environment-destroying holocausts of tomorrow.

The Case for Arms

It would create a false impression only to acknowledge the case against arms. There are also arguments in support of arms spending. In a sense, we have already touched on these arguments immediately above, but it is worthwhile to reiterate them here.

The World Is Dangerous

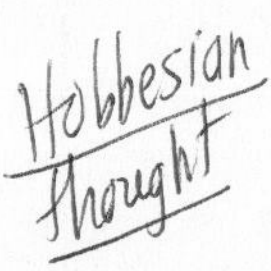

Many decision makers and social scientists argue that weapons are necessary for survival in a predatory world. As Hans Morgenthau once put it, "Men do not fight because they have arms. They have arms because they . . . fight."[9] If wars occur because humans are violence-prone or if some humans and countries are aggressive, then arms are necessary. Indeed, some also contend that, as a deterrent, arms can also be counted as a factor in preserving the peace and that disarmament might create instability or tempt aggressors, thus actually increasing the likelihood of war.[10]

Arms Aid the Economy

Arms do create employment, and technological advances do spill over into consumer products. If defense expenditures were reduced, then over time, resources would be reallocated and new economic orders established, but the exact direction and extent of reallocation is speculative, and at least short-term problems would occur. Thus, there are economic pluses for arms spending and economic minuses for disarmament without careful, long-range planning.

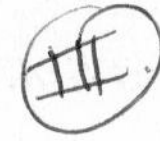

Arms Control—But

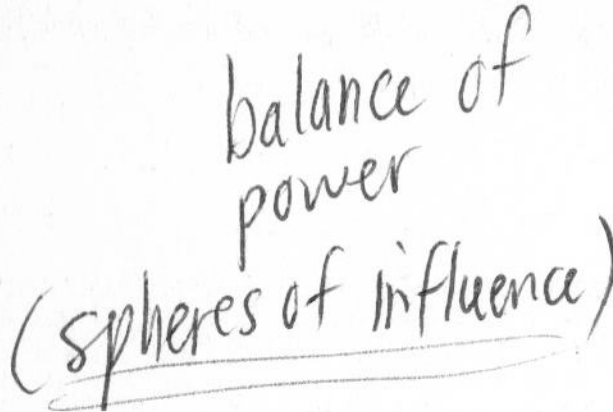

A third argument, and the one most commonly voiced, favors arms control *but* only when a favorable balance of power can be ensured. Too often, that balance is one that favors the side of the beholder. Unfortunately, that equals an unfavorable balance for the other side and gives fuel to the armament argument of its "arms control—but" advocates. It is, then, a catch-22 situation, in which absolute security for one antagonist means absolute insecurity for the other.[11]

Approaches to Controlling Weapons

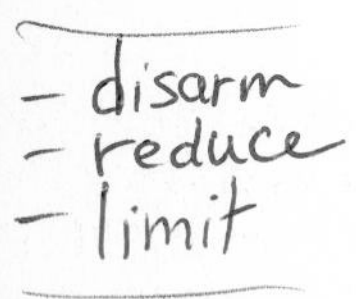

Whatever the actual merits of the arguments for and against arms, the quest for control is virtually as old as weapons themselves. That search has, through history, taken a number of varied approaches to arms control. Roughly proceeding from the most to the least comprehensive, these approaches can be subdivided into efforts to disarm, reduce arsenals of existing weapons, prevent the development/deployment of new weapons, and limit arms transfers. One representation of this range can be seen in Figure 15-3.

Disarmament

The most sweeping approach to arms control is to simply disarm. **General and complete disarmament (GCD)** might be accomplished either through unilateral disarmament or through multilateral negotiated disarmament.

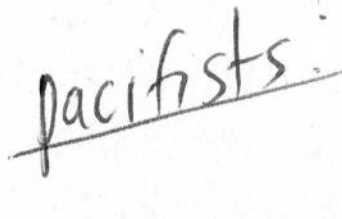

In the case of **unilateral** disarmament, a country would dismantle its arms. Its safety, in theory, would be secured by its nonthreatening posture, which would prevent aggression, and its example, which would lead other countries to disarm also. Unilateral disarmament draws heavily on the idea

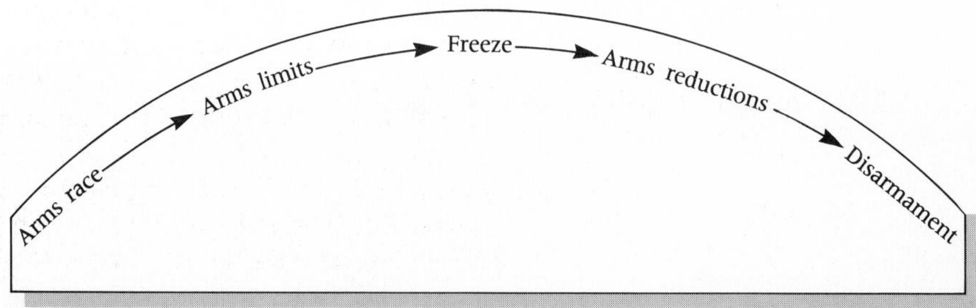

Figure 15-3. Nuclear weapons: The possibilities. *Based on a model provided by Abbott A. Brayton, Assistant Dean and Professor, East Tennessee State University.*

of pacifism, or a moral and absolute refusal to fight.[12] The unilateral alternative also relies on the belief that it is arms that cause tension rather than vice versa.

Multilateral negotiated disarmament is a somewhat more conservative approach. Advocates of this path to peace share the unilateralists' conviction about the danger of war, but they are less likely to be true pacifists, and they believe one-sided disarmament would expose the peace pioneer to unacceptable risk.

The GCD approach has few strong advocates among today's political leaders. Even those who do subscribe to the ideal tend to search for intermediate arms limitation steps. The prestigious Independent Commission on Disarmament and Security Issues, chaired by Sweden's prime minister, Olof Palme, issued a report "strongly support[ing] the goal of general and complete disarmament" but also recognizing "that this objective will not be realized in the near future."[13] Still, the quest goes on. The United Nations' Disarmament Committee has called for GCD, and the "ideal" is often valuable as a standard to measure the unacceptability of the "real."

Arms Reduction

A second approach to arms control is to reduce the number and types of weapons in existing inventories. This alternative is considered at least within the realm of possibility by most political leaders, and it is one of the main thrusts of many contemporary arms control efforts. Advocates of this approach argue that the level of existing arms is so dangerous that the mere limitation of new arms is not enough. It was at least the rhetorical commitment to this view that led President Reagan to relabel U.S./Soviet strategic negotiations as the Strategic Arms Reduction Talks (**START**) instead of Strategic Arms Limitations Talks (SALT). Figure 15-4 shows the initial U.S. START proposal.

Within the general goal of arms reductions, there are a number of differing possible avenues.

Absolute reductions. Reducing the number of existing weapons while building no new weapons is one possibility. There are a few who advocate unilateral arms reductions with the idea that this would not only break the upward arms spiral but would also be a sign of good faith that could start a downward arms reduction spiral. In 1969, for example, President Nixon announced that the United States was renouncing the possible use of biological warfare and unilaterally destroying its bacteriological weapons.

More common are proposals for negotiated reductions. In recent years, the United States, the Soviet Union, and others have all made proposals to reduce the levels of various types of nuclear weapons and conventional forces in Europe. These generally have failed because countries are reluctant to dismantle what exists and because the complexity of arms types and capabilities greatly complicates attempts to equate and count weapons systems.[14]

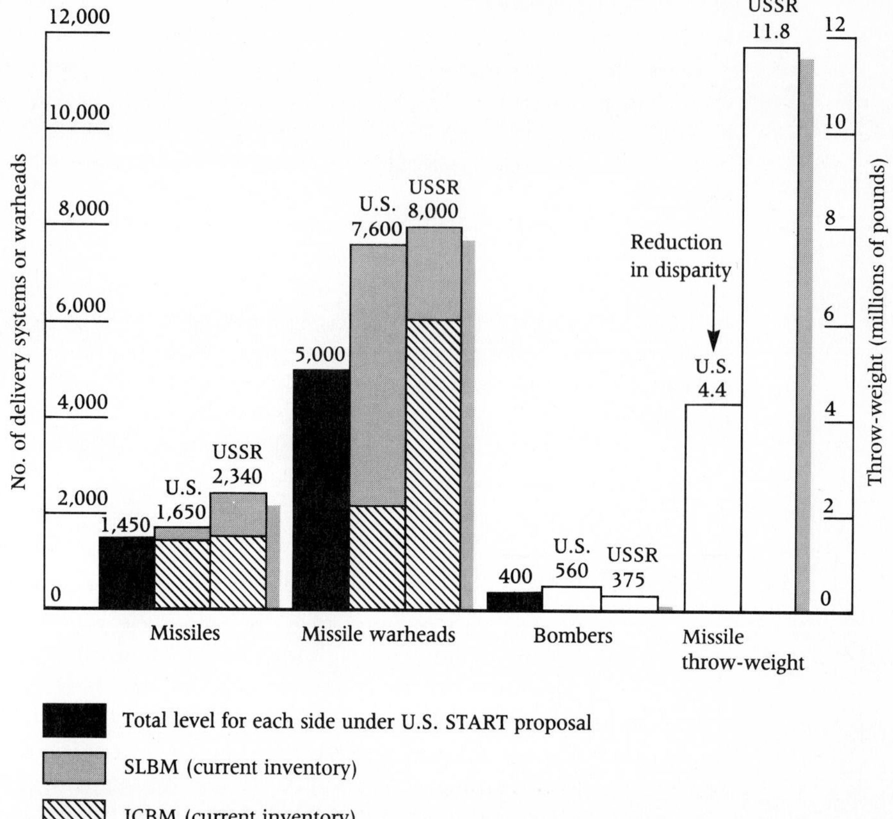

Figure 15-4. U.S. START Proposal and the strategic balance, fall 1984. *Source: U.S. Department of State,* Security and Arms Control: A Search for a More Stable Peace *(September 1984), p. 33.*

Build-down. A variation on absolute reductions proposed by the United States in the early 1980s was based on the **build-down** concept. The basic idea was that, for each new nuclear weapon a country built, it would have to dismantle two or more older weapons. This idea has a great deal of surface attractiveness, but that fades with the realization that many new weapons are more than twice as powerful as old weapons and more accurate as well. Therefore, numbers might decline, but destructiveness would increase.

Geographic reductions. Another variant on arms reduction is scaling down forces in a particular area. There have been proposals, for example, to "denuclearize" Europe completely. There have also been proposals to reduce types of weapons in limited areas, but these too have fallen afoul of fear and of what and how to count as well as the reluctance to give up prestigious weapons.

The handshake and apparent goodwill between the chief arms negotiators of the Soviet Union (left) and the United States (right) marked the beginning of strained disarmament diplomacy at the Geneva START talks in 1985.

Arms Limits

By far the most common approach to arms control is trying to limit development and **deployment** of future weapons systems. The advantage of this approach is that it avoids the difficulties of scrapping existing systems. The disadvantage, of course, is that it leaves an awesomely dangerous stockpile of arms in place. Like reductions, limits are usually attempted through negotiation, but they are also possible through unilateral action. The Soviet Union announced in mid-1984, for instance, that it would not deploy any antisatellite weapons in space as long as other countries similarly restrained themselves. Even conservatives in the Reagan administration have begun to float the idea that it may be possible to pursue arms control through "individual but (where possible) parallel policies"—that is, unilaterally or bi- or multilaterally, on the basis of parallel self-restraint rather than treaty.[15]

The idea of a **nuclear freeze** is one approach to arms limitation that enjoys considerable popular support in the United States, in Western Europe, and elsewhere. At its center, the nuclear-freeze movement advocates an immediate halt to the development, production, transfer, and deployment of all nuclear weapons and delivery systems. Beyond that point, the movement diverges. Some advocate a unilateral U.S. freeze, at least temporarily, as a "confidence-building measure" that will break the arms-race spiral and encourage the Soviets and others to follow suit. Others call for a "mutual and verifiable" freeze that either could be negotiated or could result from parallel policies of restraint by the nuclear powers.

Critics of a nuclear freeze make most of the arguments discussed above under "The Case for Arms." They argue that unilateral restraint would only encourage the Soviets by showing weakness, that it would lock in a claimed Soviet advantage in strategic weapons, and that it would eliminate most of the incentive for more meaningful arms reduction talks.[16]

It is beyond our scope here to evaluate the varying positions on a nuclear freeze. It can be confidently said, though, that the freeze movement, even if it has not achieved its announced goal, has served as a focus for antinuclear activity in the United States and has brought significant pressure to bear on the Reagan administration to pursue a more vigorous arms control effort.

There are a number of possible ways to limit new weapons, including restrictions on research and development, testing, deployment, military spending, and transfers.

Research and development. One way to avoid weapons is to practice a sort of military birth control that would ensure that weapons systems never begin their gestation period of **research and development (R&D).**[17]

The advantage of this approach is that it stops the arms race before it begins. Once R&D begins, there is a pressure on the other side to match it. Moreover, R&D begins an arms acquisition momentum that is hard to stop because the military is reluctant to give up a weapon that is in its inventory even experimentally. There are several U.S. systems, such as the cruise missile, that were begun as a potential "bargaining chip" with the Soviets, but once they were developed, the "stake" in them resulted in their becoming a permanent part of the inventory rather than being bargained away for concessions by the other side.

The difficulty in applying brakes to R&D comes from two hard-to-deny counterarguments. The first is that R&D is not really adding arms but just seeing what is possible. The second, more potent contention is that if R&D funds are not granted, the other side may get a quantum lead and advantage. Thus, R&D is persuasively portrayed as a "modest down payment on the future."

Testing. A second point at which weapons can be restrained is in the testing stage. This is technically part of R&D, but it is the critical stage when a system comes off the drawing board and is actually tried out.

Restraints on testing can be effective, even if R&D has proceeded to that point, because the technological complexity of most modern weapons systems would leave their untested reliability highly questionable. Countries would be prone to keep what they have rather than develop new, destabilizing weapons that are unknowns.

There are, however, numerous problems with and objections to testing limits. These include the arguments that other evaluation methods (such as simulation) could be developed, that **verification** of nontesting is difficult, that testing is needed to keep existing arms up to date, and even that testing can be beneficial, as in developing lower-radiation nuclear devices.[18]

Deployment. The next stage at which arms can be limited is at deployment. This approach would restrict the combat-ready positioning of weapons systems. The 1972 ABM treaty, for one, banned the further deployment of existing U.S. and Soviet antiballistic missiles. Some of the most acrimonious bargaining in recent years was over the unsuccessful Soviet attempts to prevent the deployment of Pershing and cruise missiles in Western Europe and the reciprocal and equally unsuccessful attempts to have the Soviets withdraw some or all of their SS-20s from firing positions in the European areas of the USSR. Limits can also apply to total arms bans in geographic areas, such as Antarctica.

Deployment limitations can additionally be applied to conventional weapons and to the positioning of conventional forces. Restrictions on the deployment of Egyptian and Israeli troops and weapons in the buffer area east of the Suez Canal are one successful recent example.

Although deployment limits can work, their greatest drawback is that they create the potential for dangerous violation. Nuclear missiles are increasingly mobile, and airlift and mechanization capabilities allow rapid redeployment of conventional forces. Thus, should one side choose to rapidly reintroduce its arms into an area, it would create a highly unstable and explosive atmosphere as its alarmed opponents rushed to reposition their defenses to meet the threat.[19]

Numerical limits. By far the most common approach to arms control is to limit the number or capacity of weapons and/or troops that each side may possess. Both **SALT I** and **SALT II** (as seen in Figure 15-5) relied heavily on this approach, looking to cap future expansion rather than to reduce existing levels. The **Mutual Balanced Force Reduction (MBFR) talks** in Europe between NATO and the Warsaw Pact have focused (unsuccessfully) on conventional arms in that region.

The attraction of numerical limits lies in their seeming simplicity. The attempts, however, usually founder over questions of what to count and how to equate different types of systems. Numerical restrictions alone also do not prevent the development and deployment of classes of weapons, and it is relatively simple to escalate numbers at a later date if tensions increase.

Budgetary limits. Another possible approach to arms control would be to control military spending rather than weapons as such. Limiting arms by an international agreement to limit military spending has not been seriously attempted. Its advantage is that it might avoid many existing counting and verification problems by letting each country structure its armed forces subject

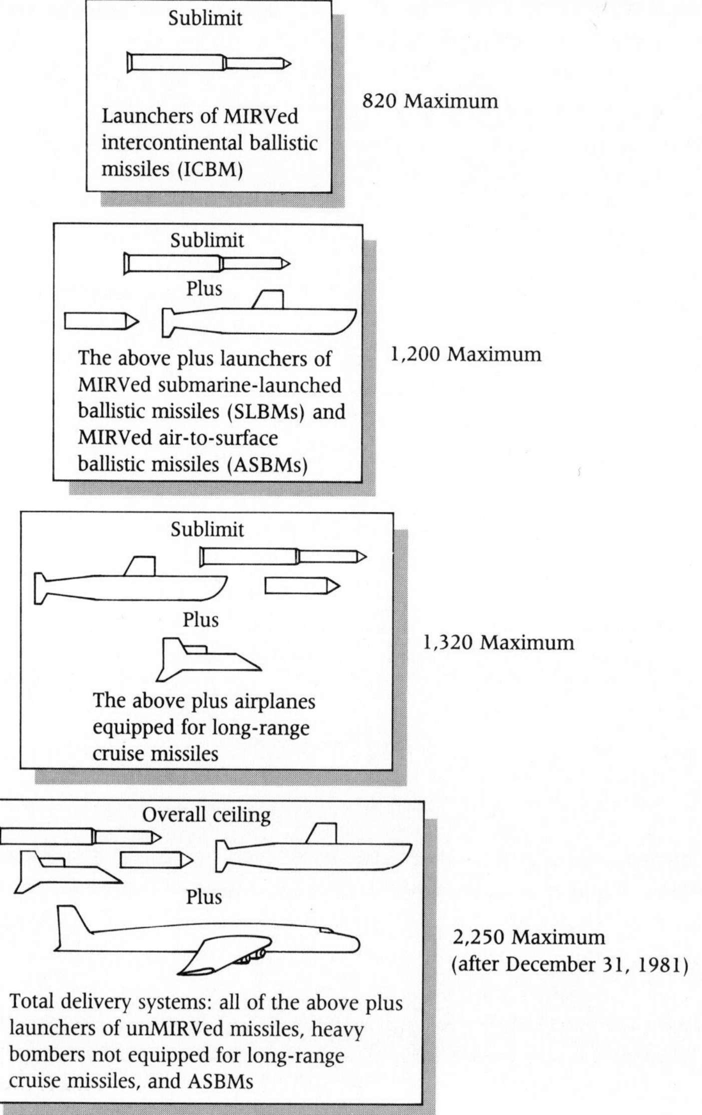

Figure 15-5. SALT II numerical limits. *Source: U.S. Department of State,* SALT II and American Security *(1979).*

only to dollar limitations. Spending might, for example, be limited to a per capita dollar figure or to a percentage of GNP.

There are, of course, substantial problems in determining and equating military budgets, as we saw in Chapter 8. Different formulas would also tend to favor one group or another. A GNP-based formula would, for example, favor rich countries, and a per capita plan might eventually leave China stronger than the United States and the Soviet Union combined. But acceptable combinations, such as per capita or GNP base, whichever is lower, might be found.[20]

Limits on Arms Transfers

Arms control can also be approached from the perspective of limiting or preventing the buying, selling, or giving of weapons or the resources and technology to create weapons.

Nuclear nonproliferation. The term **nonproliferation** commonly refers to the transfer of nuclear weapons, material, or technology from nuclear-capable to nonnuclear countries.

The *dangers* of the spread of nuclear weapons or military-usable nuclear resources (such as plutonium) or technology are manifest. By 1990, if current nuclear production and recycling plans prevail, there will be enough separated plutonium in world commerce to produce 88,000 nuclear weapons.[21] The number of states with the theoretical capability of acquiring nuclear arms is expanding, and that increases the potential of having nuclear states without stable political systems and without elaborate safeguards to prevent the accidental release of an atomic holocaust.

Nuclear proliferation also increases the chance that one state will attack another to prevent its acquisition or expansion of nuclear weapons. The Soviets solicited U.S. views on a possible preemptive attack on China's nuclear facilities in 1969, and in 1981 Israeli jets bombed an Iraqi nuclear reactor to prevent the building of an Arab bomb. Finally, proliferation also enhances the possibility of terrorist use of nuclear weapons, either through the support of a nuclear government or through theft of a weapon.[22]

The *attempt to halt* the spread of nuclear weapons has had some success and has centered on the Non-Proliferation Treaty (1968). Nuclear powers pledged to refrain from transferring "whatsoever nuclear weapons" and agreed that they would not "in any way . . . assist, encourage, or induce any non-nuclear state to manufacture or otherwise acquire nuclear weapons." Nonnuclear countries agreed not to receive or construct nuclear weapons and also to reach agreements with the International Atomic Energy Agency (IAEA) to establish safeguards to ensure that nuclear facilities would be used exclusively for peaceful purposes.

The Non-Proliferation Treaty was an important step forward and has been signed by more than one hundred countries. As such, it serves as an important symbol, and many countries such as Japan and Australia remain nonnuclear despite their capability to achieve the dubious status of member of the atomic club.[23]

Despite these successes, however, the treaty and the world commitment to nonproliferation have their *limits*. In the first place, many countries have not agreed. Pakistan, Israel, Brazil, Argentina, and South Africa are all examples of countries that are nuclear-capable and are nonsignatories.[24] It is widely rumored that Israel and South Africa already have the bomb, and Pakistan makes little secret of its intent to acquire nuclear weapons to "balance" India's capability.

A second limit is that there continues to be a significant level of nuclear material and technology transfer. These transfers are purportedly for peaceful purposes, but IAEA attempts to establish safeguards against military conversion have been only partly successful. For example, over forty nonnuclear signatories have not reached safeguard agreements with the IAEA, in part because such agreements reflect a "limitation on sovereignty."

A third difficulty is that there is heavy political and diplomatic pressure on nuclear supplier countries to transfer resources and technology for peaceful, but convertible, nuclear facilities. Countries that export nuclear resources or technology are supposed to ensure that nuclear-importing countries will not use the transfers for military purposes, but sometimes they do not. Third World countries historically oppose nuclear weapons but view the control of nuclear power by the developed countries as a new attempt to continue a dependency relationship. Consequently, supervision by the IAEA or restrictions set by nuclear exporters are sometimes resented.[25]

There have also been disputes between the United States and its European allies, which construe nonproliferation, in part, as underwriting previous U.S. dominance of the world market in supplying nuclear fuel and power plants. The continuing energy crisis and the urge to be energy-independent are further economic/diplomatic motives to import nuclear capability. Supplying nuclear capability is big business in an economically troubled world.[26] The result is that resources and technology have continued to flow from the nuclear to the nonnuclear world. The sale to Iraq of enriched uranium by France and plutonium-producing technology by Italy led to a 1981 Israeli raid that bombed Iraq's reactor, and in 1984 the United States agreed to sell China nuclear power plants with only oral assurances that they would not be misused for military applications. Thus, the problem of nuclear proliferation continues. The Non-Proliferation Treaty has had some impact, as have the self-interested and altruistic limits set by many potential nuclear importers and exporters. Proliferation does continue, though, and renewed efforts to tighten control on transfers and use, while avoiding a dependency relationship, are necessary if nuclear weapons are not to become as global in their possession as they are in their destructiveness.[27]

Transfers of conventional arms. The international flow of **conventional arms** receives less popular attention than nuclear proliferation, but it also constitutes a serious problem. The reported world arms trade for 1982 was $36.5 billion, or about 2 percent of all world trade. This massive movement of arms increases destructive potential. Iraq's acquisition of sophisticated Exocet missiles, for example, significantly escalated the Persian Gulf War to include attacks on international oil shipping. Arms importing is also a signif-

"What a shame that our weapons get used this way!"

icant financial drain on the LDCs, which account for 82 percent of all arms imports.[28] In just the five years between 1978 and 1982, the LDCs received weapons worth $120 billion that could have been better spent on economic development. Somewhat mitigating that fact, however, is the concentration of 42 percent of all sales and aid in the Middle East. Thus, the economic burden to most LDCs is much less than aggregate figures indicate.

Little is being done about the conventional arms trade, and indeed the prospects for control are even less bright than for nuclear weapons. From the importing countries' perspective, weapons are necessary for real and perceived defense needs and for prestige. From the suppliers' perspective, weapons are a way to win and support friends and are good business besides.[29] There is even some theoretical doubt about the argument that arms transfers lead to increased violence. In fact, one study found that arms transfers actually increase stability.[30]

Whether or not, in a given set of circumstances, arms transfers enhance or detract from stability, and whatever the relative cost to poor countries, the unrestrained arms trade is a problem in need of solution. If, for example, arms transfers could be governed through the United Nations or some other neutral agency, then perhaps legitimate defense needs could be met and, at the same time, the arms acquisition spiral could be checked.

The History of Arms Control

The next issue we need to consider is the state of progress in the field of arms control. If, as we have seen, arms have ill effects; if, as we have also seen, statesmen have almost uniformly condemned the arms race; and if, as is also true, there are a variety of approaches to controlling arms, then we should ask: What have we done about it? The answer is: A little but not nearly enough.

Arms Control before the Nuclear Era

Attempts to control arms and other military systems extend to almost the beginning of written history. In 431 B.C. Sparta and Athens negotiated over the length of the latter's defensive walls, and the Greeks also prohibited incendiary weapons.

In more modern times, the Rush-Bagot Treaty (1817) between the United States and Canada has for over a century and a half secured the world's longest undefended border. Nineteenth-century Europe also saw disarmament calls from figures such as Russia's czar and France's Emperor Napoleon III, but it was not until the Hague conferences (1899, 1907) that the first multilateral arms negotiations took place. Nothing was done at those meetings about general arms levels, but some restrictions were reached on poison gas and other weapons use.

The horror of World War I increased world interest in arms control. The Washington Naval Conference (1921–1922) succeeded in establishing a battleship tonnage ratio among the world's leading naval powers and, for a time, headed off a naval arms race. In 1925 the League of Nations appointed a Preparatory Commission for the Disarmament Conference, which led to the (unsuccessful) World Disarmament Conference (1932). There were also a number of other bi- and multilateral arms negotiations and agreements in the 1920s and 1930s, but they all had little impact in the face of an increasing avalanche of aggression that culminated in World War II.

Recent Arms Control Efforts

The urgency of arms control was spurred by the unparalleled destruction of World War II and illuminated by the atomic flashes that leveled Hiroshima and Nagasaki. The horror of what had just been was thus magnified by the apocalyptic vision of what might be. As early as January 1946, the UN created an Atomic Energy Commission to limit the atom to peaceful use. Later that year, the UN also called for the "general regulation and reduction of armaments and armed forces" and established a Commission for Conventional Armaments.

Accomplishments. Progress during the four decades that followed these initiatives has been slow, but it has occurred. We have, in our earlier discussion, noted several arms treaties, but they bear repeating in Table 15-1, which lists the treaties and pertinent details.

Table 15-1. Arms Control Treaties.

Treaty	*Provisions*	*Date Signed*	*Signatories (as of 1982)*
Geneva Protocol	Bans the use of gas or bacteriological weapons	1925	118
Antarctic Treaty	Internationalizes and demilitarizes the continent	1959	23
Limited Test Ban	Bans nuclear tests in the atmosphere, in outer space, or underwater	1963	126
Outer Space Treaty	Internationalizes and demilitarizes space and the moon and other celestial bodies	1967	112
Latin American Nuclear Free Zone	Bans nuclear weapons from Latin America	1967	25
Non-Proliferation Treaty	Prohibits the transfer, giving, or receiving of nuclear weapons or nuclear materials or technology for other than peaceful purposes	1968	120
Seabed Arms Control	Bans placing nuclear weapons in or under the seabed	1971	100
Biological Weapons Convention	Bans the production and possession of bacteriological and other toxic weapons	1972	126
SALT I	Limited the number and types of U.S. and USSR strategic weapons (expired 1977)	1972	2
ABM Treaty	United States and Soviet Union agreed to limit antiballistic missile sites (two each) and to no further ABM development	1972	2
Threshold Test Ban	Limits underground tests to 150 Kt for United States and Soviet Union	1974	2
Environmental Modification	Bans environmental modification as a form of warfare	1977	50
SALT II	Limits the number and types of USSR and U.S. strategic weapons (not ratified but tacitly observed by both sides)	1979	2
Physical Protection of Nuclear Material	Provides standards for protection of materials during shipment and recovering lost/stolen material	1980	34

Based on U.S. Arms Control and Disarmament Agency, *Arms Control and Disarmament Agreements: Texts and Histories of Negotiations,* 1982 edition (Washington, D.C.: Arms Control and Disarmament Agency, 1982).

Shortcomings. As our discussion has amply indicated, there have been many frustrations and failures for each success in arms control. At the conventional level, the Mutual and Balanced Force Reduction talks in Europe have languished. After real hope in the 1970s, nuclear arms talks fell into almost total disarray in the early 1980s. The SALT II Treaty existed in a sort of twilight zone for several years, unratified yet generally observed by Moscow and Washington. Nuclear relations went even further awry because of the East/West confrontation over the deployment of U.S. missiles in Western Europe and in the face of generally deteriorated relations. In the winter of 1983–1984, the Soviets broke off both the START and the **Intermediate Range Nuclear Force (INF) talks** for over a year. Thus, the lights in the negotiating halls were dark while those in the armament factories continued to burn. In early 1985, the two sides finally again sat down in Geneva, but even the most optimistic were predicting long, arduous negotiations.

Barriers to Arms Control

At this somewhat discouraging juncture we should ask, "Why?" Why can't we achieve arms control? We need it, we say we want it, we negotiate about it, yet the race goes on. Why? There are several answers to that question, and in this section we will examine the barriers to arms control.

National Pride

The Book of Proverbs tells us that "pride goeth before destruction," and that statement is as applicable to the modern arms race as it was in biblical times. Whether we are dealing with conventional or nuclear arms, pride is a primary drive behind their acquisition.

The pride factor, of course, is seldom stated in those terms. Rather, it is discussed in terms of the dangers of being behind an opponent. But you can clearly hear the pride in President Reagan's justifying the massive military buildup as a remedy for the fact that "America had simply ceased to be a leader in the world," but now in response to "a national reawakening of a new sense of responsibility, a new sense of confidence in America," the United States was once again striving "to play its proper role in the world."[31]

The have-nots. For newly independent and/or less developed countries, arms represent a tangible symbol of sovereignty. Often amid poverty, the military can be a flashy, assertive showpiece of a country's "equal" status. In addition to urging the acquisition of planes, tanks, and ships, pride promotes the proliferation of nuclear power. Pakistan's nuclear project, for one, is partly the result of nationalistic and pan-Islamic pride. As one Pakistani official complained, "The Iranians have oil, Indians have . . . the Device [bomb], it's only fair that Pakistan should have at least the bomb," or as another said, "The

Nuclear arms control has been slow and uncertain. But there has been progress. Here Presidents Carter and Brezhnev sign the SALT II Treaty in 1979.

Christian, Jewish, and Hindu civilizations have [the bomb]. . . . Only the Islamic civilization [is] without it."[32]

The haves. Pride also affects countries with substantial conventional and/or nuclear arms inventories. Both the United States and the Soviet Union are prone to project themselves as in second place militarily, and as in the classic slogan of the car rental business, those in second place need to try harder. Further, even though both the Soviets and the Americans profess a willingness to accept "parity," the tendency to overestimate the other's strength plays in with pride to promote a quest for superiority, which is impossible for two opponents to achieve simultaneously.

What to Count

A related equation problem is what to count. A long-standing point of disagreement in Soviet/American arms talks is whether to count the considerable inventory of British and French nuclear arms. The Americans insist that in bilateral talks only American and Soviet weapons are on the table and that the British and French systems are independent. The Soviets assert that American/British/French weapons are part of an alliance system and should be counted as one.

The rise of China's nuclear capability shows signs of further adding to this counting controversy. Inasmuch as the Soviets must devote some weapons to deterring their quasi-hostile neighbor, Moscow is more likely to be concerned with "equal security," while the United States will probably continue to favor equal (U.S./USSR) numbers.

Divergent Approaches

Earlier in this chapter we saw that the arms race is subject to a chicken-and-egg controversy. Which came first, tension or weapons? That same issue plagues arms control. American arms control policy making, for one, has long been divided between those who would reduce arms first and those who would reduce tension first. The Carter administration initially leaned toward the arms-first approach, but the Reagan forces began by believing that meaningful arms talks were impossible with a belligerent Soviet Union. Similarly, the Soviets' withdrawal from all nuclear arms talks in late 1983 through early 1984 was in part prompted by their reaction to the Reagan hard line. In short, the question is, where do you start? Do you try to ease political differences/tensions or do you negotiate weapons reduction? The answer, it would seem, is both.

Complexity of Weapons Systems

A fourth barrier to arms control is the extreme complexity of the weapons systems involved. This is especially true for nuclear weapons. The main problem is how to compare apples and oranges. Technologically, a missile is not just a missile. How, for example, do you compare U.S. missiles, which are less powerful but more accurate, and the Soviets' gargantuan but less sophisticated ICBMs? How can the fact that Soviet ballistic missile submarines are more vulnerable than their U.S. counterparts be factored into a formula to achieve parity? Given the mix of systems, how many bombers equal an ICBM, and how many ICBMs equal a SLBM? These equations have been made even more complex by the Reagan Strategic Defense Initiative (**Star Wars**). If, as the Soviets insist, the (as yet undeveloped) weapons are negotiable, what is their trade-off value?

The point is that simple numbers mean little in arguments, particularly of the nuclear variety. In addition to a vast array of different types of weapons, factors such as quality, capability, capacity, and vulnerability all greatly complicate the equation process. The result is that negotiations are extremely difficult, and agreements are subject to domestic political attack by opponents who mislead the public by pointing out numerical "inequities" without accounting for offsetting technological factors.

Suspicion

As with Og and Ug, doubts about the other side's motives are a prime barrier to arms control. The discussion of perceptions in Chapter 2 pointed out that there is a propensity to see an opponent as more hostile and more directed than we see ourselves. According to this process, any proposal for arms control we make is self-perceived as a genuine effort to achieve peace. An opponent's offer, by contrast, is viewed as a grandstanding attempt to sway world opinion that must be suspiciously examined because it is undoubtedly an attempt to gain an advantage.[33]

Verification

Because of suspicion, justified or not, the problem of verification is yet another hurdle in the arms control race. Monitoring compliance with any arms agreement is important, not only to detect cheating but also as a way to ease tensions caused by suspicion and worry about possible cheating.

As our discussion of spying in Chapter 10 indicated, there have been great advances in the national technical means (NTM) of monitoring weaponry. Yet the progress in NTM capability has been matched and sometimes exceeded by our ability to improve and conceal weapons. Quantity is easier to monitor than quality, and, for example, the introduction of multiple-warhead (MIRV) missiles has made it difficult to keep track of how many warheads an opponent has. The introduction of long-range, small, mobile missiles has also complicated verification. A cruise missile, for one, can be hidden in a barn, a tunnel, or a tractor-trailer truck.

One possible advance in monitoring procedures would be the introduction of on-site "inspections" that would permit neutral inspectors or representatives from the other side to visit military installations and sites of suspected cheating. Unfortunately, such a procedure can be construed as an abridgment of sovereignty or a license for spying, and the Soviets are particularly suspicious of on-site inspection proposals.[34]

Possible Cheating

We can list the potential for cheating as a separate barrier to arms control, although in essence it is a melange of factors relating to suspicion, complexity, and verification. Given our suspicions, the difficulty of verifying what the other side is up to, the complexity of weapons (which makes it difficult to agree on the nature of something that both sides accept as existing), and the stakes if the other side gains an advantage, the issue of cheating is a major obstacle to arms agreements.

Do countries cheat? That question is a major battleground in the mid-1980s as the Soviets and Americans begin a new round of nuclear negotiations. Both sides have accused the other of cheating on SALT II and other treaties, but the supposed violations are less than certain. The United States has claimed, for one, that the Soviets are developing an SS-25 missile in violation of SALT II. The Soviets counter that they are merely modernizing their old SS-13 missiles. For their part, the Soviets denounce Washington for funding ballistic missile defense projects in violation of the Anti-Ballistic Missile (ABM) Treaty. Washington counters that research and development lasers and other electronic-transfer weapons are not covered by the ABM Treaty.

The point is that gross violations of Soviet/American treaties do not seem to have occurred. The complexity of armaments has, however, led to charges that depend on one's point of view, and the difficulties of verification heighten already strong suspicions by both sides.[35]

Domestic Factors

A variety of domestic factors also undermine arms control. *Economically,* arms are big business, and economic interest groups pressure their governments to build and to sell weapons and/or arms-potential technology such as nuclear plants. In America industry has been a prime supporter of the MX missile and stands to lose billions if the project is scrapped, as Table 15-2 indicates.

The armaments industry is also important in the Soviet Union. Nicknamed "the metal eaters," arms manufacturers form a power bloc in Soviet politics, or as one view has it, "The United States *has* a military-industrial complex; the Soviet Union *is* a military-industrial complex."[36]

Additionally, there are often *bureaucratic* elements in alliance with the defense industry. In the Soviet Union, the uncertain process of leadership change gives a strong voice to the military. A leader who has achieved his position with the backing of the military is unlikely to force his benefactors to reduce their arms and budgets.

The military establishment is less influential in the United States, but it is still a powerful force. Because of its connections with economic interest groups, its support in Congress, and its technical expertise, the Pentagon has been able to exert considerable restraint on U.S. arms control efforts.[37]

Table 15-2. MX missile contractors.

Company	*Contract*	*Plants*
Martin Marietta	$380,000,000	Colorado, California
Rockwell	371,000,000	California
Northrop	187,000,000	California, Massachusetts
Morton Thiokol	149,000,000	Utah
Boeing	133,000,000	Washington State
Aerojet Strategic Propulsion	122,000,000	California
GTE Sylvania	110,000,000	Massachusetts
AVCO	108,000,000	Massachusetts, Pennsylvania
Hercules	106,000,000	Utah
TRW	80,000,000	California
Westinghouse	36,000,000	California
Honeywell	22,000,000	Florida

Based on Defense Department sources published in *The New York Times,* December 7, 1982, p. D1.

Finally, in more democratic systems, arms control becomes entangled in the *electoral process.* The positions of policy makers in the executive branch and legislators in Congress are affected not only by what they think but also by the partisan implications of their positions.[38] Particularly because arms control is such a complex subject dealing with such a dangerous issue, advocates from all perspectives are apt to oversimplify and to appeal to popular emotions in a bid to gain support. For its part, the American public has highly divergent views on arms control. The vast majority fear nuclear weapons and favor arms control. Yet, in 1984, 61 percent also agreed that the Soviets "have cheated on just about every treaty . . . they've ever signed," and 58 percent agreed that in past agreements "the Soviets always got the better part of the bargain."[39] These countervailing attitudes make arms negotiations seem almost as dangerous as a nuclear battlefield to elected officials.

Arms Control and the Future

The final question we must ask is "What of the future?" The answer, as with much of international politics, is that the case history is discouraging, the prognosis is guarded, but there are glimmerings of hope.

Among the forces working for arms control is *the chance to limit new technology.* One of the more fruitful areas of arms control has been the effort to limit the spread of weapons. Nonproliferation has had a fair amount of success and is supplemented by geographic nuclear-free zones (such as Latin America). Space is a new frontier, and treaties may be possible to expand current agreements in this area. At this writing, for example, there are beginning moves toward U.S./Soviet talks on banning antisatellite weapons and other aspects of what is called "Star Wars" technology. In short, restricting the proliferation of weapons and the development/deployment of new types of weapons is a more probable area of success than reductions/limits on existing systems.

A second hopeful sign is *domestic pressure.* Mass concern with the possibility of nuclear war has never been higher. The antinuclear movement in Europe has been particularly spurred by the deployment of U.S. Pershing and cruise missiles in NATO countries. There is also a strong movement in the United States, which has recently focused on the nuclear-freeze issue.[40] Such domestic pressures are, of course, of less consequence in nondemocratic political systems, but there are some signs of antinuclear sentiment in East Germany, Rumania, and even the Soviet Union itself. Additionally, the overall budgetary cost of military systems is generating a negative reaction in the United States and elsewhere. Especially in the West, then, but to a degree everywhere, the cost and horror of extensive nuclear and conventional weapons systems may serve as a source of restraint.

International initiatives are a third source of hope in the continuing effort to make progress. Despite periodic breakdowns, arms control talks between the United States and the Soviet Union have become a virtually ongoing process. The norm is now to negotiate. It is easy to be discouraged by what remains to be done, but the achievement of thirteen multilateral and nine bilateral U.S./Soviet agreements in the last two decades is cause for hope.

There is also considerable effort on the multilateral level. The United Nations serves as a focus of effort and information and, in particular, may serve as a potential inspection agency, as the International Atomic Energy Agency now is with respect to the Non-Proliferation Treaty.[41]

In sum, then, there is a need and there are possible solutions. The question is whether we will do enough, soon enough.

Summary

From the point of pure rationality, arms control, or the lack of it, is one of the hardest aspects of international politics to understand. Virtually everyone is against arms; virtually everyone is for arms control; yet there are virtually no restraints on the explosive arms race in which we are all trapped. It is a story that dates back far into our history, but unless progress is made, we may not have a far future to look forward to.

There are many powerful arguments against continuation of the arms race. Arms are very costly, in direct dollars and in indirect impact on the economy. Arms are also very dangerous and add to the tensions that sometimes erupt in violence. There are also arguments in support of arms spending, including their necessity for protection in a dangerous world and their favorable impact on some aspects of the economy.

There are a number of approaches to uni-, bi-, or multilateral arms control, including disarmament, arms reductions, limits on the expansion of arms inventories, and prohibitions against conventional arms transfers and nuclear proliferation. There are also a number of junctures at which arms control can be applied, including the research and development, testing, and deployment stages. It is also possible to apply budgetary limits to arms spending.

For all the possibilities, the history of arms control has not been highly successful. There have been some important successes, though, such as the ban on atmospheric nuclear testing. Despite the widespread agreement that something needs to be done, there are formidable barriers to arms control. National pride is too often associated with the possession of weapons. There are disagreements about how to count weapons and whose weapons to count. The complexity of weapons makes trade-offs between different systems difficult to equate. There are high levels of suspicion of motives, concern about cheating, and doubts that verification methods can adequately monitor agreements. Finally, there are heavy domestic pressures from the military-industrial complex and sometimes from the public against arms control.

For all these barriers, the possible consequences of not reaching arms control makes it imperative that efforts be continued and redoubled. There are also some limited signs for cautious optimism, including the chance to limit new technology, increased public pressure to act, and numerous international initiatives on the issue.

Terms

Build-down—A reduction strategy whereby for each new weapon built, two or more older weapons would have to be destroyed.

Conventional arms—Nonnuclear arms.

Deployment—The actual positioning of weapons systems in a combat-ready status.

General and complete disarmament (GCD)—Total disarmament.

Intermediate Range Nuclear Force (INF) talks—U.S./USSR talks on medium-range missiles such as the Pershing and SS-20; these talks collapsed when the Soviets withdrew in late 1983. Intermediate range nuclear forces are also called Theater Nuclear Forces (TNF).

Mutual Balanced Force Reduction (MBFR) talks—Discussions between NATO and the Warsaw Pact on the reduction of conventional arms in Europe.

Nonproliferation—A prohibition against the transfer of nuclear weapons, material, or technology from nuclear-capable to non-nuclear-capable countries.

Nuclear freeze—A proposal to halt immediately the development, production, transfer, and deployment of nuclear weapons.

Research and development (R&D)—The period in weapon system acquisition (research, design, testing, evaluation) prior to deployment.

SALT I—The Strategic Arms Limitation Treaty signed in 1972.

SALT II—The Strategic Arms Limitation Treaty signed in 1979 but withdrawn by President Carter from the U.S. Senate before ratification in response to the Soviet invasion of Afghanistan.

START—Strategic Arms Reduction Talks; the Reagan administration's designation of strategic arms talks with the Soviets.

Star Wars—The popular name given to the Reagan administration's proposals to develop land- and space-based ballistic missile defense systems. Formally called the Strategic Defense Initiative.

Unilateral—Said of action taken by one side without parallel action by another.

Verification—The process of checking on the other side's arms control compliance.

Notes

1. *Time,* January 2, 1984, p. 37.
2. Speech of March 11, 1985, quoted in *Washington Post,* March 12, 1985.
3. Robert W. DeGrasse, Jr., "The Military: Shortchanging the Economy," *Bulletin of Atomic Scientists* 40 (May 1984): 37.

4. For a review of the defense spending/inflation relationship, see Harvey Starr, Francis Hoole, Jeffrey A. Hart, and John R. Freeman, "The Relationship between Defense Spending and Inflation," *Journal of Conflict Resolution* 28 (1984): 103–122. Also see Frank Blackaby, "Introduction: The Military Sector and the Economy," in *The Structure of the Defense Industry: An International Survey,* ed. Nicole Ball and Milton Leitenberg (New York: St. Martin's Press, 1983), pp. 9–10.
5. Gavin Kennedy, *The Economics of Defense* (Totowa, N.J.: Rowman and Littlefield, 1975), pp. 184–192.
6. Starr et al., "Relationship," pp. 118–120.
7. For a recent study that finds little evidence of the arms-race model, see Miroslav Nincic, "Fluctuations in Soviet Defense Spending," *Journal of Conflict Resolution* 27 (1983): 648–660. For a general review, see James E. Dougherty and Robert L. Pfaltzgraff, Jr., *Contending Theories of International Relations,* 2nd ed. (New York: Harper & Row, 1981), pp. 333–338.
8. Lloyd Jensen, *Explaining Foreign Policy* (Englewood Cliffs, N.J.: Prentice-Hall, 1982), pp. 240–242; Dougherty and Pfaltzgraff, *Contending Theories,* pp. 335–336.
9. Hans Morgenthau, *Politics among Nations,* 5th ed. (New York: Knopf, 1973), p. 398.
10. Michael Intriligator and Dagobert L. Brito, "Arms Races Lead to the Outbreak of War," *Journal of Conflict Resolution* 28 (1984): 63–84.
11. For an example, see Seymour Weiss, "The Case against Arms Control," *Commentary* 78 (November 1984): 19–23.
12. For an exposition of this view, see Thomas Merton, *The Nonviolent Alternative* (New York: Farrar, Straus, Giroux, 1980). Also see Philip Towle, *Arms Control and East-West Relations* (London: Croon-Helms, 1983), pp. 9–21.
13. Independent Commission on Disarmament and Security Issues, *Common Security: A Blueprint for Survival* (New York: Simon & Schuster, 1982), p. 139.
14. On the problem in nuclear arms, see Richard Burt, "Reducing Strategic Arms at SALT: How Difficult, How Important?," in *Arms Control and Military Force,* ed. Christoph Bertram, published for the International Institute for Strategic Studies (Montclair, N.J.: Allanheld, Osmun, & Co., 1980), pp. 113–123. On the problems of conventional force reduction in Europe, see Robin Ranger, *Arms and Politics, 1958–1978* (Toronto, Ontario: Macmillan, 1979), pp. 193–197; and Robert A. Gasset, "Force Reductions and the Security of Europe," in *Arms Control and the Defense Posture of the 1980s,* ed. Richard Burt (Boulder, Colo.: Westview Press, 1982), pp. 39–58.
15. See Kenneth L. Adelman, "Arms Control with and without Agreements," *Foreign Affairs* 63 (Winter 1984/85): 259.
16. Kevin N. Lewis, "Negotiating a Nuclear Freeze," *Strategic Review* 12 (1984): 29–35. For an advocate, see Robert Drinan, *Beyond the Nuclear Freeze* (New York: Seabury Press, 1983); an opponent's view is in Richard Burt, "Implications of a Nuclear Freeze," *Department of State Bulletin* 83 (June 1983): 28–30. The Soviet view is in S. Korshunov, "Arms Freeze: For and Against," *International Affairs* (Moscow), March 1984, pp. 120–127.
17. This section relies considerably on J. I. Coffey, "New Approaches to Arms Control in Europe" in Bertram, *Arms Control and Military Force,* pp. 14–16.
18. See Martin B. Einhorn, Gordon L. Kane, and Miroslav Nincic, "Strategic Arms Control through Test Constraints," *International Security,* 8 (1984): 114–119; and Peter C. Hughes and William Schneider, Jr., "Banning Nuclear Testing," in Burt,

Arms Control, pp. 21–38. Despite these objections, it is true, as Einhorn and associates point out (p. 151), that test constraints are a "major step . . . toward reasserting control over technological dynamics which have tended by their own imperatives to determine strategic and political options."

19. Coffey, "New Approaches," pp. 21–23.
20. Ibid., pp. 11–14. Also see Abraham Becker, *Military Expenditure Limitations for Arms Control,* a Rand Corporation study (Cambridge, Mass.: Ballinger, 1977).
21. Paul Leventhal, "Getting Serious about Proliferation," *Bulletin of Atomic Scientists* 40 (March 1984): 8.
22. For the possibilities and dangers of proliferation, see Lewis A. Dunn, *Controlling the Bomb* (New Haven, Conn.: Yale University Press, 1982), pp. 44–94.
23. A general overview of the Non-Proliferation Treaty is in Stockholm International Peace Research Institute, *The NPT: The Main Political Barrier to Nuclear Weapons Proliferation* (New York: Crane, Russak, 1980).
24. India, France, and China are the nuclear-armed countries that have not signed the Non-Proliferation Treaty.
25. Fergus Carr, "The View from the Third World," in *Nuclear Proliferation in the 1980s,* ed. William H. Kincade and Christoph Bertram (New York: St. Martin's Press, 1982). Also see Olga Sukovic, "Non-Proliferation and Developing Countries," in *The Arms Race in the 1980s,* ed. David Carlton and Carlo Schaerf (New York: St. Martin's Press, 1982), pp. 219–230.
26. On trade, see William Waler and Mans Lonnroth, "Proliferation and Nuclear Trade," *Bulletin of Atomic Scientists* 40 (April 1984): 29–33. Also see Pierre Lellouche, "The Dilemmas of Non-Proliferation Policy: The Supplier Countries," in Carlton and Schaerf, *The Arms Race,* pp. 175–204.
27. For suggestions, see Dunn, *Controlling the Bomb,* pp. 95–148.
28. U.S. Arms Control and Disarmament Agency, *World Military Expenditures and Arms Transfers, 1972–1982* (April 1984).
29. For a skeptical view of limits, see Richard Betts, "Arms Trade Control," in Burt, *Arms Control,* pp. 109–141.
30. See discussion in Jensen, *Foreign Policy,* p. 179. For the view that arms increase conflict, see National Policy Panel on Conventional Arms Control, *Controlling the Conventional Arms Race* (New York: United Nations Association, 1976).
31. Speech to American Legion, February 22, 1983 in U.S. Department of State, *Realism, Strength, Negotiation: Key Foreign Policy Statements of the Reagan Administration* (Washington, D.C.: U.S. Government Printing Office, May 1984), p. 2–3.
32. Quoted in Dunn, *Controlling the Bomb,* pp. 45 and 44. The reference to Jewish civilization pertains to Israel's almost certain possession of nuclear weapons.
33. For example, see Michael Nacht, "The Bad, the Dull, and the Empty: Multilateral Arms Control and the Soviet Union," in *Arms Control: The Multilateral Alternatives,* ed. Edward C. Luck (New York: New York University Press, 1983), pp. 97–112.
34. Stephen M. Meyer, "Verification and Risk in Arms Control," *International Security* 8 (Spring 1984): 111–126. Also see David Hafemeister, "Advances in Verification Technology," *Bulletin of Atomic Scientists* 41 (January 1985): 35–40.
35. For contrasting views on the cheating issue, see Colin S. Gray, "Moscow Is Cheating," pp. 141–152; and Michael Krepor, "Both Sides Are Hedging," pp. 153–172; both in *Foreign Policy* 56 (Fall 1984). Also see Thomas K. Longstreth, "Report Aims to Sabotage Arms Control," *Bulletin of Atomic Scientists* 41 (January 1985): 29–34. For a brief journalistic review, see *Time,* December 3, 1984, pp. 19–21.

36. For a look at the defense industry in a variety of countries, see Ball and Leitenberg, *Structure of the Defense Industry.*
37. Steven E. Miller, "Politics over Promise: Domestic Impediments to Arms Control," *International Security* 8 (Spring 1984): 79–84. Also see William L. Hyland, "Institutional Impediments," in Burt, *Arms Control,* pp. 97–108; and Paul A. C. Koistinen, *The Military-Industrial Complex: A Historical Perspective* (New York: Praeger, 1980). A good popular account of bureaucratic infighting can be found in *Time,* December 5, 1983, pp. 18–37.
38. Miller, "Politics over Promise," pp. 84–88.
39. Daniel Yankelovich and John Doble, "The Public Mood: Nuclear Weapons and the U.S.S.R.," *Foreign Affairs* 63 (1984): 41–42.
40. For a good review of freeze proposals and pros and cons, see U.S. Congress, Senate Committee on Foreign Relations, *Nuclear Arms Reduction Proposals,* Hearings, 97th Cong., 2nd sess. (1982).
41. William Epstein and Alfonzo Garcia Robles, "U.N. Disarmament Campaign," *Bulletin of Atomic Scientists* 40 (March 1984): 37–39.

16

Economic, Social, and Environmental Issues and Responses

The sun with one eye vieweth all the world.
Shakespeare, King Henry VI

In this, the fourth and final section of our text, we have been examining the forces of world cooperation that address global problems. The topics we have covered so far are international law, international organizations, and arms control. Additionally, in the preceding three chapters and, indeed, in many sections of the book, we have touched on the economic, social, and environmental issues that face the world. This final chapter will review briefly the related problems we face in these areas and assess the cooperative international efforts to address these issues. As we shall see, economic, social, and environmental concerns are closely interrelated, and, to a substantial degree, progress or lack of it in one area advances or retards progress in the others. Therefore, in a sense, this chapter's division of these topics is a pedagogical device.

The interrelationship among economic, social, and environmental issues also means that our discussion of some of the institutions that promote and practice international cooperation is necessarily fragmented. Keep in mind, though, that these organizations are wholes and that they treat the social and economic problems as they are—as parts of an interrelated whole. Among the many institutions mentioned in this chapter, keep two in particular focus. They both represent important efforts in the area of comprehensive international integration. One, the *United Nations,* already discussed at some length in Chapter 13, is active globally on the entire range of issues that face the world.

The other step along the path toward integration is the *European Communities* of Western Europe. This important regional effort has achieved a high level of integration, primarily on economic issues such as trade and monetary regulation but also on social and political issues. Among its other institutions, it has an executive authority, a judicial branch, and the world's first popularly elected international parliament. It is not yet a "United States of Europe," but there are many who hope the integration will culminate in such a union, and there are signs that their goal may someday be realized.

To Care or Not to Care

Before proceeding on our survey of international cooperation, it is important to answer the question: Why should we care about or do anything to assist the poor, malnourished, illiterate, and medically uncared-for peoples of the world?

The Case for Doing Nothing

There are those who argue that attempts to go to the aid of all the less developed countries (LDCs) of the world are both *futile* and *beyond our responsibility.* The American diplomat and scholar George Kennan, for instance, has written with respect to food shortages and overpopulation that "we in the United States did not create the problem . . . and it is far beyond our power to solve it."[1]

" GIVE ME YOUR RICH, YOUR FAMOUS, YOUR NOBEL LAUREATES, YOUR RUSSIAN POETS AND POLISH EMISSARIES, YOUR RESPECTABLE WHITE ANTI-SOVIETS YEARNING TO BREATHE FREE...... "

Another, and even stronger, set of arguments against aiding the poor is based on the contention that such aid is counterproductive and even dangerous. Some see aid as *counterproductive* because they claim it increases, rather than eases, the problem. If, for example, you provide food and medicine to the already overpopulated LDCs, you only encourage more childbearing, decrease infant mortality, and increase longevity. All these effects only serve to worsen overcrowding.

The idea that aid is actually *dangerous* is even more emotionally powerful. To make this case, a **lifeboat ethic** analogy is often used. The world, it is argued, is a lifeboat that can support only so many passengers. The industrialized countries are in the boat. The billions of poor are in the sea, in peril of drowning and clamoring to get in. The dilemma is that the lifeboat is incapable of supporting everyone. If everyone gets in, the lifeboat will sink, and all will perish. The answer, then, is to sail off with a sad but resolute sigh, saving the few at the expense of the many in the interest of common sense.[2]

The Case for Selective Assistance

The lifeboat ethic is a stark choice, and its advocacy is too stressful for all but a few. Still, its rationale is appealing to some, and it has led to a "middle ground," sometimes called *social triage.* This phrase is an analogy to the medical term triage, the practice of dividing patients into three categories: (1) those whose illnesses/injuries are so minor that they will recover without medical assistance, (2) those who are seriously ill/injured but who can recover with medical aid, and (3) those who are so seriously ill/injured that they will die despite best medical efforts.

Good medical triage practice calls for concentrating on the second group, and that idea can be applied to international economic and social policy as well. The idea here is that the industrialized countries should identify those LDCs that are the strongest but still need assistance and aid them while not wasting resources trying to falsely and dangerously support and encourage the terminally poor.[3]

The Case for a World Effort

A third approach to the world's economic and social problems is to cooperate in an attempt to address all the issues in all areas of the globe. Those who make this case put forth a number of arguments in favor of their position or in criticism of the lifeboat/triage mentality.

Humanitarianism. A first argument is that we have a responsibility to our fellow human beings. This, of course, is a matter of philosophy and cannot be "proved" empirically, but each reader should ask himself or herself the question: What is my obligation as a human? The pope, for one, has strongly joined those who argue that we all indeed ought to be our brothers' keepers. John Paul II recalled, in September, 1984, the Gospel of Matthew, in which Christ said, "As you did it to one of the least of these my brethren, you did it to me." Christ, the pontiff told a throng of 150,000, "is speaking of what today we . . . call the North/South contrast," and, like Christ, the pope warned, "the poor South will judge the rich North." Whether one is Catholic or not, John Paul's is a powerful admonition.

Violence avoidance. A second argument is that, as we have seen, the poor are becoming increasingly hostile toward the wealthy. The poor are also potential nuclear powers, and the prospect of embittered, atomic LDCs is a strong reason to act to ease the causes of despair.

Spaceship Earth. It can also be argued that we are not in (or out of) a lifeboat but, rather, we are all on a spaceship, **Spaceship Earth**, and our fates are all inseparably intertwined. The growth of population is not just a problem of the poor. Instead, the resource depletion and ecological damage caused by a 5 billion and growing population threaten the future of all people.

Faulty analysis. Those who favor a global effort also attack the analysis of the lifeboat/triage advocates. Globalists point out that population can be controlled, that development is possible for all people, and that wealth can be shared without destroying the prosperity of the haves. It will hardly mean poverty, for instance, if Americans increase aid by the amount they spend on wine, beer, and liquor. We will, in the course of this chapter, further examine several of these analytical disputes.[4]

Globalists also point out that we partly misidentify the problem. For example, is the problem lack of food, or is it overconsumption by some? Are there too few natural resources, or are the existing stocks being squandered by the resource-rapacious North? In short, are the problems we face caused by the poverty and population of the South or the dietary and industrial gluttony of the North? Globalists would stress the latter.

Economic Issues and Cooperation

In Chapters 11 and 12 we saw that there are many difficult *economic issues* on the contemporary international scene. Not only is there the basic division and tension between the developed North and the less developed South, there are also intra-North and intra-South issues in areas such as trade and monetary relations.

Further, as this study has stressed, there is an increasing degree of world economic interdependency. Trade dependency makes a country like Zaire very important to the United States. Monetary ties mean that an economic crisis in Poland or Argentina can create severe economic tremors in Western financial institutions because of the loans made to those countries and the possibility of their default. In short, then, the world has become economically intertwined in many ways, and the problems of one country or area often have widespread international impact.

Economics is an important basis of international power, and countries continue to use their economic muscle to promote their self-interest. That self-interest, though, and a degree of altruism have led to increased *international cooperation* to achieve economic stability and prosperity. These cooperative efforts can be roughly divided among those that center on trade, those that are involved with international monetary institutions, and those aimed at multilateral development. There are also a number of comprehensive efforts, which we will examine first, that span all three dimensions of international economic cooperation.

International Comprehensive Cooperative Efforts

A number of developing and established organizations and interactions address the scope of international economic issues.

The United Nations

The UN serves as an umbrella organization for economic issues through the General Assembly and the United Nations Economic and Social Council. The **United Nations Conference on Trade and Development (UNCTAD)** was founded in 1964 to address the economic concerns of the LDCs. It and the LDCs' "Group of 77" have become a focus of demands for the New International Economic Order. The actual programs of UNCTAD have been limited, but it has served as a forum of interaction between North and South and as a vehicle for highlighting the needs of the South.[5]

Intra-North Cooperation

A primary focus of cooperation among noncommunist industrialized countries (Western Europe, Japan, United States) is the twenty-member Organization for Economic Cooperation and Development (OECD). The OECD is involved in a wide variety of North economic issues and also, through its Development Assistance Committee, in extending aid to LDCs.

Economic Summitry

A relatively recent development in economic cooperation is the periodic meetings of heads of state to discuss economic issues. Beginning in 1975, the leaders of the United States, Japan, Germany, France, Britain, Italy, and Canada have met annually.[6] There has also been, as noted in Chapter 12, summit interaction between North and South leaders at the Cancún Conference. It is as yet unclear whether this will evolve into a regular process, but there will be pressure to do so.

Regional Comprehensive Cooperation

There are several multipurpose regional economic organizations.

The European Communities (EC). By far the most extensive cooperation and the most highly integrated regional effort can be found in Western Europe. The **European Communities (EC)** has evolved through several stages since World War II. As it stands, it represents the best hope for those who believe in international integration. The European Communities is the overarching organization that was formed by the linking in 1967 of the previously existing European Coal and Steel Community (ECSC, founded 1952), the European Atomic Energy Community (EURATOM, 1958), and the **European Economic Community** (**EEC**, 1958), or Common Market. Each of these three organizations continues to maintain a distinct legal identity, but their activities are increasingly coordinated through the policy-making and judicial institutions of the European Communities (a now somewhat misleading plural, which perhaps would be better thought of in the singular, *Community*).[7]

As a developing integrated unit, the EC is a major international actor, at least economically. With Spain and Portugal as new members, the EC population will rise from 270 to 320 million. Its GNP will equal $2.5 trillion, larger than that of the United States and twice that of Japan. The EC's percentage of world trade will be approximately 34 percent, almost triple that of the United States. The EC, in short, is an economic Goliath.

The EC's *organizational structure* is extremely complex, and its full exploration is beyond our needs here. A brief look, however, is important in order to illustrate what sort of international integration is possible. Figure 16-1 gives a brief overview of that structure. The elements of the EC include a council, which reflects the views of the member states, and a commission, which is meant to reflect the interests of the EC as a whole. Legislatively, there is the 410-member European Parliament. Not only is it popularly elected, but its

The 1985 summit meeting among the leaders of the Western industrial powers is one example of the need for and attempts at consulting and cooperating economically.

political parties form across national lines; for example, socialist representatives from each country unite to form a transnational socialist party within the parliament. There are also judicial elements, including the Court of Justice, which hears disputes that arise under the treaties that established the EC and its constituent units, and a Court of Auditors, which examines EC budgets. There are also a number of consultive, advisory, and other subsidiary EC institutions such as the Economic and Social Committee and the European Investment Bank.

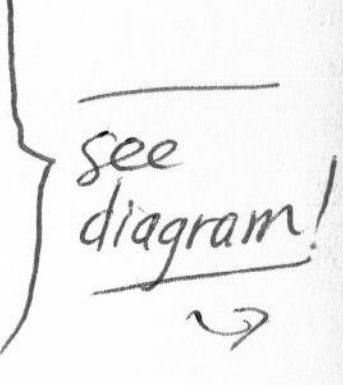

In terms of *policy,* the EC has been most successful at integrating economic activity. Trade relations, both within the EC and externally, are governed by EC policy. The EC has moved toward eliminating nearly all trade barriers between members, and it negotiates unified trade relations between its members and other governments. It has also made great progress toward establishing a Common Agricultural Policy (CAP) in areas such as commodity supports, pricing, and health and standards regulations. For all the progress, however, agriculture remains an often touchy issue within the EC. In 1984, for example, the EC finally resolved a five-year-old dispute over England's resentment because of its level of contributions to the $24 billion EC budget (1984). Agriculture subsidies account for two thirds of that budget but primarily benefit French and German farmers. The EC is also active in industrial coordination and encouragement. It has also achieved a substantial degree of monetary synchronization through the European Monetary System (EMS), although a common European currency does not yet exist.

The trend toward integration through the EC has been least successful in the *political* arena. National rivalries still exist, and a recent poll shows remark-

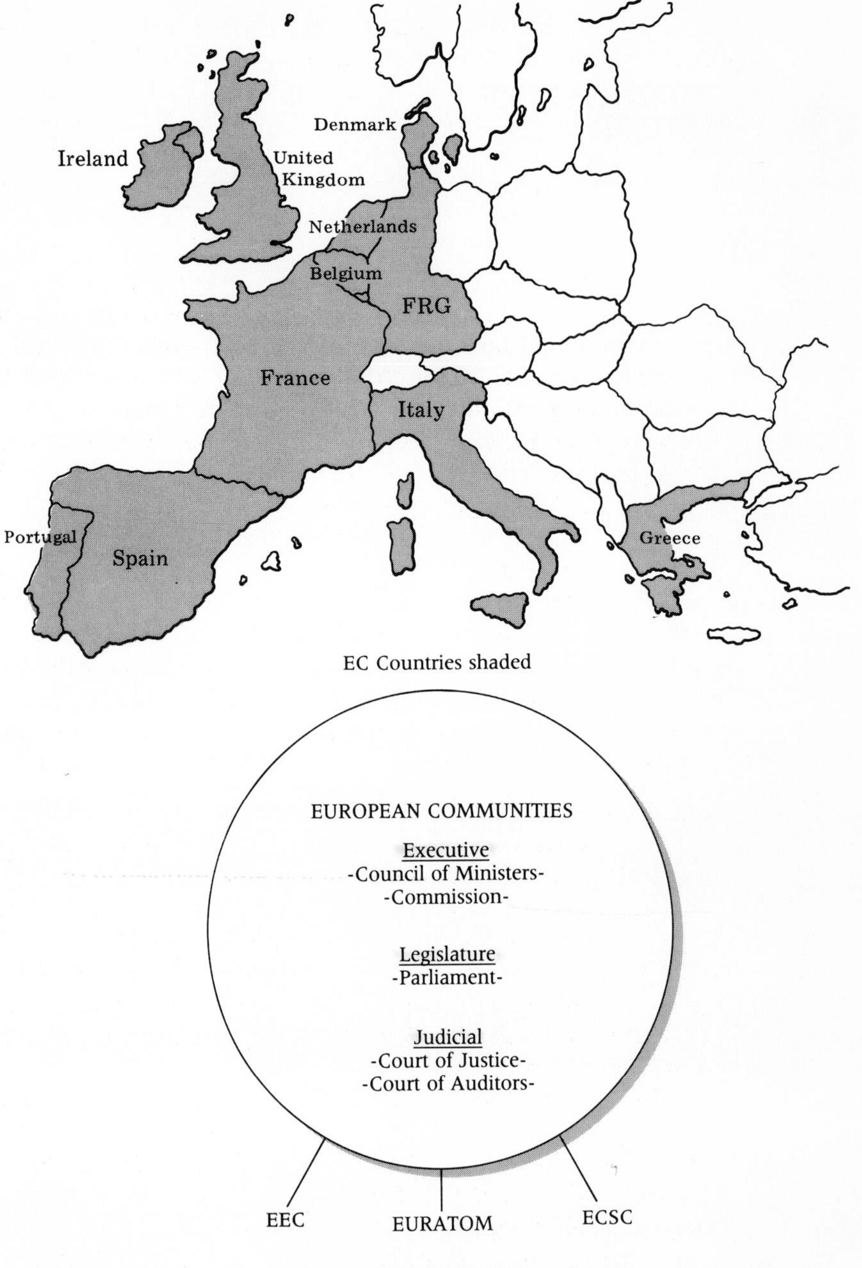

MEMBER COUNTRIES (Year of Entry)

France (1967)
Germany (1967)
Netherlands (1967)
Belgium (1967)
Luxembourg (1967)

Italy (1967)
Denmark (1973)
Great Britain (1973)
Ireland (1973)

Greece (1981)
Spain (1986)
Portugal (1986)

Figure 16-1. Membership and organizational structure of the European Communities.

ably different European attitudes on economic and other nationalistic issues.[8] Most Europeans favor closer economic ties. Of those with an opinion, 54 percent favored ending remaining trade barriers, 63 percent favored a uniform social welfare, and 59 percent favored the free migration of labor within the EC.

More mixed results were found on whether Europeans thought that integration would benefit their children. Nearly four times (39 percent) as many answered yes as no (10 percent), but over half (51 percent) were not sure. Further, 45 percent thought their members of the European Parliament should primarily protect national interests, while 42 percent thought the parliament members should take the view of the EC overall. A hopeful note was that people in the newer EC countries (e.g., Great Britain) were much more nationalistic on the question, while in the original six a majority of respondents were integrationists. Finally, on some issues, nationalism still held strong sway. Only 25 percent wanted a single EC ambassador to replace the individual countries' diplomats in Washington and Moscow, and 75 percent rejected the idea of a single EC Olympic team at the 1984 games.

Thus, the dream that some have of a fully integrated Europe remains, at best, on the far horizon. Yet the distance that remains to go should in no way detract from the progress that has occurred. It is a testament that the EC has survived and advanced despite great difficulties, occasional crises, and persistent tensions. A great deal has been integrated, and even where it has not, Western Europe is, in the words of one analyst, "in the process of permanent consultation on everything."[9] The bottom line is that the EC exists.

Other regional economic organizations. The *Council for Mutual Economic Assistance* (CMEA) is the Soviet bloc's answer to the EEC.[10] The CMEA is primarily a trade organization, but it is also involved in some aspects of intrabloc monetary and resource policy. In recent years the CMEA has been strained by a number of issues. Soviet dominance has not been able to quiet Eastern European economic nationalism and resentment over hikes in Soviet oil prices and other policies designed to cut Eastern Europe's drain on the Soviet economy. Thus, troubled economic times are straining the ideal of socialist economic solidarity.[11]

The *Council of Arab Economic Unity* is a pan-Arab economic organization that includes the Arab Common Market and the Arab Monetary Fund. Its effectiveness has been limited by the strife in the Middle East. The *Economic Commission for Africa*, with fifty-two members, was established in 1958. It has helped establish organizations involved in banking, trade, resource utilization, and other economic areas, but a lack of resources and African turmoil have limited its development.

Trade Cooperation

The most common form of economic cooperation involves agreements and organizations to regulate trade.

World trade. On a global level, the **General Agreement on Tariffs and Trade (GATT)** was founded in 1947 to promote free trade. Its initial membership of twenty-three has expanded to well over one hundred. The association of the Soviet Union with GATT in 1983 as an observer marked an important step toward expansion of GATT's influence.[12] Recent world economic difficulties have caused a resurgence of protectionist sentiment, as reviewed in Chapter 11, and GATT's progress has been slowed, but it continues to represent a successful effort to reduce tariffs and expand trade.

Regional trade. There are also a substantial number of regional trade organizations working to promote cooperation in their areas (see Table 16-1). The impact of these organizations has been mixed, but at the least, they are important symbols of the attempt to achieve trade cooperation.

Commodities agreements. A final form of economic cooperation is a commodity agreement, or cartel. This form of cooperation among suppliers was discussed in Chapter 12. We can briefly note, however, that attempts to regulate production and prices have had some stabilizing effect, though not on the scale of the OPEC effort.

Monetary Institutions

Another growing area of international cooperation is the regulation of currency exchanges. As trade and the level of other international financial transactions have increased, the need to facilitate and stabilize the flow of dollars, marks, yen, pounds, and other currencies has become vital. To meet that need, a number of organizations have been founded. The most important of these is the **International Monetary Fund (IMF).**

The International Monetary Fund. The IMF began operations in 1947, has 146 members, and receives its funds from member contributions and also from internal sources such as interest on loans to borrowing countries. The primary role of the IMF is to stabilize currency by granting loans to countries

Table 16-1. Regional trade organizations.

Name	*Founded*	*Membership*
Andean Group	1969	5
Association of South East Asian Nations	1967	5
Caribbean Community and Common Market	1973	12
Central American Common Market	1961	5
Economic Community of West African States	1975	15
European Free Trade Association	1960	6 non-EEC, W. Europe
Latin American Free Trade Association	1960	11
West African Economic Community	1972	8

Note: The EEC, CMEA, and Arab Common Market are discussed in the text.

that are experiencing balance-of-payments difficulties because of trade deficits, heavy loan payments, or other factors.

The extension of credit by the IMF to financially distressed countries is an important function. It allows them to meet their obligations and helps stabilize the exchange rate of their currency. In recent years the IMF has especially concentrated on loans to LDCs. At the end of fiscal year 1982–83, the IMF had an extended credit line of $25 billion, of which countries actually borrowed $10.3 billion.[13]

Although the IMF has played a valuable role, it has not been above criticism. Indeed, in recent years, the IMF has been one focus of struggle between the North and South. That discord stems from two facts. First, voting on the IMF board of directors is based on the level of each member's contribution to the fund's resources. That formula gives the United States nearly 20 percent of the vote, with Britain, France, Germany, and Japan each in the 4–6 percent range. Along with Saudi Arabia (3.28 percent), these countries command nearly half the votes in the IMF.[14] This apportionment has led to Third World charges that the fund is controlled by the North and is used as a tool to dominate the LDCs.

The second criticism of the IMF is that it interferes in LDCs' domestic affairs. About 60 percent of the loans granted by the IMF are subject to strict conditions requiring that the borrowing country take steps to remedy the situations that caused its balance-of-payments deficit. On the surface, the policy of requiring sound economic reform sounds prudent, but in reality it has its drawbacks. First, LDCs charge that it interferes in their sovereign domestic processes. Second, the required reforms, such as drastic budget cutting, may be politically unpopular or even impossible and may lead to political instability or even to the overthrow of the embattled government.[15] The answers, as with most things political, are not easy, and it is likely that the IMF will continue to be criticized by some in the North for "bailing out fiscally irresponsible" poor countries and by some in the South for being a vehicle of continued "Euro-American domination of the Third World."[16]

Other monetary institutions. Although the IMF is the most important international monetary institution, there are several others that make contributions. On a global scale, there is the *Bank for International Settlements* (BIS), with twenty-nine (mostly European) members. The BIS is primarily a meeting ground for its members' central banks, and it is involved in exchange rates, lending practices, and other factors that affect the Eurocurrencies. Finally, there are a number of regional monetary policies and institutions such as the European Monetary System and the Arab Monetary Fund, which have been discussed as part of their umbrella organizations.

International Development Cooperation

A last type of multilateral economic cooperation is in the area of granting loans and aid for the economic development of LDCs.

The International Bank for Reconstruction and Development. The IBRD, or **World Bank**, is the most significant development agency today. The bank began operations in 1946 and has over 140 members. It is associated with, but independent of, the United Nations.

The World Bank is involved in making international loans for development. Its resources come from members' contributions and from interest earned on loans. In fiscal year 1983, the IBRD made 129 loans, totaling nearly $12 billion, to forty-three countries. Interest rates on loans vary, depending on the borrower's financial ability and other factors, and averaged about 8.2 percent in 1984. In that year, the bank also instituted variable interest rates, which fluctuate according to world inflation.

The International Development Association. The IDA is technically a separate institution but in fact is a subsidiary of the World Bank. It was created in 1960 and has a separate pool of funds drawn from member contributions. It has 131 members, and it focuses on making loans, usually at virtually no interest, to the poorest countries. In fiscal year 1984 the IDA extended $3.6 billion in credit to forty-three countries.[17]

Like the IMF, the IBRD and IDA, as a collective, do a great deal of good, but they have also become a focus of struggle between the North and South. The first problem, as with the IMF, is the voting formula on the boards of executive directors. In 1984 the United States had 19.4 percent of the IBRD and 19.6 percent of the IDA vote. Germany, Japan, Britain, and France collectively accounted for an additional 23.3 percent of the IBRD and 25.1 percent of the IDA vote. These proportions lead to charges of inequity by the LDCs.

The terms of the loans are a second source of contention between North and South. The World Bank is caught between many in the North who want to concentrate on "businesslike," interest-bearing loans and the South's demands that more loans be unconditionally granted to the poorest countries at low or no interest.[18]

A third difficulty for the World Bank has been the desire of contributors to gain political mileage from their foreign aid. This has led some to argue that bilateral loans and aid can be better directed at friendly countries and that bilateralism more closely identifies the donor country as a benefactor. There have also been grumblings about loans to communist countries, dictatorships, and other regimes disliked by one or another of the World Bank's main backers. In short, there are attempts to politicize the supposedly nonpolitical bank.[19]

The International Finance Corporation. The IFC was established in 1957, has 124 members, and is a semi-independent affiliate of the World Bank. The IFC makes loans to LDCs to promote private-sector development, whereas the IBRD and IDA make loans for public projects. In fiscal year 1984 the IFC approved $595 million in loans to enterprises in thiry-five countries. The IFC, more than other multilateral banks, has been favorably received in the United States because of its capitalism-promoting lending policies.[20]

United Nations agencies. In addition to the World Bank affiliates, a number of UN agencies are involved in development programs. The largest is the *United Nations Development Program*, formed in 1966 to provide technical assistance to LDCs' development projects. In recent years UNDP has been under severe financial strain, with, in 1982, donor pledges of $272.5 million, equal to only about half of its need for project commitment.[21]

Regional development agencies. Finally, there are a number of regional development institutions (Table 16-2). These vary greatly in funding and success, the Inter-American Bank being the largest and most active. The advantage of the regional banks is that they are governed by the region's countries, often the LDCs, and are not dominated by the Euro-American complex. The disadvantage is that they have scarce resources. In 1980, for example, the African Development Bank was able to loan only $200 million despite its region's tremendous needs.[22]

Economic Cooperation: A Summary

We began by noting that economic affairs are a vital part of the international power structure and that economic policy is largely conducted according to short-term self-interest. That once was the whole story, but things are changing. As we have just seen, there are a variety of organizations, almost all created in the last few decades, designed to promote international economic cooperation. It is easy to be impatient with their slow progress, but that is inappropriate negativism. They are a break with the totally self-interested past. They have made important contributions already, and they are a start on what is possible. In short, like all the cooperative efforts we are reviewing in these concluding chapters, they should be viewed as progress.

Social Issues and Cooperation

Another set of pressing problems for the world community involves the human condition. These issues are, in part, economic in nature and are being addressed by the international economic cooperation efforts just discussed. There are

Table 16-2. Regional banks.

Name	*Founded*	*Members*
African Development Bank	1964	51
Asian Development Bank	1966	29
Caribbean Development Bank	1969	11
Inter-American Development Bank	1960	42

also, however, specific efforts to deal with such concerns as population, living conditions, and human rights.

Population

Identifying the population problem is simple: there are too many of us and we are reproducing too quickly. There are now almost 5 billion people in the world.

Think of that for a moment! Five billion—

5,000,000,000!!!

At least given current economic conditions, we are finding it difficult to feed that population and to provide for its other needs without depleting our resources and polluting our environment.

Further, the population continues to expand at an unacceptable rate. It took all of human history, to 1830, for the population to reach 1 billion. Now we are adding about a billion people every decade, as shown in Table 16-3. Even given a recent easing of the world birthrate, we will have over 6 billion people by 2000 and over 11 billion by 2100.[23]

Causes of the Population Problem

Fewer deaths. There are a variety of reasons for the rapidly expanding population. One is fewer deaths. There is *lower infant mortality.* Medical advances mean that fewer babies die. In addition, there is increased *longevity.* People live longer. These two factors combine to mean that even in areas where the birthrate declines, the population growth rate sometimes continues to accelerate. Africa's birthrate declined from 48.3 births per 1,000 population in 1960–1965 to 46.7 in 1980–1985. Yet the annual population growth increased from 2.44 percent (1960–1965) to 3.01 percent (1980–1985).[24]

Poverty. There is a frequently heard argument that overpopulation causes poverty. The seemingly reasonable logic is that with too many people, especially in already poor countries, there are fewer resources, jobs, and other forms of wealth to go around. Logical on the surface as that argument may sound, it is not true in a strict sense. More accurately, and to the contrary, it is poverty that causes overpopulation. The least developed countries tend to

Table 16-3. World population increase.

Year Span	*Population*	*Time Factor (Years)*
to 1830	1,000,000,000	Several thousand
1830–1930	2,000,000,000	100
1930–1960	3,000,000,000	30
1960–1975	4,000,000,000	15
1975–1985	5,000,000,000	10

What will life be like if the world population continues to expand at its current rate?

have the most labor-intensive economies, which means that children are economically valuable because they help their parents farm and/or, somewhat later, provide cheap labor in mining and manufacturing processes. Thus a nonindustrial economy encourages population growth. Between 1960 and 1976, as an illustration, the population growth rate in most of the world's most highly technological societies was between 0 and 0.9 percent. The growth rate in the least technological countries was between 2 and 2.9 percent.[25]

Cultural attitudes. In many societies, cultural attitudes have come to reflect economic utility. Having a large family is an asset in terms of societal standing and is also a "major emotional counterweight to the tedium of a bleak struggle to keep alive."[26]

The International Response to the Population Problem

If we reject the implied lifeboat argument that we ought to let more poor children die in infancy and allow impoverished adults to die in their forties and fifties, then it is necessary to address the birthrate as the method for controlling population.

The move to deal with population through international cooperation is relatively recent. Its growth is symbolized, however, by the 1984 World Population Conference in Mexico City, attended by representatives from 160 countries.

Social solutions. One set of solutions to the population increase involves social approaches to birthrate reduction. These include providing information, encouragement, and devices for birth control. Many of these efforts must come through national governments and other domestic agencies. There are, however, various forms of international assistance, either through bilateral aid or through multilateral efforts such as the United Nations Fund for Population Activities.

A related effort is to improve the status of women, because women who are more fully and equally employed have fewer children. This effort is, again, just beginning but is symbolized by the Voluntary Fund for the United Nations Decade for Women and the 1982 Convention on the Elimination of All Forms of Discrimination against Women.[27]

Economic solutions. The evidence that poverty causes population means that the prime effort must go into easing the poverty gap both between countries and within countries. Thus, efforts must be made to develop the Third World and to equalize income distribution within countries, as discussed in the first part of this chapter, if population is to be controlled.

Food

The question of food is closely related to population, and as the population grows, the adequacy of the food supply becomes an increasingly critical issue.

There are two basic food problems. One is the *short-term food supply.* Regional shortages are responsible for real human suffering. Hunger—indeed, starvation—is most common in Africa, where more than thirty-five countries face what one official termed a "catastrophic shortage of food." In addition to the tens of thousands who have died, agriculture insufficiency has a host of negative economic impacts that range from sapping the vigor of the population to consuming development funds for food relief.

Second, the *long-term adequacy of the food supply* is also a significant concern. A combination of population control and agricultural development is necessary to ensure that the world's appetite does not outstrip its agriculture. Failure to meet human needs will mean a protracted world food crisis, carrying with it the potential for political instability.

Causes of Food Problems

Underproduction. One cause of hunger is the inability of production to keep up with population in many areas of the world. Advances in mechanization, fertilization, plant and animal disease control, and other techniques are offset by declines in acreage, by agricultural food disruption due to urbanization, by ecological damage, and by other factors. The result is that Third World per capita food production is barely expanding (from its poverty base) and constantly hangs on the edge of calamity.[28]

Overconsumption. A second cause of hunger is the maldistribution of food. There is, in the world, sufficient food and agricultural capacity to meet needs. Resources and consumption, however, are concentrated in a relatively few countries. In the last thirty years, agricultural production has increased three times as fast in the North as in the South. In the developed world, daily food consumption averaged a waist-expanding 3,440 calories a day, 50 percent more than in the LDCs. Nutritional content represents an even greater gap, with protein deficiency particularly common among the poor. Finally, and ironically, the United States actually pays farmers to keep land out of production while starvation stalks the children of Africa and elsewhere.

The International Response to Food Problems

Numerous international efforts are underway. Some deal with food aid to meet immediate needs, while others are dedicated to increasing future agricultural productivity.

Food aid. Donations of food to areas with food shortages are a short-term necessity to alleviate malnutrition. The bulk of food aid has been bilateral, the United States' *Food for Peace* (or Public Law 480) program being the world's largest effort. In its more than thirty-year history, P.L. 480 has distributed more than $30 billion in food and agricultural assistance, and its current annual budget is in the $1 billion range.[29]

There are also a number of multilateral food aid efforts. The UN's *World Food Program* is the largest. It distributes food to needy nations and includes the International Emergency Food Reserve, which maintains a reserve food stock targeted at 500,000 tons.

Agricultural assistance development. The development of agricultural techniques and capability, especially in the LDCs, is crucial if there is any hope of future self-sufficiency. On a bilateral basis, many countries' aid programs include development aid.

There is also a multilateral effort. The oldest agency is the *United Nations Food and Agriculture Organization* (FAO), which was founded in 1945 as part of the UN and which has 147 members. It distributes approximately $150 million annually in food aid and technical assistance. The FAO has been subject to criticism for a variety of its policies, including putting too much emphasis on short-term food aid and not enough effort into long-range agricultural reform. That, in addition to the growing recognition of the food problem, has led to the establishment of several other global food efforts.[30]

A key event in these efforts was the 1974 World Food Conference held in Rome. That meeting established the *World Food Council* (WFC). The WFC coordinates food efforts in the UN system and is composed of thirty-six members nominated by and responsible to the Economic and Social Council (ECOSOC).

A second organization to arise from the 1974 Rome convention is the *International Fund for Agricultural Development* (IFAD). This organization began operations in 1977 and has been heavily supported by OPEC, which donated 43 percent of the IFAD's initial three-year, $1 billion capitalization. The IFAD is particularly dedicated to agricultural development projects in the poorest LDCs.

These efforts are supplemented by the Consultive Group on Food Production and Investment and the Consultive Group for International Agricultural Research, which are UN-associated organizations involved in various donor, investment, and research efforts in agriculture. Finally, there are a variety of regional and specialized organizations that address agricultural issues.[31]

Food and Future Cooperation

Like most of the cooperative efforts we are reviewing, the global response to hunger and the need for agricultural development has just begun and is small relative to the problem. Yet aid for famine relief and for development does flow in the billions of dollars. Further, the various organizations serve as major clearinghouses for information on problems and possibilities. Finally, these organizations and their efforts are a start. Progress has been unsteady, but the only reasonable direction is forward, and the world has begun down that path.

Quality of Life

Food and water are the basis of life, but there are many other factors that contribute to the quality of life. Here, too, there is great disparity in regional conditions, and there are also global efforts to upgrade the human condition.

Health. The state of medical care, sanitation, and other medical conditions is, in some areas, below a level imaginable by most readers of this book. The international response to that need is coordinated by the *World Health Organization* (WHO). The 156-member UN consultive organization is involved in a wide range of medical, pharmaceutical, and sanitation efforts. It also serves as a focal point for the gathering and dissemination of information.

The efforts of WHO and other agencies are reflected in decreases in infant mortality and increases in longevity. Perhaps even more dramatically, the value of the international health effort is reflected in the crusade against smallpox. That scourge, which had plagued humankind throughout history, stood at over 131,000 annual cases in 1967. In that year WHO began a ten-year campaign to eradicate the disease, and by 1977 the world smallpox incidence was confined to one case in Somalia. There has been no recurrence, and smallpox will kill no more, as a direct result of international cooperation.

Education. Promotion of education remains primarily a national function, but there are a number of small international efforts. In the UN, the United Nations Educational, Scientific, and Cultural Organization (UNESCO) sponsors several programs. Many IGOs and NGOs are also involved in education. Literacy is slowly becoming the norm rather than the exception in the world,

Food aid is helping to ease, but not eradicate, world malnutrition and starvation.

and in 1976 it stood at nearly 60 percent in the LDCs. That leaves approximately a billion adults illiterate worldwide—a continuing impediment to personal and economic development.[32]

Welfare. There are also a variety of efforts to meet the needs of distressed groups. The Office of the United Nations High Commissioner for Refugees, which won a Nobel Peace Prize in 1981, spends about $500 million annually attending to the needs of populations displaced by war and political turmoil. It is assisted by some 200 private agencies.[33] The International Labor Organization seeks to improve world working conditions, the United Nations Children's Fund (UNICEF) is concerned with child welfare, and there are UN programs devoted to migratory workers, the disabled, the aged, women, and other disadvantaged groups.

Human Rights

A final area of international social concern is human rights. This was discussed extensively in our chapters on ideology and morality and international law, but it is appropriate to review some of the problems and cooperative efforts here.

Rights that most Americans, Canadians, Western Europeans, and others would consider routine are equally routinely denied to a substantial part of the world's population. Various classes of citizens are discriminated against because of race, religion, ethnicity, sex, or some other inborn characteristic. Political torture is commonplace, and free speech, assembly, and movement are regularly denied. In short, conscious violations of human rights by some is a major source of deprivation and suffering for many. Although widespread abuses continue to occur, the international atmosphere that once tolerated such practice has begun to be increasingly a source of criticism and even action.

The United Nations. The UN is the main focus of global human-rights activity.[34] The basis for UN concern is the organization's charter, which touches on human rights in seven places. More specific is the *Universal Declaration of Human Rights,* adopted by the General Assembly in 1948. This document of thirty articles proclaimed as a "common standard" an array of rights "for all peoples and all nations."[35]

To further extend these rights, two multilateral treaties, the *International Covenant on Civil and Political Rights* and the *International Covenant on Economic, Social and Cultural Rights,* were put forth by the UN for ratification in 1966 and, as of 1984, had been agreed to by seventy-five and seventy-seven states (not including the United States), respectively. In addition, there are nineteen other UN-sponsored covenants governing genocide, racial discrimination, women's rights, slavery, refugees, and stateless persons. Organizationally, these agreements and human rights in general are monitored (with debatable effectiveness) by the UN Commission on Human Rights, and there are current efforts to draft documents setting standards for the treatment of children, migrant workers, and prisoners.

Regional human-rights efforts. There are also a number of regional conventions and organizations that supplement the principles and efforts put forth by the UN. The most well developed of these are in Western Europe and include two covenants and the European Court of Human Rights as well as a Commission on Human Rights.[36]

The least progressive area is Asia, which has neither a regional covenant nor an organization. The Soviet bloc countries are also without their own standards. They are judged, however, according to the 1975 *Helsinki Agreements.* This was signed by thirty-five countries, including the Eastern European states, and expresses the intention of all signatories to respect human rights. The Helsinki Agreements and subsequent meetings of the signatories have provided an excuse for Western leaders to criticize the Soviets and arguably have encouraged the Poles and other dissidents.

Nongovernmental organizations. Additionally, there are a substantial number of NGOs concerned with human rights. Some of them, such as Amnesty International and the Red Cross, were discussed in earlier chapters. These groups work independently and in cooperation with the UN and regional organizations to further human rights, and they add to the swelling of information about and criticisms of abuses.[37]

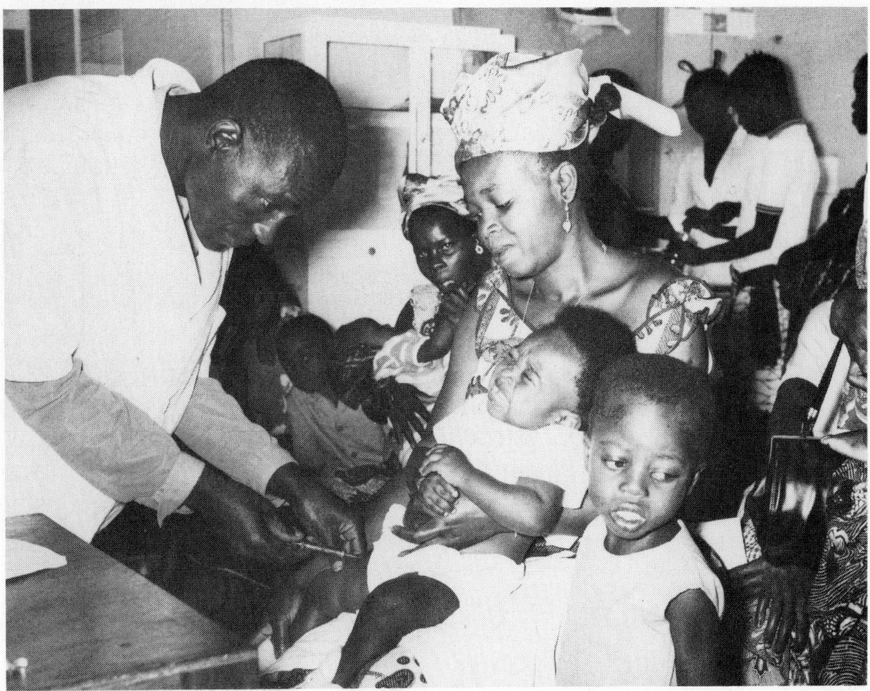

This World Health Organization-sponsored doctor working in Zaire is part of the effort to make life liveable in the less developed countries.

Impact of human-rights activity. Earlier, in our chapter on ideology and morality, we saw that there has been a gratifying growth in human-rights consciousness and conscience. Modern communications and changing attitudes have made abuses more visible and less accepted. The enforcement of human rights is still largely blocked by the stricture of sovereignty, but that is slowly being eroded. Under pressure, partly international, white Rhodesians turned power over to black Zimbabweans. The white South Africans still resist, but a few concessions have been made. Western leaders now ask their Soviet counterparts about political prisoners, who are now imprisoned, put in mental institutions, or exiled rather than shot. Progress is slow, many still suffer, but it is better than before.

Resources and Environment

Throughout history, humans have treated their world as a "given." It is there, it will always be there. It will yield the necessities of life, and it will absorb what is discarded. For several millennia that disregard proved justifiable. The earth was generally able to sustain its population and replenish itself.

The exploding human population, with its spiraling appetite for resources, has changed that. Not only are there five times as many people as there were a century and a half ago, but their technological "progress" has multiplied their per capita resource consumption and their per capita waste and pollutant production. The result is that the world faces the potential of no longer being able to sustain its population acceptably, or, to put it as an equation:

Exploding population	×	Spiraling per capita resource consumption	×	Proliferating waste and pollutant production	=	Potential catastrophe

Resources

There have long been warnings that the earth's resource bounty was not limitless, but amid seeming plenty, they were voices in the wilderness. The energy crisis of the 1970s, our obsession with oil, and our realization that petroleum was being rapidly depleted elevated resource conservation from a concern for dilettante do-gooders to the front of national and international policy concern.

The Cries of Alarm

Recent decades have witnessed a large number of warnings that we are using our resources too quickly. More than any other single document, these concerns are symbolized in the 1972 study *The Limits to Growth*, published by the Club of Rome.[38] That study concluded that if the world system continued on its path of exponential population growth and exponential resource depletion, collapse would be the inevitable outcome.

Since that time, studies by individual analysts, governmental commissions, and private organizations such as the Club of Rome or World Watch have uniformly concluded that the rate of resource consumption is a matter of serious concern.[39] It should be noted that not all these studies are as dire in their predictions as *Limits to Growth*, and as we shall see, some are even optimistic.[40] Almost all, however, express at least moderate concern about oil, other minerals, fisheries, and water.

Energy. The heaviest resource drain is on energy sources, including oil, natural gas, coal, and wood. Table 16-4 shows the 1975 and projected 1990 energy use of these sources (except wood) and of alternative, renewable energy supplies.

Projections of future use are tricky, as, in some cases, are estimates of future reserves, but if assumptions are anywhere near correct, then most energy resources are threatened. Oil, at 1981 consumption rates, may be exhausted by the year 2014. Natural gas supplies may be depleted at about the same time. Coal is a bright spot. Current reserves will last over 200 years, and potentially recoverable coal will last until the year 3600.[41]

Table 16-4. Global energy use.

	1975		1990		1975–1990
	10^{15} Btu[a]	Percentage of Total	10^{15} Btu	Percentage of Total	Percentage of Increase
Oil	113	46	179	58	58
Coal	68	28	77	20	13
Natural gas	14	19	66	17	43
Nuclear/ hydro	19	8	62	16	262

[a]That is, quadrillions of British thermal units.

Source: Council on Environmental Quality and Department of State, *The Global 2000 Report to the President*, vol. 1 (Washington, D.C.: U.S. Government Printing Office, 1980), table 10, p. 31.

Coal, however, is a major pollutant if not controlled. Further, if it is required to supply greater percentages of energy, it will be depleted more rapidly. If, for instance, coal had to shoulder the entire 1990 world energy demand of 384 quadrillion Btu, then known reserves would be depleted in about forty years.

Wood is a special concern with energy, environmental, and economic impacts. Over 1 billion people still depend mainly on wood as an energy source. Wood cutting is leading to widespread deforestation, with replanting efforts at only about 10 percent of maintenance level. In addition to a projected 25 percent wood shortfall by the 1990s, deforestation has a number of negative environmental consequences, including soil erosion, the silting up of rivers, canals, and dams, and a loss of the conversion of carbon dioxide to oxygen by trees, which means both lower air quality and rising ambient temperatures.[42] The wood shortage also has an adverse economic impact on LDCs. Not only are prices high, consuming 35–40 percent of a poor family's income in some African cities, but even where it can be cut, wood is so scarce that in some regions each family must spend from 250 to 360 workdays per year simply gathering wood.[43]

Other minerals. There is also considerable pressure on other minerals, many of which are important to a modern, industrial society. Table 16-5 shows the life expectancy of selected minerals at a static and at a projected increasing demand.

Water. "Water, water, everywhere, nor any drop to drink," cries Coleridge's Ancient Mariner, and his plight may foreshadow the shortages of the future. The seemingly simplest and most abundant of resources, water, is coming under increasing pressure. A 200–300 percent increase in water use is expected between 1975 and 2000. As a result, water will be in scarce supply in most of Europe, Asia, and Africa and in a substantial part of the United States, as shown in Figure 16-2.

Table 16-5. Mineral life expectancy.

Mineral	*Percentage of Reserve Used Annually*	*Percentage Projected Demand Growth*	*Year of Depletion, Static Demand*	*Year of Depletion, Projected Demand*
Silver	5.5	2.33	1996	1993
Zinc	3.9	3.05	2002	1995
Mercury	4.6	0.50	1998	1997
Sulfur	2.9	3.16	2010	1999
Lead	2.7	3.14	2013	2001
Tin	2.3	2.05	2017	2007
Copper	1.6	2.94	2049	2012
Nickel	1.1	2.13	2062	2039

Based on figures in Council on Environmental Quality and Department of State, *The Global 2000 Report to the President,* vol. 1 (Washington, D.C.: U.S. Government Printing Office, 1980), table 8, p. 29.

Fisheries. Although fish are a food and might have been included in our coverage of that topic earlier, they are not generally "raised" and, thus, are more properly a resource. In any case, many more are being eaten than are being spawned. The world fish catch of 70 million metric tons in 1970 was enough to supply 27 percent of the protein requirement of the world's population then. The supply, however, is static, and the population will nearly double between 1970 and 2000, meaning that fish will contribute only 14 percent of world protein requirements. Growing demand and static supply are producing heavy pressure to expand fishing operations beyond the ability of the fisheries to replenish themselves.

The world resource picture, then, is not particularly bright. Many resources (e.g., minerals) are not renewable, and even those that are (forests, fish) are being used faster than they can reproduce. Many analysts have reacted to these projections with alarm. They see the potential for human suffering caused by economic deprivation. They predict an increase in international violence as countries clash over scarce resources. Still other analysts predict or even advocate the end of democracy as authoritarian regimes are required to control the resource-hungry masses.[44]

Calls for Calm

There are other analysts, however, who do not share this doomsaying view. Instead, they argue that we will be able to meet our needs and continue to grow economically through conservation, population restraints, and, most important, technological innovation. This upbeat view has earned this group the sobriquet *"technological optimists."* The optimists argue that potential shortages can be met by technological advances. New technology can find and develop oil fields. Synthetics can replace natural resources. Fertilizers, hybrid seeds, and mechanization can increase acreage yields. Desalinization and weath-

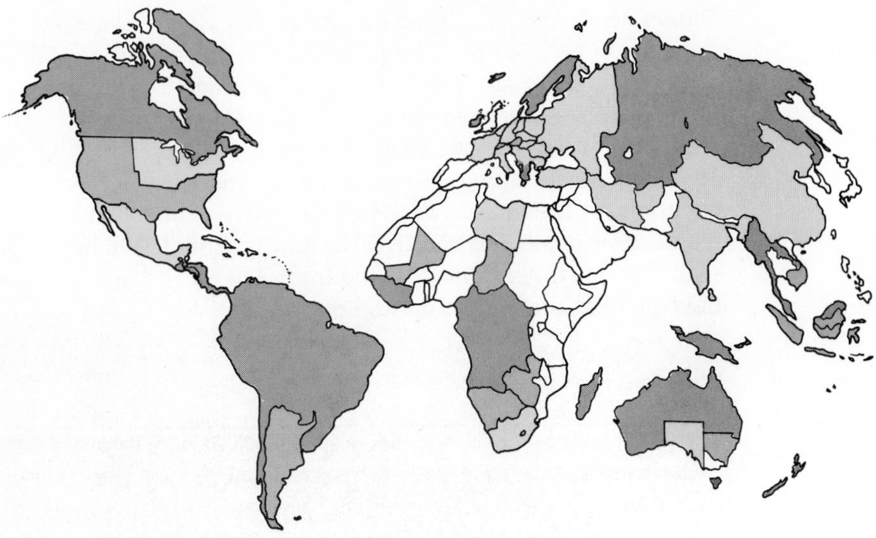

Thousands of cubic meters of water per person per year

High (more than 10) | Low (5-1)

Medium (10-5) | Very low (1 or less)

Figure 16-2. Projected per capita water availability, 2000. *Source: Council on Environmental Quality and Department of State,* The Global 2000 Report to the President, *vol. 1 (Washington, D.C.: U.S. Government Printing Office, 1980), figure 7, p. 25.*

er control can meet water demands. Energy can be drawn from nuclear, solar, thermal, wind, and hydro sources. In short, as one study concluded, "The real limits to growth, rather than being scientific and technological, are political, social and managerial. They can, with effort and good will, be overcome."[45]

Resource Scarcity: The International Response

Which view, optimist or pessimist, is correct? The answer is probably some of both, but there can be little doubt that major efforts are needed for the development of new technologies while also encouraging conservation and planned parenthood.

Yet, international cooperation in the resource area is only slowly developing. One level of activity is the collection and distribution of *information* by private organizations, such as the Club of Rome and World Watch, by individual governments, as in the *Global 2000 Report,* and by international organizations, such as the UN's Committee on Development and Utilization of New and Renewable Resources.

There are also organizations of resource suppliers and users that have information and also may be involved in *pricing and production planning*. OPEC is one example, as is the industrialized countries' counterpart, the International Energy Agency. Also in the energy area, the International Atomic Energy Association helps provide information for the peaceful use of nuclear power.

Finally, there are a few efforts at *regulation and rational development.* An International Seabed Authority (ISA) is in its early formation stages under the Law of the Sea Convention, discussed in Chapter 14. The ISA will (try to) regulate seabed mining. Fishery conservation is carried on mostly by coastal countries, at least partly in their own interest, but there has been a start on multilateral regulation through the International Whaling Commission and such regional organizations as the Inter-American Tuna Commission and the International Pacific Halibut Commission.

Environment

The state of the world's biosphere is closely related to many of the economic and resource issues we have been examining. Like the concerns over those issues, international awareness and activity are relatively recent and are still in the early organizational stages.

Environmental Concerns

Books have been written on the threats that exist to the environment, and it is tempting to emphasize the potential disasters that lurk in the not-too-distant future. In the interest of brevity, however, simply consider the following.

Desertification. More of the world's surface is becoming desertlike because of water scarcity, timber cutting, overgrazing, overplanting and because crop and animal wastes that ordinarily recycle nutrients into the soil are now being burned as energy sources. The desertification of land is increasing at an estimated rate of 30,600 square miles a year, an area the size of Austria. During the last fifty years, approximately 400,000 square miles of once-agricultural land has become barren desert.[46]

Ocean pollution. There is mounting pollution of the world's oceans, with some areas, such as the Baltic Sea, Black Sea, and Mediterranean Sea, in special danger. Pollutants come from a variety of sources such as synthetic chemicals, metallic compounds, and the escape or dumping of radioactive fission products and waste, but the greatest damage is being done by petroleum spills and other forms of release. In 1973 over 6 million metric tons of petroleum hydrocarbons entered the ocean from a variety of sources.[47] Precautions have helped stem that black tide from some sources, but others have increased. Tanker incidents doubled (to seventy) between 1973 and 1980, and the volume of oil spilled rose 800 percent (to 800,000 metric tons) during that period.[48]

Fresh-water pollution. Pollution of lakes and rivers is moving from a domestic to an international question. In addition to lakes and rivers which form international boundaries (the Great Lakes, the Rio Grande) or which flow between countries (the Rhine River), fresh-water pollution occurs from

Every year an area of the world equivalent in size to Austria becomes desert because of environmental abuse.

acid rain and other contaminants that drift across borders. Polluted domestic rivers also carry their discharges to the sea. Finally, water (and air) pollution is often the result of activity carried on by multinational corporations in LDCs. In short, domestic pollution is often an unwelcome immigrant.

Air and atmosphere pollution. The air we breathe is also becoming polluted in part by the drift of pollution across international borders. Higher in our atmosphere, carbon dioxide concentrations are up 15 percent in this century and are increasing by 2 percent a year. This increase will affect precipitation patterns and also raise world temperatures. Even a one-degree centigrade increase will mean the warmest weather in a thousand years, and a few more degrees would mean substantial icecap melting and the flooding of coastal areas such as New York City, Buenos Aires, and Shanghai.[49]

Additionally, the discharge of fluorocarbons and nitrous oxide is attacking the ozone layer. One estimate is that, at current rates, the stratospheric zone will be reduced by 16.5 percent by the turn of the century, resulting in an increase in ultraviolet radiation, which, in turn, will cause an increase of as many as 1.5 million new cases of skin cancer annually.[50]

Environmental Cooperation

International cooperation to meet environmental concerns has been slow. It is beset by a combination of related economic and political barriers. Less developed countries are too often willing to accept environmentally damaging practices by local or multinational corporations in return for industrialization. Environmental controls are expensive, and to a degree, industrialization money flows to cheap production areas. When, for example, Anaconda Copper was faced with a $200 million cost to meet U.S. clean air requirements, it shut down its Montana smelting plant and shipped the arsenic-laden ore to Taiwan for processing. Many LDCs are unwilling and unable to risk that sort of loss or to put their products at a cost disadvantage in trade by adding pollution control costs.[51]

Despite these formidable economic impediments, efforts at environmental cooperation are underway. The United Nations has been involved in a number of efforts, beginning with the 1972 Conference on the Human Environment in Stockholm, which began the multilateral dialogue. The United Nations Environment Program was established as a result of that conference, and it is currently making limited expenditures in a number of areas. Another specialized UN agency, the International Maritime Organization, has been involved in preventing marine pollution from international shipping. Also under UN auspices, the United Nations Development Program and the UN Commission on Transnational Corporations are involved in LDC development. Finally, there are a number of regional environmental efforts, such as the International Commission for the Protection of the Rhine Against Pollution, and also bilateral negotiations and agreements in the area.[52]

International Economic, Social, and Environmental Cooperation: The Prospects

On reading this chapter, like those on international law, international organization, and arms control, it is easy to be discouraged. The problems are immense and complex. Barriers to cooperation are formidable. In many cases, failure to find a solution carries the potential of the direst of consequences.

The current level of cooperation, when compared with these stark realities, seems woefully inadequate.

GLOOM!? Perhaps not!

The message here is not to adopt a "whistling past the graveyard" or an optimistic "it's darkest before the dawn" approach. As comedian Eddie Murphy observed, "Sometimes it's darkest just before the light goes out completely."

Don't sell the early efforts too short, though. It is only during this century, and really since World War II, that the need to cooperate has penetrated our consciousness and our conscience. The intervening four decades is a microsecond in human history. In that sense, much has been done.

Still, much remains to be done, and we have so little time to do it. There may, after all, be only a few microseconds left.

Summary

This chapter has been about the socioeconomic issues that face the world and whether we should take the view that we are in a lifeboat or a spaceship. Increasingly, but only slowly so, we are taking the attitude that we are indeed on Spaceship Earth and that we have a responsibility to and a stake in the status of all the people of the world.

There are a variety of weighty issues that need to be addressed. Economic cooperation is probably the most advanced of all cooperative efforts. The United Nations maintains a number of efforts aimed at general economic development, with an emphasis on the less developed countries. At the regional level, there are a number of organizations. By far the most developed of these is the European Communities, which is the great hope and example of those who favor international integration. There is also a great deal of trade cooperation, and great strides have been made through the General Agreement on Tariffs and Trade toward promoting free trade. Among monetary institutions, the International Monetary Fund is the primary organization dedicated to stabilizing the world's monetary system. There are also a number of international organizations established to provide developmental loans and grants to countries in need. The best known of these is the World Bank, which consists of several interrelated subsidiaries.

Population is another significant problem facing the world, with the global population about to break the 5 billion mark. Thus far the international effort has been limited, but the 1984 World Population Conference in Mexico marks the beginning of a greater level of consciousness and cooperation. Food is another, and closely related, problem. There is a need to supply both short-term food aid and long-term developmental assistance to agriculture. A number of international efforts exist in this field, such as the United States Food for Peace program and multilateral programs through United Nations–associated agencies.

The health of the world's population is another focus of international effort, the World Health Organization being the lead agency. The United Nations Educational, Scientific, and Cultural Organization is the best known among a number of international organizations involved in education.

Human rights is another growing area of international concern and is one of the most difficult to work in because violations are usually politically based, so that efforts are often resented and rejected by target countries. The greatest progress has been made in adopting a number of UN declarations, such as the Universal Declaration of Human Rights, and multilateral treaties that define basic human rights. The enforcement of human rights is much less well developed, but the rising level of awareness and disapproval of violations on a global level is having a positive impact.

Yet another problem area is preservation of our natural resources and the environment. Most analysts view this as a serious problem, although there are those who minimize the degree of danger. At this time, efforts at meaningful international cooperation are just beginning.

In reviewing the efforts at international cooperation in the areas discussed in this chapter, we return to the question of standards of judgment. It is easy to view the vast extent of the problems facing the globe, to measure the limited effort being made to resolve them, and to dismiss the entire subject of international cooperation as superficial. It is true that not nearly enough is being done. But it is also true that only a very few short years ago nothing was being done. From that zero base, the progress made since World War II is encouraging. The only question is whether we will continue to expand our efforts and whether we will do enough, soon enough.

Terms

European Communities (EC)—The Western European regional organization established in 1967 that includes the European Coal and Steel Community (ECSC), the European Economic Community (EEC), and the European Atomic Energy Community (EURATOM).

European Economic Community (EEC)—The regional trade and economic organization established in Western Europe by the Treaty of Rome in 1958; also known as the Common Market.

General Agreement on Tariffs and Trade (GATT)—The world's primary organization promoting the expansion of free trade. Established in 1947, it has grown to a membership of over 100.

International Monetary Fund (IMF)—The world's primary organization devoted to maintaining monetary stability by helping countries fund balance-of-payments deficits. Established in 1947, it now has 146 members.

Lifeboat ethic—The argument that there are not enough resources to go around and, therefore, the wealthy should not try to aid the weakest countries.

Spaceship Earth—The argument that the fate of all the world's people is inseparably intertwined and that if we do not aid the needy, we are not only derelict in our responsibility, we are also, in the long term, working against our own best interest.

United Nations Conference on Trade and Development (UNCTAD)—The United Nations organization that is concerned mainly with the economic needs of the less developed countries.

World Bank—A collective term for the closely linked institutions of the International Bank for Reconstruction and Development, the International Development Association, and the International Finance Corporation. All three, with different foci, make loans to countries for economic development. 

Notes

1. George F. Kennan, "The Impending Food-Population Crisis," in *The Theory and Practice of International Relations,* 6th ed., ed. William C. Olson, Davis S. McLellan, and Fred A. Sondermann (Englewood Cliffs, N.J.: Prentice-Hall, 1984), p. 273.
2. This was pivotally argued by Garrett Hardin in "The Tragedy of the Commons," *Science* 162 (1968): 1243–1248, and in "Living in a Lifeboat," *Bioscience* 24 (1974): 561–568. Hardin discusses food aid. In addition to the "lifeboat ethic," this argument is referred to by the first title, "Tragedy of the Commons," which refers to the overgrazing by and subsequent damage to the cattle herds on English villages' commons, which could be used freely by all.
3. The idea of triage can be seen in William Paddock and Paul Paddock, *Famine—1975, America's Decision: Who Will Survive?* (Boston: Little, Brown, 1967), especially chap. 9.
4. An overall review is James W. Howe and John Sewell, "Let's Sink the Lifeboat Ethic," in Olson, McLellan, and Sondermann, *Theory and Practice,* pp. 281–284.
5. For a recent negative review of UNCTAD, see Robert Ramsay, "UNCTAD's Failures: The Rich Get Richer," *International Organization* 38 (1984): 387–397.
6. A recent look at the work of these meetings is Nicholas Bayne, "Western Economic Summits: Can They Do Better?," *World Today* 40 (January 1984): 4–11.
7. Good basic overviews are Juliet Lodge, ed., *Institutions and Policies of the European Community* (New York: St. Martin's Press, 1983); Ali M. El-Agraa, ed., *The Economics of the European Community* (New York: St. Martin's Press, 1980); and Anthony J. C. Kerr, *The Common Market and How It Works* (Elmsford, N.Y.: Pergamon Press, 1977). For a more theoretical work on collaboration and integration, see Douglas Dosse, David Gowland, and Keith Hartley, eds., *The Collaboration of Nations: A Study of European Economic Policy* (New York: St. Martin's Press, 1982).
8. *New York Times,* May 28, 1984, p. A6.
9. For a recent series on the EEC, see *New York Times,* March 21 and 23, 1982, pp. A3, A4. On the question of sovereignty and integration, see Paul Taylor, *The Limits of European Integration* (New York: Columbia University Press, 1983).
10. There are a few non–Eastern European members such as Outer Mongolia, Cuba, and Vietnam.
11. Joze M. Van Brabant, *Socialist Economic Integration* (Cambridge, Mass.: Harvard University Press, 1980); and *New York Times,* May 10 and October 19, 1983, pp. A3, D1. Michael Marrese and Jan Vanous, *Soviet Subsidization of Trade with Europe* (Berkeley, Calif.: Institute of International Studies, 1983), is a technical look. Also see Raul Marer and John Michael Montias, "The Council for Mutual Economic Assistance," in *International Economic Integration,* ed. Ali M. El-Agraa (New York: St. Martin's Press, 1983).
12. For some background, see M. M. Kostecki, *East-West Trade and the GATT System* (New York: St. Martin's Press, 1978).
13. International Monetary Fund, *Annual Report, 1983* (Washington, D.C.: International Monetary Fund, 1983), especially tables 20 and 21. A useful summary history of the IMF is in Hans-Eckart Scharrer, "The IMF—a Success Story?," *Intereconomics* (July/August 1984): 158–166.
14. Scharrer, *Intereconomics,* pp. 177–179.
15. For a review of the recent works on the LDCs and the international monetary

system, see G. K. Helleiner, "The Less Developed Countries and the International Monetary System," *World Politics* 36 (1983): 147–164; also, Tony Killick, *The IMF and Stabilization: Developing Country Experiences* (New York: St. Martin's Press, 1984).

16. For recent articles on criticism and defense of the IMF, see *Time,* May 21, 1984, p. 76, and July 2, 1984, pp. 49–50.
17. For a review of the IBRD and IDA, see *The World Bank Annual Report, 1984* (Washington, D.C.: World Bank, 1984). For a useful summary of World Bank history, see Otto G. Mayor, "Development without Miracles: The World Bank after Forty Years," *Intereconomics* (July/August 1984), pp. 167–172.
18. Criticisms and proposals are in Frances Stewart and Arjun Sengupta, *International Financial Cooperation* (Boulder, Colo.: Westview Press, 1982), pp. 53–57.
19. On U.S. policy, see Jonathan E. Sanford, *U.S. Foreign Policy and Multilateral Development Banks* (Boulder, Colo.: Westview Press, 1983).
20. Ibid., pp. 66–67.
21. *Annual Review of United Nations Affairs* (Dobbs Ferry, N.Y.: Oceana, 1983), p. 203.
22. Stewart and Sengupta, *International Financial Cooperation,* p. 58.
23. For a good review on population projections, see Paul Demery, "A Perspective on Long-Term Population Growth," *Population and Development Review* 10 (1984): 103–126.
24. See Robert McNamara, "The Population Problem," *Foreign Affairs* 62 (1984), tables 1 and 2, p. 1111.
25. Esten Boserup, *Population and Technological Change* (Chicago: University of Chicago Press, 1981), table 14.1, p. 175. Also see Karen Michaelson, ed., *And the Poor Get Children: Radical Perspective on Population Dynamics* (New York: Monthly Review Press, 1981), p. 19 and *passim* on the general role of political economy; Robert Repetto, *Economic Equality and Fertility in Developing Countries* (Baltimore: Johns Hopkins University Press, 1979), pp. 1–5, 156–175.
26. Howe and Sewell, "Let's Sink the Lifeboat Ethic," p. 284.
27. The convention had forty-eight ratifications by May 1983, not including the United States.
28. The exact state of the agriculture/population balance in the future is, of course, speculative. For a guardedly optimistic view, see Nurul Islam, "Food," in *Population and the World Economy in the 21st Century,* ed. Just Faaland (New York: St. Martin's Press, 1982), pp. 23–49.
29. See U.S. Department of State, *International and Security Development Cooperation Program,* Special Report 108, April 4, 1983, table II.
30. For criticisms, see *New York Times,* November 9, 1981, p. D1.
31. On the major organizations, see Raymond F. Hopkins and Donald J. Puchala, "Perspectives on the International Relations of Food," *International Organization* 32 (1978): 581–616. The entire Summer 1984 issue of *International Organization* was devoted to the food issue. For lists of Third World agriculture organizations, see *Encyclopedia of the Third World,* rev. ed., vol. 1 (New York: Facts on File, 1982), pp. 22–23; and *International Organization* 32 (1978): 869–871.
32. World Bank, *World Development Report, 1981* (Washington, D.C.: World Bank, 1981), table 1, pp. 134–135.
33. *New York Times,* October 15, 1981, p. A6.
34. The discussion of the UN relies on Nicholas G. Onuf and V. Spike Peterson, "Human Rights from an International Rights Perspective," *Journal of International Affairs*

37 (1984): 334–337; A. H. Robertson, *Human Rights in the World* (New York: St. Martin's Press, 1982), pp. 24–79; Egon Schwelb and Philip Alston, "The Principal Institutions and Other Bodies Founded under the Charter," in *International Dimension of Human Rights,* 2 vols., ed. Karel Vasak (Westport, Conn.: Greenwood Press, 1982), pp. 231–302; and Philip Alston, "The Alleged Demise of Political Human Rights at the U.N.," *International Organization* 37 (1983): 537–550.

35. The text of the Universal Declaration of Human Rights and other UN documents discussed in this section can be found in *International Human Rights Instruments of the United Nations, 1948–1982* (Pleasantville, N.Y.: UNIFO, 1983).
36. Regional efforts are discussed in various articles in Paul Sieghart, *The International Law of Human Rights* (Oxford, England: Clarendon Press, 1983), pp. 391–422. On the general subject of human rights and the Third World, see Thomas M. Franck, *Human Rights in the Third World Perspective,* 3 vols. (London: Oceana, 1983).
37. Sieghart, *International Law,* p. 442; also, Chiang Pei-heng, *Non-Governmental Organizations at the United Nations* (New York: Praeger, 1981).
38. Donella H. Meadows, Dennis L. Meadows, Jorgen Randers, and William W. Behrens, III, *The Limits to Growth* (New York: Universe Books, 1974).
39. The Club of Rome is so named because its founder, Aurello Peccei, lived in Rome. World Watch is based in Washington, D.C., and was founded by another noted analyst, Lester R. Brown.
40. For a review of the work of the Club of Rome and its various reports, see Nicholas Greenwood Onuf, "Reports to the Club of Rome," *World Politics* 36 (1983): 121–146.
41. These and other figures, unless otherwise noted, are based on Council on Environmental Quality and Department of State, *The Global 2000 Report to the President,* vols. 1 and 2 (Washington, D.C.: U.S. Government Printing Office, 1980).
42. World Bank, *World Development Report, 1981,* p. 41.
43. Ibid. Also see McNamara, "Population Problem," p. 1119.
44. For a review of some of these arguments, see Robert Miewald and Susan Welch, "Natural Resources Scarcity," in *Scarce Natural Resources: The Challenge to Public Policymaking,* ed. Robert Miewald and Susan Welch (Beverly Hills, Calif.: Sage, 1983), pp. 9–21.
45. Denis Gabor and Umberto Colombo with Alexander King and Riccardo Galli, *Beyond the Age of Waste: A Report to the Club of Rome* (New York: Pergamon Press, 1978), p. 229.
46. U.S. Council on Environmental Quality, *Environmental Trends,* July 1981, p. 310.
47. R. Michael M'Gonigle and Mark W. Zacher, *Pollution, Politics, and International Law* (Berkeley: University of California Press, 1979), table 2, p. 17.
48. Council on Environmental Quality, *Environmental Trends,* p. 328. Figures are approximate; long tons converted to metric tons for comparison.
49. *Global Report 2000,* vol. 1, p. 36.
50. Ibid., p. 37. Council on Environmental Quality, *Environmental Trends,* p. 331; and Allen L. Price, *The International Law of Pollution* (Westport, Conn.: Quorum Books, 1983), p. 21.
51. On the trade-cost factor, see Seymour J. Rubin and Thomas R. Graham, *Environment and Trade* (Totowa, N.J.: Allanheld, Osmun & Co., 1982).
52. A good look at U.S./Canadian environmental interaction is John E. Carroll, *Environmental Diplomacy: An Examination and a Perspective on Canadian-U.S. Transboundary Environmental Relations* (Ann Arbor: University of Michigan Press, 1983).

The Tempest: An Epilogue

Tomorrow, and Tomorrow, and Tomorrow: A Prologue

Where I did begin, there I shall end.
***Shakespeare,* Julius Caesar**

So here it is some months later, and we are at the end of this book and this course. Finals await, and then, praise be, vacation. That well-deserved break from your academic labors brings you to an implicit point of decision about what to do with this text, the other course readings, and the knowledge you have gained from your instructor. One option is to sell what you can back to the bookstore and forget the rest. I can remember from my undergraduate days how attractive an idea that sometimes seems.

But then, again, is that really the best option? Probably not. We began our semester's journey with the idea that we are all inescapably part of the world drama. There may be times when we want to shout, "Stop the world, I want to get off," but we cannot. We have also seen that we are both audience and actors in the global play's progress. At the very least, we are all touched by the action in ways that range from the foreign designer jeans that we wear to, potentially, our atomized end.

We can leave it at that, shrug our shoulders, and complain and mumble at the forces that buffet us. But we also can do more than that. We don't have to be just passive victims. We can, if we want and if we try, help write the script. The plot is ongoing and improvisational. The final scene is yet unwritten. We are not even sure when it will occur. It could be well into the far distant future—or it could be tomorrow. That, more than any particular point of information, is the most important message here. You are not helpless, and you owe it to yourself and your fellow humans to take an active role in your life and in the world's tomorrows.

There are great needs in the world today. War continues to kill without conscience. A billion-dollar diet industry prospers on widespread fat in some countries, while in others infants and the elderly starve to death in the dry dust. As if localized malnutrition were too slow and selective, we globally attack our environment with the waste products of our progress, and the human population tide threatens to bring new truth to the old phrase about "being eaten out of house and home." Of even more immediate peril, an expanse of nuclear mushroom clouds could instantly terminate our biosphere's more evolutionary decay.

To face these problems, we have, at best, a primitive political system. Sovereignty strengthens nationalities but divides the world. Frontier justice is the rule. As in a grade B western, all the actors carry guns on their hips and sometimes shoot it out. The law is weak, and the marshals have more authority in theory than in practice.

There are few anymore who really try to defend the system of assertive sovereignty as adequate for the future. Clearly, it is not. What is less certain is what to do next and how to do it. Cooperation, humanitarianism, enlightenment, and such words provide easy answers, but they are largely empty in their vagueness. In practice, the answers will be much more difficult. They will involve tough choices: giving up some things now so that they will not be taken later; being less sovereign; curbing our lifestyle; risking arms control in the hope of avoiding nuclear war; thinking of the world in terms of "we."

At every step there will be those who urge caution, who counsel self-preservation first, who see the world as a lifeboat. And maybe they will be right—but probably not. We *have* begun to move toward a more rational order. The last four chapters clearly show that. But they also show how limited and fragile that progress has been. That is where you come in. Your job is to work to make the world the place you want it to be. It is your job to consider the problems, to ponder possible solutions, to reach informed opinions, and to act on your convictions. Think? Yes, of course. But also DO!! That is what is really important.

We began this study with the thought from Shakespeare's *Henry V* that "the world [is] familiar to us and [yet] unknown." The author's hope is that this text and course have made the world more familiar, less unknown. What you do with what you have learned is now the issue. Will you treat this moment as an end? Or is it a beginning? Heed, if you will, the counsel of Shakespeare's King Lear:

Be governed by your knowledge and proceed.

Index

Boldface terms are glossary terms. Boldface page numbers refer to the pages on which the terms are defined.